An HR Guide to Workplace Fraud and Criminal Behaviour

An HR Guide to Workplace Fraud and Criminal Behaviour

Recognition, Prevention and Management

MICHAEL J. COMER
TIMOTHY E. STEPHENS
Cobasco Group Limited

GOWER

Mind Maps® is a Registered Trade Mark of The Buzan Organization and is used with enthusiastic permission. Original concept supplied by Buzan Centres Ltd, 54 Parkstone Road, Poole, Dorset BH15 2PG.

Published by
Gower Publishing Limited
Gower House
Croft Road
Aldershot
Hants GU11 3HR
England

Gower Publishing Company
Suite 420
101 Cherry Street
Burlington, VT 05401-4405
USA

British Library Cataloguing in Publication Data
Comer, Michael J.
  An HR guide to workplace fraud and criminal behaviour :
  recognition, prevention and management
  1. Employee crimes 2. White collar crimes 3. Personnel
  management
  I. Title II. Stephens, Timothy E.
  658.3'14

ISBN: 0 566 08555 0

Library of Congress Control Number: 2003057140

Typeset by Sparks, Oxford, UK – www.sparks.co.uk
Printed and bound in Great Britain by MPG Books Ltd, Bodmin, Cornwall.

Contents

'IT DEPENDS WHETHER YOU WANT TO DO IT TEN TIMES A NIGHT,
OR JUST SAY YOU HAVE'

List of Figures

List of Tables

List of Mind Maps®

THE DANGERS OF LATIN

Foreword

by Spot the dog

Every dog has its day

It is the ultimate irony that towards the close of his career, when the few faculties he ever had have long since evaporated, that my master – Mike Comer – should be coming into vogue. It really is a funny old world and proves that you should never have thrown out your purple flared trousers and yellow Hush Puppies because every dog has its day and what goes round, comes round. If Mr Comer can come into fashion, anything can.

It is even funnier that the man who has made a career out of being a reactionary, sexist, anti-authoritarian should be allowed to write anything intended to help human resources and other nice people. He tells me that he has more or less relented and before he pops his clogs wants to build bridges, having at long last recognized that the alliance between HR, security, audit and compliance is critical in the fight against fraud and other security risks. What is amazing is not that the aged guru should have at last come to this conclusion – which has been obvious to me for most of my life – but that he should do an about-turn without any hint of shame.

The dangers of Latin

At a recent fraud conference, George Staple QC, a very distinguished man and a top lawyer in a leading City firm, former head of both the Fraud Panel and the Serious Fraud Office, introduced Mr Comer as 'the international doyen of fraud specialists' or words to that effect. Mr Comer suspects anything in Latin and was thus unsure what 'doyen' meant. He crawled to his feet and was about to give the distinguished QC a kick in the pants when someone pointed out that what Mr Staple had said was a compliment and wasn't even remotely Latin. Mr Comer, being unaccustomed to compliments, took time to regain his *compos mentis* before delivering an hour's tirade on the devastating impact that Latin has on the lives of ordinary folk. He never gives up, especially when he is wrong.[1]

Putting it in writing

For those of you who have cleverly avoided having to read Mr Comer's stuff or listen to him drone on at seminars, I should explain how I, a simple spotted mutt, ended up writing a foreword to what is supposed to be a serious textbook for humans. The truth is that no human (and especially Mr Staple) would agree to having their names associated in print with the author. It is one thing saying something fleetingly nice about the geriatric guru at a fraud conference and quite another committing it to paper. In short, I got the job because no one else would do it. *Stercus accidit*: or as they say, 'shit happens'.

---

[1] I don't think I was wrong. Just see how many times Latin phrases appear in this book

The geriatric devil child

Through some baffling quirk of nature, Mr Comer has always seemed able to get people to tell him the truth, or at least most of it, and to do things that they would rather not do. I am sure that the people at Gower never wanted to commission him to write this book, but somehow here it is. You may be familiar with films and books on Damian, the fiendish child, and Chuckie, the devilish doll. Mr Comer is the geriatric equivalent.

Making things happen

Things just seem to happen when Mr Comer is around. For example, the other day we were just sauntering along Victoria Street in London, minding our own business. I was hallucinating about nice juicy bones and lamp-posts and Mr Comer about his increasing band of grandchildren and his new Scotty Cameron putter when – all of a sudden – our paths were crossed by a couple of young heavies who rudely asked for fifty pence for a cup of tea. They obviously did not appreciate the dangers of interrupting the ex-guru when he is deep in thought and, after a two hour interrogation – held on the pavement in the pouring rain and in front of a growing crowd of Japanese tourists who thought they were on *Candid Camera* – the heavies confessed to three bank robberies and, worse still in Mr Comer's eyes, to being supporters of Birmingham City Football Club. Instead of getting fifty pence, the heavies face five years in the cooler. The first lesson from this is that you can always get humans and humanoids to tell the truth, providing you have a cunning plan. The second is never ask Mr Comer for money.

Commendations and condemnations

Over the past forty years Mr Comer has interviewed many hundreds, if not thousands, of people: appearing in all shapes and sizes, nationalities and sexes in all parts of the world and in cases of varying complexities. In some he has cleared people wrongly under suspicion, but in the majority he has exposed guilty secrets by using the cunning plan described in this book. On a few occasions he has failed to get anywhere, but in a painfully extended career as an investigator and as a witness in criminal and civil courts he has been commended more times than his ass has been kicked. This is not a bad record for an investigator trapped in a time capsule in a lawyer's world.

Learning from mistakes

As will become obvious, Mr Comer is not a qualified psychologist, accountant or even an estate agent but he has built on his GCE 'O' level certificates in scripture, woodwork and geometrical drawing to become a keen interpreter of human behaviour, learning what works and what doesn't. This book is the result of mistakes made over forty years as a practitioner and, in a very narrow way, as an academic.[2]

---

[2] Mr Comer served as a Visiting Professor at Cranfield Institute of Technology and is currently a Visiting Fellow at the Scarman Centre, University of Leicester. He is also Past President of the European Chapter of Certified Fraud Examiners and, believe it or believe it not, a member of MENSA

The most important lessons

In a rare burst of lucidity, Mr Comer told me that the most important lesson he has learned is that people too quickly dismiss their instincts that something is wrong. He says if something does not look or sound right, the chances are it is iffy and must be dealt with. In short, if something is too good to be true, it is. Secondly, problems do not get better by themselves and unresolved suspicions of deception leave a cloud hanging over innocent people while evil escapes unscathed. This is a very bad scene.

We dogs are totally different and if we don't like someone, we just bite them. This is a natural animal instinct but humans try to consciously control everything and would rather be deceived than face the truth. Just ask yourself: 'When did I last bite someone in anger?'

Acknowledgements

Mr Comer has asked me to thank Mike Williams, who drew the cartoons for this book. I have never met Mr Williams although I have corresponded with him and spoken to him on the telephone. He seems a pleasant sort of bloke even though his accent is difficult to understand, the more so since he had his National Health dentures fitted. Mike Williams is what is known as a 'Scouser' and lives in the Wirral, which is perilously north of civilization, bordering even on Scotland, with all that entails. A sense of humour is essential to survive in such extremes and Mike Williams has a good one. He too is a keen interpreter of human behaviour, particularly in pubs, bars, bingo halls and bookmakers' shops which he seems to frequent a lot. He claims he only goes in them to stimulate the right hemisphere of his brain and to get ideas for cartoons, but I think he may be dissembling the truth and is really a voyeur. Anyway, if you don't like the words, I am sure you will appreciate the cartoons.

I have also been instructed to thank Patrick M. Ardis, of the Woolf Ardis law firm in Memphis, Tennessee, and David H. Price of Ealing, who were dragged in by Mr Comer to co-author *Bad Lies in Business*, which was also about deception and is fortunately out of print except for the Thai and Brazilian editions. It is to their credit that Mr Ardis and Mr Price have managed to disassociate themselves from this book, although it does contain many of the ideas they developed together.

Mr Comer also acknowledges some good work by Don Rabon of the North Carolina Justice Academy and Avinoan Sapir of LSI in Phoenix, Arizona, on the analysis of written statements. He is especially grateful to Tim Stephens on whom most of the techniques in this book have been tried and tested *ad nauseam*. However, his family seems to like him and so do dogs of the more intelligent variety.

Enjoy the book; I guarantee it will make you a happier person and far more effective in dealing with deception. It will also give you a good insight into the twisted mind of a fraud investigator, but you can pick out the good bits and ignore the rest.

HE WAS DETERMINED NOT TO BE CAUGHT IN A LIE

Prologue

Monkey waves

In the summer of 1999, Herman Snooks, a sandal-wearing, ginger-haired research scientist from Newbury, Berkshire – in a moment of extraordinary genius – invented an electronic device which was about the size of a ballpoint pen and emitted what he called 'monkey waves'. These invisible and silent surges concatenated, reversed and redirected the brain's alpha and beta waves, thereby compelling human targets to tell the truth, the whole truth and nothing but the truth, regardless of the consequences.

Revealing the truth

It was an extraordinary invention that gave new meaning to the phrase 'to get on the same wavelength as someone else'. Victims who were enveloped by the waves had an unfailing reaction: they blinked hard four times, scratched their noses twice and then exploded with the truth. There was no stopping them and honesty would pour out like a raging torrent. Once removed from the beams, the victims reverted to deceptive normality but, as if in their worst nightmare, they remembered every word they had said while under the influence. The way they tried to recover and explain away their eruptions of unexpurgated truth was pitiable and the panic-ridden aftermath was the most disturbing of all. Grown men turned into blubbering imbeciles.

> *The truth really hurts, especially when you had no intention of telling it*

Herman tested the device on his neighbours, friends and family with astonishing results. His wife pleaded guilty to voting for New Labour and is now in a mental home, his teenage kids admitted to being multimillionaire drug pushers with massive real estate investments in Highgate and his mother-in-law confessed that she was undergoing sex change therapy and planned to become a professional wrestler. This last disclosure did not surprise Herman, but the others were shocking.

Clever investments

Other successes followed quickly, including sudden, unexplained bursts of honesty by car salesmen, pension advisers, social security claimants and, to everyone's total amazement, even estate agents and accountants. People could not stop themselves from telling the truth and Herman soon became very wealthy by making astute investments in all manner of honest enterprises. He thus avoided telecoms shares. His device changed his world by guaranteeing he only reacted to the truth. He could do no wrong and every decision was a winner.

Knowing the truth makes life easy

The bubble bursts

But it was all too good to be true and Herman became overconfident and went one step too far. He should have known the bubble had to burst and when it did it was in the most spectacular way imaginable. The downfall started when Herman beamed the gadget at the judge, defendants, witnesses and lawyers in a high-profile televised court case, much like the OJ Simpson trial. The tumult that followed, when justice collapsed under the unacceptable burden of the deep truth, does not bear repeating. The bottom line was that Herman was pilloried and the device seized, classified as 'top secret' and sent to the Pentagon for analysis amid great judicial and political rumblings of 'anarchy', 'communistic-inspired revolution' and 'black magic'. A few people said the device was an al-Qaeda plot to bring down Western economies by compelling accountants to tell the truth: others said the Martians were behind it. But they all thought that Herman had stockpiled better and more powerful weapons of mass detection and was a permanent danger.

Politicians close ranks

Politicians everywhere could see the implications, were the device to become generally available. 'If we are made to tell the truth and cannot spin,' some said, 'our world, as we know it, will come to an end. This is an intolerable attack on democracy: it must be banned forthwith or even quicker.' Laboratories were commissioned to develop antidotes to the diabolical beams; pills were invented and one enterprising scientist designed a wave-proof helmet and mouth guard – much like that worn by Hannibal Lecter in *The Silence of the Lambs*. This worked well, but politicians who tested the prototype were not convinced that it conveyed the right image.

They said: 'Aren't we admitting, if we wear it, that we need it and, if we need it, aren't we acknowledging that we tell lies? What the heck shall we do? This is scandalous. It gives us no room for manoeuvre and a world without spin is not worth living in.'

Political enemies, who had agreed on nothing for decades, became as one in swearing themselves to secrecy and condemning Herman's invention. 'It's a monkey on our back', they moaned. Parliament was put into indefinite recess and some MPs went on permanent sick leave, while others disappeared on world cruises.

London abandoned

Travel agents in London SW1 and Islington could not figure out why there was such a sudden rush of last-minute bookings for sponsored political fact-finding trips to the Himalayas and the Upper Volta. Haunts used by politicians and journalists, such as steam baths, bingo halls, massage parlours and expensive restaurants, were deserted and for the first time in over thirty years, table one at Langan's restaurant in the West End of London was available to non-politicians. It really was that bad!

Paranoia ran wild, and people who thought they had been beamed but hadn't confessed to everything imaginable and to lots of things that weren't. Stock markets collapsed when at annual general meetings directors, who had heard secret rumours about the device and were fearful they might be beamed midway through presenting their annual results, took the safe course and told the truth about the shocking state of their businesses. Staff working in Buckingham Palace resigned in droves, but did not think even once of speaking to Max Clifford or tabloid journalists. It was that bad, it really was.

Academia

Universities, research centres, laboratories and other repositories for academics shut their doors, forcing their occupants to seek meaningful employment as plumbers and butchers or, in one case, even as an investigator. Scientists quickly recalibrated the results of widely accepted research projects, admitting that smoking was extremely healthy, that Big Macs were highly nutritional, and that Viagra had previously hidden side effects such as multiple slipped discs and inflamed knees. Sales plunged.

But the most embarrassing scientific turnaround was from NASA, which admitted that it had never landed a rocket on the moon and that the photographs of the astronauts jumping about with flags and golf clubs had been staged in a disused warehouse in the Bronx. It really was that bad, it was. And all because of Herman.

Authors

Gurus who had written management texts stood in queues outside bookshops to buy up entire stocks of their own works so they could be burned. Amazon.com sold out overnight. Tom Peters reissued his landmark book with the new title *In Search of Flatulence* and *The One Minute Manager* was changed to *Late is Better Than Never*. It was bad. Really bad. Fear that the truth might strike anyone down at any time created pre-emptive panic and the effect was universal. No one was safe.

The closure

Very serious consideration, at the highest levels,[1] was given to having Herman assassinated. But in the end, as is often the case, common sense based on bribery prevailed and under an oath of absolute secrecy Herman was given $50 million to destroy his invention and all plans, specifications and prototypes which, being an honest man, he did. This is probably why you have never heard of the device before now.

For readers who are interested in the ending to this story, Herman changed his name and is now living happily in Mexico with his sixth wife, Bernard. His beard has gone and he is heavily

---

[1] i.e. Alistair Campbell

into designer clothes, Cartier watches, polo shirts, Volvos, crocodile shoes, dark glasses and silk socks. He is sometimes mistaken for a fraud investigator and this irritates him.

At it again

While technically in semi-retirement Herman invented an electronic collar that translates barks, mews and other sounds made by dogs, cats, rabbits and other furry and feathery creatures into plain English, Japanese and Yiddish. Don't ask why he included English and Japanese, but that's just the way it was. The beta version is working well and Herman has spent many happy hours discussing the works of Van Gogh and Rembrandt with his gerbil, Basil.

Sadly, Herman knows that the device can never be marketed commercially. *Entre nous,* the drawback is that most domestic pets are totally obsessed with their genitalia and bowel movements. Worse still, apparently innocent barks, mews, grunts and squeaks decode into awfully bad language and pets are not up to snuff on either political correctness or discretion. They are also sexually indiscriminate and spend most of their waking hours figuring out how to roger their colleagues.[2] To release the contraption on the open market – thereby empowering billions of pets to swear at and inform on their owners – would cause an international uproar of unparalleled proportions. And just think what the taxman would do if he could turn all domestic pets into whistle blowers; the mind boggles at the thought.

The latest invention

You have to admit that Herman, although a brilliant inventor, is more than a tad unlucky in his selection of commercially viable ideas. He has said if he ever gets over the problems with his animal invention, he will release an even more advanced computer that will enable people to communicate effectively with their teenage kids and elderly parents. As we speak, this contraption requires the processing power of 200 paralleled Cray computers and is about the size of ten London buses. Herman is confident, given the advances in microtechnology, it can be miniaturized to fit into a pen. The truth is that most things can if you make them small enough.

This book won't fit into a pen, but it will make you almost as effective as Herman, and without the downside.

---

[2]   To that extent they are much like politicians

PART **1** *The Problem of Deception*

'THAT'S IT, POTTER, YOU'LL MAKE A GREAT ACCOUNTANT'

1 *Introduction*

Lies are the truth to people who don't know better

Lies in business

Most days of your life you are deceived. *Think about it*! No, please, really think about it. Take it on board at a conscious level: look upwards and to your left.[1] *Deception is a really bad scene.*

The cheque is in the post

A TYPICAL DAY?

You got out of bed, read lots of lies in the newspaper; watched the breakfast show, with people pretending to be happy early in the morning; walked to the station with your neighbour who told you he had just been promoted, when you know he had been fired; caught the train, but could not get a first-class seat because the compartments were full of fare dodgers; came into the office, spoke to your colleagues who said your new employee was doing fine, when you know he is not; received a call from Bill Smith saying that he could not come to work today as he was ill; attended meetings; approved a bunch of purchase invoices for payment; signed a few expense statements, some of which looked a bit dodgy; telephoned a customer who promised you the cheque was in the post; called your banker, but his PA told you he was in a meeting and would call you back; had lunch with a job candidate and then lost to him at golf because he cheated. You then returned home; spoke to the kids, who told you they had no homework and were going to a disco; watched television, read your emails and responded to them and then clambered into bed, pretending you had a bad migraine.

How many lies were you told during this very ordinary day? Did you do anything about them? Were any of them really important?

The fact is that most people would prefer to be deceived than be perceived as being distrustful

In the majority of cases, the lies you are told are insignificant, but sometimes they have very serious consequences. In his book *Rogue Trader*, Nicholas Leeson said:

---

[1] We will explain later the reason for this

BUYING TIME

'I put the phone down. These conversations were always the same with Mary [Mary Walz was his functional manager whose career was seriously damaged by Mr Leeson's dishonesty]. She tried to give me some kind of tough instruction, but I always deflected her so she ended with the promise of another chat tomorrow. This was fine by me. Each tomorrow I passed was another day … I just needed to buy time.'

When Tony Railton, an auditor from Baring's head office, was sent to Singapore to sort out the trading positions, Mr Leeson said:

INCREDIBLE EXPLANATION

'I wondered what Tony Railton had uncovered. My list of deceit was too long … it could have been anything from the Balance Sheet to the Citibank account or to the 88888 account. I waited for him. Then the penny dropped and then the millions dropped. I realised Railton was asking me a question rather than accusing me of fraud … and wrestling me to the ground in a citizen's arrest. If he was asking a question he might not know the answer.

'"It's a consolidation account we use, something like the gross account reporting we do for you," I said airily. This was all gobbledegook. He couldn't possibly swallow this one. I put one hand out of sight below my desk and pinched my thigh to stop myself from laughing at my own idiocy. My explanation made no sense, but it was the best I could come up with on the spot and he believed it.'

For every credibility gap, there is a gullibility fill …

Fortunately you may never be confronted with someone quite like Mr Leeson but, just the same, there are hundreds of occasions every year when it would be to your advantage to extract the truth from people who don't want to tell it. Whatever job you do, your success ultimately depends on your ability to sort out the good from the bad and to deal, effectively and politely, with deception.

All lies in jest, until a man hears what he wants to hear and disregards the rest[2]

The cunning plan

This book explains how and why lies are told and how you can deal with them whatever job you do. There are two main sorts of lies. The first is the achievement lie, which is told in order to lead you down the garden path so that you give a job to a bad candidate, part with your money or do something else that is against your interest. The second sort is the exculpatory lie, used to hide wrongdoing and normally told after the event, such as in a disciplinary interview or when someone is challenged for doing something wrong.

---

2   Paul Simon, *The Boxer*

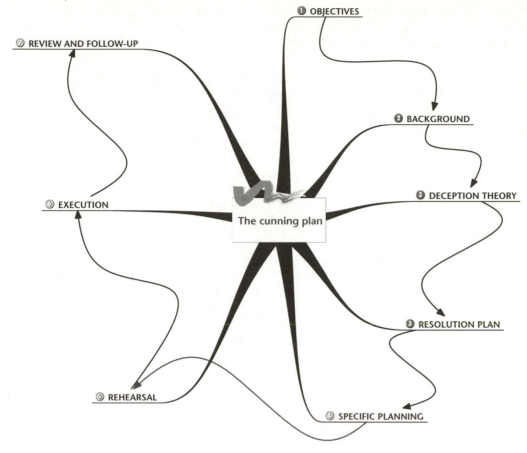

Mind Map® 1   Elements of the cunning plan

But either way, the fact is that the clues to deception are overwhelming, providing you register them at a conscious level. Once you have done this, the initiative swings in your favour. You must decide what your objectives are: do you want to deal with the lie or let it pass? If you decide to expose it you must plan and rehearse your approach and then execute it in a clinical and low-key way (see Mind Map 1). And the more you practice, the better you will become.

By working through this book, you should become almost as successful as Herman in dealing with hot air and deception in business. If you want, you will also be able to develop non-verbal methods of communicating with your pets, other humans and humanoids who don't understand plain language.

This book is intended as a practical guide primarily for human resources specialists and line managers who want to improve their performance and that of their organization based on four principles:

- Dishonesty, violence and other unpleasant behaviour is caused by humans.
- Every process, operation or asset is safe if the only people who have access to them are honest.

- Decisions will always be much more effective if they are based on the truth.
- People who act dishonestly should be identified, exposed and removed from further temptation as quickly and as quietly as possible; they should be punished and made to repay.

Good lies you can still continue to enjoy as they will do you no harm. Some of the techniques suggested in Chapters 6 and 7 are only appropriate for really tough interviews where gross deception is suspected and where the stakes are really high. The chances are that in the sorts of interviews you have to conduct you will not have to use these, but it is important that you should know about them so that you can use diluted versions in your day-to-day work.

If you think telling the truth is difficult, try lying

Buying this book

If you are reading these words in a bookshop and considering whether to buy the book, remember that even if you don't plan to read it, you can still benefit greatly from buying it. The reason it has a gaudy cover and big letters is so that you can leave it on your desk or take it with you into meetings instead of your Filofax or mobile telephone. Just let everyone see it and you will have improved your chances of not being deceived by 75.876 per cent.

Better still why not buy three copies: one for the office, one for your personal use and keep the last on your golf trolley. Do this and you will increase your chances of finding the truth simply by letting people know that you are aware of the possibilities that they might try to deceive you. If you want to improve your chances of finding the truth to 98.617 per cent you should open the book in meetings, flick through the pages, look at the person you suspect might be dissembling the truth and say: 'Aaaah ... that's it. I knew it was in there somewhere'. This will unnerve most liars.

Structure of the book

GENERAL

This book covers lies in all shapes and sizes, and the situations in which they most commonly occur (Figure 1.1).

The book is written in a modular, mildly progressive format, in four main parts:

- Part 1 (Chapters 1 to 4) covers the *problems* of deception, both oral and written.
- Part 2 (Chapters 5 to 8) deals with *countermeasures*, from generic questions through to the policies and procedures needed to assure an honest workforce, a personal manifesto to make sure you do not go the way of the Enron directors, and how to interview people suspected of fraud.
- Part 3 (Chapters 9 and 10) contains solutions to HR problems from malingering, through to harassment and fact finding and applying the cunning plan to other situations in which deception could be a factor.
- Part 4 (Chapter 11) may be the most important of all because it applies to the rare, but very important, cases when you may be called to give evidence in court or an employment tribunal.

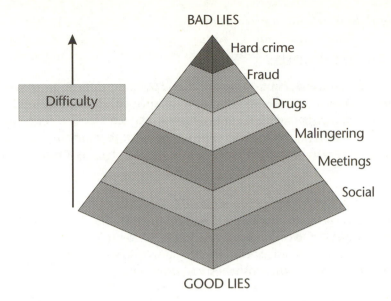

BAD LIES

Hard crime

Fraud

Difficulty

Drugs

Malingering

Meetings

Social

GOOD LIES

Figure 1.1   Tough and easy interviews

MIND MAPS® AND DIAGRAMS

Humans absorb information in different ways. Some prefer visual stimulation, others auditory, sensory or emotional channels. Mind Maps, which were invented by Tony Buzan (former editor of the *Mensa International Journal*, coach to both the British Olympic rowing team and chess squad, and an all-round clever clogs), are excellent tools for summarizing complex relationships in a visual format. Experience shows that highly intelligent people like Mind Maps: if you have bought this book, we are sure you will like them. If you have just borrowed it, you won't. If you want, you can download a free demonstration copy of a superb Mind Mapping program from www.mindjet.com. If you want bigger and better versions of the Mind Maps you can get them from our site at www.cobasco.com; they are free of charge and you can adapt them as you want.[3]

There are also lots of diagrams, 'word bites' and illustrations. Again, some people will like them and others won't. But most people remember messages in diagrams better than they do plain text, simply because their brains are hardwired to do so. If you like diagrams and other stuff, great. If not, don't worry. It probably means that your primary channel of communication is other than visual and this is not really a problem, unless you plan to become a creative accountant or fashion designer.

TABLES

There are many tables in this book, which summarize what would otherwise be massive amounts of text. The problem with tables is that people skip over them, blank out and glaze over and thus miss important messages. We strongly recommend that you take a few minutes to read each table carefully and use a highlighter pen to mark those bits you think could be important to you.

---

[3]   Providing you don't remove our copyright symbols, in which case your computer will self-destruct

You can learn a lot from tables, if you read them

ADAPTING THE TECHNIQUES

The techniques in Chapters 6, 7 and 10 are directed at the most difficult interviews of all for human resources – those where serious malpractice is suspected. These are referred to as 'tough interviews'. However, the approaches suggested may be adapted for any meeting or interview in which it is important to get the truth from people opposed to telling it.

Being able to recognize lies and to deal effectively with them is a really valuable tool, which will:

- ensure that your decisions are based on accurate information;
- avoid unpleasant surprises in your business and commercial life;
- make you more capable and confident in your job, whatever it is;
- enable you to conduct audits and special investigations more effectively;
- enable you to find the truth when dishonesty is suspected.

By understanding the nature of deception, obtaining the tools and honing your interview skills you can quickly get to the truth in 97.24 per cent of all cases and you can do so politely, in your own way and without causing controversy.

Who knows wins

We also hope you will find this book interesting and fun. Not everyone has a sense of humour and the idea of having fun at work may be abhorrent. This is a serious book, but humour has its place and helps you remember important points because it registers in the brain in a different way from most other memories.

INTERVIEWING SKILLS

This book covers 'interviewing skills', which can be defined as:

- the capability to find the truth;
- in all situations;
- in compliance with the law and ethical standards, through specified *processes*;
- in a way which leaves everyone involved with the most *positive feelings* possible under all of the circumstances.

Interviewing skills consist of two main elements: *capability* and *understanding*.

Capability is based on a deep *understanding* of the nature and mechanics of deception, and the ability to be able to deal with the conflict between the liar's:

- subconscious (which will usually try to tell the truth) and controlled consciousness (which may wish to misrepresent it);
- memory (which will know the facts) and imagination (which will distort them to suit the liar's conscious objectives).

The memory and subconscious are referred to as the 'two monkeys' that sit on the liar's back, constantly reminding him of the truth

Understanding is the second vital element of interviewing skills, and includes:

- An *appreciation* of the questions we can ask and statements we can make to get to the truth, and especially:
  - The capability to *influence* and *persuade* the liar to the point where he loses all confidence in his ability to cope with the anxiety created by his deception.
  - The capability to *recognize* when the suspect is confronting himself with the dilemma (the 'pivotal point') of whether or not to release his anxiety by telling some or all of the truth.
  - The capability to create *rapport* and *empathy* with the suspect to enable him to resolve this dilemma by telling the truth and to clear up other matters with which he may have been concerned while retaining his *self-respect*.
- An *acceptance* of the ethical, moral and social values concerned, including:
  - human rights,
  - privacy,
  - the policies and procedures in your organization,
  - the applicable laws, rules, procedures and codes of practice against which our actions will be judged by others and, more importantly, by ourselves as professional interviewers.

The definition includes three very important words, and these are 'respect', 'rapport' and 'empathy'. Let's look at these words in more detail.

Respect

We should always show respect for the person who tells lies, no matter how bad a person he really is, and must never become emotionally involved, through anger, sarcasm or discourtesy. Respect means honouring the suspect's legal rights and treating him fairly. It also means that you can sleep soundly at night, knowing you have done your best and have acted professionally.

Rapport

Rapport is defined as *'the process of establishing and maintaining a relationship of mutual trust and understanding between two or more people'*. It means 'seeing eye-to eye' or 'getting on the same wavelength' as someone else. It does not mean being condescending or obsequious. We should always try to establish rapport with the subject of an interview, while remaining firmly in control.

There is overwhelming evidence that people tell more of the truth, more often, to people they believe really understand and empathize with them. As a rule, if you show someone you don't like him by what you say, how you say it, or through your body language, he will not like you, and rapport goes out the window.

Within the first few seconds of meeting someone, you will subconsciously decide – based on their 'emblems' (see Chapter 4, Table 4.9) – how your relationship will develop (see Figure 1.2).

Figure 1.2   Who will you get on with?

To establish rapport we must take conscious control of our prejudices and first impressions. The ways in which we can consciously establish rapport are described in Chapter 5, page 133, but please remember the word: it is very important.

Empathy

This is another weighty word and goes a step beyond 'rapport', bordering on a low-level telepathy. It means that we are able to put ourselves in the other person's shoes, appreciate how he feels and, among other things, use this understanding to bring him face to face with reality, so that he tells the truth.

Where a liar is fighting with the two monkeys of subconscious and memory and deciding whether to tell the truth or not (the 'pivotal point'), an empathetic approach is critical. Chapter 5, page 223 says more about empathy, but remember that, like rapport, it is a really influential word. And you must have lots of it.

Empathy is sympathy without sadness

THE DEEP TRUTH

Really skilful interviewers don't just find the truth about the topic in which they are interested. They find the deep truth and get a brain dump from the subject of all matters that could be of interest. Once issues of immediate concern have been dealt with, they move on to explore other areas in which the subject may have been involved or may possess knowledge of naughtiness by others.

From now on you should focus on finding the deep truth and trying to get the subject to tell you *everything* that could be important, rather than just a confession to the limited matters at hand.

The person who confesses is a most valuable source of information on other matters

Disclaimers

LEGALITY

Every reasonable effort has been made to ensure that everything in this book is legal in civilized jurisdictions (i.e. excluding Cheam and Islington) and complies with legal, human rights, privacy and other legislation. However, neither the authors, publishers or Spot the Dog can be held responsible for the outcome of any particular interview and, in really difficult cases, especially involving criminal prosecution, you should seek specific legal advice.

It is also possible that some of the techniques for finding the truth – especially if they are quoted out of context – could be offensive to liars and people who believe in tooth fairies and that the rights of crooks, cheats and ne'er-do-wells should always prevail over those of their victims. We do not apologize for this but later on we include a specific health warning because it is totally contrary to human nature to ask questions that elicit the truth. Everything we suggest is fair, ethical and directed towards finding the truth, which means clearing the innocent as well as exposing the guilty. If readers of the *Independent* and residents of Cheam and Islington don't agree, so be it.

SEXISM AND OTHER STUFF

Women make superb interviewers, mainly because their brains have evolved more efficiently than men's (see Chapter 3, page 37). However, given that the population is divided almost equally between males and females,[4] it is amazing that proportionately less women are *detected* in dishonesty. This could be that they are innately more honest than men, more clever, or, more likely, both.

To simplify sentence construction, the masculine gender is used throughout and we hope this does not offend anyone.

Smile and the world smiles with you!

---

[4]   Except in Cheam and Islington

GIVING THE GAME AWAY

Some people might believe that writing books like this helps liars plan their defences and therefore should be suppressed. This is wrong and, on the contrary, the more the liar knows and becomes anxious about the clues he is emanating into the ether, the more likely he is to fail.

THE TURN IN THE BARREL

Where a person is being questioned about dishonesty, the world ceases to exist outside the room in which the interview is taking place. Family, friends and other problems disappear into the background while the subject focuses on surviving the interview. At this time, it is a closed world in which the more he understands, the more difficult it becomes to repress the truth.

Liars know too much. If you think telling the truth is difficult, try lying. When it is your turn in the barrel, things look different

Misconceptions and myths about deception

WHAT INTEREST IN SOLUTIONS?

There are few subjects which are as fraught with misconception, danger and emotion as the art of deception and the quest to identify and isolate its symptoms. Paradoxically, once symptoms have been recognized, there appears to be little interest in actually resolving them. This unwillingness to expose deception is clearly demonstrated in a recent book by a respected academic which devotes 220 pages to reviewing abstruse publications by his colleagues on the nature of lies and four and a half pages on how to resolve them!

It is easier to identify a problem than to suggest a solution

It is easy to discover when people are lying: in fact we are flooded with clues. What you do once you are put on notice is an entirely different matter, and it is in this area that the void of knowledge and lack of applied techniques are at their most extreme. No one, except for a few American investigators and lawyers, seems prepared to offer advice on how lies should be tackled and the deep truth exposed, except in the case of exculpatory lies. This is another paradox because, for the reasons explained later, it is much better to catch lies in the achievement stage, before the damage has been done.

People want to know how to detect lies but not how to tackle them

Getting to the deep truth can be simplified as a three-stage process:

1   Recognizing that a lie has been told.
2   Using interviewing skills to get to the deep truth.
3   Using a legal and morally defensible process.

Stages 1 and 3 are easy and, for this reason, everyone seems to have concentrated on them, including academics, lawyers etc., etc. Police training throughout the world is focused on

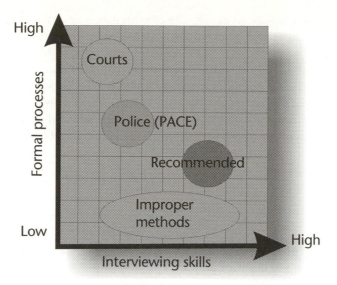

Figure 1.3   Interviewing skills and processes

process rather than on deep-truth interviewing skills. If you don't believe this, just read the transcript of the interview with OJ Simpson (http://simpson.walraven.org) which from a procedural point of view was uncontentious but which had no chance of ever getting off the ground and into the deep truth.

Process suppresses skills

This is not to say that processes are not important, but they must be set against the skills and techniques necessary to get to the deep truth. Figure 1.3 shows the relationship between skills and processes and the fact that the two must work together.

Without process controls, 'skills' may go over the line into extreme areas such as violence, torture, deprivation and truth serums. However, the methods currently used by law enforcement agencies are too process-orientated and do not encourage the use of interviewing skills. The result is that the deep truth never surfaces.

Putting down in writing the skills, tools and techniques needed to get to the deep truth in all situations – involving achievement and exculpatory lies – is difficult and if there has been any applied research on the subject, it is not visible.

Many groups are involved in the detection and resolution of deception, including academics – ranging from anthropologists, psychologists, psychiatrists to zoologists – politicians, lawyers and do-gooders down to the great unwashed such as police, customs, the intelligence services, auditors and business managers. Their work is fragmented and often conflicting.

A POTENT HEALTH WARNING

The point of the above is not just to take a gratuitous smack[5] at academics, lawyers and others who have the luxury of second guessing, but to issue a potent health warning. This book

---

[5]   However satisfying this might be

is based on over 40 years of applied experience of both achievement and exculpatory liars, including successes, failures and many hard-learned lessons. Not every technique can be proven scientifically or measured, and in the abstract some – especially those at the pivotal point – may appear clichéd or pedestrian.[6] Some ideas may not be suitable for the golf club or the Women's Institute. It is up to you to decide how you will deal with deception, but it is evil and ruins the lives of honest people. We hope this book will help you until such time as something better comes along. It should also lead you to conclude that prevention is far better than cure because once you are forced to deal with exculpatory lies it could be too late.

Prevention is better than cure

Conclusions

The bottom line is that people will always answer questions and admit the truth providing you have a cunning plan and use your powers of persuasion.

UNDER-AGE DRINKER

In an American case a man with a shotgun appeared before the cashier in a small grocery store and filled up a paper bag with the contents of the cash register. Nothing unusual in that, you say, but not satisfied with just the cash the robber saw a bottle of whisky on the shelf behind the trembling cashier and ordered him to hand it over. The cashier said he would not do so as the robber was under age. The robber claimed he was over 21, but the cashier argued. The argument went on for a few minutes but was resolved when the robber produced his driving licence showing his name, address and photograph, proving that he was over 21. The cashier examined the licence, remembered the details, and handed over the whisky. Two hours later the robber was caught sitting in his apartment counting the cash, with the bottle unopened.

This case demonstrates that anxiety can cause people to do things they would otherwise not do. You can always get to the deep truth by using a cunning plan: someone will always give the game away.

BUZZ LIGHTYEAR

In November 2002, the *Daily Telegraph* reported an interesting case involving the *Toy Story* character Buzz Lightyear. For those of you not involved in academia, Buzz is a small spaceman whose main catchphrase is 'To infinity and beyond'. A thief hiding in the bushes after stealing a Buzz Lightyear toy from a shop was caught after Buzz blurted out one of his catchphrases. Police with sniffer dogs were about to give up the chase for the thief who had set off the store's alarm, when the intergalactic law enforcer blurted out, 'Buzz Lightyear, permission to engage'. The thief realized the game was up when a police dog ran to his hiding place and began growling at him.

---

[6]   But they usually work

The first rule of interviewing is never give up and the second is if one person won't tell you the truth, somebody else will. If you want to really find out what is going on in an organization, go to the area where smokers congregate, speak to the tea ladies or the chauffeurs or play golf with the senior managers. The world is full of Buzz Lightyears who blurt out the truth and all you have to do is to recognize it at a conscious level and then deal with it.

'THINGS HAVE NEVER BEEN THE SAME SINCE HE BOUGHT THAT
BLOODY BOOK'

2 *Taxonomy*

If at first you don't succeed, try lying

The basics

WHAT IS A LIE?

A lie is a communication which the person conveying it:

- does not believe to be true; *or*
- has good reason to suspect is incorrect *(that is, wilful blindness).*

A lie is communicated with the conscious objective of misleading the victim to achieve an advantage for the liar or for someone else.[1] Thus, to tell a lie the liar must first know the truth. Truth is the baseline cognitive state and a lie a distortion of it.

> *The liar always makes a conscious decision to lie.*
> *A person lies because the truth is not to his greatest advantage*

A liar has conscious control over most of the words he utters, or the content of his story, but in all cases unconscious clues – including incongruencies in the syntax, paralinguistics, non-verbal communications and attitude – will always give the game away.

CLUES FROM EVERY PORE

Sigmund Freud said, 'He that has eyes to see and ears to hear may convince himself that no mortal can keep a secret. If his lips are silent, he chatters with his fingertips. Betrayal oozes out of every pore.'

> *A liar will always fail against an effective interviewer*

As we shall see in Chapter 3, the human brain is hard-wired in a way that makes repression[2] and concealment of the symptoms of deception impossible, simply because emotions and autonomic actions driven by the lower – reptilian and mammalian – brain cannot be hidden. In simple terms we can consider a liar's memory and subconscious as two monkeys sitting on his back, chattering away, creating anxiety, and liable at any moment to blurt out the truth.

---

[1] St Augustine defined a lie as 'an intentional negation of a subjective truth'
[2] Unconscious concealment

CHANNELS OF COMMUNICATION

Untruths – which will have one or more critical issues – can relate to future intentions, and are thus usually classed as 'achievement lies', or past events, usually 'exculpatory lies' that can be communicated in what we will refer to as a 'story' (Table 2.1).

This is the first table. Please don't just gloss over it, but read it carefully. It is important.

Table 2.1   Methods of communicating lies

Channel of communication	Delivery of the lie		
		How expressed	Examples
Verbal Consisting of content, lexicon and syntax		Speech Auditory	In face to face conversations In meetings During negotiations Over the telephone
	V I S U A L	In writing	In correspondence In forms In statements and affidavits In accounting and financial records In spreadsheets In business proposals In agreements and contracts In academic research and surveys
Non-verbal		Other than in writing	In pictures, photographs and diagrams In physical objects
			Sign language, flags, smoke signals and symbols
		Emblems	In appearance, such as clothing, hair or jewellery In appearance of an object, such as an office or a car
		Body language Kinaesthetic	Through gestures Facial expressions Proximity or personal space
		Paralinguistics Phonetics	Non- verbal sounds such as grunts and sighs Speed, tone and pitch of delivery
		Sensory	Smell (olfactory) Touch (tactile) Taste (gustatory)
		Extrasensory	Demeanour Attitude Telepathy

Channels of communication can also be summarized in the following way (see Mind Map 2).

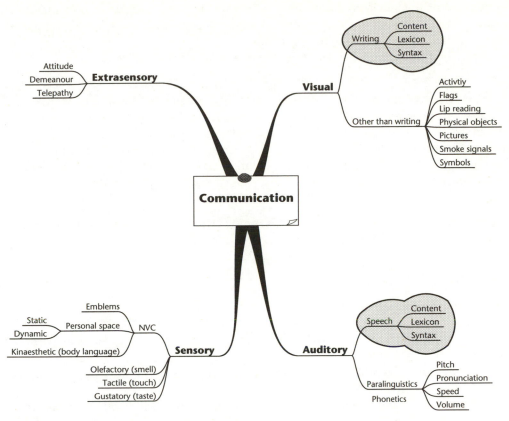

Mind Map® 2   Lies and channels of communication

Mind Map 2 shows that there are four channels through which we can communicate with others, the two most important are:

- auditory (hearing);
- visual (seeing).

We will discuss these channels of communication and their significance when we talk about finding the truth in Chapter 3. However, it is important to recognize from the outset that people always communicate:

- what they intend to communicate (conscious communication);
- other things they do not intend to disclose (unconscious communication).

Unintended or unconscious disclosures – which include body language, paralinguistics, proximetics, kinetics, attitude and emotions – are very important in guiding us to distinguish truth from lies. We will return to this point later.

Often lies will be communicated through more than one channel. For example:

THE TASTY DISH

A menu might give a written description which is nothing short of mouth-watering; the chef might tell us that the meat is delicious and arranges it so that it looks appetizing and covers it with a sweet- smelling sauce. The waiter may provide us with a knife so sharp it would cut through concrete. Only when we start eating the meat do we realize that it tastes like an old sock and is as tough as an army boot.

Lies usually come in clusters, with signals through the different channels of communication being incongruent. The liar has no conscious control over such incongruencies.

COMPONENTS OF A LIE

A lie consists of a number of components:

- The *content*, which is the words the liar consciously selects (or fails to select) in giving his story.
- The *syntax*[3] or the technical construction of the sentences in the story, which is mainly driven at an unconscious level.
- The tone, volume and speed with which the explanation is given: called *paralinguistics*, again usually directed at an unconscious level.
- The *non-verbal communications* (or body language), some of which may be consciously controlled, although most come straight from the autonomic system and are instinctive.

In a truthful story all of these components are more or less compatible, but in lies there is usually a conflict between them or incongruencies which reveal the underlying untruth.

THE ALIENS

In the mid-1970s mysterious circles and patterns appeared in fields of wheat and corn throughout the UK and the tabloids spread doom and gloom, as they do, to the effect that aliens had landed. In one case the words 'We are not alone' appeared in the patterns, thus confirming that aliens spoke English. Granny Smith immediately placed a curfew on her cat and Tommy Jones would not eat meat for weeks. There was great panic and the tabloids had a field day.

However, within the statement the lie is glaring, because aliens would have said '*You* are not alone' or '*Earthlings* are not alone'. The fact that the syntax included the personal pronoun 'we' showed that the supposed aliens included themselves in the same category as humans. Eventually, two jokers from Southampton admitted their responsibility.

---

[3] Including the person's lexicon (or dictionary of words he uses), semantics and pragmatics (the meaning he attaches to words)

The problem with stories like the above is that humans tend to make deductions from apparent facts and thus come to the wrong conclusions. For example, the fact that the Southampton cornfields incident was a sham does not mean that all such cases fall into the same category and it is quite possible that there are aliens out there.

As we will see later the pronoun 'we' – and syntax, generally – is very important in detecting deceit. In many cases syntax conflicts with the content of the story.

THE PRIZE WINNER

Soon after the hoax was exposed, the same Granny Smith received a very posh letter announcing, 'I am pleased to inform you that you are to receive a cash amount. We are currently holding a corporate cheque for £50,000 and await the filing of your Winnings Claim Form.'

Read the sentence carefully and you will see that no one was saying that Granny Smith would get anything more than a 'cash amount' and certainly not the fifty thousand smackeroos she expected. Incongruencies also appear between other channels of communication and particularly between content and non-verbal communication.

The truth lies in detecting small deviations and incongruencies, but the problem is that we do not think deeply enough about what we hear, see, feel or read and ignore our unconscious concerns. This is a bad mistake.

The truth is always in the detail

THE COMPONENTS OF A STORY

A 'story' is the total proposal, explanation, statement or answers a person gives about a particular matter and it may contain both truth and lies. They may be 'freestyle' when the person has total control over what he communicates or 'guided' when a template is provided by questions asked by an interviewer or in a form left blank for completion. As we will see later, it is often easier to find the truth in freestyle stories. Stories may be oral or written.

Freestyle, and some template, stories usually consist of a background introduction (or scene setting), factual and emotional clarification and one or more topics, scenes or events in:

- *a prologue*: the introduction to the matter concerned;
- *critical issues*: the key aspects of the proposal or explanation;
- *an epilogue*: the closing of the matter concerned.

A story, whether initially in writing or transcribed later, takes on an identity of its own, distinct from the reality it purports to represent. For example, an event that took two hours in real life may be represented in the story by one line of text or a very short oral explanation, whereas something else that was over and done with in two or three minutes may, in the mind of the subject, justify pages or hours of explanation (see Figure 2.1).

The fact that the person allocates a disproportionate number of words to a topic indicates it is very important to him: it should therefore be important to you. The same is true of the sequence in which topics are dealt with.

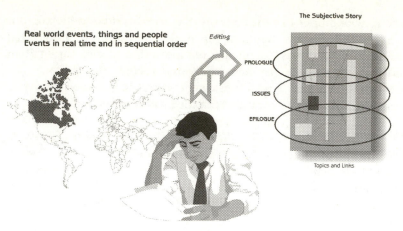

Figure 2.1   Real and story or subjective time

In most truthful freestyle stories, whether written or oral, the divisions between the prologue, critical issues and epilogue are more or less equal and comments in the background consistent with emotions and the sequence of scenes or topics. In deceptive stories the prologue and epilogue may be extended, usually because the liar unconsciously prevaricates before bringing himself to address the critical issues and, when he does, he may extend the epilogue to soften its impact. Such prevarication is true of a deceptive story as a whole, for sentences within it and within answers to specific questions. For example, the pseudo-denial by Bill Clinton:

> *I would like to tell the American people, and I will say it again, I did not have sex with that woman, Monica Lewinsky.*

This is an instance of an extended prologue, within an answer, and, as we will see later, it is also a subjective truth. Both are strong indicators of deception.

Types of lies

GOOD AND BAD LIES

Not all lies are intended to cause the victim harm.

> *Example*: A doctor may understate the seriousness of an illness to reassure his patient that he will recover. A smarmy employee might compliment the boss on his new tie when it looks like a dog's blanket. A golfer may boast about the length of his drive or the fisherman the size of his catch. Such lies are unimportant and, in fact, if we always challenged them we would soon become very unpopular.

Altruistic, boastful, joking, social or *good lies* involve no serious penalties if exposed, and may even be authorized by the victim, or justified by the circumstances in which they are communicated. If good lies don't exactly make the world go round, they do little harm either.

Bad lies have a negative or evil intent. They are not authorized by the victim, justified by the circumstances or expected. They are normally intended to cause damage to the victim or to someone else. Their discovery would normally result in adverse consequences for the liar. In some cases bad lies become so ingrained that they are accepted, including: 'The cheque is in the post', 'Mr Smith is in a meeting and cannot take your call, but will call you back straight away', or 'Billy is sick this morning and will not be able to come to work'. They are still damaging and should be dealt with.

This book concentrates on bad lies

ACHIEVEMENT AND EXCULPATORY LIES

Lies can be told to provide the liar with a *benefit not already obtained* and these are called 'achievement lies'.

> *Example:* The job candidate may claim to have a degree in zoology when he can't tell a camel from a goat, a car salesman might lie about the age of a car or the number of previous owners to get a better price, the social security claimant might feign illness when he is as fit as a butcher's dog, and the businessman might try to convince a banker that an investment is sound when it is built on sand.

Achievement lies are usually based on a *falsification* (rather than concealment) of what we can regard as a *central issue* in one or more of three aspects:

1   *Personal* misrepresentation.

> *Example*:
> • The liar claims to be someone he is not. This is essentially identity theft, which is an increasingly nasty problem (see www.identitytheft.com).
> • He claims a relationship he does not have (for example, a woman claims she is the widow of President Abacha of Nigeria and has $25 million ready to send to you).

2   *Physical* misrepresentation.

> *Example*:
> • The liar misrepresents the quality or quantity of goods being delivered.
> • He deceives an insurance company over the extent of damage to his car.
> • He falsifies an injury to claim compensation.

3   *Commercial* or *financial* misrepresentation.

Example:
- The liar produces false accounts to obtain a loan from a bank.
- A manager overstates the results of his department.
- A potential borrower pretends to own assets he does not own.
- He exaggerates the gains to be made from an investment.
- He claims false professional or other qualifications to obtain employment.
- He inflates his performance.
- He anticipates results not yet achieved.

In such cases, liars must *create* explanations, forge or falsify documentation or *make up* falsehoods to achieve their objectives and cannot claim the right of silence. For example:

THE ESTATE AGENT

The house was described in the glossy brochure as 'boasting a wonderful outlook over the rolling hills with planning consent to build an observatory over the adjacent wildlife park.' When you go to look at it, and find that it is in the middle of an abattoir, not unreasonably you ask the estate agent to explain. He cannot respond: 'I am saying nothing until I have first spoken to my lawyer.'

In *achievement lies*, the liar cannot refuse to answer: he has to falsify. Also, achievement lies are very dangerous for the liar, because they leave him little opportunity to provide a plausible excuse if they are detected.

Exculpatory lies usually occur after the liar has obtained an advantage and are necessary to justify or substantiate an earlier deception. There is a close relationship between achievement and exculpatory lies (see Figure 2.2).

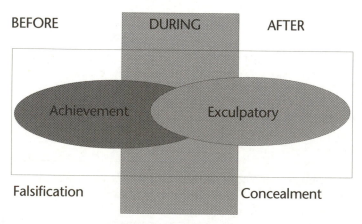

Figure 2.2   Achievement and exculpatory lies – showing that an achievement lie today may have to be explained away by an exculpatory lie tomorrow

The relationship between achievement and exculpatory lies is important, especially from a fraud prevention point of view, because the more false detail the liar can be committed to at the achievement stage, the more likely it is he will be deterred or detected. Moreover, barefaced achievement lies may be impossible for the liar to explain later on. Ways of dealing with achievement lies are discussed in Chapter 10, page 356.

For every exculpatory lie there has already been an achievement lie that succeeded

CONCEALMENT LIES AND FALSIFICATIONS

Lies can be used to *conceal* information adverse to the liar, such as responsibility for a criminal act, a bad credit record or previous deception. Concealment is used in both achievement and exculpatory lies.

Concealment lies are used to deceive the victim by:

- failing or refusing to answer questions;
- feigned cooperation;
- suppressing or evading the truth;
- attacking the victim, physically or verbally, as a means of deflecting his questions.

Concealment lies are the most common and the most beneficial when viewed from the position of the liar. If they are challenged, the liar is usually able to say that he misunderstood the question or forgot to mention an important detail. In 95 per cent of cases, lies occur because a person does not tell the *whole* truth. If he succeeds, the interviewer is to blame because he did not ask the right questions and press for detailed answers.

Every concealment is a step away from the truth while
every falsification is a step towards finding it

AN EXAMPLE OF CONCEALMENT

'I understood Michael Heseltine wanted to know whether I had a "financial relationship" with Ian Greer by which Fayed money could have found its way into my pocket … the term "relationship" implied some element of continuity. The receipt of two single commission payments … carrying no implication of further obligation does not constitute a "relationship". This has been described as a semantic distinction, but I was answering the question I was asked. If I had been asked whether I had ever received a payment of any kind from Ian Greer I would have said that I had. But that was not the question.'

Neil Hamilton MP before the Select
Committee on Standards and Privileges

In *falsifications*, the liar has to make up a story or invent details that are not true. Falsification calls for good imagination, excellent short-term memory, anticipation, composure, assertiveness and confidence. What starts out as a concealment can quickly turn when the victim challenges it, forcing the liar to falsify.

There is no excuse for a barefaced lie and a skilful liar will try to make sure that, if he is compelled to give an answer, the words he actually utters are as near to the truth as possible.

These, as we will see later, are referred to as 'subjective truths' and their recognition is very important in exposing deception.

REHEARSED AND SPONTANEOUS LIES

Most achievement lies are rehearsed and some salesmen are trained in delivering them.

PENSION SWITCHES

Thousands of British workers were persuaded to remove their pension funds from 'earnings related' to individual 'money pool schemes'. Investigations revealed that salesmen, working for apparently reputable companies, had systematically lied about the benefits of making the switch, primarily to increase their own commissions.

A liar may also rehearse for exculpatory interviews but will still be unable to suppress all clues and incongruencies in the various channels of response. On the contrary, the fact that a liar has rehearsed his responses may make him more vulnerable to surprise questions.

DIRECT AND INDIRECT LIES

Lies may be communicated directly to the intended victim or they may be relayed through a third party who has himself been deceived.

Example: A parent who believes incorrectly in his child's innocence will be a fierce defender.

LIES IN WRITING

Even when the liar has extensive time to plan and write down his untruths, he still leaves clues. This includes achievement lies, such as false business proposals, application forms, or Nigerian 4-1-9 scam letters (see the excellent site www.ed-u.com/nigerian-scam-letters.htm), and exculpatory lies, such as false statements and affidavits in legal proceedings or in correspondence.

PASSIVE AND ACTIVE COLLUSION

Experience suggests that over 90 per cent of all deception involves collusion between two or more people, which can be viewed in two categories:

- *Active collusion*, in which all the people involved participate and share in the benefits and are personally liable if the dishonesty is detected.
- *Passive collusion*, in which people know of dishonesty by others but do not benefit or participate or report their suspicions and are not at risk of criminal prosecution. The Buzz Lightyear example in Chapter 1 is an example of how the liar can be exposed by others, possibly inadvertently.

In most cases of fraud there will be a number of passive colluders or bystanders, most of whom do not wish to become involved or to voluntarily report their suspicions. However, they often retain detailed records, copies of correspondence, tape recordings and diaries for their own protection if they ever fall under suspicion. Establishing that such unofficial and personal records exist and obtaining them is critically important in interviews with witnesses.

INDIVIDUAL AND TEAM LIES

Lies can be told by one person to another or they may involve groups of people who actively collude together to deceive others.

> *Example*: Many employees of the failed Bank of Credit and Commerce International (BCCI) maintained false achievement lies of the bank's finances for many years. In fact, BCCI is alleged to have had a special office whose only job was to create fraudulent documentation.

Members of collusive groups usually rationalize their behaviour as acceptable and take strength from each other. They will sometimes dress, look and act alike to reinforce the bond between them. When they involve collusion, lies are usually easier to prove, simply because the people involved are scared that their associates will capitulate to save their own skins. Their fear is usually justified and someone will always inform on the others. Collusion is always a fertile ground for developing witnesses and informants.

Why people tell lies

People tell lies because they believe at the time it is to their advantage to do so or to help someone else. Men tend to tell more self-serving lies – even good ones, such as boasting about their golfing prowess – than women, and this seems to be in their nature. Women are much more likely to lie to help someone else to prevent their feelings being hurt.

In most frauds the liar has no alternative but to lie if he wishes to achieve an advantage and a confidence trickster cannot elect to remain silent or claim the 'Fifth Amendment'. When a story is challenged, the liar has three options:

- fight;
- flight;
- appease.

Reactions to any threat are triggered by the limbic system (see page 35), are often based on fear and are, initially at least, unconscious. Neurotransmitters bursting out of the lower brain may, or may not, be refined by the upper brain before the liar says or does something, but even when he consciously tries to control his reaction, he will radiate with clues to deception.

Exculpatory lies are normally in response to a challenge and are communicated for a number of reasons. The most important is that the liar wants to give the impression of innocence and thus appease his opponent. He knows refusal to answer will be treated with suspicion and is tantamount to a fight.

The liar answers questions because he believes he can bamboozle the interviewer by deception, evasion, concealment and all the other tools available to him. The decision to answer questions is usually taken consciously.

In some cases the liar will refuse to answer questions but will present a plausible justification for non-cooperation, the most usual being based on legal advice which he may, or may not, have taken. He may claim mental or physical incapacity or make promises to answer in the future, which he has no intention of keeping.

The lack of an endgame

In both achievement and exculpatory lies, the liar seldom plans his endgame with precision and his thinking is essentially short term.

THE ROUNDABOUT	
A fraudster working for a bank created fictitious loans for non-existent borrowers and converted the funds to his own use. As they became due for repayment he created new and larger loans, siphoning off further	funds. When he was caught he was asked how he planned to bring the fraud to a close. He looked puzzled and said, 'I never thought about it. I was just living from day to day.'

This lack of planning for the endgame is a serious problem for the liar which can be exploited by asking the right questions at the appropriate time (see pages 216/217). It is, as they would say in Latin, his Achilles heel.

'WE ALWAYS GET MRS BIRT TO CHECK OUT JOB CANDIDATES AS HER
CORPUS CALLOSUM IS MORE DEVELOPED THAN OURS'

3 *The Human Mind*

Never believe in superstition as it makes you unlucky

Introduction

This chapter examines some of the important psychological, physiological and other theories that have proven themselves important in practice, and sets the background for getting to the deep truth. Its bottom line is that the symptoms of deception can never be hidden, mainly because contention between different elements of the brain when lying always surfaces in recognizable profiles. We usually know when we are being deceived; we just don't want to deal with it.

Darwin said that repressed emotion always surfaces

Freud's model of the mind

Sigmund Freud theorized that there were divisions in the human psyche (Figure 3.1).

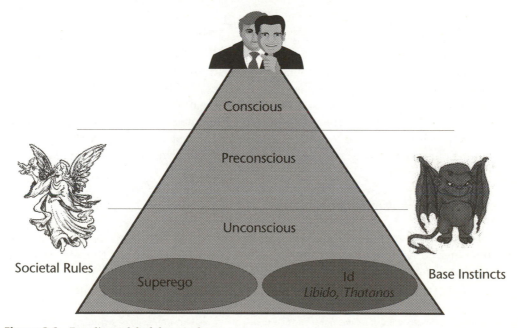

Figure 3.1   Freud's model of the mind

Although Freud believed that his model was representative of physical structures in the brain, he was never able to prove it. However, recent research using magnetic resonance imaging (MRI) seems to confirm that at a subconscious level only reality and deep truth exists, and that the subconscious cannot lie. Jung believed the subconscious to be the reservoir of 'transcendent truth' and that it dominated human behaviour.

Freud also identified what he regarded as the main drivers of human behaviour: *eros* or libido, which centre on life's pleasures and erotic thought, and *thatanos* or death instincts. Unsurprisingly, the erotic bits have been given the most attention, especially in such academic journals as the *Sun* and *Mirror*, but the death wish instincts are also important. They explain why smokers are not deterred by death warnings on tobacco or why some people are sadists or masochists.

Experts in subliminal advertising – especially those employed by Silk Cut cigarettes – have replied upon the instinct of self-destructive behaviour to the extent that the urge for a drag is excited by advertisements that non-smokers would regard as bizarre. In short, the 'smoke this and die a painful death' warnings are a great way of increasing sales. Similarly, if you believe that banishing smokers to a freezing spot alongside the dustbins deters them, dream in technicolour: they love it and are encouraged by the pain.

Freud also suggested that unconscious emotional responses always occur ahead of conscious reactions to the same input, but may be repressed before intruding into awareness, concealed by mental constructions (such as self-deception) or through obsessive behaviour, such as repeated washing of the hands or cleaning of the carpet. Even then, the repressed thoughts continue to affect conscious behaviour.

Freudian theories thus suggest that to succeed with deception, a liar has to block out damaging information from his subconscious, especially his real memory, feelings and attitudes. He then has to consciously present the filtered results. This is very difficult for even the most accomplished liar to do. The subconscious and memory are monkeys on the liar's back that make him anxious and may cause him to blurt out the truth.

The subconscious is the first monkey on the liar's back.
The second is his memory

It is obviously impossible for us to remain in conscious control of everything we do. For example, it is estimated that the human brain receives 2 million bits of information every second. If we had to deal consciously with our breathing or the carbon dioxide levels in our blood, we would never cope. The subconscious represented mainly in the limbic system (cerebellum or mammalian brain) and brain stem (or the reptilian brain) are the autopilots, controlling our vital bodily or autonomic functions, most of which are hard-wired and, to a large extent, non-variable.

Question: Why are you breathing so heavily?

Until you thought about this question, you were not consciously aware of your breathing, but now you are.[1] It is a simple example of how stimulation can bring thoughts from our unconscious into awareness.

---

[1] You thought to yourself 'Bullshit', but now you are thinking about your breathing: go on admit it

Question: When people dress, why does a woman put her left arm in first and men their right? And why do they cross their legs in different ways?

Most people react to deception at an unconscious level and may have an intuitive feeling that they are being misled without quite knowing why. For example, we notice other people's body language and emblems and, once we have made an unconscious determination, our minds may become closed to further input. To get to the deep truth it is imperative that we remain alert to everything around us and elevate our suspicions to conscious level.

If it does not look or feel right, ask yourself, 'Why?'
Never consult a psychiatrist whose office plants have died

The brain and mind

EVOLUTION (IN VERY BASIC TERMS!)

Some 3.5 billion years ago (can you even imagine how long ago that was?) single cells floated around the planet, with no brains, spines, eyes, ears, legs or even golf clubs. The best they could do was to drift towards a light source and if they bumped into something, chomp away at it. You can still see this behaviour today as kids chomp away in McDonald's. Bumping into things and then chomping at them is an inherited instinct.

Darwinism, which has held to be accurate except in the case of investigators, proposes that the human gene pool was refined as a result of natural selection, sexual selection and inherited instincts.[2] Faculties that were useful were incorporated and subsequently hard-wired by the development of new cells in both the body and brain. Patterns that were beneficial to survival were replicated and those that weren't were thrown in the bin through a process known as atrophy. If lying had been bad for survival of the species – any species – it would have atrophied during earlier evolutionary periods. The fact is that deceptive instincts and abilities are ingrained in humans, animals and – according to Prince Charles – in plants, because they are useful.

Some researchers believe that deception is instinctive and is the baseline cognitive state, overridden in humans by conscious intervention. We are not clever enough to know the answer, but nature suggests that both hard-wired and learned deception evolves depending on the ability of opponents to detect it.

The rule in life is 'If you don't use it, you will lose it'

BRAIN HARDWARE

The basics

The human brain, at its present state of evolution, is a complex, modular system (rather than a homogeneous lump of stodge), around three pounds in weight and consisting of the useful parts not atrophied from reptilian and mammalian eras, plus a newly added (i.e. 60 million years ago) cerebrum, or outer brain (Figure 3.2).

---

[2] Lamarkianism

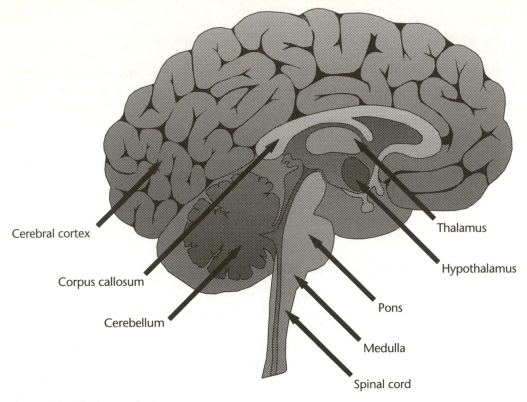

Figure 3.2 The human brain

We can summarize the components of the human brain, as in Table 3.1.

The amygdala plays an important role in lots of things, including deception. It is one of the basal ganglia, small islands of grey matter in the limbic system, and consists of two almond-shaped, fingernail structures that are reciprocally connected to most brain areas. Its main task is to filter and interpret incoming sensory information in the context of survival and emotional needs and to trigger appropriate responses. It also encodes or lays down emotional memories.[3]

Sensory receptors (such as eyes, ears, nose, mouth, hands) detect something and then direct signals to the appropriate part of the brain, which fires up neurons and sends them on. Senses and movements on the right side of the body are processed by the left hemisphere and vice versa (except for smell which is handled simultaneously by both hemispheres). Funny that!

Engineers (bless them) see the brain in a slightly different way and represent its processes as shown in Figure 3.3.

The engineering representation is important because it shows the connection between a sensory input and the resulting action, passing through a number of conscious filters. As we will discover later, when a person is being deceptive, some of these filters break down.

---

[3]   Definition based on www.ascd.org/pdi/brain/amygdala/html

Table 3.1   Important elements of the human brain

Area of the brain	Sub area	Evolutionary stage	What it does
Forebrain or upper brain			
Cerebral cortex *A thin sheath covering the cerebrum and cerebellum*			Super fast transmission system between most areas of the brain
Cerebrum *Gives humans 'self-awareness' – or consciousness Split into two hemispheres which appear identical but in fact operate differently It controls impulses*	Occipital Lobe	Human	Visual processing and some memories
	Temporal lobe		Sound and speech, spiritualism and some memories
	Parietal lobe		Movement, calculation, recognition and some memories
	Frontal		Integrated functions, thinking, conceptualizing, also consciously processes emotion and stores some memories
	Motor cortex		Handles bodily movement
Midbrain			
Corpus callosum *Transmission system*	Connects the left and right hemispheres	Human	A sheath-like membrane connecting the two hemispheres of the brain
Hindbrain or lower brain			
Limbic system or cerebellum *Totally unconscious Creates impulses*	Known as 'the little brain'	Mammalian	Directly connected to the cortex
	Thalamus		The brain's central switch
	Hypothalamus Pituitary gland		Adapts the body to the environment
	Hippocampus		Lays down and controls long-term memory
	Amygdala		Deals with emotion and especially fear. Acts as memory store for emotions
Brainstem		Reptilian	Handles transmissions to the body, determines the brain's level of awareness, regulates breathing, heart beat and blood pressure etc. Also directs most eye movements

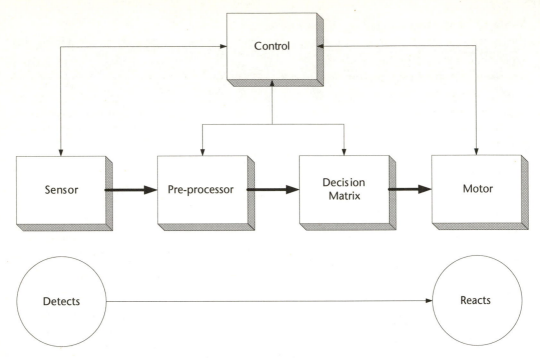

Figure 3.3   An engineering representation of the brain

The different areas of the brain are related through a web of more than a 100 trillion (again just think how many this is) neural connections, which receive and send a complex array of neurotransmitters for even simple tasks.

Darwin made a Freudian slip: what he meant to say was 'survival of the fattest'

Hemispheres of the brain
Divisions
The human brain is divided into two hemispheres each with the same component parts (except for the old pineal gland):

The left hemisphere is concerned with:

- *logic* and analysis and is conscious of time;
- verbal communication and *words*;
- *control*, linear, serial and sequential thinking;
- movements and sensory input on the right side of the body;
- dissection and separation of thoughts;
- autonomic control of the right side of the body.

It processes information in a logical way and is closely associated with a person's conscious state. When different parts of the brain are in contention for control, it is usually the left hemisphere cortex that acts as the final arbiter and failure in this control region can be disastrous for the liar.

The right hemisphere is concerned with:

- creativity and perception;
- *visual* communication, pictures and even Mind Maps;
- *imagination*, mood and emotion, *including humour;*
- movements and sensory input on the left side of the body and the autonomic management of most non-verbal communications;
- whole or holistic relationships;
- synthesis and connecting things together;
- autonomic control of the left side of the body.

The right hemisphere of the brain processes information in a non-sequential, spatial, holistic and relational way and is closely associated with a person's subconscious.

Twice as many twins are left handed (20%) as single births (10%)

Job gravitation, hobbies and personal interests
People tend to behave and take up interests and jobs that match their dominant hemisphere. This is admittedly a sweeping statement but most accountants, actuaries, lawyers and even some investigators are left hemisphere dominant whereas HR specialists and artistes tend to be driven, more often, by the right hemisphere. There are exceptions and a few accountants, such as some of those employed by Enron and WorldCom, are dominated by their right hemispheres and thus may be exceedingly creative.

Getting on the same wavelength
You can predict, more or less, how a person will react once you determine which hemisphere is dominant and if you wish to create rapport with a left hemisphere driven, dreary and humourless accountant,[4] you should try a logical, step-by-step unemotional approach. With an arty, creative, right hemisphere inclined advertising executive, you should normally work on a more visual, intuitive and emotional basis. If you try things the other way around, you are unlikely to succeed. As we will see later, establishing rapport, or 'getting on the same wavelength', is important.

You can establish rapport with anyone, if you try

Men and women
It may not be politically correct to repeat what scientists have said about the evolution of male and female brains, but it is relevant. Men, traditionally, have been the hunters, gatherers, stalkers and rogerers while females have evolved as nurturers and homemakers. Thus male and female brains have advanced in slightly different ways. It is a physical reality that the corpus callosum (which acts as the conduit between the right and left hemispheres of the brain) has a greater bandwidth in women than men.

---

[4] And believe it or not there are some like this!

A PROVEN FACT

MRI scans reveal that between 14 and 16 areas in both hemispheres of a female brain are active when she is communicating face to face. These areas decode words, note non-verbal communications and result in what is known as 'woman's intuition'. A male brain uses only four to seven areas for identical tasks because it has evolved for spatial tasks rather than for communication.[5]

Women are thus hard-wired to multitask faster and more efficiently than men, process seamlessly in both hemispheres of the brain and are more prepared to take emotional stimuli on board. Men tend to be more pedantic and logical although, as in all walks of life, there are exceptions to every rule.

The term 'opposite sex' was not coined by accident

DECISION CONFLICT

The brain is the ultimate in multitasking and multi-programming. It is like a giant committee of the Women's Institute when discussing whether to serve cream teas or muffins at the village fete. All relevant sectors of the brain – logical, emotional, visual, sensory and so on – are canvassed, in milliseconds, on what to make of a stimulus. Each involved area has an input with the frontal lobes of the cerebrum normally trying to resolve disputes, before sending signals to the motor cortex for action to be taken.

It is generally believed that stuttering is caused through interference by the right hemisphere in verbal construction and linguistics delivery handled primarily by the left. Similarly, there is an illness called the 'alien hand' in which (usually) the left hand opposes actions both contemplated and completed by the right. It is very common in investigators, whose right hands often don't know what the lefts are doing.

ALIEN HANDS

In one sad case a lady would pick her dresses from the wardrobe with her right hand and the left would put them straight back.[6] She could not pack suitcases. One man used to put his cufflinks on with his right hand and immediately take them off with his left.

KNEE-JERK REACTION

A tap on the knee of a person sitting down with his legs crossed produces a message to the spinal cord, which sends a pre-processed message to the leg to respond with an upward jerk. The brain is not involved in this movement and hence the phrase a 'knee-jerk reaction'. The body uses such reflex arcs when a rapid reaction is needed.

---

[5] See *Why Men Lie and Women Cry*, Allan and Barbara Pease, ISBN 0 75284 727 9
[6] This might explain why it takes your wife so long to get ready to go out

When a person is anxious, under pressure, fearful, angry or lying, the cerebrum (upper brain) has difficulty controlling other parts that are inputting, contending or thrashing about to be heard. One reason for this is that the neurotransmitters going up from the limbic system are more powerful than those coming back down from the upper brain. However, as adults we regard it as 'immature' to react to emotional stimuli and try to suppress them.

One of the most important results of brain thrashing is when the limbic system causes uncensored bodily movements and especially facial expressions. Such 'micro-expressions' occur for milliseconds usually before the upper brain can control them and produce a more reasoned reaction.

LOUISE WOODWARD

You may remember the case of the young British nanny – Louise Woodward – who was accused of killing a baby in the USA. At her trial, when she was asked whether she killed the baby, she said, 'No', but a micro-smile seemed to influence the jury, who found her guilty. This was a great shame if, as she claimed, she was innocent.

Micro-expressions are very important

BRAIN FINGERPRINTING

Brain fingerprinting works by flashing words or pictures relevant to a crime or other incident, together with irrelevant words or images. When the subject recognizes information brain pulses, called MERMERS (or P300 waves), are involuntarily emitted around 300 milliseconds after stimulation. Thus when details of a crime, for example the scene of a murder, are shown to the guilty subject he MERMERS, where innocent people do not. This activity can be detected on a headband equipped with sensors and MRI scanning.

To find the truth, we have to overload the liar's brain (see the difference between creating fear – a definite no-no – and increasing anxiety, page 60 to 61) so that he loses confidence in his ability to succeed. This is referred to as the pivotal point and it is critical in finding the truth.

Most liars succeed because they are not taken to the pivotal point

NEUROLINGUISTIC PROGRAMMING (NLP)

You either like NLP or you don't and even its greatest supporters have difficulty in explaining what it is. The simplest definition is that 'NLP concerns itself with modelling existing cognitive processes, and designing interventions, based on redirecting resources that the person already has.' The word 'neuro' refers to an understanding of brain functions; 'linguistics' to communication; and 'programming' is the behavioural and thinking patterns that people follow. The pseudo-science was founded by John Grinder and Richard Bandler in 1975 and has come into and fallen out of favour ever since.[7]

---

[7]   The website www.skeptic.com sets out to debunk NLP and it is well worth visiting

The bottom line from a practical viewpoint is that there is a two-way feedback between a person's inner thought processes and his actions. In simple terms, the subconscious will normally drive most non-verbal communications, paralinguistics and so on, but if an external stimulus can be introduced there will be a corresponding impact on the person's thinking, feelings, attitudes, anxiety, verbal responses and so on.

NEUROLINGUISTIC PROGRAMMING

NLP is the art, science or pseudo-science concerned with programming the brain (see www.NLP.org) to act in a certain way. For example, if you consciously feel the emotion of happiness, neurotransmitters will be sent to the amygdala and you will genuinely feel happy. Moreover, the more you repeat the process (called 'feedback'), the more the emotion becomes a reality.

If a child is feeling unhappy, with his head down and perhaps in tears, the mother's normal reaction is to place her fingers gently under his chin and raise it: the child cheers up. This is another example of NLP. It is very difficult to remain depressed when your eyes are open and looking upwards. If you don't believe this, try it.

LOOK UP NOW

Look towards the ceiling for a minute or two. You may even feel happy that you bought this book.

Recent research, including MRI scanning, confirms this feedback relationship between the brain and bodily movements. Neurotransmitters, coming from the amygdala, result in facial expressions, such as smiles and other activity. But consciously driven activity can affect the brain, including emotions. Thus the old saying 'smile and the world smiles with you' is true.

In all interviews we should consider using NLP and feedback techniques to our advantage. The way of doing this is described later but you should always programme yourself when dealing with suspected liars by imagining two monkeys on their backs.

More on channels of communication

PRINCIPLES

Primary channels of communication are normally aligned with the dominant hemisphere of the brain. For example, right hemisphere-inclined people react better to visual input and are less linear in their thought processes; they also react strongly (both positively and negatively) to emotional and sensory stimuli. The language a person uses and his eye movements (see Table 3.2, column 3) when processing and retrieving information will *usually* reveal his primary channel of communication.

Table 3.2 Primary methods of communication for right-handed people

For right-handed people		
Dominant method of communication	Examples of language used	Eye movement when retrieving from memory for a right-handed person (see page 51) *Eye movement when calculating or imagining something*
1	2	3
Auditory Usually left hemisphere dominant	'I haven't *heard* any reason why I should help' 'It *sounds* to me that you have already made up your mind' 'You are barking up the wrong tree'	Horizontal and left Then straight ahead *Horizontal and right* *Then straight ahead*
Visual Usually right hemisphere dominant	'I don't *see* why you have asked to see me ...' 'It *looks* to me that you have already made up your mind ...' 'In my *view* ...' 'You cannot *read* too much into this' 'You're *looking* at the wrong person' 'We don't see eye to eye'	Upwards and left Then straight ahead *Upwards and right* *Then straight ahead*
Sensory and emotional Usually right hemisphere dominant	'I *feel* you are looking in the wrong direction' 'You are not *handling* this very well' 'Just get off my *back* ...' 'I do not *believe* ...' 'That is really *heavy* man' 'It *strikes* me you are on the wrong track'	Downward Eyes closing or fluttering Expression before verbal statement *To the right* *Verbal statement before expression*

There is a very important point to note in relation to Table 3.2. It is that there is an exception to every rule. To test how a person reacts you should ask a few control questions, which are non-threatening, and monitor his eye movement. This will set the baseline standard against which you can monitor his response to relevant questions.

When you are watching people in live interviews on television, determine their primary method of communication and observe their eye movements – it will soon become a habit

HOW INFORMATION IS CONSCIOUSLY ABSORBED

People become consciously aware of information through their sensory receptors (eyes, ears etc.) and process it through their primary channel of communication: some people learn best by listening, others by reading or watching and others by touching, feeling or through emotional stimuli. Experience shows that visual inputs have a very powerful effect on all people and for this reason, your appearance, the way you present documentary and other evidence and the layout of the room in which the interview is held are all very important.

VISUAL INPUT
Images sensed by the right visual field of both eyes are processed by the left hemisphere of the brain and vice versa. Thus, documents and other visual prompts will have the greatest emotional impact	when they are presented into the subject's left field of vision because they hit his emotional right hemisphere. We will come back to this important point later on (see page 136).

Impact is enhanced when all channels are used together

UNIQUE COMMUNICATION CODES

Everyone uses reasonably consistent protocols for communication, both linguistic and non-linguistic. For example, some people use hand movements a lot and others don't; others use big words[8] and complex syntax, some speak slowly and others quickly. Deviations to a person's baseline communications code – in response to a specific question or stimulus – are normally a strong sign of deception.

Generally highly educated or intelligent people use non-verbal communication less than dummies.[9] But please remember everyone has his own baseline communications code.

Communication codes are disturbed by anxiety caused by being deceptive

Our communication codes are mainly determined at an unconscious level, except when we try to impress others by using big words or by 'dumbing down', for example in the mistaken belief that we can establish rapport with a rapper by talking rap[10] or by trying to get on the same wavelength as teenage kids by doing moonies. Artificial changes to your communication codes can make you look a plonker and destroy, rather than create, rapport.

Linguistic codes (which are part of the wider communication codes) are also reasonably consistent but may change over time with the adoption of vogue words: these days everything seems to be an 'issue' or a 'fury' or, in government circles, 'an initiative'. Sometimes organizations and divisions within them create their own vocabularies and linguistic codes. There is nothing sinister in this and it simply goes towards building group identity and rapport. However, the use of common codes tells you that people are part of a group.

Sometimes the extended use of esoteric linguistic codes can cause problems.

---

[8] Their lexicon or dictionary
[9] Possibly because dummies are further down the evolutionary chain
[10] Never try doing this: it will make you appear a condescending nerd and will destroy rapport (no pun intended)

THE INTERNATIONAL COMPANY

Supposedly to simplify communications, a leading international company used acronyms in place of virtually all proper nouns. It did not refer to the Marketing Department but to 'EMCS' (Marketing Central Services) and it referred to the Human Resources Department as 'GER' (Global Employee Relations). In its reports it did not refer to John Smith, but to 'JS', or to Bill Jones, but to 'WEJ'. It had printed a glossary of over 500 acronyms, which employees (and external consultants) were expected to learn. There was no consistent structure to the acronyms. For example, common sense would suggest that the first letter should always be the geographical area ('E' for Europe, 'G' for global and so on) but this was not the case. An enormous amount of time was thus wasted in trying to decipher what was meant. There were also serious misunderstandings, which were put to rest when a senior manager sent out an instruction that in future 'all UOAANST[11] would cease'. This caused an uproar, but it made the point.

We should consciously tune in to a subject's communication codes – think what he is really saying and why. We should also remain on the lookout for changes in his codes, or incongruencies between his various channels of communication, because these are always good clues to deception.

EMBEDDED COMMANDS

Obviously people do not *always* stick to their primary channel of communication or codes, nor do they think exclusively with one hemisphere of the brain. To complicate matters further, the subconscious registers communications totally missed at a conscious level. Subliminal advertising[12] or muzak to encourage sales in retail shops are examples of communications aimed directly at a person's subconscious. These are sometimes referred to as 'voice to skull' communications because they bypass conscious filters.

We often pay too little regard to the importance of smell and its impact on the subconscious. The Greek Orthodox Church incorporates all five senses into its services, including the burning of incense. Aromatherapy was first practised by the ancient Egyptians and there is a strong connection between the impact of smell and memory.[13]

DEBT COLLECTION AGENCY

A London debt collection agency sprays demanding letters with a clear non-smelling solution of the pheromone andosterone. This odourless stuff is normally emitted from men's armpits[14] to warn away others, but it improved debt recovery by over 17%. The trouble is, pigs like pheromones and eat the letters and women find them a turn-on.

---

[11] Use of acronyms, abbreviations and non-specific terms, i.e. UOAANST
[12] There is still a big debate over whether this works: the balance of professional opinion is that it does in certain circumstances
[13] Aroma processing is wired directly into the limbic system, where much memory is stored and emotion resides
[14] Don't ask how the chemical is collected

DEJA VU

Some scientists believe that deja vu is a phenomenon where a smell too faint to be consciously recognized registers in the subconscious, triggering memory and an inexplicable sense of familiarity.

KEYBOARD ERRORS

When the odour of jasmine or lemon was diffused into a room, keyboard errors fell by 30%. According to research by Neil Martin of Middlesex University, smell has a significant effect on the way people behave. Subjects were asked to smell a number of odours including chocolate, spearmint, coffee, almond, strawberry, baked beans, rotting pork and garlic. They sat in special smell-proof rooms and wore clouded goggles and earplugs so that they were forced to concentrate on the smells provided to them. While they sniffed away, their brain activity was monitored. Chocolate consistently suppressed theta waves, making it more difficult for the subject to concentrate or carry out complex tasks.

The human brain is truly amazing: some people are able to speak in reverse and to decipher a tape recording played backwards. The subconscious also reacts to what are called 'embedded commands', and these are very important. They can be considered an adjunct to neurolinguistic programming.

DON'T SPILL THAT!

When Johnny walked across your new carpet carrying an overfull bowl of mulligatawny soup and you told him, 'Don't *spill* that', that is exactly what he did. Until now, you probably thought he was a careless little critter and deserved a smack round the ear. You could be right, but chances are his subconscious recognized the embedded command *'spill that'*, which is precisely what he did.

If you are not convinced about embedded commands, let's look at another example:

DON'T LIE

If you want to challenge a lie, you should emphasize the word TRUTH. This seems, in practice, to be recognized as an embedded command.

NON-VERBAL COMMUNICATION

The reptilian-mammalian heritage

Our reptilian and mammalian ancestors communicated primarily through body signals. Rita Carter in *Mapping of the Mind* (ISBN 0520219376) states:

MAPPING OF THE MIND

Once, no doubt, all living things communicated only to the extent that they reacted to changes in others' behaviour or appearance in much the same way as they reacted to environmental signs. Those that were good at reading these changes must have had a major advantage. If you react to a neighbour's reaction to a rustle in the bushes rather than hear the rustle itself, you speed up the process of fleeing from a potential predator. Similarly, those that gave big noticeable reactions must have given a survival benefit to those around them, so their genes were passed on preferentially.

In this way Darwinian selection must constantly have improved communications between individuals until some species became adept at reading the slightest facial expression, body movement or visible physiological change in others of their kind.

Hominids, blessed with their free moving, flexible hands developed gestures, which were supplemented by proper language some two million years ago. This gave humans the tool needed to elevate themselves to a higher level of consciousness ... while still retaining many of the other forms of communication.

Try describing a spiral without using your hands. It is also much easier to point to an object rather than describe it. Thus body language is still an integral part of human communication and a lot of it is instinctive and unconscious. As we shall see later, body language is very important in building rapport.

As finders of the truth we should be primarily concerned with four main aspects of non-verbal communication:

- personal space;
- emblems;
- body language;
- facial expressions.

What we do about this form of communication is explained at page 189 but first we should have a basic understanding of its significance. Body language can be driven unconsciously by the lower brain when it is really significant or consciously controlled, when it is less important. We will describe later how conscious and unconscious non-verbal communications can be profiled and how you should react.

Personal space

All people have an elliptical zone around their bodies, which their reptilian brain unconsciously defines as their personal space and in which they feel comfortable (see Figure 3.4). It is an embodiment of the inherited instinct to establish territorial possession.

The phrase 'Too close for comfort' has a deep meaning as does 'Looking over my shoulder', 'Keep at arm's length' or 'Get out of my face'

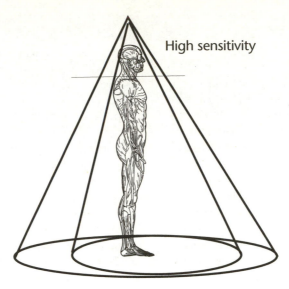

High sensitivity

Figure 3.4   Personal space

Remember the saying 'Keep at arm's length'

People raised in large cities and in large families tend to be comfortable with smaller personal zones, but whatever their history the way a person stands or sits in relation to others is part of his communications code. Research indicates that psychopaths and hardened criminals are very sensitive to violations of their personal space.

Liars usually change their baseline communications code by trying to increase their personal space by:

- moving their body away from the interviewer;
- leaning backwards and especially towards the nearest door;
- moving their chair away from the interviewer;
- walking around.

They may also sit with their legs in a position to make a run for the door.

THE START OF THE MEETING

Bill Jones walks into your office and you guide him to a chair, which he immediately pulls away from you. This deliberate move to increase his personal space should alert you to the possibility that he intends to mislead you or, at least, sees you as an opponent.

Liars may also try to protect their personal space by erecting large barriers, such as crossing their arms high on their body or over their genital regions, protecting themselves with a file or standing behind a piece of furniture. They may also build protective barriers around their desks, such as laying out files, fruit, drinks etc. in a set defensive pattern.

People also find comfort in occupying territory they believe belongs to them. For example, board members usually take the same seat at every meeting, and if someone changes the routine everyone becomes uncomfortable. The same applies to animals. Try entering a dog's kennel and see what happens.

Anxiety usually increases when there is an unauthorized intrusion into a subject's personal space, especially when he is approached from behind or when you upset his ritual (like moving the towel on a German holidaymaker's sunbed). But if you consciously invade someone's personal space to increase his anxiety, you must be careful, as you can never tell whether the anxious result is because the suspect feels 'pinned down' or whether your socks smell.

We have unconscious protocols for setting our positions with other people. Maybe you haven't noticed this, but it is true. When you happen to meet Joe Jones in the corridor you will both unconsciously negotiate a position with which you are comfortable. There will be a certain distance between you and you will align at an angle which will be to the left or right. If one of you changes position the other will normally move. Just try it.

Personal space also has some interesting sub-plots. In most cases the guilty suspect will try to distance himself from incriminating evidence and especially documentation. Thus if you hand a damaging exhibit to the subject and he quickly drops it on the desk, hands it back or shoves it away (usually in small increments while it is in his space), you know it is causing him anxiety (see Figure 3.5).

You can increase this anxiety by pushing the offending document back into the suspect's personal space and in his left field of vision. This, again, is a useful NLP technique that appears to work in practice because it impacts on the liar's more emotional right hemisphere.

Emblems

An 'emblem' consists of all those visual, verbal and sensory images through which a person, consciously and unconsciously, presents himself to the world, including clothing, hairstyle, glasses, shoes, tattoos, jewellery, the tone and strength of his voice and the accessories and accoutrements he uses and the people who accompany him.

You can tell a lot about a person by the company he keeps

It also includes other sensory images such as smell (nice perfume or bad breath) or touch, such as the strength of a handshake. Emblems are an inherited instinct intended to show, or impose, the social status of the animal.

Indicative of innocence

Indicative of guilty knowledge

Figure 3.5 Handling incriminating evidence

In the olden days, great store was put in physiognomy and the supposed relationship between a person's looks and his character. To an extent, we all still react to a person's physical appearance and form conclusions based upon it.

Emblems are selected both consciously and unconsciously to represent the way the person feels about himself and how he would like others to perceive him.

The trouble with emblems is that we tend to accept them without thinking. This is a big mistake because the impression we form may permanently influence our transactional relationships.

THE TRAMP

An actor dressed as a tramp stopped people in Victoria Street in London and asked them for directions to the Houses of Parliament. Some people avoided him; most were curt and did not want to be bothered. The next day, in exactly the same spot, the actor was dressed as a top businessman and asked the same question. The responses were fast and friendly.

We are also subliminally influenced by a person's accent and we all tend to work on stereotypes.

BRUMMIES ARE NOT TO BE BELIEVED?

A report from Doctor Mahoney and colleagues from the Worcester College of Further Education was presented to the British Psychological Society in the autumn of 1997 and concluded that people speaking with a Birmingham (or 'Brummie') accent are twice as likely to be convicted or, if not convicted, disbelieved in court. The doctor and his team hired male actors to reproduce interviews with suspected armed robbers and cheque fraudsters. The actors used Brummie, 'standard' and other regional accents before a panel of 119 students from the college. The results showed a dreadful bias against Brummies, who were seen as 'less intelligent', 'working class' and 'socially incompetent'. This is extremely interesting, as many of the students on the panel were from the Birmingham area and the city produces many highly intelligent people including, even, some lawyers and investigators.

Thus the rule is to be very careful with emblems, both your own and your interpretation of others. Look, listen and smell carefully and consciously determine what the person is telling you about himself. Pay particular attention to incongruencies between a person's emblems and his communications through other channels.

Body language
Chapter 4, pages 115–117 goes into interpreting body language signals in depth, so it is not necessary to repeat them here, except to say that the liar's body is like a monster BBC transmitter, driven by unconscious commands from the limbic system and reptilian brain, often resulting in contention and conflict with the cerebrum.

For example, some hand movements (called *manipulators*, see Chapter 4, page 118) are used unconsciously to relieve stress. Actions like rubbing the back of the neck, putting hand to mouth, crossing arms and legs or brushing non-existent dust off clothing are examples of manipulators. If the person is deprived of the comfort of these, anxiety is increased. For example, if a person is getting comfort from crossing his arms high up his body, we can increase his anxiety by handing him a piece of paper to examine, thereby compelling him to change his position. Also, if we unobtrusively mimic manipulators or comment on them he will stop using them and will be denied their soothing effect.

Other non-verbal communications are called *demonstrators* and these again are hand movements (like describing a spiral) used to reinforce a verbal explanation. When being deceptive a liar's demonstrators usually stop or deviate from his baseline patterns.

Facial expressions

In 1862, Guillaume Duchenne carried out experiments on facial expressions and especially smiles. He discovered, by applying small electrical currents to his patients' faces, that genuine smiles (thereafter known as 'Duchenne smiles') were quite different from those that were artificial, mainly because in the latter the *pars lateralis* (bloody Latin again) did not move and some muscles in the cheeks remained passive (see Figure 3.6).

Figure 3.6 Duchenne's experiments. (Poor victim: he only intended going out to buy some milk for his cat. But note the striped trousers, suggesting that the patient is an English solicitor, and Duchenne's knotted eyebrows, suggesting that he should not become a used car salesman.)

In our world there are seven primary facial expressions:

- anger;
- anxiety;
- disgust;
- fear;
- happiness;
- sadness;
- surprise.

In most cases, an expression representing a genuine emotion is spontaneous and takes place before any associated verbal response. Spontaneous reactions are driven by the lower brain. With feigned expressions of emotions the reverse is true and they are often preceded by micro-tremors around the eyes and mouth that give the game away.

Eckman and Friesen (see www.2cs.cmu.edu) have proposed a Facial Action Coding System, based on the relationship between expression and emotion. They identified 46 different Action Units (AU), which are mainly unconscious, and 14 miscellaneous mainly conscious expressions. For example AU 20 is called the 'lip stretcher', which involves the *risorius w/ platysma* muscle (Figure 3.7); the 'lip corner depressor' involving the *depressor anguli oris* (or *triangularis*) muscle (Figure 3.8).

This is all very interesting stuff, but the expressions were all posed mainly in response to stimulation by smell: in the case of Doris (Figure 3.7) by showing her a Big Mac. To that extent the results have to be regarded as artificial and in any case do not take you very far. You could hardly say to her: 'Look here, Doris, I know you are unhappy because your *risorius w/ platysma* muscle has pulled your expression into AU 20.' Try this and you are likely to get a smack with her handbag.

The problem is not in recognizing when a person is lying, but what you do about it

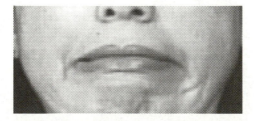

Figure 3.7   Does this remind you of anyone? Her name is Doris.

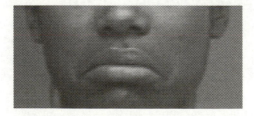

Figure 3.8   Looks like Tiger Woods after missing a 40-foot 'tap in' putt

However, the Eckman–Freisen research is important in confirming the relationship between apparently genuine emotion and facial expressions. We will return to this point in Table 3.8, page 63.

A person's eye movements, including their direction (left, right, up or down), the size (or dilation) of their pupils, gaze intensity and blinking rates are mainly driven unconsciously and, when a person is lying, are different from his normal communications code. The normal reaction when a person is recalling from memory (probably true) or constructing a story (probably false) can be summarized as in Table 3.3.

Table 3.3 Eye accessing clues

Channel of communication or type of memory being accessed	Construction of a lie		Remembering the truth	
	Eye movement from the subject's position			
	Vertical	Horizontal	Vertical	Horizontal
Visual	UP	RIGHT	UP	LEFT
Auditory	AHEAD	RIGHT	AHEAD	LEFT
Emotional	DOWN	RIGHT	DOWN	LEFT

A LITTLE TEST

Try this little test: concentrate on which way your eyes are drawn in answering the following questions.

- What is the date of your mother's birthday?
- What is the result of multiplying 72 by 6?

It probably won't work because you are thinking consciously about eye movements, but unconsciously to the first question your eyes would drift to the left (and up if you are trying to picture her) and to the second question your eyes will be pulled to the right.

There are obviously exceptions to the rule,[15] but it is very easy (with a little practice on your granny or by watching politicians on television) to work out what the subject's baseline patterns of eye movements are and to determine which way they move when they are truthfully retrieving facts from memory or untruthfully contriving them in the imagination. You then have to remain consciously alert to changes in the response to relevant questions.

Eyes left usually means the truth is being told

The direction of a person's gaze, his rate of blinking and the size, or dilation, of his pupils tells you a lot about what he is thinking. If you are sexually interested in someone, the chances are that you will unconsciously focus on their mouth: if you are not, the direction of the gaze is towards the forehead, unless you are severely anxious, when you may try to avoid all eye contact or just stare (see Figure 3.9).

---

[15]   Especially with left-handed people

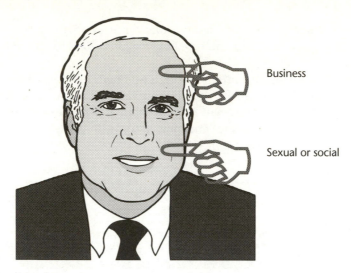

Figure 3.9   Direction of gaze

Never say to someone, 'You can't look into my eyes and say that'

Normal eye contact is for around 40 per cent of the time a person is speaking and 75 per cent when he is listening. The baseline human blink rate is six a minute and the average gaze for between one to ten seconds. Remain consciously aware of a subject's baseline behaviour and deviations from it: these are often signs of deception.

People's pupils become enlarged (dilated) when they are emotionally aroused and blinking rates noticeably increase or decrease. These can all be considered as deviations from the person's baseline communications code and you should consciously register them.

Memory and imagination

TYPES OF MEMORY

Input to memory is encoded in a number of ways, both consciously and unconsciously, and can be considered under four main headings (Table 3.4).

Each type of memory has short-term and long-term stores hard-wired into the brain in the areas shown in column 2 of Table 3.4. What moves between them and when is usually directed at an unconscious level.

Experiments suggest that information is held in memory in chunks and that it has many handles through which it can be retrieved. The short-term memory in the cerebrum can normally hold between five and nine topic-related chunks, after which it becomes overloaded and either throws the excess into the waste bin or files it for the long term. Each experience is encoded in chunks in different parts of the brain and can be considered to be a highly complicated relational database.

We can, of course, override the unconscious processing of memory and make a conscious decision to remember something such as an important telephone number, name or date. We may make a note to remind us, but the irony is that when we do this, our subconscious reminds us at the appropriate time and we never have to refer to the note. Similarly, if we set our alarm clock to wake us for work particularly early, our subconscious will wake us up every 90 minutes throughout the night.

Table 3.4 Types of memory

Type of memory	Function AREA OF THE BRAIN IN WHICH STORED	Examples
1	2	3
Procedural	How to perform tasks CEREBELLUM AND PUTAMEN	How to ride a bicycle or drive a car How to get home from work
Semantic	Relating to ideas and concepts CORTICAL AREAS AND TEMPORAL LOBE	Recognizing different colours Feelings and emotions Shapes and colours Relationships
Episodic	Relating to events, people, facts and learning ENCODED BY THE HIPPOCAMPUS AND STORED IN CORTICAL AREAS	Birth dates of your children What you did last week What someone told you yesterday Your last annual appraisal
Emotional	Emotional experiences Amygdala in the LIMBIC SYSTEM	Stored in the amygdala and very difficult to forget

You can never forget something you really want to remember

Episodic memory (relating to people, places events etc.) is the most short-term and transient. Some input is consciously or subconsciously flagged as important and is retained in long-term memory: unimportant matters are not flagged and recollection quickly degrades.

Other inputs may not be consciously flagged on being laid into memory but still can be quickly retrieved when prompted by a cue. *For example, the cue of 'What were you doing on 11 September 2001?'* will undoubtedly remind you where you were and what you were doing, mainly because of the emotion involved and the scale of the visual impact. The cue of 18 February 2002, may not have the same effect unless, of course, it was your wife's birthday and you forgot it and found your supper in the dog rather than in the oven.

The more handles, or cues, there are, the easier it is to remember

THINGS WHICH ARE NOT FORGOTTEN

Whether they like it or not, criminals and liars unconsciously commit emotional details of their dishonesty to memory; 'handles' guiding them to stores in the lower brain will trigger other parts of memory into action, such as the date their dishonesty started, what their feelings were at the time, what they did and thought about doing with the money and who else was involved. Once one handle gets pulled, neurotransmitters fire away and activate other memories.

When someone responds to a question with 'I don't remember', this may or may not be true. Everything depends on what the person is being asked to remember, the type of memory involved and the number of handles potentially available.

In all cases, a spontaneous statement that a person does not remember, when he has made no attempt to access his memory, is a very powerful sign of deception.

If you genuinely don't remember, how do you know there is anything to forget?

REHEARSING FALSE EXPLANATIONS

In some cases, a liar will carefully rehearse how he plans to deal with questions and will try to commit the answers to memory, but they will go into a different area of the brain to a real experience.

MEMORY CORRUPTION

Extracted from *Mapping of the Mind*:[16] [Most] memories are not pure recordings of what happened but are heavily edited before being laid down. The process of falsification gets another boost each time memory is recalled. As we go over things that happened we add a bit, tweak a bit, lose a bit, tweak a fact here, tinker with a quote there and fill in any little bits that may have faded. We may consciously embellish the recollection with a bit of fantasy – the biting comment that we wished we had said but that was only thought of later. Then this new, re-edited version is tucked back in storage. Next time it gets an airing it may pop up with the fantasy comment still attached, and this time it will be difficult to distinguish it from the genuine memory. So by gradual mutation our memories change.

However, MRI studies suggest that the brain activity used in recalling pure memory differs from that which produces a false recollection.

When interviewed, the liar may deliver his answers too quickly or have varying response times that do not correspond with the complexity of the question or matter concerned. He may spontaneously list out alternatives, but they will normally be concerned with the content of the story. Unless he is an exceptional liar, his answers will lack commitment and his non-verbal responses will not be synchronized.

Evidence that answers have been rehearsed is often a strong sign of deception

THE BENEFITS OF RECOVERING MISPLACED MEMORY

A great deal of information which appears to have been genuinely forgotten can still be re-trieved, providing the right stimulus is provided and handles pulled. In Chapter 10, page 424, cognitive and other methods of helping witnesses dig deep into their memories are explained. Most are based on presenting the subject with as many handles as possible to help him retrieve memory chunks. Similarly, by asking the right questions, we can cause a suspect to bring disa-greeable information to a conscious level, which obliges him to either tell the truth or repress it, significantly increasing his anxiety. Either way, he is faced with a problem.

The memory is the second monkey on the liar's back.
Liars have more memory failures than truthful people

---

16   By Rita Carter, ISBN 0520219376

PRACTICAL DIFFERENCES

The truth comes from memory and is consistent with the person's unconscious deep knowledge. When a person lies, he has to overrule his subconscious, wipe the truth from his memory and draw the detail from his imagination.

Truth comes from the subconscious and memory.
Memory is recalled in the past tense

The difference between memory and imagination is true whether the lie is a falsification or a concealment and whether the response is rehearsed or not. In concealments the liar has to select from memory only those portions of the truth he wishes to reveal, and has to imagine that the remaining negative detail does not exist. In falsifications he has to invent something that did not happen. Lying successfully is very difficult, since the liar has to try to juggle a number of connected elements (see Table 3.5).

Table 3.5 Difference between memory and imagination

CHANNEL OF COMMUNICATION Elements of a lie	True and from memory and subconscious	False and consciously drawn from the imagination
	Examples	Examples
VERBAL The content of what the person says; the story	Natural and spontaneous, consistent in detail Demands the right to explain Commitment to the explanation	Censored and lacking detail Claims the privilege of silence Uncommitted
VERBAL The words used. The syntax or construction of the story	Consistent with the content	Inconsistent with the content
VERBAL AND VISUAL How the answer is delivered: sometimes known as 'para-linguistics'	Relaxed and confident Possibly angry at accusations of responsibility	Cautious Will not make an enemy of the questioner
VERBAL, VISUAL AND SENSORY The person's attitude to honesty and the offence in question	Consistent and likely to condemn the act in question	Inconsistent and insincere; unlikely to condemn the act in question
VERBAL, VISUAL AND SENSORY Emotional reactions	Superficial Non-verbal expression appears before a verbal response	Repressed The verbal response appears before the non-verbal reaction
VISUAL AND SENSORY Non-verbal, body language clues	Consistent with the words used. Hand movements will be mainly demonstrators, which emphasize points being made	Defensive, inconsistent with the words used. Hand movements are restricted to manipulators, which are soothing movements

Making sure that all of these elements are consistent, especially with the liar's normal or baseline behaviour and communications codes when not lying, is virtually impossible.

If there is one single indicator of deception, it is the incongruence of a person's responses when compared to his normal baseline behaviour

The difference between memory and imagination has a computer equivalent. The first is similar to a computer chip that can be accessed rapidly at any point. Memory has separate brain areas for storing visual, auditory and sensory information. Data drawn from memory can be repeated consistently and confidently, and the visual, auditory and sensory responses are congruent.

Imagination is like a tape that starts as a blank and records lies as they are told. The tape has to be replayed carefully to check earlier answers each time a new question is asked. Moreover, the tape may have no track – or a corrupted track – for visual and sensory information, and thus responses are likely to be incongruent.

Transactional analysis

THE THEORY

Professor Eric Berne, a distinguished American psychologist, developed a theory called 'transactional analysis' (TA), which suggests that in our relationships with other people (called 'transactions') we adopt one of three ego states, referred to as 'parent', 'adult' or 'child'. Parents are further sub-divided into 'critical' or 'nurturing', and children into 'rebellious' or 'adaptive'.

These roles, shown in Figure 3.10, are further illustrated in Table 3.6.

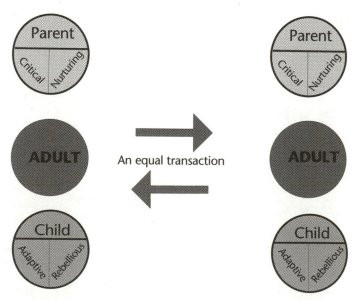

Figure 3.10   Transactional analysis

Table 3.6 Roles in transactional analysis

Ego state	Primary channel of communication	Role model example *Attitude*
Parent: critical	Whatever is normal for the person concerned plus emotional	Father or mother who disciplines a child *Assertive, disciplinary, punishing, censuring*
Parent: nurturing		Father or mother who nurtures and comforts a child *Consoling, teaches, guides, mentors, encourages, empathizes, helps sort out problems*
Adult	Normal for the person concerned	The usual ego state in business *Controlled – logical – responsible – political – unemotional*
Child: adaptive	Whatever is normal for the person concerned plus emotional	Emotional and willing to comply *Willing, cooperative, loving*
Child: rebellious		Awkward and looking for trouble *Truculent, angry, emotional etc.*

TA is relevant in all meetings and interviews and we must elevate our subconscious behaviour to a conscious level.

TA is a very powerful tool in establishing or destroying rapport

EQUAL TRANSACTIONS

Transactions are regarded as 'equal' when the parties to them accept their roles. Equal transactions build rapport. In business, most transactions take place on an adult-to-adult level and can be regarded as more or less 'equal' (Table 3.7).

Table 3.7 Equal transactions

Person 1	Person 2
Adult	Adult
Child	Child
Critical parent	Adaptive child
	Rebellious child
Nurturing parent	Adaptive child
	Rebellious child

Equal transactions are normally harmonious and rapport building and they can be consciously controlled.

DRIVING OFFENCES

If you are pulled over by a traffic cop on the way back from a boozy night at the golf club annual dinner and dance, the worst thing you can do is to get off on the wrong transactional footing, if you want to avoid a night in the slammer. Get out of your car, nice and quietly, walk slowly towards the officer in an appeasing way, perhaps gesturing by clasping your hands to your forehead, and make a conciliatory remark such as, 'I am so sorry, officer, I just did not see that pink elephant. How could I be so stupid?' You might get your ass verbally kicked but you should escape, simply because few animals attack if they already know they have won.

If you sit in your car, with a defiant expression, or your wife comes out with a load of verbals such as 'Tell the pig who you are, Stan, and that you play golf with the Chief Constable', you have had it. Getting to the right transactional relationship is the key.

UNEQUAL OR 'CROSSED' TRANSACTIONS

Negative emotion – usually fear, anger or anxiety – is generated when one person tries to impose a transactional role on another that he is not willing to accept. For example, you will become angry if you treat a colleague on an adult-to-adult basis but he treats you as he would a child. Such misalignments are referred to as 'crossed' transactions, and they always generate strong emotions. You can totally unbalance people by deliberately crossing a transaction.

NEGOTIATION OF TRANSACTIONAL ROLES

Transactional roles are usually negotiated (much like personal space) between the parties at an unconscious level and are dynamic over the course of a meeting or interview. Most people are not aware of ego states or how they affect them and thus lose the opportunity to get into the transactional relationships that lead to the deep truth. Moreover, the opening phases of a conversation with someone you have never met before usually set the transactional relationship for everything that follows.

First impressions will be influenced by various factors, including:

- The person's position, reputation, wealth etc.
- The location at which the meeting takes place, including visual, auditory and sensory inputs.
- The person's intended or unintended emblems, such as clothes, hair, office, car or speech.

The lesson is always to try to consciously register transactional roles, emblems and communications codes and to get to the deep truth by arriving at the position where you are a nurturing parent and the subject an adaptive child.

The deep truth comes in the relationship between a nurturing parent and an adaptive child

CONSCIOUSLY CONTROLLING ROLES

If you want to raise the temperature of an interview or meeting and, for example, challenge the honesty of the other party, you must be prepared to cross the transaction and become a critical parent. If you want to establish rapport, you must recognize the other person's ego state and act accordingly. If you want to put someone off, adopt the role of a rebellious child.

Police officers and lawyers in court are perceived to be, and often act as, critical parents. In fact, the environments in which they operate and their personal and associated emblems, including uniforms, helmets or wigs, are deliberately used to reinforce a critical parent role and to increase anxiety in the minds of people around them. The fact that people in positions of authority rarely consciously move to become nurturing parents is one reason why there are so few deep confessions in court, and why those made to police are sometimes alleged to have been obtained through oppression.

If you can't understand people, don't interview them.
If you can't become a nurturing parent, you will never get to the deep truth

BIG TIPS

Research in the US shows that waiters and waitresses who touch their customers get 20% greater tips than those that don't.

The light physical contact shows they are interested and nurturing.

Emotions: from anxiety and panic to relief

WHAT ARE EMOTIONS?

Emotions may be defined as 'strong, positive or negative feelings' and they are usually an important factor in deception. They affect both the subject and the interviewer and are mainly triggered in the lower brain at an unconscious level.

THE EMOTIONAL PATH

Emotion always surfaces either obviously or by displacement into other verbal, non-verbal or sensory disclosures. The stronger the emotion, the more obvious are its symptoms and the more difficult to repress.

The normal sequence of emotions involved in deception is illustrated in Figure 3.11.

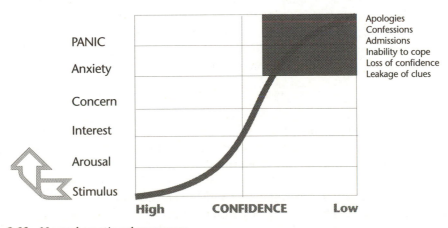

Figure 3.11 Normal emotional sequences

A person's ability to reason decreases as his emotions move up the scale. When anxiety turns to panic, the liar finally loses confidence in his ability to succeed with lies and at the 'pivotal point' (see Chapter 7, pages 168–172 and 180) may try to negotiate to minimize the consequences of his acts before accepting the truth.

We are primarily concerned with seven emotions:

- anger;
- anxiety;
- disgust or contempt;
- fear;
- happiness or deception delight;
- sadness;
- surprise.

These all originate mainly in the lower brain and are neurotransmitted to the cerebrum (to be precise the ventromedial or subgenual cortex), which consciously examines them before sending signals to the motor cortex for action. There are two potential problems for the liar. The first is that the emotional neurotransmitters going from the amygdala to the cortex are more powerful than the ameliorating signals going the other way. The second is that, to achieve the fastest survival reaction when facing a severe threat, the amygdala can go straight to the motor cortex. Thus, in genuinely emotional reactions, body movements and facial expressions occur before any conscious verbal reaction driven by the upper brain. We will see the significance of this hard-wiring when we try to distinguish genuine from feigned anger.

SCRATCHING

If you have a genuine itch, the chances are you will scratch it five times. If you	consciously move to make a scratch it will be more or less than five times

HAPPINESS AND DECEPTION DELIGHT

Some people enjoy lying and this is especially true of achievement lies when the victim is being misled and taken like a lamb to the slaughter. The liar feels that he is in a dominant position and his approach is akin to an attack. Ways of dealing with achievement lies are discussed in Chapter 10, page 356 and they are, unfortunately, very common in business. Delight or happiness are the starting emotions for achievement lies because the liar is in the driving seat. This can quickly turn to anxiety when the lie is challenged.

FEAR

Fear is a very strong emotion, initially based on an unconscious perception of a specific external threat, like being chased by a sabre-toothed tiger; or your wife after the neighbour's party. In the modern day truth-and-lies world, fear may result from, amongst other things:

- torture and physical pain (i.e. working for an investigations consultancy);
- an improper threat to lock him up or beat him (as above);

- loss of livelihood, family or friends;
- not being believed;
- becoming involved in something he would rather avoid;
- some other reason unknown to the interviewer.

You should never assume that the reason for a person being afraid is because he is guilty of the matter in which you are interested. Innocent people can be afraid, for genuine reasons. Thus, fear is not an emotion you should stimulate, although anxiety is.

Usually genuinely frightened people don't have the time to be anxious

ANXIETY AND PANIC

Principles

Although fear and anxiety are closely related, the latter is internally generated through a combination of factors resulting in an elaborate and continuing neurotransmitted dialogue between the lower and upper brains. Anxiety is mainly a conscious emotion and it can result in near panic when the person internalizes that he is unable to cope. Whereas fear is a response to a specific threat, anxiety is usually caused by a combination of small factors, which accumulate to become overwhelming.

Anxiety in a guilty suspect varies directly with:

- His analysis of the situation, including:
  - the strength of the evidence currently against him and the potential penalties (this is the balance at the pivotal point),
  - other evidence he believes might be *discovered and not just that which the interviewer has currently available*,
  - his perception of the skills of the interviewer,
  - his ability to explain and evade questions,
  - his ability to succeed with an attack.
- The penalty if earlier lies are revealed.
- Other unrelated problems such as:
  - poor mental and physical health,
  - tiredness.

The more the liar has to falsify an explanation, the more his anxiety increases. And it is not always one large problem that causes anxiety, but rather a combination of small issues which cumulatively lead the suspect to conclude that he cannot cope. This is an important point to remember. Although we would always like to have overwhelming evidence, the fact that we have many small items of incriminating intelligence, or use NLP techniques, can be just as effective in increasing the suspect's anxiety and getting him to the pivotal point and then to the deep truth.

Raising the pavement

If most people were asked to walk on a narrow kerbstone at the edge of a pavement, the probability is that they could do so successfully and without anxiety because they have the balancing skills to succeed.

However, if the pavement were raised, so that there was a sheer drop of 30 feet over the edge, the balancing skills needed would be just as before. But anxiety, caused by the consequences of failure, would increase, in turn leading to a possible loss of balance. A few people might try to walk along the edge and succeed. Others would try and fail, but the majority would take the safe course and either refuse the invitation, or accept but leave a wide safety margin so that they would not fall off the edge. The same principles apply to deception and are manifested, primarily, in a lack of commitment that results in panic when the penny drops that the person simply cannot cope. In finding the truth, this is referred to as the pivotal point.

Always raise the pavement to get to the pivotal point

ANGER

Anger is a negative, initially unconscious, emotion directed externally and is consistent with a person's decision to fight rather than flee. It may also be a battle against reality. Anger may spring from frustration, anxiety or fear, or from some totally unrelated reason; in the animal kingdom, it is used to establish dominance or protect territory. The basis may be genuine, or contrived, but in most cases anger is intended to cause the adversary to withdraw and run off.

Some people will take a conscious decision to simulate anger, again to frighten off an opponent, but the difference is obvious (see Table 3.8).

You should remember that an angry person is directly connected to, and thrashing with, his subconscious and is vulnerable to making mistakes, Freudian slips and blurting out the truth. If you can talk him out of his anger, you are likely to get to the deep truth (see the methods of dealing with anger in Chapter 7).

SADNESS AND DEPRESSION

Depression can be regarded as anger directed inwardly and is often an isolation from reality. It usually has the same roots as anger and leads to increased, rather than reduced, anxiety and can result in a mental block. However, depression is often an unconscious excuse in anticipation of failure. Signs of depression include:

- complaints about poor health and particularly mental problems;
- self-pity;
- paranoia;
- comments such as *'I wish I had never been born'*;
- self-deprecation, e.g. *'No one will ever believe me', 'I am not clever enough to lie'*.

It is also not uncommon for suspects to feign depression to get the interviewer to pull back, using phrases such as *'If this doesn't stop, I will kill myself'*. Depressed people do not usually confess and the ways in which a subject can, and should, be talked out of this negative emotion are explained in Chapter 7, page 188.

Table 3.8 Genuine and contrived anger

Genuine anger (driven unconsciously by the sympathetic system)	Contrived anger (conscious action by the parasympathetic system)
Bodily signs	
Adrenalin flush, fast heartbeat and heavy breathing	Normal heartbeat
Apparently enlarged body	Normal, ambivalent or 'image-managed' posture
Pallid complexion (often extreme)	Flushed or reddened complexion
Face inclined forward	Face pulled back
Tightly drawn lips	Exposed teeth
Profuse sweating	No discernible activity
Hair standing on end	
Dry mouth caused by reduced salivation	
Clenched hands or pointing finger gestures	
Fixed stare with dilated pupils	Variable gaze
	Displacement movements to relieve tension, such as false scratching, rubbing hands, winding his watch or cleaning glasses: gasps and sighs
Voice	
Raised with a fast delivery	
Attitude and demeanour	
Not quickly forgotten	Transient
Will not defer to interruptions by the interviewer and will be assertive	Will usually defer to interruptions
May terminate the interview and storm out	Very unlikely to terminate the interview
Focused on a specific issue or event	Unspecific, often unjustified and at the start of the interview
Throwing or breaking things	Threatening but not doing
Timing	
At any time in an interview and usually in response to a specific statement	Usually at the start of an interview, without any obvious reason
Non-verbal expression appears before a verbal outburst and is symmetrical	Verbal outburst precedes the non-verbal expression. The facial expression may be asymmetrical
Justification	
Often a good basis for complaint	Spurious grounds for complaint
Anxiety decreases	Anxiety remains

Other characteristics of deception

A COMPLEX ARRAY

There is also a range of other emotional and emotionally based reactions that can surface during an interview.

SELF-DENIAL

The human body has a powerful ability to anaesthetize itself against pain, and the mind has an equivalent capacity to block out unpleasant facts from consciousness. This self-denial may take a number of forms, both conscious and unconscious (see Table 3.9).

Table 3.9   Examples of self-deception

Category	Effect	Examples and comments
Repression	Keeping bad news from the consciousness	*Like the ostrich: burying his head in the sand*
Denial	Deliberate refusal to accept things as they are	*Pure self-deception and a most common feature in lies*
Projection	Refusal to see himself as being personally involved	*Seeing the problem in an impersonal way. For example, Richard Nixon often referred to himself in the third person as 'The President'*
Obsession	Displacing anxiety to a manual task	*Compulsive washing of hands etc.*
Isolation	Acceptance of the facts while not accepting blame, guilt or emotion	*Admitting the transgression but without intention or guilty knowledge*
Rationalization	Consciously defending, justifying or downplaying the bad news	*Minimizing the seriousness of the problem*

> *Inattention to painful truths shelters us from anxiety*

Before the truth can emerge, we may have to bring the liar to face the truth at a conscious level and to overcome his self-denial. There are two main ways of doing this and both are founded on the relentless pursuit of detail, what you believe to be the truth and arousal of the two monkeys: the memory and the subconscious.

This action will either lead the subject to lose confidence in his ability to cope with the continuing anxiety created by deception, or to be forced into telling more and more extreme lies.

> *When in doubt, press for detail*

NEGOTIATION

The subject may seek clarification, usually at the pivotal point, to help him decide whether or not he should confess. The object is usually to help him decide whether the consequences of confession are tolerable and whether he has more to gain by telling the truth than not. Symptoms of negotiation include:

- Asking for clarification about the possible outcome: 'What usually happens in cases like this? Do they get reported to the police?'
- Posing hypothetical questions about the possible consequences: 'I didn't do it, but if I said I did, what would happen?'
- Accepting a justification for their action, without specifically acknowledging guilt: 'You are right in suggesting this started by mistake.'
- Seeking sympathy: 'How would you feel in my position?'
- Asking to speak off the record.
- Body posture opens or leans forward: arms and legs may unfold.
- Eyes look upward, with slow blinking or head drops.
- Rubs chin: his chin may appear to quiver.

You must recognize negotiating symptoms and take your time. It is likely that the suspect will be communicating on an emotional and sensory level and you must mirror this. It is not the time to say too much and under no circumstances should you discuss the potential penalties or make any promises that cannot be kept (see Chapter 7, page 231).

ACCEPTANCE AND ADMISSION

If the suspect believes he has more to gain by confessing than from continued denial, he will begin to make admissions. Signs of acceptance include:

- tears and deep sighs;
- eyes looking downward, often accompanied by slow blinking and with virtually no eye contact with the interviewer;
- head and shoulders drop;
- body posture opens further and the suspect may appear to look smaller;
- appears that he is about to faint.

Again, such communication will be at an emotional level and you must remain patient, adopt the role of a nurturing parent and help him get the monkeys off his back. We will return to this point in Chapter 7, page 223.

CONFESSION: THE DEEP TRUTH

It is one of the great ironies of life that most religious orders see confession as a positive, natural and healing process, whereas lawyers and smelly socks[17] seem to assume that they can only be obtained through improper means. In a tough interview, the suspect definitely finds confession cathartic.

Over the years we have tried to find what caused suspects to confess. We did this after the deep truth had been revealed, empathetic relationships established and a bond of mutual trust formed with the suspect, by simply asking them.[18] People said they confessed because at the time they were convinced that:

---

[17] 'Smelly socks' is a generic term relating to people who live in a dream world, believe in Father Christmas and the tooth fairy, and think that the Data Protection Act achieves any useful purpose for honest humans
[18] 40 years later we still get Christmas cards and emails from people who have confessed

- The truth would emerge regardless.
- They could not cope with the anxiety created by their own deception.
- They had lost confidence in their ability to succeed with lies.
- They believed that telling the truth might be beneficial to:
  - gain an advantage,
  - minimize punishment,
  - start life again,
  - feel better,
  - clear the position for colleagues,
  - avoid disadvantages,
  - avoid the involvement of family,
  - terminate the investigation,
  - prevent matters becoming worse,
  - avoid their home being searched,
  - avoid the involvement of police,
  - avoid dismissal,
  - avoid publicity for the case.
- They were able to internally excuse their own behaviour and save face with their family and colleagues, both in defending the transgression and their admission of it.

They also said they believed that the immediate consequences of confession were tolerable and that they could rebuild their lives. It should be noted that very few showed any genuine signs of remorse.

PROJECTION AND REVENGE

The relationship between a suspect, who has confessed, and the interviewer is usually very close, often based on a child-to-child transactional relationship. Most suspects are relieved that they have told the truth. However, in the days immediately after the interview, when the suspect has discussed his confession with his colleagues and lawyers, it is not unusual for him to turn and make allegations of improper treatment and to go on the attack. There is little you can do about this except to know in your heart that you have acted properly, fairly and reported the facts accurately.

Monkeys on the liar's back

Always remember that the liar has two monkeys on his back (see Figure 3.12). The subconscious monkey always wants to blurt out the truth and give away what the person is really thinking, his emotions and attitudes. It is the ultimate 'supergrass'. It is a very dangerous monkey, and the liar has to try to keep it carefully and consciously under control. The memory monkey also knows the deep truth: it is a database of unbridled accuracy. When set free, it will always state the facts.

Figure 3.12   The two monkeys – the subconscious and memory

From now on, when you are confronted by someone you suspect is not telling you the truth, put on some new spectacles and look at him in a different way.

So from today onwards become a keen observer of human behaviour and remember the monkeys on the liar's back. It will make you a much more effective truth finder!

'I HAVE TO TELL YOU, MR PARKER, YOUR CONVICTIONS FOR MURDER
ARE A POTENTIAL RED FLAG'

4 *Signs of Deception*

The total amount of evil in a person remains constant

Introduction

Finding the truth is a seven-stage process (see Mind Map 3).

This chapter examines how a liar leaves clues as a direct result of his conscious objectives and, much more importantly, scattered unconsciously in ways he never intended.

MILLER'S LAW[1]	
In order to understand what a person is telling you, you must first accept that what	he has said is the complete truth and then ask yourself what it is true of.

The bottom line is that there are so many clues that we cannot consciously remember them all and have to rely on our subconscious to warn us. Once we get the warning – which may be as weak as an intuition – we have to decide if the matter is important and, if it is, to elevate our suspicions to a conscious level and deal with them.

Thus dealing with deception is a three-stage process:

- Let our feelings and intuition run free (that is, don't immediately suppress them and test the story against the clues you can consciously remember).
- Decide whether the suspected deception is important: if it is not, just enjoy it. But if it is important, take a conscious decision to deal with it.
- Adapt the cunning plan to suit the circumstances.

The Mind Maps in this chapter summarize everything and Chapters 6 and 7 set out the methodology for handling tough interviews where fraud or other gross deception is suspected.

Deciding that a person is not telling the truth is the easy part.
Dealing with it is more difficult

---

[1] George Miller, US psychologist

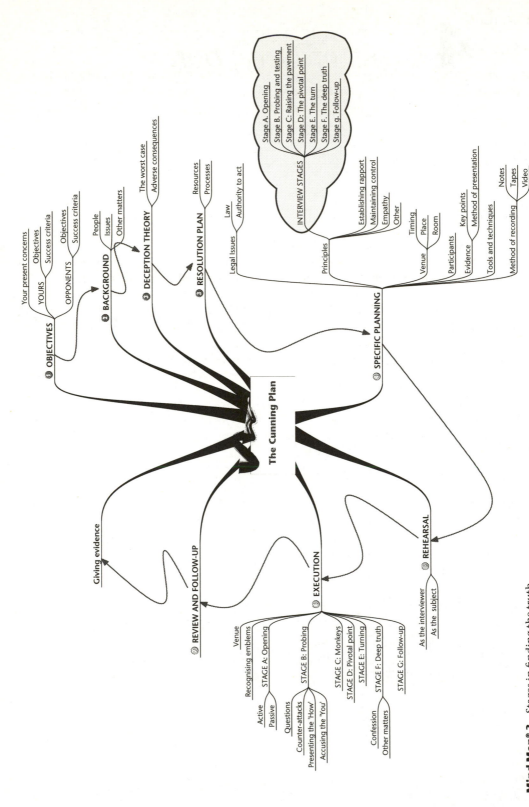

Mind Map® 3 Stages in finding the truth

The liar's *conscious* objectives

BACKGROUND

In most cases, a liar has conscious objectives, which are to distort what he knows to be the truth and to communicate the modified story to another person with the intention of misleading him. Achievement lies are told before the event, to provide the liar with a financial or other benefit and are usually based on falsification.

Everything is said for a reason

Exculpatory lies are usually told after the event with the conscious objective of:

- *Permanently removing suspicion* or stopping the enquiry:
  - by attacking,
  - by convincing you of his innocence.
- *Escaping*, taking a line of appeasement, without incriminating himself:
  - by *avoiding making admissions* and ensuring he does not increase the evidence against himself in any other way,
  - by diverting, distracting, *evading* or attacking so that the matter is not effectively pursued.
- *Finding out what you know* and planning so that he can take appropriate action.
- *Minimizing the penalties*, if there is no escape.
- *Frustrating follow-up action by further attacks*.
- *Possibly returning to the deception* as soon as he believes it is safe to do so.

These conscious objectives are mainly achieved by concealment and falsification of the content of a story. Few liars appreciate the importance of syntax, paralinguistics, non-verbal communication and attitude. Even if they did, they could not consciously control them. Also, lying is easier when the liar knows he has left no repudiatory evidence.

Liars usually concentrate on the content, but know too much.
They fail to say things an honest person would

If the liar cannot succeed with an achievement lie, possibly because he is effectively challenged, his fall-back position is to try to escape by removing suspicion: if this is not possible he will fall back to minimizing the penalties or making sure action cannot be taken against him, so that he can walk away to fight another day, with another victim. In fraud cases, achievement liars usually revert to their dishonesty once they believe it is safe for them to do so. Thus, this makes it imperative that suspicions of dishonesty are resolved. However, in most cases, liars and fraudsters have not planned their endgame and this is their weakest link.

If you currently have suspicions, you should make every effort to resolve them

ACHIEVEMENT LIES

These lies, which are an integral part of most frauds, hit you when you least expect them. The liar chooses the time, the circumstances and the weapons: everything is in his favour but he will usually assess his chances of success and decide whether or not to engage in what is effectively a fight with the victim. If the fraudster believes the balance is not in his favour, he will deflect to another victim, to another time, place or another method. Thus, a deep awareness of your risks and the circumstances in which you may be deceived is a great defence. That is why this book should be carried with you at all times. Also the personal manifesto (Chapter 5) should ensure that you do not become the victim of achievement lies. They are always preventable if you ask the right questions at the right time.

> *For every credibility gap, there is a gullibility fill.*
> *If it looks too good to be true, it is*

EXCULPATORY LIES: PERMANENTLY REMOVING SUSPICION

Objective

Totally stopping an investigation and removing himself from suspicion is an ideal outcome for the liar and he has two options, based on the 'fight, flight or appeasement' decision discussed in Chapter 2, page 27.

Attack

The option to attack will be used if the liar believes it will achieve his objectives.

AN ATTACK: THE SWORD OF TRUTH

'If it has fallen to my destiny to start the fight to cut out the cancer of bent and twisted journalism in our country with the simple sword of truth and the trusty shield of British fair play, so be it. I am ready for the fight.'
Jonathan Aitken, former Defence Minister, author of the book *Nixon: A Life*, and later jailed for perjury

'A few weeks later, there was a moment of absolute stillness in the court as Jonathan Aitken, once dubbed the tallest, handsomest man in British politics, bent over to study the documents that had just been placed in his hands. They revealed that the testimony he had recently given on oath had been a lie.'
The *Guardian*

The attack may include:

- *Challenging*:
  - the motives, authority, skill or independence of the victim or the interviewer,
  - the evidence.
- *Threatening or using*:
  - violence,
  - legal action,
  - any other action that could damage the victim, including blackmail.
- *Interfering with the evidence*:

- destroying records,
- threatening witnesses,
- creating false evidence and alibis.
- *Complaining*:
  - about alleged unfair treatment,
  - about infringement of his human or other rights.

Attacks – especially at the start of an interview, or during it, when they are unjustified in the circumstances – are usually contrived to deflect you off course.

NOW WHAT DO YOU HAVE TO SAY ABOUT THAT?

In a very high-profile British murder case, an experienced detective began to interview a 15-year-old suspect in the presence of his lawyer. The detective opened the interview politely and explained to the suspect how it would be conducted. Without warning, the suspect leapt from his chair head-butted the detective (breaking his nose) and said, 'Now what do you have to say about that?'

An attack may also come at any point when the suspect believes the balance falls in his favour and can be encouraged by your lack of confidence or determination. Thus, it is critical that you remain in control of every important interview, because if you fail to do so you increase the chances of an attack. The good news is that the subject who launches an attack and fails is extremely vulnerable, and thus you should look upon anger as a step towards reaching deep truth.

Strong objects cannot be shaped without the application of heat

Convincing of the truth
The liar will try to convince you of his innocence, but if the right questions are asked, this is a dangerous course, requiring him to falsify information and to tell barefaced lies. More often the liar will give the impression of truthfully answering questions but, in doing so, he leaves abundant clues. These are analysed later.

EXCULPATORY LIES: TO ESCAPE

Objectives
If the liar believes he cannot stop the investigation – through an attack or convincing you of his innocence or appeasement – he must either make sure that he does not make the case against himself any worse, or try to cloud the issues sufficiently to prevent any action being taken against him. Again, he is unlikely to have planned his endgame.

Avoid making admissions
The liar may avoid making admissions in a number of ways, including not appearing for the interview at all, refusing to answer questions, evasion, feigned anger or sickness, alleged memory failures plus a host of other tactics described later in this chapter. By deciding to answer questions the suspect consciously enters into a battle of wits that he believes he can

win and, unless you can take him by surprise through your own cunning plan, his prepared responses may prevail.

Liars are more evasive than honest people

Finding out what you know

The liar may also ask questions ('fishing questions') to find out how much you know and what action you plan to take. This, again, is much like a game of poker and you must control any disclosure. If you say too much (perhaps through the questions you ask) the liar is able to plan future answers and actions, interfere with witnesses or destroy evidence. For this reason, the fact that you have suspicions should be treated in confidence, especially when fraud is suspected. It is critical that the suspect is ambushed.

Minimizing the penalties

Where a suspect's guilt is overwhelming, he may try to minimize his punishment by providing a plausible excuse, the most common being that he is suffering from a terminal illness or has a personal crisis of some sort, the common theme being that people should take pity on him.

Excuses are the manifestation of the 'flight' or 'belly up' decision by animals who know they have lost the fight. Experience shows that many excuses are totally false but even so, people seem to accept them. Even the highest courts in the land fall for sob stories without verifying them and thus allow villains to walk away laughing.

Thus the rule is that if at any time an excuse is presented, consider it to be no more than an achievement lie and deal with it accordingly.

GOD'S LITTLE MIRACLE

Tommy Taylor stole £100,000 from ABC Ltd and admitted his sins to his manager. If anyone was facing a term of imprisonment, Tommy was; until God intervened. The day after making his admissions, Tommy and his crying wife saw the head of personnel and explained that he had a terminal illness and was unlikely to live for more than a few months. A letter from his doctor – backed up by very bleak test results – confirmed the tragic news.

Human resources recommended that Tommy be allowed to resign and die in peace, and any idea of prosecuting him was abandoned. In fact he was given time (something of an irony under the circumstances) to repay.

A few months later, Tommy appeared on a national television quiz show and was a picture of health. God had intervened with a miraculous cure and, six years later, Tommy is still alive and well and probably still cherishing the letter, supposedly from his doctor, and test results which his wife had dutifully forged on her laptop computer.

Never accept an excuse without verifying it

Frustrating follow-up action by further attacks

It is not unusual for people who have confessed to change their minds and make complaints of unfair treatment or to threaten blackmail. Such allegations, which can be days or even months later, can be successfully defended if the interview has been properly conducted and recorded.

Always expect a counter-attack and never give in to blackmail

TACTICS

To achieve his objectives a liar may consciously use a number of tactics in the following ways.

Silence or explanation

Innocent people who believe they are being wrongly accused usually demand the right to explain. Their emotions run deep and are consistent. They are committed to their positions and little will deflect them. On the other hand, liars frequently claim the privilege of silence – either directly or, more usually, through their legal advisers.

Innocence demands the right of explanation.
Guilt claims the privilege of silence

In 99.24 per cent of cases, refusal to answer a question has to be viewed as an admission that there is no believable explanation. Of course, there are exceptions, such as where a person has been treated unfairly by the organization concerned or has no confidence that his explanation will be reported accurately. Genuine cases of this nature are very rare. It is also very unusual for a suspect to commit himself so that he accepts personal responsibility for refusing to answer questions. Usually his failure to answer is blamed on his legal advisers, some feigned illness, deafness, inability to speak the language, muteness, unavoidable absence on a prolonged trip to Mongolia, family catastrophe, religion, curvature of the earth – or legitimized in some other way.

Silence is an admission that there is no believable answer

Concealment and falsification

Both consciously and subconsciously, liars do not want to get caught in a barefaced lie for which they have no plausible excuse. Thus, where you permit him to do so, the liar will conceal the truth rather than falsify it (Table 4.1).

When you are in doubt over whether a person is telling the truth or not, press for more detail and make him falsify. Pin down his explanation, listen carefully and get more and more detail. In this way the liar's confidence decreases, anxiety increases and his non-verbal and verbal clues spiral out of control. You then confront him with these as part of the cunning plan.

The devil is always in the detail

Table 4.1   Concealment and falsification

Concealment	Falsification
He omits to mention important and usually incriminating information	*He makes up facts, events and other things that did not take place*
He does not have to remember what he has already said and is therefore less likely to give a conflicting answer	*He has to be careful to make sure untrue details provided are not contradictory and to avoid 'Freudian slips'*
If it is discovered that he did not volunteer the truth when asked, he can always say he had forgotten the detail or misunderstood the question. There is usually a plausible excuse for concealment	*If the suspect is caught in a falsification, he may be unable to provide a plausible excuse. There is no excuse for a barefaced lie*
Low anxiety	*High anxiety resulting in the surfacing of repressed emotions through non-verbal and other communication*
This is the safe course, chosen by 99 per cent of all liars in 90 per cent of all cases	*Inexperienced liars and suspects under professional questioning falsify rather than conceal*

The clues

It does not matter how skilled the liar is, his conscious and unconscious objectives will always leave clues to deception (Table 4.2).

Table 4.2   Objectives and clues

Objectives CONSCIOUS *Unconscious*	Where the lie is revealed				
	Content *What he says*	Syntax *Words used*	Paralinguistics *Ancillary verbal communication*	Non-verbal *Body language*	Attitude
ATTACK	Treated as a separate response (see this chapter page 92)				
CONVINCE BY FALSIFICATION	See page 95	See page 103	See page 112	See page 115	See page 121
AVOID MAKING ADMISSIONS					
EVASION					
FINDING OUT WHAT YOU KNOW					
Lack of commitment					
Reducing anxiety within the response					
Attitude					

Also, the liar's attitude will be revealed mainly in the content

There are also peripheral clues, in content, syntax and so on, arising from the way a liar seeks to minimize punishment and frustrate follow-up action. In fact, we are flooded with signs of deception but often fail to consciously register and deal with them.

We may unconsciously recognize a lie, but consciously fail to challenge it

Unconscious symptoms of deception in the content

GENERAL

We can easily recognize a liar's conscious objectives by relying on our deception theory and resolution plan but unconscious clues are less easy to spot although they are equally important. But please remember, there is seldom one perfect clue to deception, short of a full confession. We must always look at clusters of responses and gauge them against the subject's baseline responses to non-threatening, or 'control' questions. We must also look for incongruencies in the different channels of communication (oral, visual, paralinguistics and body language).

Incongruency is the best single indicator of deception

However, the four most important clues that a liar unconsciously leaves are:

- lack of commitment;
- reducing anxiety within his response;
- from his attitude and especially not doing and saying the things an honest person would;
- not reacting as an innocent person would.

These are discussed below.

LACK OF COMMITMENT

Generally

Most liars (but there are always exceptions) will make every effort to avoid being caught in a barefaced lie for which they have no plausible excuse. They will dance like a dervish around difficult topics, squirming and using every option to avoid commitment. The liar will try to keep his options open, so that he is not pinned down to a barefaced lie or any other position from which he cannot escape and will consciously use a number of techniques, such as evasion, appeasement, deflection, ambiguity etc. to do so.

Liars rarely answer a relevant question with a binary 'yes' or 'no'

Even when a person seems to be committed to an explanation, the syntax used can still give the game away.

THE BODY[2]

'Around 5:00 am/5:30 am I, John A. Woods Jr, was in the process of giving my son, John A. Woods III, his scheduled feeding. During this feeding he bucked and fell approx. 2 ft to the floor, hitting his head on the floor.	His body landed head first; I attempted to catch him but was unsuccessful. When I picked him up he cried for about 90 sec. then started to gag. His eyes were glazed. I immediately called 911.'

Can you spot the hidden clue? It is that he referred to the 'body' (a dead one) before it supposedly hit the floor.

Lack of commitment is often concealed by alleged memory failures such as:

- 'I am not sure about this …'
- 'Don't hold me to this …'
- 'To the best of my recollection …'

Such phrases are always an indication of deception, especially when the subject has made no effort to access his memory. You should never let them succeed with this ruse.

It is a proven fact that liars claim to have more alleged memory failures than truthful people. If someone genuinely does not remember, how does he know there was anything to forget?

Subjective truths

A liar will unconsciously try to reduce his anxiety when giving a false explanation and this may be achieved by omission, deflection or other contrivances. Perhaps more importantly, he will try to make sure that the precise words he utters are technically true or justifiable and these are referred to as 'subjective truths' or 'internalized definitions'.

TONY BLAIR AND THE SECRET UNDERSTANDING

Tony Blair was asked about a secret agreement between him and Gordon Brown to the effect that he would resign and let the Tartan Terror take over as Prime Minister	before the next election. Blair said, 'What Gordon and I say when we are asked this question is "no".'

Think about it. What Mr Blair said is subjectively true in his own mind, even if there is an agreement in blood, more so if it is not a 'secret'. The wording is typical of a subjective truth and, therefore, of deception. Time will tell whether Mr Blair and the Tartan Terror have such an agreement, 'secret' or otherwise.

---

[2] From the excellent site www.theirwords.com

THE AFFIDAVIT

John Smith was accused of taking bribes from a customer and in his statement to the Employment Tribunal he said:
'I have been accused of taking money from a customer. *I would like to state* categorically that I have never taken money. I know the company's policies *and I would be stupid* *to risk my job by doing anything underhand.* I do know the customer concerned and from time to time have played golf with its Managing Director, but I would like to repeat that I have never taken money, except for small winnings on our games.'

There is no doubt that he 'would like to state' but he is not actually stating it. Equally, the voluntary admission over golf winnings was a pre-emptive defence or a denial of an allegation not made. The statements are typical of deception.

Bill Clinton also relied on subjective truths.

NOT A SHRED OF EVIDENCE

During an interview with Jim Lehrer of PBS, Bill Clinton said: 'There is not a single solitary shred of evidence of anything dishonest in my public life'. Most people hearing this would understand it to be a total denial of wrongdoing and Mr Clinton clearly intended this to be the case. However, more careful reading shows that Mr Clinton did not deny acting dishonestly: merely that there was no evidence of it. His further qualification concerning dishonesty in his 'public life' suggests that the denial did not apply to his private life.

BILL CLINTON

No one could forget President Clinton's emphatic, but rehearsed, finger jabbing denial that: ' I would like to tell the American people, and I will say it again, I did not have sexual relations with that woman: Monica Lewinsky'.

This apparent denial was based on his internal rationalization that what he was saying was true, and resulted from his very mealy-mouthed definition of 'sexual relations'. At another point in his testimony we find another classic statement: 'It all depends what the definition of "it" is'. It should be noted that were Neil Hamilton's definition of 'relations' to be applied (page 25) to this story, a single rogering would not have qualified!

A classic example of a subjective truth is the statement made by a person who stole £100,000 through a wire transfer fraud. He said: 'As I told Mr Smith last week, I did not take the money'. The statement that he 'told Mr Smith' is subjectively true (and thus minimizes the liar's anxiety in saying it) even if he did make the transfer as, in fact, he did. It is also true because he did not take 'money' but merely rearranged a few electronic impulses.

Subjective truths often appear in pseudo denials (see page 88). For example, when the subject is told, 'I think you are involved in this, Bill', he responds, 'I would have been crazy to do that', which is subjectively true and not a denial.

Job candidates are great at subjective truths and the phrase 'I pursued a degree course in mathematics' does not mean that he caught up with it and actually qualified.

Subjective truths can arise because the liar has rearranged his memory (see page 54) and given himself the benefit of the doubt. His anxiety in delivering the lie is thus reduced because he has rewritten history. This is a very common form of deception in business, which makes it imperative that you have an accurate record of conversations in which achievement lies may have been told.

THE TRUSTY BUSINESSMAN

A businessman and an apparent pillar of society routinely makes promises which, possibly, he may intend to keep at the time. However, on reflection, he believes they were too generous and convinces himself he did not say he would do something, merely that he would 'do his best' or would 'consider' doing what in fact he had promised.

The routine is made even more abhorrent because he systematically delegates execution to his deputy, who denies all knowledge of any promises made by his boss. The only way to deal with such people is to tape-record their every word.

Truth is always in the detail and subjective truths must always be challenged.

Not answering the question

Although it is rare for a person to accept personal responsibility for saying, 'I am not going to answer that question', there are many other ways in which the liar can achieve the same result including:

- waffle and ambiguity;
- answering a question with a question such as *'What do you expect me to say?'*;
- attacking or praising the question such as *'That is a good question'* or *'I don't know how you can ask me that'*;
- avoiding detail, often claiming loss of memory;
- answering a totally different question *(this is a common ploy by politicians)*;
- limiting phrases such as *'That's about all I can tell you', 'I can't think of anything further', 'That's about it.'*

DISCONTINUITY PHRASE

The subject said: 'We went to the billiard hall, then to the pub and began to drive towards Central London. Later on, we called in at the club'. The phrase 'later on' is a discontinuity statement indicating that something has been omitted (and probably important) between 'starting to drive towards Central London' and calling at the club.

It is truly amazing how often politicians are allowed to escape in television and radio interviews without answering the question.

THE HEAD IN THE SAND AND THE TARTAN TERROR

Or as George Carman QC said of The Right Honourable David Mellor MP: 'He buried his head in the sand, thus exposing his thinking parts'. On Sunday 26 January 2003, Tony Blair was interviewed by Sir David Frost. Quentin Letts reporting in the *Express* said:

'Later stages of the interview were devoted to domestic problems: college fees and immigration. Mr Blair's tone deepened. Maybe he thinks these are more of a threat to his electoral chances. And then, just as the distinguished guest was at last relaxing, old Frostie produced a kidney punch. He asked about Mr Blair's relationship with Gordon Brown. Could both men still be in their jobs in a year's time? Would Gordon soon be looking for a new place to live? Mr Blair stared in astonishment. Motionless. When he recovered himself he said lamely: "Gordon does a fantastic job." "Marvellous," said Frostie, with a clap of the palms.'

What Sir David should have done was to press home the question, maybe by crossing his transactional relationship with the Prime Minister and to continue doing so until he got an answer. Why he did not do this raises more questions than answers, but it is typical of all humans in that they would rather be deceived than confront a lie.

The golden rule is to make sure that every relevant question is fully answered.
Relevant questions have to be repeated before a liar gives a meaningful answer

Generalizations

Generalizations may be used to craft a false explanation by drawing in general practice to avoid answering a specific question.

OJ SIMPSON AND THE BRONCO

Tom Lang:	And where did you park it when you brought it home?
OJ Simpson:	Ah, the first time probably by the mailbox. I'm trying to think, or did I bring it in the driveway? *Normally, I will* park it by the mailbox, sometimes …
Tom Lang:	On Ashford, or Ashland?
OJ Simpson:	On *Ashford*, yeah.
Tom Lang:	Where did you park yesterday for the last time, do you remember?
OJ Simpson:	Right where it is.
Tom Lang:	Where it is now?
OJ Simpson:	Yeah.
Tom Lang:	Where, on …?
OJ Simpson:	Right on the street there.
Tom Lang:	*On Ashford?*
OJ Simpson:	*No, on Rockingham.*
Tom Lang:	You parked it there?
OJ Simpson:	Yes.

In this case, Mr Simpson's generalization that the car was 'normally' parked on 'Ashford' was flushed out by specific questions, revealing that it had been parked 'on Rockingham' where it was found in a blood-drenched state. The interviewer should have pressed home this deception by asking, 'Then why did you try to mislead us by implying that you had parked it on Ashford?' In a very poor interview, he did not do this and in fact had no plan to bring OJ to the pivotal point. Had he done so, the result of his criminal trial might have been totally different.

Responding to a specific allegation with a generalization is a sign of deception

Suppressing guilty knowledge

The fact is that in most cases the liar knows too much, has to suppress the truth and has to be careful he does not inadvertently leak clues.

KNOWING TOO MUCH

Some sensitive files were stolen on a Saturday from a storeroom in company Y's offices. Employees were told only that 'information' had been stolen over the 'weekend' and asked to write down in free style all they knew about the thefts. One statement said:

'I had nothing whatsoever to do with the removal of the *files* and I can account for every second of my time last *Saturday* 14th.'

He knew and said too much and he later admitted his guilt. It is a great shame that not all cases are this simple.

Liars always know too much

The way a subject reacts to documentary and other exhibits (which have a powerful visual impact on the right hemisphere of the brain) can also tell you a great deal about his guilt or innocence, as in the following example.

THE ARSON CASE

Two very serious fires had been started on board a British seagoing oil tanker (a very large crude carrier). They could have killed the 54 crewmen. The police in the country concerned had investigated the cases and advised that the fires had been accidental. We were called in to investigate and immediately searched the ship from top to bottom and found a third fire, in a storeroom, which had not flared. We took photographs of the piles of wood, newspaper and about 50 empty matchboxes and hundreds of matches. We also tried to raise fingerprints from the matchboxes, but without success. We did find some fingerprints on a light switch, but

they were far from illuminating!

The photographs were enlarged and stuck all over the walls of the cabin in which it was planned that the crewmembers would be interviewed. The matchboxes were laid out on a table and the fingerprint slides cut to the same size as the matchboxes and set out in front of them. The impression was that fingerprints had been raised from the matchboxes.

Other evidence suggested that one or more of five crewmembers could have been responsible for all three fires. The first suspect was asked into the interview cabin. He appeared fairly relaxed.

The first question was: 'Is there any reason

why your fingerprints should be on all of those matchboxes?'

He asked where the matchboxes had been found, what the photographs were all about and tried quickly to put the question in context. He had no objection to providing his fingerprints. Subsequent questions established his innocence.

The second suspect came into the cabin and immediately his eyes focused on the photographs, matchboxes and fingerprint slides. When we asked the question: 'Is there any reason why your fingerprints should be on all of those matchboxes?' he did not ask any questions about them, but sat silent for a full two minutes and then said 'Yes'.

He gave an unconvincing explanation that he may have handled all of them while working in the ship's bar. Five minutes later he confessed to starting the fires and gave details that only the arsonist would know. He also explained his motive and made a voluntary written statement.

This is a classic example of the suspect knowing too much and of not asking the questions an innocent person would ask.

Liars don't ask the questions an innocent person would.
Guilty people make assumptions of facts known only to the perpetrator

Disclosing inconsistent detail

An absence or excess of detail is vital in assessing the truthfulness of a story. Some people have good memories while others cannot even remember their wife's birthday or wedding anniversaries (bless them!). Absence of detail should always be treated with suspicion, especially when the person's memory – on other events at around the same time or regarding topics of equal importance – is good.

Inconsistencies indicating deception include:

- lack of detail relating to significant, and especially emotionally charged, events;
- jumbled sequences of important topics within a story;
- significant changes in an explanation to fit newly revealed facts;
- failure to explain an admitted inconsistency;
- Freudian slips;
- admissions of having failed to volunteer information, possibly in response to a 'blocking question' (see page 194);
- rigid recollection of some facts (such as times) but not others of equal significance.

Other inconsistencies, such as variations in estimates of time, distance, size etc. are not necessarily indicators of deception, but they should still be carefully examined.

Unnecessary or apparently irrelevant detail may unconsciously expose a chain of events or subject matter which the subject has tried to conceal.

WHAT IS OJ CONCEALING?

Vannatter:	You haven't had any problems with her lately, have you? (This is a bad, negative, leading question.)
OJ Simpson:	*I* always have problems with *her*, you know? *Our* relationship has been a problem relationship. Probably lately for *me*, and *I* say this only because *I* said it to Ron yesterday *at the* – Ron Fishman, whose wife is Cora – at the dance recital, when he came up to me and went, 'Oooh, boy, what's going on?' and everybody was beefing with everybody. And I said, 'Well, I'm just glad I'm out of the mix.' You know, because I was like dealing with him and his problems with his wife and Nicole and evidently some new problems that a guy named Christian was having with his girl, and he was staying at Nicole's house, and something was going on, but I don't think it's pertinent to this.

There was a reason why OJ did not simply reply to the awfully bad question with the word 'yes' rather than go into the unnecessary detail about Ron, Cora etc. The likely answer is that he unconsciously associated these people with a real problem that he did not want to reveal. Unfortunately, he was never asked to explain so we will never know the answer.

Consistent detail – in response to both control and relevant questions – indicates that the subject is being truthful.

There is no such thing as irrelevant detail.
The subject says everything for a reason

REDUCING ANXIETY WITHIN THE RESPONSE

Generally

The liar will try to reduce his own anxiety by consciously avoiding a barefaced lie, avoiding detail, by evasion, deflection and so on. But he will be also driven by his subconscious monkey to make sure that anxiety is reduced and this may be manifested in the content, syntax, paralinguistics and non-verbal communications of his responses. Obviously, the lack of commitment discussed above minimizes anxiety but there are subtler and more telling clues, and failure to deny an accusation is the most telling.

Falsely denying an allegation requires commitment and raises anxiety.
For this reason, liars don't react in the way an honest person would

Failure to deny

It is critical that you confront a liar with what you believe really happened and with the symptoms of his deception (see pages 88 and 219). The way he reacts to accusations such as:

- 'Bill, I have to say that I believe you took the money.'
- 'The evidence shows clearly that you did this.'
- 'I can see no other explanation than you did this.'

is critical.

A truthful denial of an accusation is normally a positive and committed assertion, such as 'I did not do it', and when the syntax used is in the first person singular, past tense, the denial is usually true. Most guilty people cannot commit themselves to utter this barefaced lie but will use pseudo denials, objections, partial denials and subjective truths.

Any deviation from a first person singular, past tense denial must be regarded with suspicion

Frequently, as in the case of Bill Clinton (see page 79), they will prevaricate and use superfluous words before and after what appears to be a denial. A person making a false denial is at great risk from a statement along the following lines.

THE ULTIMATE IN COMMITMENT

'So, Bill, there can be absolutely no doubt about this, can there? If I prove that what you have said is not true, the only explanation is that you have told a barefaced lie and deserve all the punishment possible: isn't it?'

In over forty years of practical experience a proven liar has never once answered this question with a simple 'yes', although many people wrongly suspected have.

THE GREAT ANSWER

In one case, where a dishonest but legally qualified senior manager was confronted with this question, he responded: 'This is not fair. If you have this evidence, you should tell me before I answer that question'. As always, it is a different matter when it is your turn in the barrel.

If the response to the statement is in the affirmative, the liar is denied a plausible excuse.

F LEE BAILEY AND MARK FUHRMAN

F Lee Bailey: Do you use the word 'nigger' in describing people?
Mark Fuhrman: No, sir. (A subjective truth because he does not use the word currently.)
F Lee Bailey: Have you ever used that word in the past ten years?
Mark Fuhrman: Not that I recall, no. (Lack of commitment.)
F Lee Bailey: So anyone who comes to court and quotes you as using that word in dealing with Afro-Americans would be a liar …
Mark Fuhrman: Yes, they would. (Again, a subjective truth, depending on Mr Fuhrman's definition of an 'Afro-American'.)

Tape recordings made between 1985 and 1994 by Laura Hart McKinny, who was carrying out research for a film script, of conversations with Mr Fuhrman revealed that he had used what became referred to as the 'N-word' on no less than 40 occasions to denigrate black citizens of Los Angeles (i.e. but not necessarily 'Afro-Americans'). This evidence, which the jury believed, confirmed OJ Simpson's defence claim that he had been framed by racially motivated cops and was the turning point in the trial.

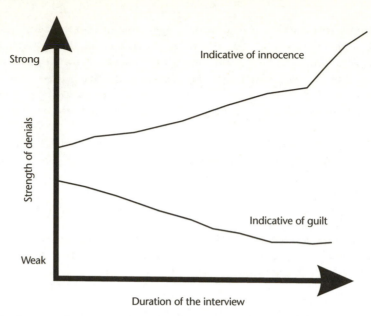

Figure 4.1   Declining and increasing strength of denials

Liars are also much more passive in the way they respond to accusations and, when these are repeated throughout the interview, their pseudo denials become weaker (Figure 4.1).

Feigned anger over being accused is transient and quickly dissipates. On the other hand, innocent people, wrongly accused, react strongly and their protests increase if the accusation is repeated. Their anger is deeply felt and, usually, not quickly dissipated.

An objection sounds like a denial but it is far from it. A statement along the lines of 'I could not have taken [Note: not 'I did not take'] the money *because* I did not know the combination of the safe' is almost certainly untrue. An objection usually contains a justification within the sentence concerned, which probably results from the liar's unconscious acceptance that he knows his denial is unconvincing and which he internalizes for reinforcement. Objections often include the word 'because' and are a strong clue to deception.

A pseudo denial will often contain superfluous words which are an indication of the subject's prevarication in bringing himself to address a critical issue.

For example: 'You have accused me of a very serious offence that strikes at the heart of my relationship with the company and I would like to tell you I did not do it.'

It should be noted that this statement also contains a subjective truth, as there is little doubt the liar 'would like to tell you'. He is not saying that this is what he is actually telling you!

No one in the UK will ever be able to forget the recent case of Neil and Christine Hamilton who were arrested on suspicion of rape, based on a story which was brokered by the publicist Max Clifford.

NEIL AND CHRISTINE HAMILTON

Neil Hamilton said: 'Given that the name of Max Clifford has been mentioned in this context, a man that brought you "Freddy Starr ate my hamster", and can be believed to that extent, there is no truth whatsoever in the allegations.'

Taken by itself, the prevarication before the pseudo-denial is very suspect, but in the same interview the Hamiltons made many FPSPT (first person singular, past tense) denials which were totally committed. The lesson is that clues come in clusters and seldom is a single statement conclusive of deception.

Superfluous words at the end of a pseudo-denial indicate a lack of commitment. For example, the statement 'I did not do it, *as such*' tells you all you need to know, that the denial was too committed for the liar's comfort.

The various forms of denials and pseudo denials can be summarized as in Table 4.3.

Any deviation from an FPSPT denial through a single word or short phrase should be treated with suspicion

Finally, the English upper classes (including royalty, politicians and those investigators who wear 'Hush Puppies' and red suspenders) have what appears to mere mortals to be a pretentious habit of referring to themselves with the reflexive pronoun 'one', such as *'One would not do such a thing'*. This subtle way of avoiding the dreadfully committed pronoun 'I' should be treated with suspicion unless the person concerned is a Raving Rupert or an estate agent.

Because so much emphasis is placed on the strength of denials, you may believe that a liar could prepare himself to respond in the right way and thus deceive you. This is not the case.

YOU WILL NEVER GET ME

At a celebratory dinner following a very successful investigation when ten employees confessed to fraud, a senior manager told the investigators, 'I am bloody amazed that these guys confessed. If ever you came after me, I would say nothing'. One investigator – who did not like or trust the senior manager – replied, 'It's a different matter when you are in the barrel, Bill. If ever we had to interview you, you would be a soft touch, so remember that.' Everyone went quiet but the matter dropped.

A couple of years later investigators discovered that the senior manager had incurred thousands of pounds in costs by entertaining his mistress at a local hotel but had them misdescribed as dinners or meetings with clients, trade union representatives etc. and paid for by his employer. The hotel reported the investigation to the senior manager, explaining that it had no alternative but to supply the correct documentation. When the manager appeared at the first interview with the investigators he said, 'I remember what you told me at that dinner. I am dead in the water and I will tell you everything. I do not want to go through the pressure of trying to lie to you. I have not slept for days thinking about this moment.'

Deception seems easy until it is your turn in the barrel.
If you think telling the truth is difficult, try lying.
Making first person singular, past tense denials is hard if you are lying: they are too committed

Table 4.3   Summary of denials and pseudo-denials

Wording of the apparent denial	Interpretation
'I did not take the money' 'I did not do it'	FPSPT, bold, brief and totally committed *Probably true*
'I don't steal' (in response to a specific question: 'Did you take the cash from the safe?')	This is not a denial to a specific accusation but a generalization and is *probably false*
'I *would not* steal from the company' 'I should like to think I would never be suspected of that'	Conditional-passive *Probably not true*
'I could not have taken the money, *because* I did not have the keys to the office'	This is an objection *Probably untrue*
'I know in my own *mind* I am innocent'	Any reference to his internal thoughts, 'heart' or 'mind' should be treated with great care *Probably untrue*
'There is not a shred of *evidence* and no *proof* that I took the money'	This may be a subjective truth, but is not a denial *Probably untrue*
'I have been with the company for forty years and have *worked hard and loyally*. I am upset that anyone should think I was responsible for this. I did not do it'	Extended introduction to what appears to be a bold denial *Probably untrue*
'I had a great time in Florida and the hotel was great. The hire car was excellent, *but I did not meet any nice-looking blondes with long legs*'	Denial of an allegation not made and *probably false*
'I did not take the money, as such'	End softening and extraneous words after the denial *Probably untrue*
'*I know you may accuse me of taking the money, as well as all of the other things, but I would like to make it clear* that I do not need to do this'	Self-deprecation and a denial of an allegation not made: a pre-emptive denial *Probably untrue*
'Oh, and I suppose you believe I stole the crown jewels as well?'	Joking or dismissive reply *Probably untrue*
'If I had, do you think I would admit it?' 'No one would admit to that, would they?'	Not a denial and *probably untrue*
'You have accused me of taking the money and of falsifying the accounts. I have never taken any money from this company'	Limited denial: does not deny falsifying the accounts *Thus the allegation not denied (i.e. he falsified the accounts) is true*
'There will be no whitewash in the White House. The "President" would not do such a thing.' President Richard Nixon in referring to Watergate	Projection to the third person *Probably untrue*

'I know you will not believe me, but I am telling you I did not do anything wrong' or 'I am not clever enough to lie'	Self-deprecation and a subjective truth *Probably untrue*
'I did not take the money simply because I did not know the combination to the safe'	An objection and *most likely false*
In response to the question 'Did you take the money?' the subject replies 'no' and has words before or after this binary answer such as 'No. I was not there' or 'The reply to that question is "no"'	*Probably untrue*
In response to the question 'Did you take the money?' the subject replies 'I would be crazy to do that'	Subjective truth and *probably untrue*
When asked a non-threatening question the subject responds 'Are you accusing me?'	*Probably guilty*
In response to the question 'Did you take the money?' the subject replies 'No'	*Probably true*

Irrelevant support

A truthful person will usually be confident in his own position and will convey his explanation. He will also answer closed (binary) questions with a committed 'yes' or 'no' with no prevarication before or softening words afterwards. Liars, knowing the weakness of their position, will often go too far in trying to convince you by providing inappropriate support for a false explanation.

> *For example*: 'I did not steal the money and if you don't believe me, you can ask my mummy; she will tell you I don't steal and that I always eat up my cabbage.'

They may also suggest corroboration for their lies from a source that is impossible to verify. For example: 'Bill Smith would confirm my explanation, but it is a great pity he died last week'. Dishonest job candidates often use the same ploy by claiming to have worked for companies they know have gone out of business.

Contextual clarification

Liars are hindered by the fact that they do not understand how an innocent person would react and may seek clarification through phrases such as: *'I am not sure what I should say about that'*, *'I am not sure what I am expected to say'*, or *'How should I know that …?'* Such phrases should be treated with suspicion.

Other anxiety reducing responses

The liar will unconsciously use a range of techniques to reduce his anxiety when delivering an untruthful response. Possibly the most important are his use of manipulators, defensive body language and from his attitude, but other clues are summarized in Table 4.9, page 117.

Clues from an attitude

Liars, like alcoholics, are inclined to minimize the seriousness of their problems by using soft, non-emotive words or unwanted words at the end of an apparently strong sentence. The words 'really', 'actually' or 'as such' are good examples. They may minimize important topics with words such as: *'as an aside,' 'perhaps I should mention in passing,' 'incidentally,'* or *' by the way'*.

The liar may use self-deprecating phrases such as *'I know it sounds incredible but ...'* He may even be excessively submissive and use phrases such as: *'If you want me to say I did it, I will'*. He may introduce an excuse before one is justified or deny allegations that have not been made.

SELF-DEPRECATION IN GOLF

Some golfers who stand on the first tee of an important competition use self-deprecation such as 'I had a really late night last night and still feel a bit pickled' to unconsciously reduce anxiety by providing an advance excuse for what they fear will be a poor shot. By doing so they use neurolinguistic programming to prepare themselves for a duck hook into Granny Smith's garden.

You should not allow suspects to find comfort in self-deprecation but they should be told something along the lines: 'Forget that, just tell me ...' If your golfing partner self-deprecates say the same sort of thing and try to make him focus. If your opponent self-deprecates you might say: 'Yes, you do look a bit pickled and you are aiming miles to the left. Watch out for Granny Smith's garden.'

A suspect may refer to his own state of mind such as *'I know in my own mind I am innocent of this'* and give away other clues that he has internalized the problem. Experience shows that when a person refers to his own mental state, he is struggling with the truth. When he refers to his 'mind' or 'heart' he is usually drawing information from his imagination.

A profile in family murder cases is that the attacker will not refer to his victim by his given name or by his exact relationship. For example, he will refer to the victim as 'the child' or 'my child' rather than 'my daughter'.

Most crooks (whether white collar or otherwise) tend to be non-judgemental, do not have clearly ingrained beliefs and tend to assume everyone is as crooked as they are. In management fraud cases, the guilty person will often fail to clear himself or blame someone else. For example, if he is asked the question, *'There were four of you on duty at the time and someone took the money. Who can you absolutely clear of this?'* the person responsible will seldom give the answer 'me'. If he does, the chances are he is innocent. But if he says 'me, *because* I just love pussies', by now you should know what this means. Through such attention to fine detail the truth is exposed.

Perhaps the greatest example of attitude giving the game away is the story of King Solomon.

KING SOLOMON

Two women were in dispute over a baby: both said they were its mother. King Solomon said the baby should be cut in two and half given to each. He knew that the woman who accepted this decision was not the real mother.

Attitude is critically important in revealing the deep truth

The real bottom line is that liars do not do or say the things an innocent person would and do not show congruent emotions.

OTHER UNCONSCIOUS CLUES

Virtually all of a liar's syntax, non-verbal communication, paralinguistics, and clues to his attitude are driven at an unconscious level and are summarized in pages 92–126. But the most important thing, in all of the ways lies are communicated, is that liars do not do or say what an innocent person would do or say.

Liars focus on what they do and say but omit innocent reactions.
It is not only what liars say, but what they don't say that is important

Detailed symptoms of truth and lies

FROM OBJECTIVES TO DETAILED LEAKAGE

The truth is that we are flooded with symptoms of deceit, so much so that there are far too many to consciously remember. The good news is that all of the clues are already embedded in your subconscious and you should always try to elevate – to a conscious level – why you have the feelings you do. Detecting deception is not difficult but resolving your suspicions is less easy unless you have a cunning plan. Chapter 1 contain such plans.

Deception is communicated through one or more of five channels (see Chapter 2, page 18), the most important being auditory, in speech and paralinguistics, or visual, in writing and non-verbal communications. This section summarizes the most important conscious (IN BLOCK CAPITALS) and unconscious clues under the headings of:

- Attacks.
- What the liar says:
  - content,
  - syntax,
  - paralinguistics.
- Non-verbal communication.
- Attitude.

You will not be able to remember them all, so don't worry. The important thing is that once you believe a subject is lying, you must use a cunning plan to clear him from suspicion or nail him.

ATTACKS

Attacks are communicated through verbal, visual and sensory channels but are of such importance that they warrant being treated as a separate division. The main clues, which mainly result from the liar's conscious decisions are listed in Table 4.4, and further illustrated in Mind Map 4.

Table 4.4 Attack

Symptoms of deception CONSCIOUS and unconscious	Examples and comments	Significance 10 = High 0 = Low
ATTACK REFUSAL TO PARTICIPATE ON THE GROUNDS OF ALLEGED INJUSTICE	'You have not been fair in the past and I do not trust you' 'You cannot be trusted to report the truth' 'The Audit Department is total crap'	10
CHALLENGING THE INTERVIEWER'S AUTHORITY, MOTIVES, INDEPENDENCE ETC.	'You have already made up your mind' 'You are not interested in hearing the truth' 'You have been trying to catch me out for years' 'You have never liked me' 'You have no right to treat me like this'	10
CONTRIVED ANGER AT THE START OF THE INTERVIEW OR NOT IN RESPONSE TO A RELEVANT QUESTION	Note that the verbal outburst of feigned anger usually occurs before the facial expression and is transient. Genuine anger usually results from a specific stimulation, such as a question	10
THREATENING VIOLENCE	'I know where you live and you will be getting a visit from my brothers' 'You and I better step outside, right now and sort this out'	5
ACTUAL VIOLENCE	If the suspect attacks you, he has lost the fight	10
THREATENING OTHER PROBLEMS AND DIRE CONSEQUENCES	'If you try and carry on with this investigation I will have a few things to say to the Inland Revenue' 'I will report the company to the Fraud Squad' 'I will expose the MD for his shenanigans'	8
THREATENING LEGAL ACTION	'That is slander and I am going to my lawyer' 'I will prosecute you personally' 'You are discriminating against me'	5
CHALLENGING THE EVIDENCE	'You have no evidence of that …' 'There is no proof' 'There is not a shred of evidence in my public life of any wrongdoing' (Bill Clinton) 'You will have to prove that' 'I hope you have some evidence of that'	10

ATTACKING A QUESTION	'That is a stupid question' 'I do not have to answer that sort of crap' 'I am not going to justify that with an answer' 'I can't believe you asked me that'	8
RAISING SPURIOUS ISSUES	'Before I answer that, you better tell me about the company's problems with tax evasion'	8
FALSIFYING EVIDENCE SUBMITTING FALSE ALIBIS, DESTROYING EVIDENCE AND INTERFERING WITH WITNESSES	Producing false documents Producing deceitful witnesses Threatening witnesses	10
COMPLAINING ABOUT UNFAIR TREATMENT	'I have never been treated fairly here' 'You have always wanted to fire me'	5
SYNTAX	Using obscenities	8
PARALINGUISTICS	Shouting, fast speed of delivery	10
NON-VERBAL CLUES	Aggressive body language Using pointing gestures or a closed fist Aggressive facial expressions	10
ATTITUDE	Feigned anger Irrational justification of his position	10

The vast majority of attacks are intended to deter the victim from pursuing his rights. Ways for dealing with them are explained in Chapter 7, pages 185–186, but the rule is don't panic and treat them for what they are.

THE CONTENT OF THE STORY

The content, or what the person says *and does not say,* contains many clues to deception. You should always consciously consider why the liar:

• chose to say what he did and, sometimes more importantly, what he did not say;
• chose how to say it and in the order he did.

Clues in the content of a story are summarized in Table 4.5 and Mind Map 5.

What the suspect does not say is almost as important as what he does say

You will note that the subject has conscious control over most of the content. The same is not true on other areas where unconscious clues are scattered into the ether.

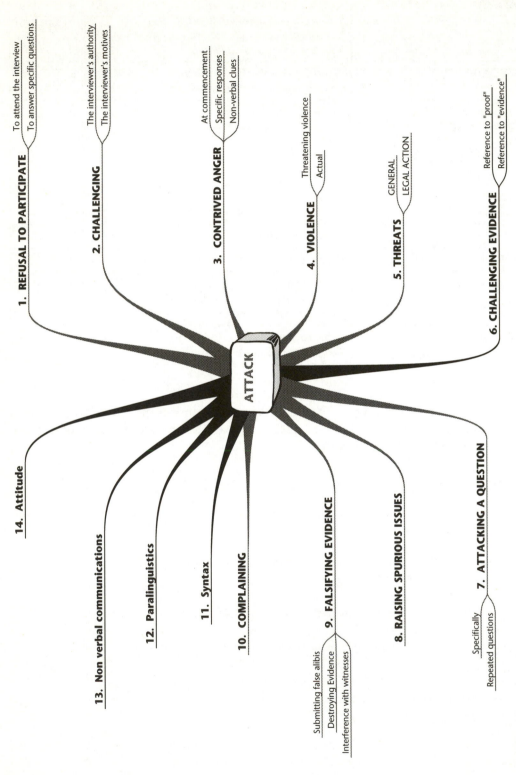

Mind Map® 4   Attack

Table 4.5   Clues in the content

Symptoms of deception CONSCIOUS, unconscious or *both*	Examples	Significance[3] 10 = High 0 = Low
AVOIDING BAREFACED LIES		
LACK OF COMMITMENT CONCEALMENT, OMISSION, EVASION, DEFLECTION ETC. DELIBERATE AMBIGUITY SUBJECTIVE TRUTHS OBJECTIONS RATHER THAN DENIALS GENERALIZATIONS FAILURE TO DENY	*'I did not have sexual relations with that woman, Monica Lewinsky'* *'There is not a shred of evidence of any wrongdoing in my public life'*	10
LACK OF COMMITMENT		
AVOIDING THE BAREFACED LIE ALLEGED MEMORY FAILURES	*'I am not sure about this, but …'* *'To the best of my recollection …'* *'Don't hold me to this … but I believe …'* *'I am not sure about this …'* *'As far as I recall'* *'I believe'* *'I would have thought'* *'I can't really remember'*	8
DELIBERATE AMBIGUITY	Long rambling sentences	10
REDUCING THE SIGNIFICANCE OF A TOPIC	*'As an aside …'* *'Incidentally …'* *'By the way …'* *'I would just like to tell you …'*	8
SUBJECTIVE TRUTHS	*'When Gordon and I are asked that question, we say there is no secret agreement'* *'I would have been crazy to do that'* *'How can you think I did that?'*	10
SELF-DEPRECATION	*'I know you won't believe this …'* *'I know this sounds incredible but …'* *'I am not clever enough to lie'* *'I know you think I am a crook but …'* *'I know I look foolish'* *'I know I will fail to convince you'*	5
Projection	*'The President of the United States would not do such a thing'*	5
Referral	*'As I told Mr Smith, I was not in the room at the time'*	10
Prevarication, especially before a pseudo denial	*'I would like to tell the American people, and I will say it again, I did not have sexual relations with …'*	10

[3]   The higher the score, the more likely the response is deceptive

Symptoms of deception CONSCIOUS, unconscious or *both*	Examples	Significance 10 = High 0 = Low
Evasion and omission	*Various techniques*	10
Contextual clarification	*'I don't know what you expect me to say'* *'How can I answer that?'*	8
Suppression of detail	*Unwillingness to falsify a statement*	10
CONCEALMENT		
FAILING TO APPEAR *In effect saying 'I don't want to answer questions, because I have no answer, but I do not want to take the responsibility for this decision on my own shoulders'*	*' I would like to see you, but my wife is ill'* *'My lawyer has told me not to see you'* *'I have had a heart attack and cannot see you, as much as I would like to help'*	8
FAILURE TO ANSWER *Usually by blaming someone else or through a legitimization*	*'I cannot answer that because of the Data Protection Act'* *'It is not company policy to discuss such matters'*	10
Inconsistent coverage of topics Sequence violations in an explanation or story	In freestyle stories or responses to open questions, the liar prevaricates and delays in reaching the critical issue and thus extends the prologue. In various topics in a story, the subject allocates a disproportionate amount of his explanation to one over another. Often the most important topic is dealt with superficially (indicating omission) or a less important topic given excessive coverage (indicating that there is some hidden reason why the subject believes this is important). In some cases, topics are dealt with out of sequence (indicating omission)	7
Omission *Limited answers* *Containment*	DELIBERATE OMISSION OF INCRIMINATING INFORMATION *'I am not going to answer unless my lawyer is present ...'* *'I don't have to answer that ...'* *'I can't answer that ...'* *'I can tell you this ...'* [probably meaning there are other things he cannot or does not wish to tell you] *'There's not much I can say ...'* *'Oh yes, and then I murdered the chairman ...'* *'I am not going to dignify that question with a reply'* *'That's a stupid question'* *'Company policy prohibits me from answering that question'* *'I cannot answer that question until I have spoken to my manager'* *'That's about all I know ...'* *'That's all I can tell you ...'* Such phrases usually mean that there is other information the liar is not prepared to reveal	10

Symptoms of deception CONSCIOUS, unconscious or *both*	Examples	Significance 10 = High 0 = Low
RELUCTANCE TO PROVIDE DETAIL	Inconsistent recollection of detail. Typically the liar will have a good and detailed recollection of non-controversial matters within the time frame concerned. Only when questions focus on critical areas will his recollection become vague. The liar is drawing the content of this explanation from imagination. He knows the more detail he provides, the greater the chance he will give contradictory answers. Thus avoiding detail seems the safe course	10
FAILURE TO VOLUNTEER	Failing to volunteer information to open or blocking questions or to admit facts which are known	7
COMPRESSION	Instead of giving detail such as *'I went to Sainsbury's and bought an egg, then to Tesco and got some bacon, then to Homebase and bought a ladder,'* the subject says *'I went shopping'*	5
Discontinuity words and phrases	*'Later on', 'The next thing we did', 'Subsequently', 'We began to discuss'* Indicates that important information has been omitted before the discontinuity word	8
Unopened or unclosed actions	*'I then left the office'* (without explaining when he entered it)	8
Inconsistent and missing detail	Different levels of detail between control and relevant questions	8
EVASION AND DEFLECTION DIVERSIONARY ADMISSIONS RAMBLING ANSWERS	*'I have made small mistakes ... I will admit that'* Long rambling answers which are off the point *'Before I answer that, I want to tell you about ...'*	10
LIMITED ANSWERS	*'Basically ...'* *'As a rule ...'*	8
ADMITTING ONLY WHAT CAN BE PROVEN	And changing his explanation in response to enticement questions (see page 212)	10
FOCUSING ON NON-ISSUES	Using ambiguous words and phrases (see also 'subjective truths') Admitting only what is provable Focusing on non-issues and elevating their importance	7
GENERALIZATIONS	In answer to the question *'What did you do last Friday?'* the suspect responds, *'I usually go to the club on Fridays'*	8

Symptoms of deception CONSCIOUS, unconscious or *both*	Examples	Significance 10 = High 0 = Low
REHEARSED ANSWERS AND FOCUSING ON NON-ISSUES	*'I could not have done it (1) because I did not have keys to the office (2) because my car had broken down (3) because I am not that sort of person (4) etc …'* Listing of this nature indicates the answer has been rehearsed	10
CONTRIVED ANGER	An honest person may become genuinely angry at suggestions that he has done something wrong. A guilty person's anger is usually contrived and short term *'Are you accusing me?'* *'That is a stupid question …'* *'I will not dignify that question with an answer …'*	8
LEGITIMIZATION	*'I would like to answer that, but it is a state secret'* *'It is not company policy to disclose this stuff'* *'I cannot answer because of the Data Protection Act'*	10
FALSE PROMISES	*'I will get the papers for you next week'* *'I have to see my accountant first'*	7
FEIGNED COOPERATION		
Feigned submissiveness and cooperation. Flattery and misplaced humour	Using permission phrases such as: *'Can I please explain …'* *'Will you give me time to think about this?'* *'You are obviously a very, very clever interviewer …'* *'I would never do anything to upset you …'*	7
Offers to confess	*'If you want me to say I did it, I will'* *'If it will help, I will take the blame for this'*	10
Responding with a question	*'Why should I do that?'* *'What do you expect me to say?'*	8
Repeating words from the question	Using some or all of the interviewer's words	7
Contextual clarification	Saying something like *'Who, me?'* when he is the only person in the room or when the question is obviously addressed to him *'How should I know that?'* *'What do you expect me to say?'* *'Why do you think I can answer that?'* *'I don't get the question'* *'I don't see what you are driving at'*	10
REPEATING THE QUESTION	Using exactly the same words as the interviewer	8

Symptoms of deception CONSCIOUS, unconscious or *both*	Examples	Significance 10 = High 0 = Low
PRAISING THE QUESTION	*'That is a great question'* *'I knew you were going to ask me that ...'* *'The answer to that question is ...'*	8
ASSESSMENT QUESTIONS	*'Have you spoken to Bill Smith?'* *'Will you be able to get the Swiss bank accounts?'* *'What do you plan to do?'*	10
ASSERTIONS OF VIRTUE		
Religious assertions Ethical assertions Other assertions	*'I have done many good things in my life ...'* *'I have always worked hard for this company ...'* *'I swear on the Bible ...'* *'I am an honest, God-fearing man ...'* *'I would never do such a thing'* *'I swear on my mother's life.'* *'Let God strike me down if I am not telling the truth ...'*	10
Abnormal assumptions		
Inside knowledge of critical issues known only to the perpetrator Failure to seek clarification	Failing to ask for clarification of facts that would not be known to an innocent person. For example, a guilty person will rarely ask about the significance of exhibits displayed in the interview room	10
Denials		
Failure to deny	See page 88	10
Passive reaction to accusations and lack of commitment	Denials get weaker as the interview progresses	8
Declining strength of denials	Throughout the interview, an innocent person's denials usually become stronger. A guilty person's objections become weaker	10
Pseudo denials *Generalizations* *Limited denials*	In response to the question *'Did you take the money?'* the suspect responds *'I do not steal.'* This is also a generalization In response to the question *'I think you are a crook and a liar,'* the reply *'I am not a liar'*	10
Objections rather than denials	A denial is a solid, usually first person, past tense statement along the lines *'I did not do it'* and is usually a sign of innocence. An objection is used because the suspect knows his case is weak and looks for reinforcement. Typical objections are: *'I could not have done it because I did not have the key to the safe ...'* *'I would not do such a thing'* *'I am not that sort of person'* *'I have no reason to do that'*	10

Symptoms of deception CONSCIOUS, unconscious or *both*	Examples	Significance 10 = High 0 = Low
Conditional denials	*'I would never do such a thing'*	7
Unsolicited denials	For example: *'I had a great time in Florida and the hotel was great. The hire car was excellent but I did not go out with any nice-looking blondes'*	7
Prevaricated denials	Superfluous words before or after the apparent denial	8
Softened denials	*'I could not have done it, **really** ...'* *'I was not there, **as such** ...'* *'essentially'* Coughing or other non-verbal sounds at the start or end of sentences	10
Motivational denials	*'I have no reason to do that'* *'I would have been crazy to do that'*	
Unjustified support	Going too far in trying to convince Referring to an unverifiable or irrelevant source for corroboration. For example, *'I did not take the money and my mummy will confirm that'* or *'Bill would confirm he gave me permission but unfortunately he died last week'*	8
MINIMIZING ANXIETY WITHIN THE RESPONSE		
Subjective truths		10
Projection	Stepping outside his own body and seeing the accused as a separate person. Referring to himself as a third party. For example, in the Watergate case, Richard Nixon did not deny erasing tapes, but used phrases such as: *'The President is innocent of this ...'* *'One would never do such a thing'*	7
Permission phrases	See above	5
Self deception and challenging evidence or proof	*'I would like to think I would not do such a thing'* *'I know in my own mind I did not do it'* *'There is no evidence of wrongdoing in my public life'* *'If you think you have the evidence, then go ahead'*	7
Self-deprecation	See above	6
Diversion to safe ground	*'Can we just go back and deal with (some minor issue)'* *'I think we should first deal with ...'*	
Reducing the significance of a response	*'By the way ...'* *'Incidentally ...'*	8

Symptoms of deception CONSCIOUS, unconscious or *both*	Examples	Significance 10 = High 0 = Low
Referral statements to a past (and successful) lie	*'In my own mind I know I did not do this ...'* *'As I said in my speech last month ...'* *'As I told Mr Smith last week ...'* *'As you know ...'*	9
Layering	This partly conscious and unconscious ploy can be confused with excessive or omitted detail. The subject starts off on an important topic, then diverts to a subtopic, then from the subtopic to a sub-subtopic and so on. The result is that the original topic is lost and this may be deliberate.	6
Avoiding binary answers	Not using *'yes'* or *'no'* without some qualification or prologue	10
Using soft words	Using *'borrowed'* rather than *'stolen'*	6
Prevarication	Using surplus or esoteric words	6
Inappropriate humour		6
AVOIDING COMMITMENT	See above	10
FALSIFICATION		10
ADMITTED LIES	Falsification is a dangerous game for a liar and calls for composure and good memory. In exculpatory interviews falsification is manifested in most of the symptoms explained above	10
Obvious lies		
Contradictions		
Changing explanations to fit new facts		
Unintended disclosures		
FALSE ALIBIS		
FALSE EXCUSES		
False and inconsistent detail		
FALSE CONVINCING		
ADMISSIONS AND CONFESSIONS		10
	'Ok, It's all down to me and only you are clever enough to have caught me'	

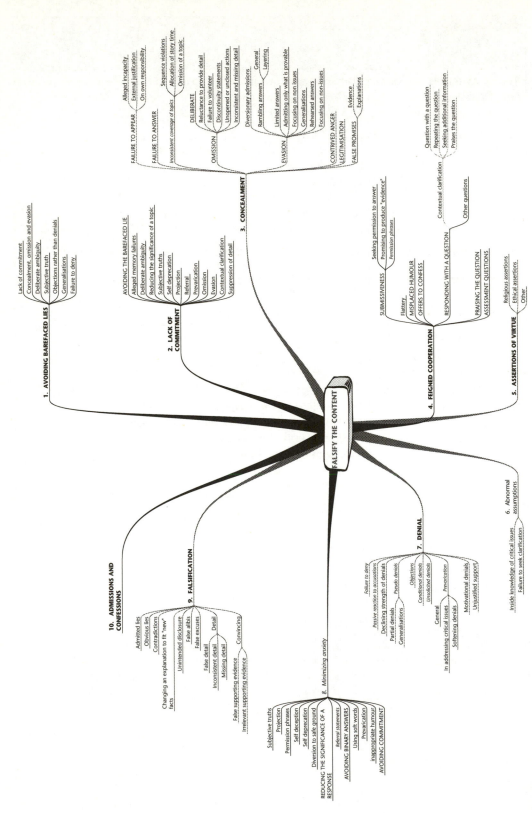

Mind Map® 5   Clues in the content

THE SYNTAX

General

The construction of sentences is mainly unconscious and based on the person's unique communications code and may be incongruent with the content of a freestyle story or an answer to an open question.

Sentence construction

The construction of sentences may be stilted, excessively short or rambling. They may also be deliberately ambiguous, riddled with subjective truths or incomplete.

OJ SIMPSON AND HIS ALIBI

In explaining what he had done on the night his wife was murdered, OJ Simpson said: 'Eight-something, maybe. He hadn't done a jacuzzi, *we* had ... [unfinished sentence but probably referring to a discussion about his wife] ... went and got a burger, and *I'd come* home and kind of leisurely got ready to go. I mean, *we'd* done a few things.'

Note also the mixture of and missing personal pronouns.

Often an incomplete sentence, or changes in content or syntax midway through a sentence, result from severe editing and are indicative of deception.

With the brain in a thrashing mode a liar may use esoteric words such as *'I am positively asserting that I can exculpate myself from this abhorrent predicament'.* Such phrasing is a sign of severe editing – a deviation from his communication code – and deceptive unless, of course, the subject is an estate agent, when any language is possible.

In another part of OJ's interview he says the following.

OJ SIMPSON

'I recall bleeding at my house. *The last thing I did before I left, when I was* rushing, was [ ] went and got my phone out of the Bronco.'

The phrase 'The last thing' suggests that something important was omitted between the time he 'recalled' the bleeding and left the house. Also the missing pronoun 'I' before 'went and got' and the change from past to present tense may also be significant. The statement is unlikely to be true.

Statements such as the above, and especially changes in tense, should be carefully analysed for their real meaning. But please remember the analysis proves nothing. It is only of any value if you consciously deal with it and it leads to other evidence, admissions and confessions.

In written stories, especially, punctuation can reveal important clues. Direct speech, reported within inverted commas, is normally a sign of commitment and is more likely to be true than not. However, if you are a follower of the comedian Billy Connolly, you will have seen him use hand signals to indicate inverted commas in parts of his speech. Liars do the same. So if someone says, ' I spoke to my wife' and signals inverted commas when saying 'wife' you know something is amiss.

Use of verbs and adverbs

- *Verb* n. a word that applies to an action (doing).
- *First person singular* 'I' 'me' or 'my'.
- *Tense* n. (Gram.) form taken by a verb to indicate the time (also continuance or completeness) of the action etc. (present, future, past, conditional, imperfect, perfect).
- *Active or passive* 'I kicked Bill' or 'Bill was kicked'.

A person may unconsciously use different verbs in a way that exposes his inner thinking. *For example, a story may contain the verbs 'said', 'tell', 'conversing', 'conversed' and 'discussed'* which appear synonymous but may reveal important differences. Analysis might reveal that the subject used the verb 'told' and the past tense when he was describing a friendly conversation and consistently used 'conversing' in the present tense when he was on the receiving end of a tirade. Such minor differences may be important and they should be consciously examined.

Liars consistently use less past tense verbs than honest people

LINGUISTIC CODES

A defendant's affidavit[4] was described by the complainant's lawyer as 'being convincing beyond peradventure'. The defendant stated that on various specific times and dates he 'went', 'saw', 'spoke to', 'bought', 'purchased' and each one was supported by detail. The critical point was precisely when and where he bought a specific item. The affidavit addressed this purchase as follows: 'During the week commencing Monday 8th April (i.e. not a specific date and time), I attended upon a retail store in Central Essex and acquired the said items.'

This sentence was a glaring breach of the defendant's linguistic code and is highly suspect.

Memory speaks in the past tense

Great care also has to be taken over verbs that do not have any associated action. For example, *'I started to mend the computer'* does not mean he mended it, or even that he made a reasonable effort to do so. 'Tried', 'thought about', 'considered' etc. (which can be referred to as 'unverbs', or 'political verbs', because the only action associated with them is cerebral) should be carefully examined for their real meaning.

CEREBRAL VERBS

You should always ask for an explanation of unfinished verbs. For example, 'I started to mend the computer.'

Question: 'Did you actually mend it?'
Reply: 'No, Tom came into the office and interrupted me.'

First person singular, past tense (FPSPT) commits a writer to an explanation. Use of other than the FPSPT or a mixture of tenses within a topic dealing with past events are all signs of deception.

---

[4]   Most affidavits cannot be considered to be freestyle stories

MORE OF OJ SIMPSON

In answering questions about the unusual way in which the Bronco had been parked Mr Simpson said, 'Well, it's parked because … I don't know if it's a funny angle or what. It's parked because when I *was hustling* and the end of the day to get all my stuff, and *I was getting* my phone and everything *off* it, when I just *pulled* it out of the gate there … it's like a tight turn.' The change of tense suggests that the story is untrue, as does the preposition 'off' rather than 'from' (the Bronco).

PAST TENSE FOR LIVING PEOPLE

In a recent high-profile case, three children had been abducted and the fear was that they had been murdered. The mother and father appeared on television appealing for their kids to be returned. He consistently referred to them in the present tense: '*are* lovely kids' etc. The mother, however, referred to them in the past tense: 'they *were* home loving and caring', revealing that she knew they were dead. She was later convicted of their murder.

Passive sentences or statements normally reflect a lack of commitment. For example, '*He was seen by us*', rather than '*We saw him*' suggests a problem. Similarly the difference between '*I went at around 10.00pm*' and '*It would have been around 10.00 that I would have gone out*' is significant: the conditional statement is suspect.

The possibilities of deception, especially in exculpatory stories can often be determined by verb usage (Table 4.6).

Any contrived avoidance of FPSPT should be treated with great caution

Adverbs are normally used to add detail to a verb by qualifying such things as who, why, how or how much etc. If the adverb or adverbial phrase is consistent with the story, and especially any emotion involved, it is normally true.

Table 4.6 Verb usage

Probably true Committed	Probably deceptive Uncommitted
PAST TENSE *I saw*	Other than past tense, especially if the syntax is contrived *'When I got to the door I could see'* *'I would have seen'*
FIRST PERSON SINGULAR	Other than first person singular
ACTIVE *'I hit Bill'*	PASSIVE *'Bill was hit'*
ADVERBS AND ADVERBIAL PHRASES *'I was very, very angry'*	Absence of adverbs and adverbial phrases, especially when recalling an emotion
SUBJECT – VERB – OBJECT *'Tom took the money'*	OBJECT – VERB – SUBJECT (or no subject) *'The money was taken by Tom'*

Use of nouns

> - *Noun* n. (Gram.) word or phrase used as name of person, place or thing.
> - *Synonym* n. (Gram.) word or phrase identical and coextensive in sense and usage with another of the same language.
>
> Nouns may be *proper* when they refer to a specific entity (such as the King) or *common* when they refer to a general class such as 'investigators'.
>   The *gender* of a noun may be masculine, feminine or neutral.

A writer may give away a great deal of information in the way in which he uses nouns and pronouns to 'label' people and things.

Changes in the use of labels when they are not consistent with the writer's likely emotions are suspect.

FROM GENTLEMAN TO YOB

'I saw this *gentleman* walking along. *He* and a *youth* appeared to be drunk. The *man* walked up to me and said, "Up yours." The *fat pig* then hit me in the face without any provocation and I fell to the ground, the youth just stood there. If I get my hands on this *yob* again I will kill him.'

The change of labels for the same person from *'gentleman'* to *'man'* to *'fat pig'* to *'yob'* is interesting. On the one hand it could accurately reflect the changing emotional state of the writer when reliving the real-world events. On the other, at the time the story was written, the writer had already decided that the man was a 'yob', so why did he refer to him as a 'gentleman'? This is inconsistent and the phrase 'If I get my hands … again' reveals that the writer was far from a passive victim and had probably already given the 'gentleman' a smack or two. The syntax throws great doubt on the truth of the story. However, the consistent use of the noun 'youth' suggests he was a passive bystander and that he could be an important witness.

Also significant is the use of a synonym (rather than a pronoun) when the person refers to himself.

PROJECTION TO A THIRD PERSON

In the 'Praise the Lord' scandal, Tammy Bakker said, 'No one would believe that *Jim and Tammy* would do such a thing.' She could have said, 'We didn't do it', which would have been much more convincing. Similarly in Watergate, Richard Nixon frequently used the word *'President'* when referring to his part in the deletion of tapes. In both cases the writers appeared to be standing outside their own bodies, thus distancing 'I' from the unpleasant truth.

Such phrasing is referred to as a 'projection' because the subject seems to disassociate himself from personal accountability.

THE FOOTBALL MANAGER

Kevin Keegan, the ex-England football manager, often referred to himself as 'Kevin', especially when he was trying to justify poor results.

Use of pronouns

- *Pronoun* n. (Gram.) word used instead of (proper or other) noun (without naming) the person, place or thing already known from the context. There are different types of pronouns. Examples:
  - personal (first person) – I, me, mine, myself;
  - personal (second person) – we, us, you, he, she, it, they;
  - possessive – my, mine, ours, hers, his, its;
  - demonstrative – this, that;
  - distributive – each, either;
  - impersonal – any, some, anyone, something;
  - interrogative – who, what, which;
  - relative – who, what, which, that;
  - reflexive – myself, oneself, one, himself.

Everyone subconsciously selects pronouns. Generally 'I', 'me' and 'my' (first person singular) indicate a positive commitment and their use in the past tense is consistent with the truth. Clumsy construction of sentences to avoid FPSPT is a clear warning of deception. Also a mixture of possessive and demonstrative pronouns, especially with the definite article 'the', can be interesting.

THE CAR

The subject said: '*My* Jaguar was parked on the drive. I had owned it for a few years. I jumped in *the* car and then it just exploded. I had nothing to do with it, honest. *That* car just went up in the air … woosh!'

Also, the stilted or exaggerated use of 'I' can be a sign of concealment or deception, possibly resulting from a discontinuity in the process of imagination.[5] For example:

STILTED USE OF FPS

'I am the manager. I know about the system. I have no reason to take the money. I do not know Bill Smith.' This extract is a sign of extreme censorship.

Normally, before the collective pronouns 'we' or 'us' or 'they' are used, the other people concerned should be introduced by name; failure to do so (i.e. the use of 'we' without explaining who is referred to) suggests that the relationship between the subject and the other party is not harmonious.

---

[5] Memory of events is usually in chronological order: imagination is jumbled

Use of adjectives

> • *Adjectives* n. (Gram.) word or phrase naming an attribute, added to a noun to describe a thing more fully.

Adjectives, and adjectival clauses, add detail to a topic and when consistently used are more likely to be truthful than not.

Use of prepositions

> • *Preposition* n. word governing and normally proceeding a noun or pronoun, expressing its relationship to another word (for example, 'at', 'in', 'off', 'to', 'with' etc.).

The liar may unconsciously use wrong or inconsistent prepositions. *In the OJ Simpson case he referred to taking his telephone 'off' his car rather than 'from' it.* Again this suggests that the explanation is unreliable.

Use of definite and indefinite articles

The use of 'the'[6] and 'a'[7] or 'an' can also be revealing. In our analysis of the dingo case (Chapter 5), the subject spoke of seeing 'a' dingo and later refers to 'the' dingo. This progression is natural: but immediately referring to an individual member of a general class as 'the' indicates deception or omission.

Conjunctions

These words, such as 'and', 'but', 'because' etc. connect words and phrases and usually indicate a continuity of thought or of memory retrieval. An absence of conjunctions is indicative of deception.

Interjections

A person may interject with an exclamation such as 'oh' or 'shit' which does not grammatically fit into a phrase or sentence. Interjections are normally true.

Summary of clues in the syntax

Clues in the syntax of a false explanation are illustrated in Mind Map 6 and summarized in Table 4.7.

---

[6]   Definite article
[7]   Indefinite article

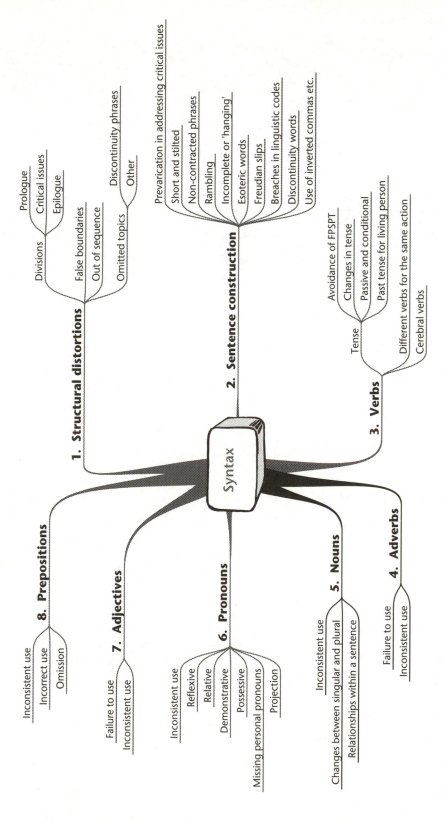

Mind Map® 6   Clues in the syntax

Table 4.7   Syntax

Category of response	Examples	Significance 10 = High 0 = Low
Structural distortions		
Distortions between real and story time and prevarication in addressing the critical issues Out of sequence and omitted topics	*In real life an event that took one hour is explained in one sentence. Another that took two minutes is explained in ten pages*	8
Sentence construction		
Prevarication	*In addressing the critical issues*	10
Use of short stilted sentences	*'I went out. We saw the car. It was a dark car'*	5
Non-contracted phrases	*'I did not go' rather than 'I didn't go'*	6
Long rambling sentences		6
Incomplete or hanging sentences	*'I went … er … no, we thought about …'*	8
Esoteric words	*'I can explicate myself from this abominable predicament'*	6
Freudian slips	*'Can I have a ticket to Titlochry please' (see page 113)*	6
Breaches in linguistic codes	*See page 104*	10
Discontinuity words and phrases suggesting a topic or detail has been omitted	*'The next thing I know …'* *'We then began …'* *'I continued …'* *'Later on …'*	8
Use of inverted commas in a written explanation	Usually means that the person does not accept the conventional interpretation of the words concerned. *'I knew the cheques were in the safe when I "left" that night'*	8
Use of verbs		
Avoidance of first person, past tense For example *'I went …'*	In English, first person, past tense is a very precise and committed style of expression. Explanations in first person singular, past tense are usually true	10
Passive rather than active phrasing Indicating lack of commitment	*'The tree was cut down'* as opposed to *'I cut down the tree'*	10
Changes, mid-story, between past and another tense	*'I went to the office and the next thing I know I am reading the computer files …'*	10

Passive and conditional tense, such as 'could', 'would' 'ought' etc. Both lack commitment	'I would have …' 'I could have …' Are non-committal and more likely to be untrue than true	10
Past tense for a living person	'They were happy kids'	10
Different verbs for the same action	'I talked to Bill then we discussed the game and chatted about golf'	6
Use of cerebral verbs *These usually mean the act was not completed*	'I then thought about going …' 'I planned …' 'I started to talk to …' 'We talked about …'	6
Use of adverbs		
Failure to use and inconsistent use	These add detail to an explanation. When the detail is relevant, the chances are the explanation is true. Apparently irrelevant detail indicates an important topic has been concealed	6
Changes, mid-story, between singular and plural	'I went towards the office and then we saw the door …'	7
Use of nouns		
Inconsistent use for the same thing or person	'I got in my **car** then drove the **vehicle** to my home'	6
Changes, mid-story, between singular and plural	'We got into the car. Then as I was driving along we saw …'	7
Relationships within a sentence	'I went with Bill, John, Fred, Doris, Ethel and my wife.' The distance in the sentence between 'I' and 'wife' suggests a poor relationship, as does the fact that she is referred to in her position, rather than by her name	8
Use of pronouns		
Inconsistent use	'I got in my car, then the bloody thing wouldn't start. Can you believe it, that car just blew up'	8
Reflexive pronouns	'One would never consider stealing from the company'	10
Relative pronouns	*Inconsistent use of pronouns*	6
Demonstrative pronouns		
Possessive pronouns		
Missing personal pronouns	'I went to the dance … then saw Bill … talked to him … drove my car to the cinema.' The missing 'I' before 'then' etc. suggests a lack of commitment to that part of the explanation	10
Projection	'The president would not do such a thing'	10

Category of response	Examples	Significance 10 = High 0 = Low
Use of adjectives		
Failure to use resulting in missing or inconsistent detail		6
Use of prepositions		
Inconsistent or incorrect use		6
Use of definite and indefinite articles		
Using 'the' to refer to an individual member of a general class without any introduction or the prior use of 'a'	Compare the difference between *I went to the dance and saw a girl'* to *'I went to a dance and saw the girl'*	7
Use of conjunctions		
Missing conjunctions	*'I spoke to the man. He said he was ill. I did not like the look of him.'* This shows a discontinuity that indicates deception	8
Use of interjections		
	'I said, "Holy shit".' Probably he did say this	8

Even with the most careful planning and rehearsal, it is virtually impossible for a liar to maintain consistency between false content and syntax; this applies whether the deception is oral or in writing. On the other hand, most people do not take syntax and semantics to a conscious level and thus miss important clues.

Listen to and read every word; think what they really mean

PARALINGUISTIC CLUES

Paralinguistics is the study of auxiliary communications such as the tone, speed, volume and pitch of a person's voice. It is distinct from the content and syntax of the communication and body language and is mainly unconsciously driven. There are exceptions – such as when someone deliberately feigns a posh accent to convince the listener he is not from Birmingham.

The liar, who has to minimize the chance of saying something from his memory or subconscious that reveals his guilt, will usually edit his replies before delivering them. Pauses, long silences, deep sighing and clearing the throat are all signs of deception, as are changes in the tone of voice and the speed of response. This speed of response, known as 'response latency', varies from 0.5 seconds for truthful replies to 1.5 seconds for lies. Response latency is important and you should consciously monitor it and interject when the suspect's brain is thrashing for an answer (see page 38).

Remember: When a person is silent, thinking about how to lie, he is at his most vulnerable

Even in writing, liars make Freudian slips which result from memory becoming confused with imagination and a fight between the conscious and subconscious monkeys. Things are blurted out that the liar never intended.

WHAT IS A FREUDIAN SLIP?

Tom asked Bill what was meant by the phrase 'a Freudian slip'. Bill said: 'It is when the subconscious kicks in with something you did not wish to say. Let me give you an example. I went to buy a ticket to visit the famous Scottish town of Pitlochry. The girl at the ticket desk was really beautiful and wearing a low-cut dress. Instead of asking for *Pit*lochry I asked for a ticket to *Tit*lochry.

That is a Freudian slip.'

'In that case', said Tom, 'I have made a dreadful Freudian slip. Yesterday I was sat at breakfast with my wife and I meant to say, "Darling, would you please pass the toast". Instead I said, "I hate you – you dreadful old cow, you have wrecked my life." I told her it was a Freudian slip and she seems to have believed it.'

Freudian slips seem to result from thrashing between the person's conscious and subconscious and are therefore very important.

Remain on the lookout for Freudian slips and challenge them.
Darwin meant to say 'Survival of the fattest'

ENRON

In the Enron case, a senior accountant meant to say, 'Ship the documents to the Feds,' but what he said was, 'Rip the documents to shreds,' and, as we know, this is what happened.

Freudian slips often appear as unfinished or 'hanging' sentences. For example, a suspect might say: 'We were just completing the annual accounts ... no, I am mistaken, we were talking about the weather.' At such points you should interject along the lines of 'Hold on a minute, Ralph, what were you going to say about the accounts?' so that you try to get him to complete the sentence.

'Insurance claims' below shows the effects of both open questions and Freudian slips.

INSURANCE CLAIMS

- 'I knocked over my mother-in-law's bicycle but unfortunately she wasn't on it.'
- 'The pedestrian panicked and had no idea which way to run, so I ran over him.'
- 'The guy was all over the road. I had to swerve a number of times before I hit him.'

Open questions get people thinking. This can be dangerous

Paralinguistic clues can be summarized as illustrated in Table 4.8 and Mind Map 7.

Table 4.8   How answers are expressed

Category of response	Examples	Significance 10 = High 0 = Low
STALLING Delayed to give the suspect the chance to prepare the reply in his imagination	Long silences between a question and answer Disjointed replies Hesitant and cautious delivery Extended silences	10
DELIVERY (partly unconscious)		
Changes in the tone pitch of the suspect's voice and speed of delivery (normally 120 to 150 words per minute)	Answers delivered slowly are more likely to be untruthful The pitch normally rises with deception and falls at the pivotal point Tone 8Hz to 12Hz micro-tremors Low volume: quieter replies may indicate deception	7
Stuttering and mumbling		8
Delayed response Delayed to give the suspect the time to prepare a lie from his imagination	Micro-delays (from a normal response time of 0.5 seconds for truthful answers to 1.5 seconds for untruthful answers) Long silences between the question and answer Disjointed replies Hesitant and cautious delivery 'Please give me time to think' 'I want to be certain, so give me time' 'You are trying to trap me'	8
Changes in volume	The volume of deceptive answers is usually lower than truthful replies (perhaps indicating a lack of commitment)	5
Extended silences		10
Looking away when replying		7
Defers to interruptions		7
Non-verbal noises		
Extended sighs Clearing the throat Odd clicking sounds Tummy rumblings Extreme flatulence (stand back) Inappropriate laughter at the start or end of a response Grunts		8

Speech errors		
Missing words Freudian slips Spoonerisms Unfinished sentences Short, jerky sentences Corrections within a sentence Starting the sentence with 'Well ...'	Again this is usually caused by a conflict between memory and imagination, conscious and subconscious. Statements like 'I never let the wail tag the dog' instead of 'tail wag the dog'	10
EMOTIONAL OUTBURSTS		
Anger Humour Tears	The main clue is that the emotion is inappropriate	8

Paralinguistics are very important

NON-VERBAL CLUES

Non-verbal communication is normally managed unconsciously by the autonomic system and accounts for over 60 per cent of the messages conveyed between humans and 10 per cent between accountants. It dates back to over 500 million years ago before language evolved and was the only way that our ancestors could communicate. It is still highly relevant.

The body language of children is usually obvious, such as placing hands over their mouths, ears and eyes when they do, say, hear or see something naughty. As we get older, these childish movements are refined and substituted by disguised actions, such as false scratching, yawns etc. but they have the same objective of covering the mouth.

Non-verbal clues are especially important in assessing whether an emotion is genuine or not.

WHAT A LOVELY BABY: THE DUCHENNE SMILE IN REVERSE

All politicians love babies for three reasons. The first is that babies don't ask difficult questions. The second is they are camera ready and bring reflected glory. The third is that they show the politician has safe hands.

But next time you see a politician holding a baby look carefully and what you will see is him saying 'Coochy coo. What a beautiful little baby you are' and then put on a patently contrived smile. This is known in the trade as a 'reverse Duchenne smile' (see pages 49 and 118). You know from the timing, lack of wrinkling around the eyes, the absence of dilation in the pupils and the uneven quick fade of the facial expression that the only thing the tub-thumper likes about babies is playing a part in their conception after an all-expenses-paid dinner at Langans (table 1).

When emotion is genuine, the non-verbal clues are driven directly from the limbic system (see page 38) and appear before any oral expression. When false, they appear in reverse order and are usually transient. If you don't believe this, look closely at politicians on television: they usually get it wrong and smile milliseconds after they say how nice the baby looks.

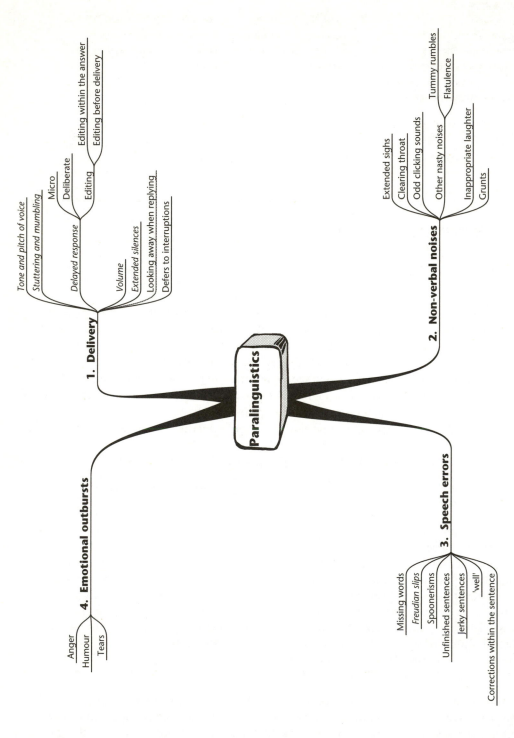

Mind Map® 7   Paralinguistic clues

Watch for incongruencies between micro expressions and those which are consciously contrived

Overall the body language of truthful subjects is more dynamic and relaxed with consistent use of demonstrators.

Believe in body language

Non-verbal clues to deception are summarized in Table 4.9 and Mind Map 8.

Table 4.9 Non-verbal clues

Body element	Symptoms of deceit	Significance
EMBLEMS (may also be unconscious)		
SURROUNDINGS DRESS ASSOCIATES VEHICLES PREMISES Transactional role Incongruence	These are visual signals reflecting how the person sees himself and how he would like to be perceived by others. For example, police uniforms, barristers' wigs, punk hairstyles. Clothes, hair and especially *shoes and spectacles* inconsistent with the person's true standing or position and displayed with the intention of enhancing his ability to succeed with an attack or to deceive the interviewer	10
Body posture		
The body is the most reliable source of non-verbal communication. Posture is a reflection of the subject's confidence OVERALL POSTURE Large limbs and trunk into defensive positions Leaning away Body changes in response to a relevant question Orientation of body Defensive angles	Leaning or turning away from the interviewer. A person telling lies will rarely sit on the front of his chair, lean forward or sit or stand frontally aligned or 'face on' to the interviewer. He will usually stand or sit at an angle using his shoulders as a defensive barrier. Crossed legs and arms: the higher they are, the more defensive the barrier Sits in a foetal position	10
	At the opening of the interview or in response to a relevant question, moves his body so that he creates a barrier with his shoulders and legs and is thus not frontally aligned Changing posture before delivering a false answer Generally the liar's main body movements are static (except when severely anxious) and are seldom inclined towards the interviewer	
Breathing	Shortage of breath Increased heartbeat Rapid pulsing of the carotid artery in the neck	5
Personal space		
Initial position Reactive movements Responding to evidence	Liars will usually try to increase the space around them. They may lean away or pull their chair away from the interviewer at the start of the interview. Liars will usually push away incriminating reminders of their guilt such as documentary exhibits	10

Body element	Symptoms of deceit	Significance
Legs		
Dynamic movements	While sitting down, moving legs towards or under the body or retracted High crossing to create a defensive barrier Crossing one on top of the other Preparing to run	10
Feet		
	Nervous tapping Raised off the ground when seated or standing	8
Arms		
	Crossed: the higher up the body the crossing of arms and the tighter they are together, the more defensive the intention Moving towards the body	10
Hands		
Manipulators are soothing, grooming movements near to or touching the body, the mouth, ears or back of the neck. They are usually an indication of deception and are a displacement activity Demonstrators are used to emphasize a point and are usually movements away from the body. Consistent use of demonstrators – in relation to control and relevant questions – are usually an indication of truthfulness	**Manipulators** Breaches of the normal communications code Hand to mouth and head gestures False scratching (a genuine scratch is usually five times, though be sympathetic to sufferers of eczema or those with fleas) Grooming gestures, such as straightening the tie Appearing to fall asleep Brushing non-existent dust or hairs off clothing Needlessly winding his watch or cleaning his glasses Hands covering stomach or genitalia Micro-expressions (see page 39) **Demonstrators** Breaches of the normal communications code Hands moving inwards and close to the body Use of hands to insert punctuation marks in conversation (such as inverted commas) Failing to touch incriminating evidence Frozen arms and hands Jerky or nervous movements Hand tremors or trembling Pointing is a sign of anger or assertiveness. When people are telling lies, they do not usually point except when angry Micro-expressions **Other movements** Excessive grip on an object Clenched fists (a sign of anger) Palms other than open; palms downwards; movements may be disguised and subtle Displayed thumbs are a sign of defiance Sits on hands or hides then in his pockets Heavy sweating	10

Body element	Symptoms of deceit	Significance
Face (may also be conscious)		
The face has over 100 separate muscle groups which produce around 20,000 expressions. It is one of the most unreliable indicators of deception. However, the face makes micro-expressions which are straight from the subconscious and last for less than a second. You will notice these	Pallid or flushed complexion Heavy sweating especially on the upper lip Poker faced 'Stony faced' **Micro-expressions** False smiles (see page 39) **Expression after an emotional outburst** Transient expressions Asymmetrical expressions: for example a 'crooked smile'	8
Eyes (may also be conscious)		
Normally gaze is for between 1 and 10 seconds with around 6 blinks per minute. The speaker has eye contact for 40% of the time and the listener for 75% of the time People who are telling the truth look more and have better and more consistent eye contact **Eye accessing clues** Left to access memory Right to access imagination	**Gaze and direction: gaze aversion** **Variable or unnatural eye contact** Generally a suspect will have poor eye contact when telling a lie. Thus the term 'shifty eyed' Looking away and especially downwards and to the right Eye contact is normally directed at the other person's forehead. When it is directed to the mouth or eyes, a sexual interest may be present Dysfunctional gaze Extended eye contact (staring) **Size of pupils** Pupils become enlarged (usually referred to as 'dilation') Whites of the eyes become more visible **Eye accessing clues** Looking to right when accessing memory **Blinking** Eyes closed Dramatic changes – increase or decrease – in the rate of blinking **Other clues from the eyes** Micro-tremors in the muscles around the eyes Sweating below the eye lids Hands over eyes usually as a disguised movement, but a reflection of 'see no evil'	8
Mouth (may also be conscious)		
	Dry mouth: sometimes the person telling lies will drink vast amounts of water. Be particularly on guard when the subject brings his own bottles of water into the interview room False yawning or any other movement that excuses the hands being put over or near the mouth Biting, licking or chewing lips Sighing and heavy swallowing Narrowed, tight lips Foam or spittle build up in the corners of the mouth	10

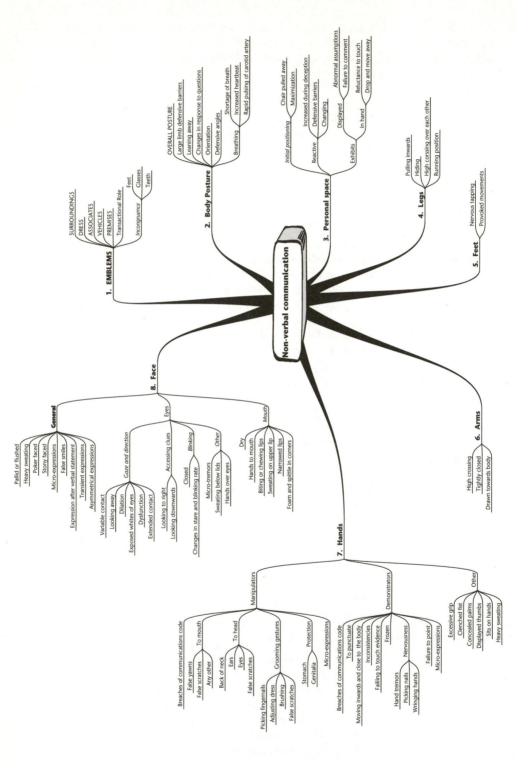

Mind Map® 8 Non-verbal communication clues

If you are not convinced about the merits of non-verbal communication, you are strongly advised to visit the website of Center for Nonverbal Studies (CNS) which is a private, non-profit research centre located in Spokane, Washington, and La Jolla, California. Underway since 1 October, 1997, the Center's mission is to advance the study of human communication in all its forms apart from language. The Center's goal is to promote the scientific study of non-verbal communication, which includes body movement, gesture, facial expression, adornment and fashion, architecture, mass media, and consumer-product design. On 12 January, 1999, CNS affiliated with the Center for Ethnographic Research (CER) at the University of Missouri in Kansas City.

The liar is well aware that subconsciously he is throwing away non-verbal clues and will try to disguise or consciously control them. This is virtually impossible and, if he knows you have noticed his struggle, it will increase his anxiety until it becomes a self-defeating spiral.

ATTITUDE

The subject's attitude, which is communicated mainly in the content, also reveals important clues to deception (see Table 4.10 and Mind Map 9).

Table 4.10   Clues in the attitude

Symptoms of deception CONSCIOUS, unconscious or *both*	Examples	Significance 10 = High 0 = Low
Absence of values		
	The liar is usually focused on short-term goals and may find difficulty distinguishing right from wrong, having few values or principles to guide him He may consider himself 'above the law' Business liars seldom show remorse (until they are exposed)	8
Attitude to dishonesty and the matter in question		
Non-judgemental of himself	President Nixon *'dissembled the truth'* President Clinton's relationship with Monica was *'inappropriate'* Clinton smoked pot, but *'did not inhale'*	10
Minimizes the seriousness of the matters in issue	Tends to minimize their seriousness, subconsciously reducing his anxiety Failure to deny Failure to become angry Contrived submission Contrived flattery	8
Unjustifiably passive Defers to interruptions Avoidance of hard words	Quietly accepts statements such as: *'I am not interested in that, Bill'* Like an alcoholic, the guilty person will usually minimize the seriousness of the problem, and will not use words like *'theft'*, *'fraud'*, *'steal'* etc.	10

Symptoms of deception CONSCIOUS, unconscious or *both*	Examples	Significance 10 = High 0 = Low
Allocation of blame		
Blaming others	The white collar fraudster will not usually blame someone else for his dishonesty. For example, when asked the question, *'Who do you think is responsible?'* he will not name anyone	7
Anonymous blame	*'The company just wants to get rid of me'* *'I am always the scapegoat'*	
Clearing himself	When asked the question *'Who can you clear of this?'* he will not usually name himself *first*. An innocent person is more likely to do so	8
Failure to deny (see content)		
	Failure and pseudo denials (see page 88)	10
Rationalization (may also be conscious)		
Generally Specific issue Internalizes Admissions without guilt Honesty	*'Anyone would do the same'* *'I don't see what the problem is'* Tends to believe everyone is dishonest *'I may have done it, but it wasn't intentional'* *'OK just say I did it'*	5
Self-deception		
Failure to accept the facts Failure to appreciate the consequences Self-deprecation Projection Unwillingness to touch incriminating evidence The false death wish (usually sarcastic or unemotional)	*'That document proves nothing'* *'He would say that, wouldn't he?'* *'I know I am stupid, but ...'* *'The Sales Director [speaking about himself] is totally innocent, I can tell you that'* *'I wish I was dead'* *'Why don't I just kill myself right now'*	8
Admits having considered the act in question		
	Will explain how he would have committed the act in question. An innocent person will rarely become involved in such a discussion. The explanation given may be obviously misleading or childish. However, sometimes the liar will give away facts known only to the perpetrator	10
REFERENCE TO HIS MENTAL STATE	*'I know in my own mind'* *'I would be bloody crazy to have done that'*	8
Reference to proof	Will tend to underestimate the significance *'You have no proof of that'* *'Show me the evidence and I will believe you'*	10

Symptoms of deception CONSCIOUS, unconscious or *both*	Examples	Significance 10 = High 0 = Low
Comments on the question	*'That is a good question'* *'How dare you suggest that'* Respond to a question with a question	9
EMOTIONS	Feigned anger etc.	8
	Fluid emotions Failure to show the emotions an innocent person would Verbal expression before the non-verbal communication	
Failure to act innocently	Failure to deny Failure to become angry or express the emotions of an honest person Goes too far to convince rather than simply convey Will usually deny having discussed the problem with his spouse or close family members as most innocent people do Admits to nothing in relation to the matter in issue, including small, irrelevant details	10
CONTENT	see page 95	
Syntax	see page 103	
Paralinguistics	see page 112	
Non-verbal communication	see page 115	

A liar's attitude is always different from a truthful person's attitude

A great example of attitude shining through the mist and of people giving away their true feelings is contained in a press release put out by the Information Commissioner. The background was that a bunch of people had set themselves up as:

- Data Protection Registration Service;
- Data Registration Agency;
- etc.

They had been extracting money from mugs who thought they were dealing with the Information Commissioner: this was a pretty clever and lucrative scam. The press release opened:

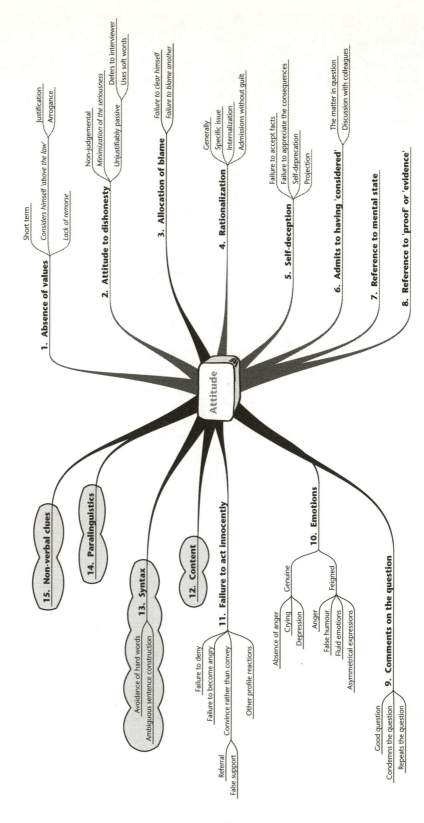

Mind Map® 9   Clues from the attitude

THE INFORMATION COMMISSIONER

'The Information Commissioner, Elizabeth France, is concerned about the volume of telephone calls and correspondence received by her Office in relation to the above businesses.'

It later went on to say: 'She has been disturbed that a number of people have been confused and troubled by the wording and tone of some of the correspondence issued by these businesses.'

It would have been much more convincing if these sentences had been juxtaposed because they suggest that she is more irritated by having to respond to telephone calls and letters than she is about the poor buggers who have been ripped off.

Putting it all together

Academic research[8] indicates that for most people the chances of detecting lies are no better than 50:50 but since the research is always artificial – based on test conditions – it is not necessarily reliable in real life. In such experiments police officers and psychiatrists fared only a little better, although some individuals were accurate in almost every case, usually by following techniques of the type described in this book. Ironically, the most effective detectors of deceit *in the test cases provided to them* were a group of criminals serving life sentences! Estate agents were not scored.

LIAR

The British television programme *Liar* asks the audience to decide which one of six candidates is telling the truth. Each candidate is asked questions, and in round one the audience dismisses the one it is most sure is a liar. Further rounds take place with a candidate being voted off each time until only two are left. They ask each other questions and the audience votes on which one is truthful. If the one and only genuinely truthful candidate of the original six is the winner, £10,000 is given to the audience. If the person voted by the audience as the truthful candidate is a liar he keeps the £10,000. As far as is known, the truthful candidate has never been voted the winner, but is often thrown off in the first round as being the biggest liar. The reason for this is that the truthful person is more likely to make mistakes and reveal small inconsistencies. For example, the only truthful candidate on one programme claimed to be a committed Christian yet, under the glare of the studio lights, she could not remember the Ten Commandments. She was immediately identified as a liar and thrown off in the first round.

The truth is that most people rely too heavily on the pure content of what is said and on facial expressions, which can be manipulated to some degree. The dark grey shading in Figure 4.2 represents their approach.

---

[8]   With all its limitations and under artificial conditions

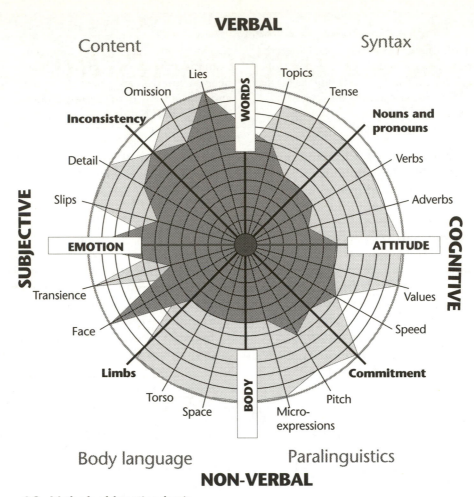

Figure 4.2   Methods of detecting deceit

Experienced interviewers take a holistic approach, *as shown in the light shaded area of Figure 4.2,* when assessing the truthfulness of an explanation and look for incongruencies rather than a single clue. This leads to far higher success rates in finding the truth. We suggest in future you take this approach.

You already know how and when you are being told lies. This is the easy part. You just have to consciously accept the reality. The following chapters explain the cunning plan necessary for dealing with them.

'I RECOMMEND BUYING THE SHARES ... THE FUNDAMENTALS ARE GOOD AND THE CASH FLOW POSITIVE AND WE DON'T EXPECT THE FINANCE DIRECTOR TO BE ARRESTED BEFORE THE FOURTH QUARTER OF 2005'

5 *Your Personal Manifesto*

Live on trust and die of flatulence

Introduction

This chapter contains a short cunning plan for you to deal with suspected deception under most circumstances and to ensure that you will:

- find the truth, or at least most of it, before making a decision or taking action;
- discharge your fiduciary duties and cover your ass if someone threatens to sue you and confiscate your Hush Puppies or Scottie Cameron putter.

Chapters 6 and 7 deal with tough interviews with fraud suspects and Chapter 10 with other specific problems, such as pre-employment screening, annual appraisals, elimination interviews and hard negotiations where deception is possible.

Detecting lies is easy: resolving them calls for a cunning plan

You are always flooded with clues that someone is lying. In fact there are so many that it is impossible to consciously register them all. All you need to consciously decide is, 'Is this person telling lies?' If the answer is 'yes', then you must proceed on that basis. Detecting lies is not the problem, but you need a cunning plan to resolve them (see Mind Map 3, p. 70).

The essence of the cunning plan is that you raise the liar's anxiety to the pivotal point at which he loses confidence in his ability to succeed with deception. At this point, you use an empathetic approach to get him to tell you the deep truth. It is that simple (see Figure 5.1).

You can apply this model to any situation where you believe deception is a possibility and where you want to get to the deep truth. We will return to the cunning plan shortly.

Important background

A LOW-KEY PROFESSIONAL APPROACH

Television detective films and soaps have misled people into believing that to get to the truth it is necessary to take on a macho, heavy-handed role, packed with testosterone. This is the opposite of what is needed and, if such tactics are used, the result is likely to be a disaster. A quiet, confident, professional, empathetic but relentless approach is the most effective way of getting to the deep truth.

Become quietly professional, but relentless

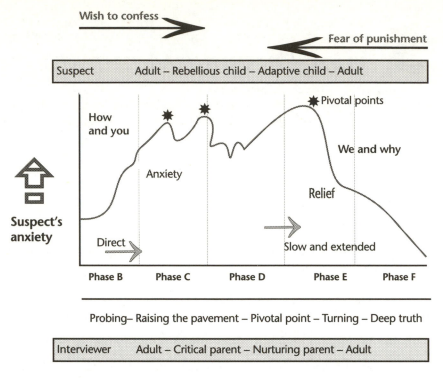

Figure 5.1   Phases in getting to the deep truth

Some of the questions and responses discussed in this book may not suit your style.

THE EMPATHETIC BANK INSPECTOR

An experienced interviewer was mentoring a team of bank inspectors. One inspector (who, ironically, became a very senior manager) could nor bring himself to turn at the pivotal point into a nurturing parent. 'I don't like people who defraud my bank', he said, 'and there is no way I can say all that crap, that I understand them or empathize with them.'

His supervisor pointed out that the empathetic turn to nurturing parent had worked successfully for the department and that he should try it. His next interview was conducted brilliantly and the suspect brought quickly to the pivotal point. 'Why did all this start, Bill? You have always been such a good employee. Was it because you simply wanted money or was there some other reason?' The suspect thought for a few moments and then in a quiet and emotional voice said: 'I took the money because my wife was ill and she needed an operation, urgently.' The inspector's face became a mask of hate and he said: 'Bollocks, what was wrong with the National Health Service? It's good enough for my family and me. It should be good enough for you.' Unsurprisingly, all signs of empathy disappeared and it took another four hours to bring the suspect back to the point where he admitted the deep truth.

The decision on the approach you use is yours, but it is critical that you select tools and techniques appropriate to the situation concerned and with which you feel comfortable.

ACTIVE LISTENING, OBSERVING AND VISUALIZATION

However, there is one critical point and that is to become an active listener and a conscious observer of human behaviour. Most people hear but don't listen, or see but don't observe, and thus miss important clues to innocence and deception.

Before every interview or meeting, make sure all of your senses are turned on and listen carefully to every word the subject says, how he says it and consciously monitor his body movements. Try to visualize what he is saying and picture if it makes sense. Tune to the emotions involved and question whether they are genuine or false. Think how you would feel in his position and assess whether his reactions are consistent with his story.

You can learn a lot by listening and looking

GET DOWN TO THE CRITICAL ISSUES

Wherever possible – and especially with people suspected of serious deception – you should try to get straight to the heart of the matter and be as direct as possible (Figure 5.2).

Chapters 5 and 6 discuss the approaches you can take on the direct path in tough interviews. However, if it becomes clear that the subject has no intention of telling the truth, you should switch your approach, take a few deep breaths and ask questions that force him into more and more detail – and lead to increasingly outrageous lies. Whatever the objective of the interview, lies to which the suspect has committed himself will come back to haunt him later on.

Ironically, if you take this indirect route, it is not uncommon to find that the suspect's anxiety is increased to the pivotal point, and he then decides to tell the truth.

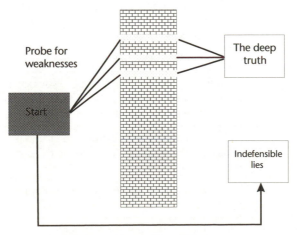

Detailed questions and incredible answers

Figure 5.2   Direct and indirect approaches

TRANSACTIONAL ROLES

You must consciously try to retain control of every interview or meeting. This may be easier said than done, especially if the suspect is an experienced crook, a senior businessman or represented by an overly hostile lawyer. However, you should always aim to start every interview by consciously taking the role of an adult and be prepared to move into compatible transactions as the interview progresses (Table 5.1).

You should remain consciously aware of the transactional dynamics in all meetings and be prepared to take action to change them.

A GOOD EXAMPLE

If you want to see a good example of transactional analysis in operation, watch the television detective programme *Colombo*. This poor, untidy creature, who falls automatically into the role of a child, customarily seems to face murderers who are pillars of society and the ultimate critical parents. Colombo establishes an equal transaction with them and from time to time gains total control by picking up the suspect's most valuable possession – usually a vase or some other fragile gem – putting them in mortal fear that he might drop it. Certainly while it is in his hands, he has the suspect's full attention.

To get to the deep truth it is usually essential that an equal transaction is created, with you in the role of a nurturing parent and the suspect accepting the role of an adaptive child. You will find that innocent and truthful subjects will be far more opposed to imposed changes in role than liars.

Pay attention to transactional roles

Table 5.1   Creating an adult role

Aspect	What you should do
Dress and emblems	You must dress and appear professional. Do not wear your bow tie or Hush Puppies. Take great care over the first impression you will create with the subject.
Interview room	The room should be clinically clean and tidy (see page 161)
Introduction	You should appear calm. Introduce yourself and your colleagues and offer to shake hands. Direct the subject to the chair in which you would like him to sit
Language	Your language should be professional and polite. Avoid childish chit-chat and humour. Try to get on the same wavelength as the subject
Body language	You should adopt an assertive, professional posture. Do not slouch in your chair
Documents to which you will refer which we call the 'key points'	You should make sure these are carefully arranged, so that their presentation is professional. Fumbling with documents will make you appear incompetent and childish

CREATING RAPPORT

Your chances of getting to the deep truth are much greater if you consciously tune to the same wavelength and channels of communication as the subject. Thus before every important interview you should have thoroughly researched his background and know what makes him tick or tock.

For rapport-building purposes, the population can be classed as introverts or extroverts and further categorized in Table 5.2.

Knowing even minor things about the subject, such as his support for Birmingham City Football Club or his love of African parrots, may be important in building rapport.

SALES TRAINING

Some sales training courses encourage salesmen in rapport-building techniques. They are taught to show a deep interest in the prospects' hobbies, families etc., to mirror his dress, body language and verbal communications even to the point that if he swears a lot, they should do the same. The theory is that by getting on the same wavelength, rapport is established and sales improve. Also, giving a small gift to the prospect or touching him has the same effect.

Table 5.2 Character types – showing how rapport can be established. However, in tough interviews you will still have to go through the roles of critical and nurturing parent to get to the deep truth

Type and characteristics	Additional ways of creating rapport
Emotion dominant (arty types) Wears his heart on his sleeve Sometimes acts in a 'childlike' way Takes things very personally and is inclined to worry Extreme mood swings Wants to please and be liked May see himself as a victim of circumstances	Move slowly, possibly on a child-to-child basis Avoid aggression Deal with problems on an emotional level (feelings etc.) Build up case slowly and logically
Sensory dominant (SAS types) High achiever Appears fearless and a risk taker Energetic and fast speech Prepared to fight rather than flee	Avoid emotions Move quickly and focus on concrete evidence (the mechanics) Deal calmly with counter-attacks Focus on the 'key points'
Logic dominant (accounting types) Superior attitude Exact, logical and precise, bordering on 'nit picking' Cold and emotionally withdrawn Logical A loner Detached and indifferent to the problem	Take a logical approach and focus on detail Make sure you are accurate Show no emotion Emphasize the key points
Ego dominant (managing director types) Assumes the role of a critical parent Condescending, haughty and conceited Pampers himself and is full of self-justification Inconvenienced by the problem	Play to his ego (initially and to build rapport as an adaptive child) Take a high-level view of the case and work on principles

You can use some or all of the approaches in Table 5.3 – at appropriate stages of the interview – to establish rapport.

Table 5.3   Methods of establishing rapport

Aspect	What you should do
Transactional role	Adopt appropriate and equal transactional roles
Primary channel of communication	Tune to the subject's primary channel of communication
Careful listening	Listen carefully to the words used: use compatible language and don't talk up or down to him. If he is a rapper, do not pretend that you are some sort of jive bunny. Always act your age!
Words	Carefully repeat some words and phrases used by the subject
Method of addressing the subject	In the early stages of the interview you may refer to the subject as 'Mister' but use his first name, at the appropriate time, to support a nurturing parent role
Body language	Consciously use positive body language: mirror his eye contact and gestures
Mirroring	Adopt similar postures to the subject and use the same type of language, words and hand movements. When he picks up his cup of tea, you should do the same
Interests – shared professional qualifications, schooling, etc.	Interests shared with the subject can be discussed to create rapport. However, make sure this does not become a displacement activity for asking relevant questions or used by the subject to ramble off the point
Emotions	Monitor the subject's emotions. Be prepared to communicate with him at an emotional level
Accusations and criticisms	Try to avoid being judgemental, but challenge all lies. Never attack the subject's character by calling him a 'liar' but you may destroy specific untrue statements by calling them 'lies'. It is, however, important to continually emphasize the embedded command 'truth' (see page 43)
Agreement	Confirm your agreement with the subject wherever you can. Try to find common ground. The more you are able to agree (even on small things), the more likely you are to get to the deep truth. The more the suspect says 'yes', the less likely he is to say 'no'
Touch	Although touching the subject must be handled carefully,[1] there is no doubt that with right hemisphere dominated (and tactile) people, touch builds rapport. However, never touch a member of the opposite sex, nor an accountant or lawyer
Appearance	Believe it or not, good-looking people are more easily accepted by others than those with faces like Ena Sharples. There is not much you can do about this if you are ugly, but it is a point worth noting
Compliments	Compliment the subject, without being patronizing

---

[1]   Excuse the pun

'We', 'us' and 'ours' are great rapport-building words, as are discussions about emotions, feelings and attitudes that hit directly on the subject's subconscious. Agreement on any point with the subject also increases rapport. However, never fall into the trap of believing that by self-deprecating you build rapport.

Create a feeling of rapport

THE MODEST AUDITOR

An auditor for a very large conglomerate would – as a matter of course – try to get others to underestimate him by saying something along the lines: 'I know I am only a stupid auditor, but please tell me ...' Rather than leading people into a trap, the words put him in the transactional role of a child and the embedded command 'stupid' stuck in the minds of auditees, who all seemed to agree with him. They also thought his approach was 'patronizing'.

Don't self deprecate: it will make your hair fall out

As Forrest Gump would say, *'That's all we have to say about rapport,'* at least for the moment, but it is a very important word.

LOSING CONTROL

Remember there are always two interviews taking place and that the subject will evaluate you and recalibrate his approach accordingly. You *may* lose control of an interview if:

- You have not fully understood the issues or have misinterpreted the facts, *so research carefully and check everything.*
- You make wild allegations, *so be careful how you phrase accusations.*
- You bluff, bluster or show that you are angry or impatient, *so remain emotionally detached.*
- You let the subject succeed with lies, *so always challenge them as politely as you can.*
- You show your nervousness, *so take a few deep breaths and focus hard on the suspect's nervousness as he has more to lose than you.*
- You do not take on board facts which contradict your opinions: *you must always keep an open mind.*

You will *definitely* lose control if you have not fully prepared for the interview, lack commitment in the delivery of questions, succumb to an attack or do not adopt the appropriate transactional role. Good planning and rehearsal can eliminate all of these problems.

THE BIG SHOT

A group of serious commercial villains employed a powerful ex-politician, who was also a brilliant lawyer, as a special adviser. He would be wheeled in to important meetings as the ultimate critical parent. Even experienced businessmen would tremble in his presence.

Lawyers had to try to negotiate a settlement with the villains and knew they risked being overawed by the special adviser. For a few thousand pounds, they retained the special adviser's ex-political boss and presented him at the meeting. For a few moments, there was a transactional battle between the special adviser and the ex-boss, which the latter won and a fair settlement was reached.

Keep control and remain emotionally detached.

DELIVERY OF QUESTIONS

Visual and other stimulation

Often questions have a much greater impact on the subject if they are delivered in conjunction with a visual and emotional stimulation, such as simultaneously handing him an incriminating piece of evidence or requiring him to look at a chart, physical object or picture. For this reason, it is a good idea to have every key point that supports the deception theory summarized on single pieces of paper which can be presented to the suspect at the appropriate time and kept within his personal space and in his right field of vision (see page 42).

Try to keep incriminating evidence within the suspect's personal space and field of vision

Using checklists

Some interviewers like to use checklists which set the questions they plan to ask. Although in some circumstances this approach may be useful,[2] it tends to make the interview too rigid and for this reason fails. A checklist may be referred to at the end of an interview, and before the subject leaves, to make sure you have covered everything you should. Lists may be used in formal interviews where you simply want to give the subject the chance to explain.

Assemble key points in the order that you will deal with them

For complex interviews, it is usually better to assemble all of the papers (summary single pages, exhibits, schedules etc.) in the order in which you plan to cover them and flag them with highly coloured Post-it® notes summarizing the key points and other matters you want the subject to explain.

If the documents can be assembled in voluminous files, so much the better, as these will make it clear to the subject that he has a great deal to answer and thus increase his anxiety.

Increase the visual impact of documents

Note taking

Taking detailed notes during an interview is a very bad practice and should be avoided at all costs. The detailed reasons for this, and alternative solutions, are explained on page 161. But

---

[2] Especially for elimination interviews (page 400)

please remember, from now on, that your chances of getting to the deep truth are significantly reduced if the suspect sees you, or anyone else, writing detailed notes. In any case, detailed note taking is usually no more than a displacement activity by inexperienced interviewers. It is really bad practice.

Note taking disturbs the subject

Taking a deep interest in the subject

You always should try to remain emotionally detached and avoid being judgemental. Even in really tough interviews your job is to find the truth, within the law, while showing respect for the suspect's rights. If you take a genuine conscious interest in him (however bad his behaviour) and try to put yourself in his position, you will find interviews much easier and more effective. You will also get more easily to the truth.

Take a deep, genuine interest in the subject

Body language and paralinguistics

You must remain consciously aware of the way in which you ask questions and the effect your body language has on the subject. Try to deliver questions clearly, without prevarication and with real commitment. Try to make sure that your body language and channels of communication are consistent with the transactional role you are adopting (see page 56). This is especially important when you are in the role of a nurturing parent, when the tone and volume of your voice should drop and speed of delivery decrease. You should feel that you are talking to a child whom you are genuinely trying to help.

Adapt your own body language

AWARENESS

You must always remain alert to the possibility that someone may try to deceive you: a little paranoia does no harm.

Never take things at face value

This does not mean that you have always to express your concerns, but you should internalize and think to yourself 'What is the angle?' and 'Is this important?' If the lie is insignificant, such as a joke or a slight exaggeration, you are best advised to simply enjoy it, unless you dislike the person concerned and want to teach him a lesson. A lot of lies fall into this 'good' category and if you challenge them all, you will quickly become unpopular. Do this and your only option will be to become a lawyer, accountant or even an investigator.

Decide which lies you wish to challenge

Stage 1: Determine your objectives

You should challenge all bad lies even if the potential consequences are tolerable. The reason for this is that if the liar thinks he has got away with a minor matter, he may be tempted to deceive you more seriously next time. Lying can reinforce itself, by becoming a normal pattern of behaviour. There is abundant evidence of this in politics. In the final analysis, lying destroys the values by which we live, corrodes trust and makes life unpleasant.

You should ask yourself: 'If I had a magic wand, how would I like this resolved?' Your success criteria might be:

* I would like him to tell me the truth so that we can deal with the problem openly;
* I would like him to learn a lesson so that he does not try to do the same again;
* I would like to maintain a friendly relationship with him.

Or:

* I want him to tell me the truth;
* I want to report the matter to the police and see him behind bars;
* I want to get our money back;
* I want personal revenge;
* I want to send a message to his colleagues not to mess with me;
* I don't give a damn about any personal relationship with him: I have had enough.

Let's assume that the matter is serious and you want to bring the deception into the open and deal with it. The rule, at this point, is to plan carefully and take your time so that you hit the liar with an ambush from which he never recovers. We call this the *first step* and it must be an ambush.

To get to the deep truth, you must also identify the liar's objectives. Most liars have not thought the endgame through and lie only for the short term. By focusing on the likely end result, you increase their anxiety, thus improving your chances of finding the truth. Remember that most liars must be brought to the pivotal point where they lose confidence in their ability to succeed with deception and accept that telling the truth is the only viable option.

Liars must be brought to the pivotal point

Stage 2: Get all of the background

Find out as much about the suspect as you can, providing this does not alert him, and try to work out what really makes him tick.

Next, analyse the nature of the suspected deception and make sure you have all the facts accurately. For each 'key point', prepare a single piece of paper which, at the appropriate time, you can push under the liar's nose.

Document the key points

Stage 3: Develop a deception theory

In important cases, take a sheet of A4 paper and fold it vertically down the middle (Mind Map 10).

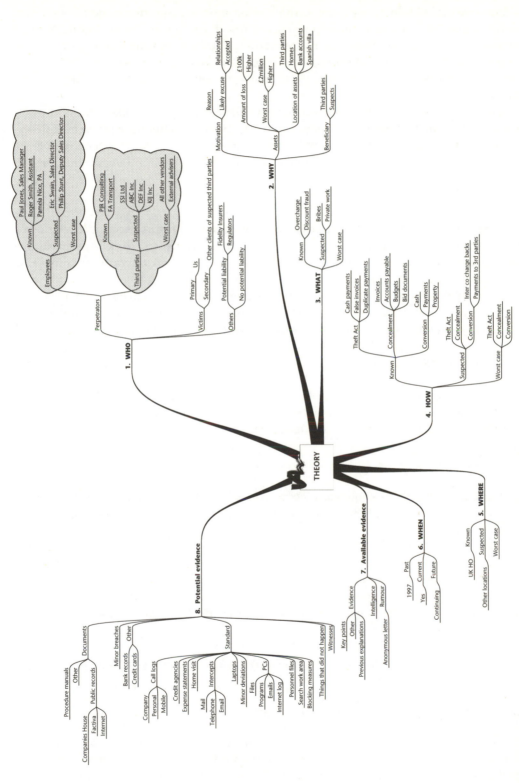

Mind Map® 10   The deception theory

In the left-hand column write down all those things that cause you concern. These may be: that a deal looks too good to be true; that the rascal does not answer questions; has told someone else something different; his shoes and socks are a bit too fancy or whatever. There is no need to be scientific about this and you should let your right hemisphere and subconscious take over. No one else is going to see your note, so don't worry and let intuition fly with abandon.

In the right-hand column write down the evidence and the intelligence (i.e. the 'key points') that support the left-hand column and your theory. Compiling a problem or deception theory is like doing a jigsaw puzzle. If a piece does not fit, then your theory is wrong and you must revise it. Often pieces that didn't initially fit result in the most important clues.

Pieces in a jigsaw puzzle

Always remember that, with deception, there is no such thing as a coincidence and you must assume that there is a reason for everything that has happened. Work on the basis that every clue is the result of a deliberate action by the liar. Next, look carefully for things that should have happened but didn't.

Consider other areas, possibly more serious, where the suspect might have tried to deceive you or others. Lying is like pregnancy; either you are or are not. Think carefully and develop a 'worst case theory'. Write this down, again on a sheet with two columns.

Develop a worst case theory

This process will result in a detailed deception theory. If you like Mind Maps, now is the time to draw one, with nice illustrations and bright colours. You must do everything you can to stimulate your right hemisphere, be creative and try to get into the liar's brain.

Think like the liar

If you have time, think about your theory overnight and if you have a colleague you can really trust, discuss it with him (or, much more preferably, her). Add to your theory as you move forward.

If you conclude that your suspicions are wrong and that you are overreacting, keep the paper in your pocket and just get on with your life. If you fear the worst, you must decide what you want to do about it, if anything.

The minute your red warning light has gone on, and you recognize that someone is trying to deceive you, the initiative swings 100 per cent in your favour. You are now in the perfect position to plan an ambush.

If you know the person is lying and he does not know you suspect, you have the advantage

Stage 4: Specify a resolution plan

This plan, based on your objectives and the deception theory, should be a step-by-step process of how your suspicions will be investigated and resolved. Your initial reaction may be to call the liar in for an interview, but you should think carefully before doing so. Are there any preparatory steps you can take, without alerting him, that will increase your chances of success in an interview? The options are described, in the context of tough interviews, in Chapters 5 and 6. These should be considered for every suspected case of deception as the more evidence you have, the greater your chances of success in the interview or meeting.

The object is to ambush the liar with his pants down

You should also consider the actions that you will take if your theory is correct or if it is wrong. These might include dismissal, termination of a contract or some other action. Also consider possible counter-attacks and false excuses that the suspect might put forward. Never assume the suspect will be a soft target and plan for the worst.

Always assume the liar will counter-attack

Whatever your wider planning decision, you *must* get as much background as possible on both the suspect and the matter in question. Obtaining this background, and the development of your deception theory and resolution plan, is an iterative, dynamic process and it is critical.

Stage 5: Specific planning

Consider whether there are any legal or other issues that could cause problems and make sure you have the authority to take the action you intend. Consider how you will get the suspect to attend the interview. If you cannot simply ambush him, make sure your invitation gives him minimal time to prepare and does not frighten him off (see page 167). If you must give advance notice, make the invitation low key, so that the suspect is confident he can succeed in deceiving you. Lead him into the lion's den, nice and quietly.

Think how you will structure the interview in the stages described in detail in Chapters 6 and 7:

- opening;
- probing;
- increasing anxiety;
- the pivotal point;
- the turn;
- the deep truth;
- follow-up.

For example, will you ask a few blocking questions to give him the chance to volunteer the truth or will you start with a bold opening statement? What sort of questions will you ask: confrontational, enticement, assumptive or accusational etc.? (see Chapter 6). A vital aspect to consider is how you will present the 'key points', other evidence and intelligence. You may decide to hold it in reserve until the subject has lied about it, or to ambush him with it. The choice is yours, but remember the way you present evidence is very important. Plan your approach carefully.

Next, plan the venue and timing of the interview. Maybe the ideal time is when you are travelling with the liar, over a beer, or in a more formal setting. You should aim to catch him at his weakest point. If he is a lark type – up early in the morning, all bright and cheerful – you may want to plan the interview for the late evening and vice versa if he is an owl. If you can catch him at a time when he is doing something he shouldn't be doing, so much the better. Always plan the venue and timing carefully: make sure they are to your advantage.

Ambushes are always more effective when the ambushee is taken by surprise

If you intend to use an interview room, make sure it is laid out effectively to give you the maximum chances of success (see pages 160 and 161). Even very small points can add to a liar's anxiety and make a confession more likely.

Carefully arrange the interview room

Think who should be at the interview; should it just be you and the liar or should someone else join in? Remember the chances of getting to the deep truth vary inversely with the number of people present, but think about it.

Also plan how you will make a record of the interview: maybe you will tape-record it, have a stenographer present or not make notes until the end. But whatever you decide, do not take detailed notes during the interview, as this will seriously distract both you and the suspect.

Stage 6: Rehearsal

If the interview is important, always rehearse it, if necessary with a colleague, your wife, kids or, in extreme circumstances, with your mother-in-law. The first rehearsal should be with you playing the role of the interviewer and the other in the shoes of the suspect. You will find this rehearsal is more than worthwhile.

Practice makes perfect

Stage 7: The execution

If you have gone through the above process, the interview should be simple providing:

- you arrive early and get into the interview room first;
- you stick to your plan and remain in control.

As explained fully in Chapter 7, page 168, the process should take you to the pivotal point, with you in the role of a nurturing parent and the liar an adaptive child. From this point onwards, you must be driven by the circumstances of the case in question, but take your time and get to the worst case and deep truth.

Never trust a man wearing more expensive shoes than your own

Stage 8: The follow-up

You should complete your notes or record of the interview and take all other actions necessary to find the truth. Try to complete this work as quickly as possible.

Conclusions

Don't let the simplicity of the cunning plan mislead you, because it works. You will find that by adapting it to suit your own style, and through practice, you will become a really effective truth finder. You can improve your chances even further if you read Chapters 6 and 7 really carefully, as the techniques can be adapted to any situation where you want to find the deep truth.

'I KNOW THEY LIKED THE BOOK ON RAPPORT BUT THIS IS RIDICULOUS'

6 *Planning Tough Interviews*

Every falsification is a step towards the truth and every concealment a step away

Introduction

Although the liar usually chooses the battleground, appears to have all of the advantages and believes he can win, the balance is always in favour of the effective interviewer, providing he plans carefully. This chapter presents an overview of the legal background and planning steps that should be considered for difficult interviews, including those shown at the top of the pyramid in Figure 6.1.

We strongly recommend that when serious fraud or other criminal acts are suspected, the case should be handled by experienced investigators and litigation lawyers, preferably in accordance with a fraud policy of the type described in Chapter 9, page 281. However, the techniques described can be trimmed down for the sorts of interviews you have to conduct.

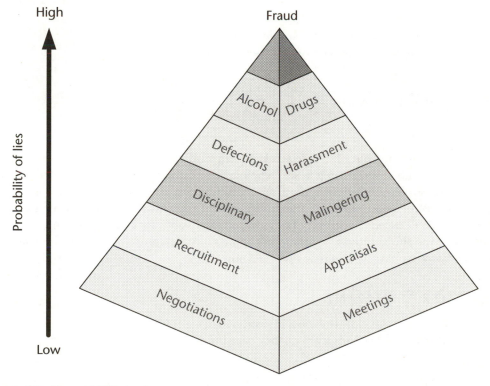

Figure 6.1 Types of HR interviews

Reasons for investigating

When suspicions of malpractice are first aroused, there is a three-way obligation to:

- the victim, enabling him, her or it to recover and prevent future problems;
- anyone under suspicion;
- honest employees: morale will suffer if they see liars escape unpunished.

Sweeping the symptoms of malpractice under the rug is not fair to the people suspected, to the victim organization or to honest employees; wilful blindness and apathy are not viable options.

BRAND MANAGER

Allegations, in an anonymous letter, were made against a senior and very successful brand manager to the effect that he had taken bribes for passing business to an advertising agency. His managers decided not to probe the allegations, foolishly believing that an investigation would result in adverse publicity. However, they transferred the manager to low-level work, but refused to explain why. He became depressed and killed himself. At the inquest the truth emerged: the anonymous letter proved to be false, and the employer was heavily censured for its lack of action.

If the suspicions of malpractice are ignored, they will reappear, usually in a more damaging form.

Fraud, malpractice and dishonesty are contagious.
If you have current suspicions you should resolve them

The legal framework

GENERALLY

In most countries, any question can be asked of anyone, subject to their not being discriminatory on grounds of such things as sex, religion, ethnic origin, nationality, age or disability. There is also an inherent right against self-incrimination and limited rights of protection against intrusion by the state into the private lives of individuals under the Human Rights laws. It should be noted it is unlikely, bordering on impossible, for a company or individual to contravene the Human Rights legislation: it applies to interference by the state. As the actor Michael Caine would say, 'Not many people know that'.

RIGHT TO REMAIN SILENT

It is a fundamental principle that people suspected of a crime have the right to remain silent and to have access to legal advice once they have been arrested or are in custody. The exceptions are:

- Certain regulatory and Serious Fraud Office and DTI investigations.
- Health and Safety enquiries.
- Tax investigations (especially under the 'Hansard' procedure.
- When required to answer under an employment or other contract (see page 326).

In all other cases there is nothing to prevent you in a fair exchange from finding the truth by asking questions, challenging, persuading, leading or guiding someone else to tell the truth. It is a game of chess and a competition in which the liar engages because he believes he can win.

Before a criminal court will accept admissions and confessions in evidence, the judge must be convinced that they were obtained fairly, without oppression, fear from threat or promise of reward.

THE POLICE AND CRIMINAL EVIDENCE ACT

The Police and Criminal Evidence Act 1984 (PACE), sets out the framework for interviews by police officers and others 'charged with the investigation of crime' when – and only when – criminal prosecution in England, Wales and Northern Ireland is contemplated. Scotland has slightly different procedures, as it would.

The English rules are vague, bordering on a subjective truth – and it is far from clear whether they apply only to full-time investigators or to anyone (such as an HR manager) who happens to be 'charged' on one occasion to enquire into a small matter. Lawyers, especially when they are on fees, disagree over the applicability of the rules, and stated cases go both ways.

However, your safe course is to assume the widest interpretation of the Act and thus, when you have reasonable grounds to believe that the suspect has committed a criminal offence and you intend to prosecute through the criminal courts, you should caution him with the words:

> 'You do not have to say anything. But it may harm your defence if you do not mention when questioned something which you later rely on in court. Anything you do say may be given in evidence.'

You do not have to caution a subject just because your mother-in-law thinks he has shifty eyes or because he has a pencil-thin moustache or fancy shoes. But if you have good reasons for suspecting the person has committed an offence and you do not administer a caution at the appropriate time, all of your interview evidence may be ruled inadmissible in a criminal court. This is true even if the suspect is subsequently re-interviewed and cautioned. Once the rules have been broken, it is very difficult to get back on track. For this reason, if you suspect a serious problem and intend to prosecute, you should make sure that all interviews are handled by an experienced investigator.

If you don't plan to prosecute, forget all about the caution

In practice, the caution is no big deal and is unlikely ever to stop an honest person from giving an explanation. If it is administered at the start of the interview, in a matter-of-fact way, possibly as part of the introductory statement, it is unlikely to frighten even the most malodorous villain.[1] However, if the caution is administered immediately the suspect makes his first damaging admission, it may be a major deterrent if for no other reason than it destroys the empathetic relationship you have already established.

When criminal prosecution is an objective, caution the suspect at the opening of the interview

If criminal prosecution is not an objective, you can forget all about PACE and cautions. You can use all of your persuasive skills to encourage a suspect to confess, but remember everything you do may be examined under a microscope in a civil court or tribunal (see Chapter 11), so do nothing you cannot honestly defend.

STANDARDS OF PROOF

To succeed with a criminal prosecution, all of the elements of the offence and the accused person's responsibility have to be proven 'beyond reasonable doubt'. This is an extremely high standard and the benefit of any uncertainty is given to the accused. It is usually critical to show that the accused acted with 'guilty knowledge' or *mens rea*.[2] There are some criminal offences where proof of guilty knowledge is not required and these (for example: failing to submit a tax return, not registering with the Information Commissioner or using a television without a licence) are referred to as 'absolute offences'.

There are two standards of proof in civil cases. The first is where you apply *ex parte*[3] for pre-emptive relief such as search and seizure or freezing orders, when you have to convince a judge based on intelligence (see 'Intelligence and evidence' below) and evidence that you have an 'arguable case'. If he agrees, some or all of the order will be granted. In such cases it is critical that you enter the court 'with clean hands' and disclose everything which could be relevant, including adverse evidence. You need not worry about this right now, and at the time your lawyers will guide you. To succeed in a civil trial you have to prove your case on a 'balance of probabilities'.

It is important to recognize the differences between criminal and civil law standards and to remember that you can succeed in a civil court even when the parallel criminal prosecution has failed. You may remember that this happened to OJ Simpson.

INTELLIGENCE AND EVIDENCE

A phrase often heard in investigations is: 'We know he did it, but we don't have any evidence'. This is rarely correct and there is nothing magic about evidence. In many cases intelligence (or information, which is essentially the same thing, and consists of knowledge, suspicions, deductions and extrapolations made therefrom) is uncovered suggesting that X did Y or something else happened. Often intelligence is not given the weight it deserves but turning it into 'evidence' calls for a combination of legal and investigative skills.

There are a number of categories of evidence in criminal cases (see Table 6.1).

---

[1]   Mainly because he has already figured out that he can beat you
[2]   More bloody Latin, but it means criminal intent or the knowledge of wrongdoing
[3]   Without the other side's knowledge or attendance

Table 6.1   Types of evidence

Type of evidence *Examples*	How it is presented in court	How it is collated by the investigator and *Presented in court*
Oral evidence *What the suspect said when he was interviewed* *What a witness said, heard etc.*	Given on oath from the witness box by a person with first-hand knowledge of the facts at issue	In statements (including his own), Proofs of Evidence, affidavits or transcripts of tape recordings *Delivered – under oath – from the witness box*
	In a written Criminal Justice Act (CJA) statement which with the agreement of the defence and prosecution is read out in the absence of the witness. It has the same standing as oral evidence given from the witness box	In CJA statements (see page 438) *The statement is read out in court without the need for the witness to attend*
Documentary evidence *False purchase invoices*	Produced by a witness as part of his oral evidence. Items which are produced to a court by a witness are normally called 'exhibits'	Originals, copies and schedules prepared by the witnesses *Produced by the witness during his oral evidence or attached to his statement*
Photocopies of original exhibits *Photocopies of sales invoices*	Produced by a witness as part of his oral evidence, providing the court is satisfied that the originals are no longer available	Copies, extracts and schedules prepared by a witness *Produced by the witness during his oral evidence or attached to his statement*
Copies of overseas bank accounts and other records	Produced by an employee from the bank concerned as part of his oral evidence or by another witness under the Criminal Evidence Act	Certified copies and schedules prepared by the witness *Produced by the witness during his oral evidence or attached to his statement*
Real evidence *Stolen goods and weapons*	Produced by a witness as part of his oral evidence	Produced in court or illustrated by photographs *Produced by the witness during his oral evidence or attached to his statement*
Tape and video recordings *Of interviews with the suspect or telephone calls made by him*	Produced by a witness as part of his oral evidence	The original recording and a transcript may be produced in court *Produced by the witness during his oral evidence or attached to his statement*
Expert evidence *Opinion by a computer technician*	Expert evidence is one of the main exceptions to the hearsay rule. The expert may give evidence under oath of his opinion concerning some or all of the facts in issue	Proof of Evidence, or statement *Delivered – under oath – from the witness box or read out to court*
Computerized evidence *Disks, tapes, printouts etc.*	Produced by a witness as part of his oral evidence. The witness must be able to establish the exhibit was produced in the normal course of business on a computer of proven reliability	Proof of Evidence or statement. Original or copies of computer media *Produced by the witness during his oral evidence or attached to his statement*

In civil cases and industrial tribunals, evidence is more usually introduced in affidavits and statements sworn under oath by witnesses and read out in their absence. This has the same standing as evidence given from the witness box.

In larger cases, juries decide on guilt or innocence based on the evidence presented to them. Juries, being constructed of those who are insufficiently astute to avoid being called to this noble service, often find the evidence in complicated fraud cases too difficult and thus fail to agree on a verdict, much to the delight of the defendant. This, unfortunately, is life and you just have to accept it.

Planning essentials

DETERMINE YOUR OBJECTIVES

You should always decide what your objectives are before conducting any important interview:

- *Find the deep truth*: to identify and deal with crooks; *preferably by criminal prosecution, civil action or financial recovery and to clear honest people of suspicion. Ideally aim to obtain a full confession as this simplifies any subsequent legal action or negotiation.*
- *Disciplinary action*: you should make sure that any proposed action is permitted under local laws. But remember that taking a soft line against dishonesty is always counter-productive. It is also true that most cases of alleged unfair dismissal are no more than a ruse to weaken the victim organization's resolve, so do not take a soft line; where necessary select experienced litigation lawyers to assist you.
- *Criminal prosecution*: this is neither an easy nor necessarily a cost-effective option. It is true to say that most victims of fraud who prosecute are disappointed with the results. However, community responsibilities are important and it is morally indefensible to let fat cat fraudsters escape unpunished.
- *Civil litigation*: this again can be a costly and difficult process, but your chances of success are generally much higher through the civil, rather than the criminal, courts. You may also consider taking civil action to recover assets, to discover evidence in the possession of the suspects or third parties, to block funds or for some other reason. If civil action is an objective, you should instruct specialist litigation lawyers, as soon as possible, and follow their advice.
- *Recovery of the amounts lost*: this should be a primary objective in the case of fraud and may be achieved, at the appropriate time, by negotiating with the criminals and their associates, through civil recovery or by claiming under fidelity or computer crime insurance. However, check your coverage now, before you need it and make sure it is appropriate.
- *Getting back to business*: investigations take time and, unless properly controlled, they can be disruptive and costly. It is thus important to keep management of the investigation separate from on-going business. Under no circumstances should the line manager responsible for the operation or area in which the problem is suspected be put in charge of the investigation. It is imperative that all serious investigations are professionally handled using specified procedures and skilled resources. The time to get these in place is now, before the worst happens (see page 281).

- *Improving controls*: as soon as possible, controls should be reviewed and, where necessary, improved but do nothing before the first step that might alert the suspects and allow them to escape.

In most cases, the victims of fraud should take the toughest line necessary to get their money back and get rid of the crooks

You should also consider the adverse consequences of pursuing your objectives. For example, the suspects may make allegations about, or threaten to expose other problems in, your organization, with the objective of stopping the investigation. The fact is that if you give in to blackmail you are headed on the path to failure and you should remember that the media is not interested in fraud unless it concerns Buckingham Palace or some sexual scandal.

Publicity of fraud cases is very rare and transient

You should agree the objectives of each interview with your colleagues and legal advisers, and decide whether or not a confession is important (see Figure 6.2).

If the evidence is already overwhelming and the objective is criminal prosecution, there may be little to be gained from interviewing the suspect, other than being able to demonstrate that by going through a low-key, formal process, he had been given the opportunity of giving his explanation. This is the safe course because a badly conducted interview may actually reduce the strength of the case or, in the worst eventuality, get it thrown out of court.

Don't go for a 'tough' interview unless you have to

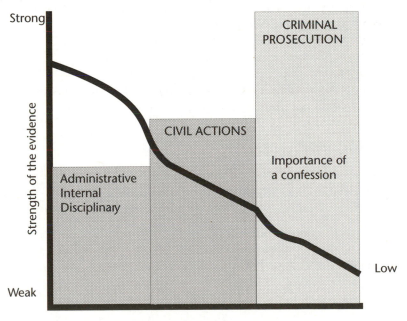

Figure 6.2   Where confessions are not necessary

On the other hand, *properly obtained and admissible* admissions and confessions are important because they:

- add support to the existing evidence and intelligence;
- disclose previously unknown offences;
- identify accomplices;
- identify control weaknesses which can be corrected;
- speed up and simplify the legal process;
- enable the victim to recover more quickly and easily;
- reduce the chance of acquittals and successful appeals against conviction.

Also, the suspect with whom you have established a close relationship may become a valuable source of information on other matters.

Good interviews are worthwhile whenever you can aim for a confession and the deep truth

AUTHORITY TO ACT

You must have the clearest understanding of your right to ask questions and the legal framework, bearing in mind your objectives and consider:

- Is the subject required to answer questions under the terms of his employment or some other contract?
- Can the subject demand that a colleague, union representative or lawyer is present?[4]
- Do you have to administer a caution – but only in cases where criminal prosecution is contemplated – to comply with the Police and Criminal Evidence Act? Chances are, unless you are a full-time investigator, you can forget about cautions.
- Can you tape-record with or without the subject's knowledge?
- Are there disciplinary or other procedures that must be followed?

You should also think about the benefits of obtaining a letter from senior management authorizing you to investigate and conduct interviews.[5]

MAINTAIN TOTAL CONFIDENTIALITY

Do not discuss the suspicions with anyone who does not have an immediate need to know. It may be repugnant, but in fraud-related cases you should assume collusion by at least one management level above the suspect's and that even honest managers may resist an investigation.

ASSUME THE SUSPICIONS ARE TRUE

The safe course is to assume that your initial suspicions are true, or even worse than they currently appear. You should not panic or rush to take action, but assemble your ideas and

---

[4]   In most investigatory interviews the answer is usually 'No' (see page 286)
[5]   Providing this does not alert the suspect to your interest in him

resources so that you can take the suspects by total surprise in what we refer to as the *first step*.

Also, unless there are exceptional circumstances, you should take no remedial – and especially disciplinary – action until you have established the facts.

Always get the facts before you take action

DEVELOP A PROBLEM AND DECEPTION THEORY

Before any interview takes place, you should have the clearest understanding of what you believe has happened, and how and where the evidence can be found:

- Who appears to be involved in the problem, based on the existing evidence? The safe course is to assume that other people are involved, possibly at more senior levels. Collusion is a factor in most fraud cases.
- Assuming the suspicions are correct, in what other – possibly much worse – dishonesty or misconduct might the suspect be involved? This is the *worst case*.
- What are the precise mechanics of the dishonesty or misconduct suspected and the worst case – the '7WH mnemonic':
  - how and how not,
  - what and what not,
  - when and when not,
  - where and where not,
  - which and which not,
  - who and who not,
  - why and why not.
- Who obtained the benefit, where and how? Consider how, in due course, you might recover your losses (if there were any).
- What evidence is there to prove or disprove the suspicions: who has it, and how can it be obtained?

Write down or Mind Map (see page 139) in as much detail as possible everything you know about the possible worst case. Keep your theory under review, with an open mind, as the investigation moves forward.

Remember, there is no such thing as a coincidence. If a fact does not fit your theory, the theory is wrong. Develop an explanation for every detail, document, coincidence or discrepancy. Summarize the key facts on which your theory is based and keep them updated. Make sure that these key facts are summarized in a way that they can be presented – with maximum visual impact – to the suspect during the interview.

DEVISE A RESOLUTION PLAN

In parallel with the deception theory, write down a resolution plan showing the steps that need to be taken, when and by whom (see Table 6.2, page 162).

Table 6.2 A simple resolution plan. Column 6 (Man days) enables budgets to be controlled. The table can be sorted by location, priorities etc.

Ref number	Location	Aspect	Priority	Action by	Man days	Action required
1	2	3	4	5	6	7
1	Birmingham	Jones	2	JEF	1	Interview Smith and Co (vendors) Obtain documents and statement
2	London SW1	Jones	1	ABC KLM	2	Observation on XYZ and Co to check deliveries and goods inwards procedure

The *first step* is critical. If the dishonesty or misconduct is still continuing or is likely to be repeated, determine where and when the first step could be taken to catch the suspects in an act, with their pants down, for which they cannot provide any plausible excuse. For example:

- while handling stolen goods or converting funds;
- while accessing premises or computer systems without authority;
- while involved in an obvious breach of procedures or deviation from honest practice;
- through pre-emptive legal actions, such as civil search and seizure orders.

It is much easier for the victim to seize the initiative if the dishonesty is continuing or might be repeated.

If the problem is not continuing, plan how and when the first step can be taken with the maximum element of surprise:

- when the suspects can be kept apart and are unable to collaborate over their explanations: this is very important;
- when important records, computer and communication systems can be secured.

Review the resolution plan and decide upon the actions that should be taken simultaneously; remember international time differences. Simultaneous actions might include interviews with other suspects or witnesses, third party audits or site visits.

Remember, make the first step a knockout blow

WHEN TO ADVISE THE POLICE

If criminal prosecution is a definite objective, the police should be informed before any internal interviews with suspects take place. But please remember:

- Your objective is probably to establish the total amount of any loss, whereas the police will focus on proving a small selection of criminal charges.
- The results of internal company interviews can be made available to the police whereas the results of police interviews will not normally be made available to you.

- Once a suspect has been interviewed by the police and cautioned, he is unlikely to cooperate in an internal investigation.

Do not be surprised if the police flatly refuse to take the case. Most police forces do not have sufficient resources and the worst thing you can do is to allow them to sit on the case for months, or sometimes years. If the police accept the case, a provisional timetable should be agreed and, if it is not realistic, you should reconsider the advisability of criminal prosecution.

Delay always acts to the victim's disadvantage

ALIGN MANAGEMENT'S EXPECTATIONS

You should ensure that senior managers fully understand the case and the time and cost that may be involved in investigating it. Many who watch television mistakenly believe that all investigations can be completed within 60 minutes including commercial breaks. This is far from the truth. The investigation should be independently conducted by internal audit, corporate security, the police or consultants, and line managers should be prohibited from interfering. Ideally, this fact should be made clear, before the event, in your security and fraud policy.

Managers are usually woefully misinformed about fraud

Obtain background information

INTRODUCTION

You should never interview anyone without being fully prepared: who knows wins.

GEORGE CARMAN QC

Mr Carman (see the excellent book *No Ordinary Man* (ISBN 0 340 82099 3) was widely regarded as the best cross-examiner in the business and was known for his pithy comments and apparently throwaway lines such as those in respect of David Mellor MP when Mr Carman said, 'He buried his head in the sand, thus exposing his thinking parts'. What was not generally known is that Mr Carman prepared in the finest detail and often took weeks to coin his memorable phrases. He also liked to ambush witnesses with evidence they did not know he had and to 'break the session overnight to give them the opportunity to fret'. He knew the value of detailed preparation in raising a subject's anxiety levels. This was described by one of Mr Carman's victims as 'being Carmanised'.

Gary Player, the great South African golfer said: 'Funny, the more I practice (and prepare), the luckier I become.'

There is no substitute for hard work

BACKGROUND ON THE SUSPECTS

It is vital that as much as possible is known about the suspects before they are interviewed.

ON SMALL DETAILS

Background analysis of the type suggested in Table 6.3 below has thrown up some critical clues and evidence. In a number of cases, suspects had authorized payments to fictitious vendors in the maiden names of their wives, to ex-employees who mysteriously appeared as vendors immediately after the suspect joined the victim employer or at addresses owned by a family member or at one of their own previous addresses. Inspection of a suspect's home revealed that he was living well beyond his means (and in one case a man on £25,000 a year had a £120,000 sports car parked on his drive). In other cases vacation addresses turned out to be a villa owned by a supplier. And in the most surprising case of all, involving manipulation of an electronic payments system, the suspect had noted the method of fraud used, as well as incriminating memory dumps, in copies of procedure manuals issued to him.

An argument is sometimes put forward – based on a misinterpretation of the Data Protection Act – that information from personnel files cannot be accessed. This is incorrect, and any data – even the most personal – can be used for the purpose of preventing and detecting crime.

THE IMPORTANCE OF PRESS REPORTS

A basic check showed that a suspect had been approved for a gold credit card issued in the name of one of his employer's suppliers. In another case, a routine check of the local press library revealed that the suspect had been provided with a £100,000 rally car and his expenses sponsored by a customer. In both cases, the suspects were given the opportunity to volunteer their benefits and failed to do so. Both were eventually prosecuted for corruption.

In important cases, try to assess the suspect's financial and domestic position, as these often establish his motive. It is also essential that you carefully analyse any explanations given by the subject. Important facts should be thoroughly checked and discrepancies should be scheduled as *key points* so that they can be presented to him at the appropriate time.

UNDERSTAND THE EXISTING EVIDENCE

Examine the evidence and the intelligence that has led to the suspicions and fully understand them. Pay particular attention to:

- The *key points* that suggest the suspect's responsibility. Make sure your conclusions are correct; look for alternative explanations; pay close attention to detail. *In due course you should summarize each key point on a single sheet of paper that can be presented to the suspect during the interview (see pages 136, 158 and 162).*

- Any *discrepancies* in the existing evidence. Developing a deception theory (see page 153) is like completing a jigsaw puzzle. If a fact does not fit your theory, the theory must be wrong. Keep an open mind. Very often the biggest breakthroughs in investigations come from what appeared to be small discrepancies. You should worry them to death.
- Things *that should have happened,* but didn't. These often appear as discrepancies or coincidences. But you should work on the theory that everything happened for a reason and was probably part of the suspect's plan.

Keep asking yourself these questions as the investigation moves forward and remain open-minded but dig deeper and deeper for detail.

Evidence is sometimes the only thing that separates the criminal from the entrepreneur

DIARY OF EVENTS

From the first moment, you should start compiling a diary of events or chronology which shows, in date and time sequence, everything that happened from all of your sources, especially telephone call logs, expense statements and correspondence. It is a critical document and puts you in control (see Table 6.3).

Columns 2 and 3 can be particularly important in international frauds, involving different time zones and public holidays. The diary of events can be kept on Microsoft Excel, which has functions for calculating the day of the week (DOW) from any date, and superb sorting and analysis tools. It is also extremely important in interviews and enables you to quickly check and cross-reference explanations given by the suspect.

In simple cases, or for critical short sequences within a bigger case, you should consider preparing a simple time bar.

Table 6.3 Diary of events

Date	Day of week	GMT	Action or event	Comments	Source	Cross-reference
1	2	3	4	5	6	7
2002						
Jan 1	Wed	14.00	Bill Smith calls John Jones (14 mins)		Call logs 1	
Jan 1	Wed	14.15	John Jones calls Zurich bank (12 mins)		Call logs 2	
Jan 1	Wed	20.30	Bill Smith entertains Robinson at Hilton Hotel (bill £145.76)		Expenses 1	

FORENSIC EXAMINATION

You should consider having some or all of the evidence forensically examined:

- ESDA testing for latent impressions of other writings.[6]
- Handwriting analysis, to prove who wrote a document.
- Fingerprinting, to prove who handled a document.
- Enhancement of audio tapes from answering, voice mail and dictation machines.
- Recovery of deleted computer files and emails.

However, it is essential that examinations are made without alerting the suspects that they are under investigation.

THE BANK OFFICER

A senior bank officer, suspected of involvement in a major fraud, denied that he had seen a letter of authority, although he agreed he had seen and signed similar documents on the date in question. Forensic examination of the letters revealed an ESDA impression of the officer's signature on the unsigned document. It had obviously been included in the pack submitted to him for signature. This evidence was vital in obtaining his confession that he had seen the document and had *not* signed it because he knew it was fraudulent.

CATALOGUE MINOR BREACHES

Minor breaches of procedures, incorrect application forms, previous false explanations, abuse of discretion, and errors or expense fiddles should be identified, catalogued and summarized on single sheets of paper as key points. These may be used during the interview again as 'key points' to demonstrate to the suspect that, whether he admits to the more serious matters or not, he is already exposed to censure and this may lead him to conclude that he has little to lose in leading you to the deep truth.

Consider covert action prior to the interview

You should consider whether it would be beneficial to take covert action, before or after the first step, to detect the suspects in a dishonest act which cannot be excused, or to trace assets or accomplices.

The possibilities include:

- *Interception and covert recording of company telephone, fax and data lines.* But first understand the legal position set out on pages 285–286.
- *Intercepting company mail (including email),* subject to the Regulation of Investigatory Powers Act (2000), page 285.
- *Installing video or audio monitors* in offices, warehouses or computer centres or on equipment which the suspects may use in carrying out the fraud.
- *Searching the suspect's work area or office.* Before doing this take a Polaroid photograph or video recording to help you make sure everything is put back in its original place.

---

[6] ESDA detects impressions made on paper from writing on other papers which at one time may have been made on papers resting above it. The leading company in the UK is Berkeley Security Bureau (Forensic) Ltd, 10 Grosvenor Avenue, London SW1

- *Searching the suspect's PC* and covertly copying his diskettes. Do not use standard software to take a secret copy of a hard disk as this may destroy the evidential value of what you find. It is much better to retain the services of a professional computer forensic technician. Consider carefully what rights you have to access the suspect's personal computer.

The possibilities should be considered and, where appropriate, included in the resolution plan. However, it is critical that the actions you take are proportionate to the seriousness of the suspected transgression.

Your action must be proportionate

Blocking measures

Also, consider any actions that could be taken, at the appropriate time and probably before the first step, which might give wrongly suspected innocent people the chance to voluntarily disclose the facts.

DECLARING A CONFLICT OF INTEREST

If an employee is suspected of running a competitive business, the employer might ask all employees – in a casual, low-key way – to submit a written declaration for 'insurance purposes' of their private interests. If the suspect fails to make a truthful disclosure, he is denied the opportunity of producing an innocent explanation later on. An honest response would normally be in the person's favour, but he can then be asked openly to produce the records of his private business interests for examination.

Whichever way the attempt goes, the results will be useful, and, at worst, bring forward the suspicions for discussion.

If the suspect does not volunteer the truth, when given the opportunity, it will make any subsequent explanations or denials less credible.

Decide on the venue

Ideally, interviews with suspects and important witnesses should be held simultaneously as part of the *first step*, at a time and place when the suspects are most exposed or where they can be taken by surprise.

Under normal circumstances, a suspect should never be interviewed by more than two people at a time, and even then the second person should try to stay out of his direct line of sight and should remain silent unless the lead interviewer invites him to speak. The relationship between the interviewer and the suspect should be a one-to-one as far as possible.

The chance of finding the truth varies inversely with the number of people present

In complex cases, more than one interview may be required with some or all of the suspects but the first is usually the most productive because it should take the suspect by surprise. It is not uncommon for suspects to refuse to attend follow-up interviews simply because they have assessed their chances of success, decided the odds are against them and elected not to engage in battle.

You may only have one bite of the apple

Arranging the interview room

The layout of the interview room is very important in all serious cases. Always try to make the suspect play away from home or in an environment with which he is not familiar. Only in exceptional circumstances should the suspect be interviewed in his home (especially if he has a big dog) or office (especially if he has a fawning PA). There are two reasons for this. The first is that the interview might be deliberately disrupted by family members or colleagues. Second, in his own environment, the suspect may feel in control.

Also, think carefully before holding the interview in your own office, especially if it is small and untidy or displays your golfing memorabilia and photographs of you and your family on holiday in Benidorm. These can put you in the wrong transactional role.

Always remember that there are two interviews taking place, and if the suspect forms an opinion about you, based on the appearance of your office, it may make it more difficult for you to adopt the transactional roles necessary to succeed.

Ideally the interview room should be small,[7] private, reasonably soundproof and away from centres of earnest activity (thus, the conference room in the accounting department may be ideal). People should not be able to look in from outside and the subject should be able to go in and out of the room without having to walk past rubberneckers.

- Telephones should be disconnected and clocks and other distractions removed. (*At the appropriate time, you must make sure all mobile telephones are turned off.*)
- The room should be clean and tidy, bordering on clinical. (*A slight scent of antiseptic or of the confessional box does no harm.*)
- Furniture should be carefully arranged so that the suspect sits furthest from the door.
- At the start of the interview you should sit behind a desk with the suspect to your right.
- Seats for any corroborating witnesses should be placed out of the suspect's direct line of sight.
- If there are any pieces of particularly incriminating evidence, such as forged documents, you should consider enlarging them and having them pinned to the walls in the suspect's direct line of sight.
- If the suspect is known to smoke, the interview should be conducted in a smoking area.[8]
- If the interview is to be tape-recorded, a test should be made to ensure that air conditioning and other ambient noise does not spoil the quality of the recording.

At the start of the interview you should sit behind a desk to the suspect's left (Figure 6.3). As the interview progresses, through the pivotal point and 'the turn', you may move from behind

---

[7]   Around ten feet by ten feet
[8]   Although denying the suspect the right to smoke may increase his anxiety it will be counter-productive in the later, empathy-building stages. Also, his smoking is likely to disturb his lawyer

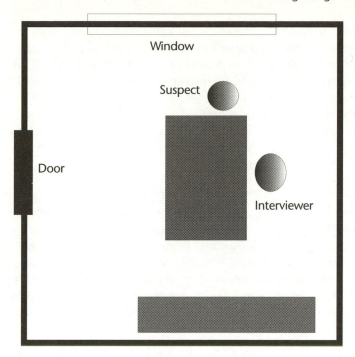

Figure 6.3   The interview room

the desk and sit alongside and close to the suspect, thus reinforcing a nurturing parent role. But such movements have to appear spontaneous and natural. At the pivotal point you should be sitting close to the suspect and to his *left*.[9]

After you have prepared the room and before the interview begins, ask a colleague who is not involved in the case to walk in and give you his first impressions. It must appear clinically professional.

Notes and records of interviews

It is important that a full and accurate record of each significant interview is prepared and retained.[10] The Codes of Practice, issued under the Police and Criminal Evidence Act 1984, make it clear that lawyers would always prefer all interviewers to make contemporaneous notes as they do themselves.[11] The advice is detached from reality if the object is to establish rapport, create a free flow of information and get to the deep truth.

If you don't agree what a discouragement of the truth contemporaneous note taking is, try pulling out your notebook at the next cocktail party you attend but don't be surprised when no one – except the odd accountant or lawyer – talks to you.

Taking notes puts people off, including the note taker

---

[9] By now you should know why
[10] You may use notes made at the time, or immediately after an interview, to refresh your memory when giving evidence in court
[11] This is why lawyers seldom get to the deep truth

Worse still, while you are concentrating on joined-up writing, you miss important clues. Contemporaneous note taking is at best a deterrent to finding the truth, and more often a displacement activity for anally retentive interviewers. It is the worst form of neurolinguistic programming and is tantamount to saying with each stroke of the pen, 'Watch out what you say, old chum, you are really in trouble.'

Contemporaneous notes may, in exceptional circumstances, be made by a corroborating witness, but this practice is not recommended, again for the reason that it deters free-flowing discussion.

THE STENOGRAPHER

American lawyers insisted that investigators had a paralegal sit in on an interview with a fraud suspect. She was also a trained shorthand writer. She was told to remain silent, sit outside the suspect's direct line of sight and just take notes. When the interview got to the pivotal point and, in an emotional state, the suspect made his first serious admission, the paralegal could not contain herself and said, 'Holy shit.' This threw the interview off track for at least an hour and could have been disastrous.

However, if a suspect is being totally unreasonable, you may decide to increase his anxiety by pulling out your notepad and committing him to false detail which he will later find impossible to defend.

In the UK you are allowed to tape-record an interview without the subject's knowledge and for complex cases this is the safe course. However, if a long and important interview is not being tape-recorded, trigger notes (such as names, addresses and other important information) may be made, but even then you must take great care. Never write anything down while the subject is speaking. Let him finish, make your note and then ask the next question.

It is critical that you do not write down anything while the subject is speaking

Notes of significant points, denials and admissions may be made at the end of the formal interview, jointly by you and any corroborating witnesses. These should then be shown to the suspect and his agreement sought. If he agrees they are correct, he should be asked to sign and date them.

A note should be made (again signed and dated) of any points with which the suspect does not agree. The notes should be annotated with the date and time they were completed and the names of the people involved. A photocopy of the notes may be handed to the subject for his retention.

Consider how the evidence will be presented

You should identify, for each suspect, the most important evidence (the 'Key Points') you have and assemble it in such a way that its presentation will have the maximum visual and emotional impact:

- Enclosing documentary and other exhibits in clear plastic envelopes and marking them with exhibit labels and different coloured Post-it® notes. *(Usually an innocent person will ask about these and what they mean: the guilty party rarely will.)*
- Preparing weighty files of 'exhibits', which may be left out on desks in the interview room although never referred to. *(The anxiety of a guilty person will be increased by these, but he won't say anything!)*
- Marking filing cabinets with the case name and exhibit references; i.e. 'Evidence against Joe Jones: Volumes 1 to 10' etc.
- Preparing single-page schedules summarizing important points: again these should be in colour, with important evidence highlighted or enlarged.

The visual impact (as well as control of the interview) can be enhanced by using small coloured tabs, positioned to indicate the relevance of each document.

The more evidence the suspect believes you have or can get, the more likely he is to confess

There are two ways in which the suspect can be confronted with key evidence. The first is to hold it in reserve until he has committed himself to a deceptive answer and then to ambush him with it.

LOOK AT THIS

'Bill, you told me a moment ago that you have never been to Budapest. You said you were absolutely certain. I would like you to tell me about this receipt which shows that you stayed "with Mrs Jones" at the Hilton Hotel, Budapest, from 1 to 12 April.' You should hand him the receipt and keep it in his personal space.

If you plan to do this, make sure you have back-up copies of the evidence.

EATING THE EVIDENCE

A young investigator found an airmail letter which totally proved a narcotics smuggling scheme. He interviewed the rather large Jamaican lady to whom it had been addressed, handed her the letter and asked for her explanation. As quick as a flash she popped it in her mouth and ate it. 'What letter?' she asked. There was no back-up copy.

Fumbling with papers in the interview reduces the chances of finding the truth, because it makes you appear incompetent and puts you in the transactional role of a child.

Once key evidence has been presented, make sure it remains under the suspect's nose and remains in his personal space.[12] You will find, with most guilty suspects, that they will unconsciously push away nasty reminders of their responsibility.

Guilty people seldom want to handle incriminating evidence, but will drop it and push it away during the interview

---

12 Do not put it back in a file or folder, but keep it in front of the suspect, so that it builds up into a large pile

The second way is to display some or all of the evidence, by mounting it on walls around the interview room or laying it out on tables in the suspect's line of sight. The VLCC arson case (page 82) is an example of this approach. You will find that the guilty person seldom says anything about displayed exhibits, although you will notice his eyes drifting towards them, especially when he believes you are not watching him. Innocent people usually comment or ask questions about displayed exhibits.

Interviews in the presence of the suspect's lawyer

The British Law Society published a paper in 1998[13] setting out the approach it recommends lawyers should take when their clients are being investigated and interviewed. It is not necessary to go into the gory detail, but sufficient to say that the recommended actions appear to be based on a compulsive interference disorder (CID) and the assumption that their clients are always innocent.

The main problem is that the charisma of the suspect's lawyer will disturb transactional relationships and unless you take care, he will capture the role of the ultimate critical parent, forcing you into the role of an adaptive child. This is very bad news.

The recommended approach is to:

- Speak to the lawyer – in the absence of the suspect – immediately before the interview starts[14] and try to agree the ground rules to the effect that he is *not* a participant, nor a witness as to fact. His job is to advise the suspect on legal matters and not to argue the case on his behalf or to impede the course of justice. He is, after all, 'an Officer of the Court' and should act accordingly.
- If you regard his client as a peripheral player or if there are mitigating factors, do not be afraid to say so. Clever lawyers will seize upon this and may change sides to support you.
- Try to establish an adult-to-adult transactional relationship with him. If this doesn't work, you should consider crossing roles in the interview (see pages 56–58) but this is a high-risk strategy.
- Don't let the lawyer argue the case in the absence of the suspect but politely point out that 'your client should answer these questions and make these points, not you'.
- Outline the proposed interview structure, without necessarily revealing all of the key points or your line of questioning. However, you must be fair.
- In the interview, direct all questions to the suspect and concentrate on him, not his lawyer, unless the latter is being unusually cooperative.

Alternatively, you may decide to invite your legal representative to attend the interview and at least put the transactional roles in balance. However, you should recognize that the probability of getting to the deep truth varies inversely with the number of people present.

---

[13] *Becoming Skilled: Active Defence*, Eric Shepherd
[14] Try to make sure he is not able to brief his client on your conversation before the interview starts

Conclusion

With this background completed, you are now in a position to move on to planning the interview in detail.

THE INTERVIEW ROOM

7 *Conducting Tough Interviews*

The interview phases

OVERVIEW

For really tough interviews there is a seven-phase process in getting to the deep truth. Please read Table 7.1 carefully, it is important.

This is the roadmap to the truth

These phases are described in the context of tough interviews but they can be modified for any situation in which deception is suspected. But in all cases the objective is to get to the deep truth fairly, and in a way that complies with all relevant laws. If you do this, all remedial actions – from criminal prosecution to warning letters – are simplified and are much less costly.

Aim for the deep truth

Many of the examples given in this chapter are concerned with suspected frauds and the sorts of cases that specialist investigators rather than the HR generalist would investigate. They are relevant because they cover the most difficult sorts of interviews and show the approach that you can tailor for other cases.

PHASE A: GETTING THE SUBJECT TO ATTEND

We strongly recommend that when you suspect serious deception, the subject should be ambushed in the *first step* and we recognize that this may not be the conventional approach. However, your objective is to find the truth and to clear the innocent as well as nail the guilty party. Experience shows that the first step must be a surprise. This makes it less likely that they can prepare excuses or interfere with the evidence.

The first step must be an ambush

The invitation for a suspect to attend an interview, or meeting, should be carefully planned (see page 169) and should be made in a low-key, unemotional way, ideally with the minimum of notice. The objective is to entice the suspect into accepting the challenge of attending an interview. You can only do this if he believes he can win or has more to gain than lose by attending.

Table 7.1   The seven phases (see also Figure 5.1, page 130)

Phase	Objectives and coverage	*Possible emotion* and APPROACH of the deceitful subject
Phase A Getting the subject to attend and the opening	Tempting the suspect to explain Creating the right impression Building empathy Stating the purpose Getting a detailed explanation	*Fear and anxiety* *Anger* FIGHT FLEE APPEASE
Phase B Probing and testing	Establishing whether the person is telling the truth or not with the interviewer acting as a human lie detector	
Phase C Raising the pavement *Putting the monkeys on the liar's back*	Pinning the subject down to detail Increasing anxiety to the point where the subject loses confidence in his ability to cope and arrives at the pivotal point	*Increased anxiety* *Depression* QUESTIONS HIS ABILITY TO COPE
Phase D THE PIVOTAL POINT *At which the suspect balances the relief given by confession and bringing the interview to an end with the potential consequences of a confession*		
Phase E Turning and empathy *Getting the monkeys off the liar's back*	Helping the subject handle the critical decision whether or not to tell the truth Taking an empathetic approach Enabling the suspect to rationalize his behaviour	*Unbearable anxiety* NEGOTIATION ACCEPTANCE
Phase F Getting to the deep truth and arriving at a soft landing	Working with him as a nurturing parent to get to the deep truth Leaving the door open for later contact	*Relief* ACCEPTANCE SUBMISSION
Phase G Review and follow-up	Transcribing notes and preparing an accurate record of the interview Reviewing your own performance, so that you can improve in the future Identifying other actions Keeping in regular contact with the suspect	*Relief* ACCEPTANCE *Anger* ATTACK

There are cases where people have no option but to attend an interview and answer questions, including investigations by the Serious Fraud Office, some health and safety enquiries, where employees are required to assist under the terms and conditions of their employment, and when you are summonsed by your mother-in-law. But, in most cases, the willingness of the subject to attend depends on your persuasive skills.

A person invited to attend a tough interview will carefully assess his position. If he believes the evidence against him is damning and that he has no chance of escape, he is likely to flee, and refuse to attend. Thus the way you invite a subject to attend an interview is important.

THE TELEPHONE CALL

You have been investigating for months and have reached the stage at which you would like to interview the suspect. You telephone him at home on a Sunday evening:

'Good evening, Mr Jones, this is Bill Smith from Audit. As you know I have been investigating you for six months and

I have the strongest evidence that you are a malodorous scumbag who has ripped off millions from Sunshine Foods. My office is jam packed with evidence that incriminates you and you are in deep shit with no chance of escape. I would like to see you at 8.30 tomorrow.' Will he come? Would you?

You might think that conversations like this never take place, but unfortunately they do. In one recent multimillion pound case, auditors telephoned the suspect at home on a Sunday evening, telling him about their investigation and asking to see him in his office the following morning, adding: 'Bring your laptop and back-up files with you'. They were amazed that the suspect did not appear but had instead run off to Brazil. When he was eventually tracked down, he claimed his laptop had fallen into a river.

The lesson is not to make a big deal of the interview or meeting but to let the suspect form his own conclusion that, if he attends, he has a chance of winning or at least coming out no worse than he went in. Ideally you should give minimal advance warning or, better still, ambush him when his pants are down (see page 158 and Appendix 1).

FALSE ARREST

A participant in a seminar on corporate fraud listened intently as the elderly speaker listed the ways in which false purchase invoices could be detected. A day or so later, he telephoned the speaker and said:

'I tried out the tests you suggested and picked up £70,000 worth of false invoices. I interviewed the head of purchasing and he has confessed. I have locked him in the lavatory but I am not sure what to do next.'

The moral of this story is that although you should try and take the suspect by surprise you should not arrest him, unless it is vital to do so and permitted under the law. Arrest means detaining someone against their will, usually with the objective of bringing them before a court. In the United Kingdom under Section 24(4)–(7) of the Police and Criminal Evidence Act 1984, 'any person may arrest anyone without a warrant' providing:

- he is in the act of committing an arrestable offence (this includes all thefts and frauds);
- he has reasonable grounds for suspecting him to be committing such an offence;
- where an arrestable offence has been committed … he may arrest anyone who is guilty of the offence or anyone whom he has reasonable grounds for suspecting to be guilty of it.

This is an important power, available to all citizens, especially if a person is caught while trying to remove or destroy evidence. All that is necessary is to tell the person he is being arrested and to take him to a police station or call for police assistance as soon as possible. Reasonable force can be used to prevent the suspect from escaping (see Section 3 of the Criminal Law Act 1967), but great care must be taken in all cases, especially when he is bigger than you, or is with his mum or his dog.

You may invite a person to attend an interview, but you should not arrest him.
Let the liar think he can win

If the interview can be arranged when the suspect is doing something he should not be doing, so much the better. For example, if an employee who is suspected of stealing can be caught loading company property into the boot of his car, the initiative swings quickly in your favour.

It is very difficult for a liar to maintain his composure when caught with his pants down

THE MALINGERER

Bill Smith, a senior manager, is suspected of malingering and taking time off to play golf, mainly with competitors and vendors and is strongly suspected of taking bribes and giving away sensitive company information. He has been absent from work for two months, claiming to suffer from 'random blackouts'. He has been invited to come into the office to discuss his problems with the head of human resources, but each time has failed to appear, claiming that he was ill and had to stay in bed.

You believe that Bill has been invited by a vendor to play in a golf competition at Wentworth on 3 and 4 June, which is some two weeks away. You know this is just too good for him to miss, so you invite him to come to the office to meet you and the head of human resources on one of these days. Bill cannot admit he is already tied up on another engagement (i.e. his important golf date) and says, 'OK, I will do my best, but I have a provisional hospital appointment in that week'. 'How are you feeling?' you ask, and he replies, 'OK, I think I am getting better but when I see the specialist I will know a lot more.'

On 2 June, Bill telephones and says he cannot make your appointment, as he has to check into hospital for the whole week, but will call you on his release. He sounds very worried and sick, as malingerers always do. You decide to ambush him when he appears to play golf at Wentworth.

PHASE A: THE OPENING

The way you open an interview is also critically important. First impressions count and you must present an adult and professional image. In most cases you should explain, through some sort of introductory statement (see page 194), the nature of the interview, your background, objectives and the process involved. You may ask blocking questions or take a more direct approach.

However, in the opening phase you should:

- make it clear that you intend to find the truth and that you have limitless time and resources available to you;
- ask questions that commit the subject to detailed explanations;
- challenge untruths;
- state what you believe the facts to be, if necessary by making direct accusations.

If you are reasonably sure the subject is not telling the truth, you should proceed to Phase B.

PHASE B: PROBING AND TESTING

In this phase you move from an adult to a critical parent role, continue to ask detailed questions and test the subject's reaction to the evidence and intelligence you have. You should focus on the key points and obtain detailed explanations on the mechanics (the 'how') of what you believe has happened. You will not remember all of the clues to deception described in Chapter 4, so rely on your intuition but elevate specific concerns into your conscious awareness.

If you believe the suspect is innocent or telling the truth or both, don't be afraid to admit it to yourself and move forward on that basis.

One of the greatest failings of inexperienced interviewers is that they will not admit to themselves that the subject is being truthful

If you believe the suspect is guilty, telling lies or you are not sure, one way or the other, you must move to Phase C.

PHASE C: RAISING THE PAVEMENT: PUTTING MONKEYS ON BACKS

It is crucial that the suspect's anxiety is taken to the pivotal point (see Figure 7.1) where he loses all confidence in his ability to succeed and is willing to accept the consequences of confessing or sees an advantage in doing so.

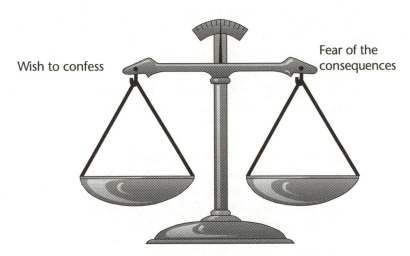

Wish to confess

Fear of the consequences

Figure 7.1   The pivotal point

You can lead the suspect to the pivotal point by taking a critical parent role and by provoking his subconscious and memory monkeys into states of intolerable anxiety by:

- preventing him from succeeding with concealment lies;
- provoking him into falsifying fine detail;
- challenging deceptive answers and non-verbal clues of deception;
- stating what you believe he did (based on the fraud and deception theories) through accusatory questions.

You should emphasize the key points and keep the documentary summaries within his personal space; make sure all questions are answered fully, react coolly to counter-attacks and make clear what you believe has happened. You must state, repeatedly, what you believe the suspect has done.

The liar is at his most vulnerable at any phase of an interview when he is:

- emotional – especially when he is angry;
- pausing for thought before answering a relevant question ('brain thrashing');
- caught out in a lie;
- forced to change an explanation or to admit he has been less than forthcoming in his answers.

However, he is totally exposed at the pivotal point. The way you handle this is critical in getting to the deep truth.

Put the monkeys on his back

PHASES D AND E: THE PIVOTAL POINT AND TURNING

In this phase the suspect will consider confessing, usually for the reasons explained in Chapter 3, page 172. If you miss your opportunity at one pivotal point, the chances are another will appear. The suspect may:

- ask bargaining questions such as 'What might happen?';
- show non-verbal and other signs of acceptance, such as dropping his head or rolling up into a foetal position. It may sound incredible, but at the pivotal point, many suspects appear to get smaller.

The suspect's primary channel of communication (both verbal and non-verbal) will almost certainly be emotional and you *must* tune to his wavelength by adopting the role of a nurturing parent. You must retain a low-key, sensitive and slow approach to the first and subsequent admissions: you should empathize with the suspect, make rationalization statements and slowly and carefully extend admissions into a confession. You should focus on the word 'we' and how the matter can be resolved.

If you handle this phase properly you should obtain admissions or confessions or conclude that the suspect is wholly or partly innocent. If you conclude he is innocent, truthful or both, you must be prepared to apologize for giving him a hard time.

Example: 'I am sorry, Bill, I had to put you through that, but it was very important to find the truth and I am satisfied that you did not … but I would like your help in moving this case forward.'

It is very rare, bordering on unique, for such an apology not to be accepted by an innocent subject. On the other hand, if the suspect has made admissions or confessions, this is where the hard work starts and you must take limitless time in getting to the deep truth.

Turn from a critical to a nurturing parent

PHASE F: GETTING TO THE DEEP TRUTH

This phase focuses on obtaining detailed admissions and confessions, using empathetic and emotionally challenging questions and getting to the deep truth. By this phase, the chances are you will have fallen naturally into the role of a nurturing parent and the suspect into that of an adaptive child. You should also explore any other cases of dishonesty that the suspect knows about and in which he may have been involved.

PHASE G: FOLLOW-UP

In this closing down phase, you will complete your notes or transcribe tapes. It is critical that records are accurate and securely retained. You should also prepare a list of further actions and review the results of the interview.

In the days following the interview, keep in contact with the suspect and try to obtain further details. Stay on cordial terms with him and speak to him as frequently as you reasonably can. Regular contact, after the interview, makes it less likely that the suspect will try to withdraw his confession, but don't be surprised if he turns against you once he has discussed his confession with accomplices, family and friends.

Types of questions

THE MENU

There are many ways in which we can deliver questions:

- some are general and set the scene;
- some will test whether the subject is being truthful or not;
- some will produce detail or fine-tune an answer;
- some will increase anxiety;
- others are empathetic and emotionally sensitive and can be used at the pivotal point to help the suspect conclude that it would be in his best interests to tell the truth.

The relevance of questions to the seven interview phases is usually as follows (Table 7.2).

Table 7.2   Question types and interview phases

The types of questions that are most applicable to the following phases	Types of questions *Transactional role*				
	General	Testing	Accusatory		Empathetic
			Probing	Increasing anxiety	
A: Opening	Introductory Statements Yes *Variable*	Possible *Adult*	No	Possible *Adult*	Possible *Adult*
B: Probing		Yes *Critical parent*	Yes *Critical parent*	Yes *Critical parent*	No
C: Raising anxiety					
D: The pivotal point		No	No	Yes *Critical and nurturing parent*	Yes *Nurturing parent*
E: Turning					
F: The deep truth		Yes *Nurturing parent*	Yes *Nurturing parent or adult*	Possibly *Adult or critical parent*	
G: Follow-up		Possible *Adult*	Yes *Adult*	Possible *Adult*	

Most questions will be directed and answered at a conscious level although, as we will see later, we can use embedded commands, NLP, non-verbal communications and other techniques to excite the monkeys on the liar's back.

CONTROL AND RELEVANT QUESTIONS

Control questions are non-threatening and are used, among other things, to monitor a subject's baseline reactions when he is telling the truth. For example, under most circumstances, the question *'When did you start working here?'* could be regarded as a control question, as could *'Do you prefer rice pudding to treacle tart?'* The problem is that what you think may be a control, and unthreatening, question may hold a dreadful significance for the subject, especially if he has just stolen Granny Smith's rice pudding. Honest people take the same level of care with control as they do with relevant questions: liars relax but don't know how to deal with them.

Relevant questions relate specifically to the matter in issue and will either require:

- the suspect to make an admission or confession;
- or to tell a lie.

Relevant questions thus stimulate an anxious response, usually within three to five milliseconds of being asked. Often the differences in responses to control and relevant questions – or 'response latency' – are glaringly obvious.

THE OJ SIMPSON CASE

OJ Simpson was interviewed by two Los Angeles detectives the day after his wife was found butchered. The full transcript of this very poor interview can be downloaded from the Internet (http://simpson.walraven.com). Detailed analysis reveals some very interesting patterns (Table 7.3).

Incongruence between the responses to control and relevant questions are vital clues

Table 7.3   Responses in the interview with OJ Simpson

Type of question	Response to control questions	Response to relevant questions
Closed questions that could have been answered with a binary 'yes' or 'no'	95 per cent of questions were answered only with a 'yes' or 'no'	None were answered with only a 'yes' or 'no' but were either prefaced by prevarication or closed with a softening phrase
Open questions	No requests for clarification were made and there was no stalling	95 per cent of questions were clarified by a question from OJ

Obviously, patterns such as those described in Table 7.3 are not proof positive of either guilt or innocence, but you should always consciously monitor the differences between the subject's response to control and relevant questions and incongruencies between content, syntax, paralinguistics, body language and attitude. This is the easy part, leaving you with the more difficult job of resolving your suspicions.

OPEN QUESTIONS

Open questions invite the subject to give an explanation in his own words, without prompting. They do not provide him with any sort of template for deception because they hide how much you know and don't know. Open questions such as:

'Why?' 'What?' 'Where?' 'Who?' 'How?' 'Tell me everything you know about …'

allow the honest subject to respond with a detailed freestyle narrative, but they require a dishonest suspect to decide how much he will say and thus take a gamble: he does not want to volunteer too much detail (through which you may trap him later); nor does he want to be caught out in an obvious concealment (see Table 7.4).

The most usual response from both honest and deceptive subjects to the question 'Tell me everything you know about x' is: 'Where do you want me to start?' Your response should be: 'Everything you think could be relevant'.

Table 7.4   Reactions in the interview with OJ Simpson

Reactions indicating innocence	Reactions indicating guilt
Gives a detailed, free-flowing account of the matters at issue, consistent with his baseline responses	Wants more information: *'Where do you want me to start?'* *'I am not sure how far you want me to go'* *'How much do you know?'* *'You tell me what you want me to explain'*
Retrieves the answer from memory: looks to the left while thinking	Creates answers in the imagination: looks to the right while thinking
Consistent detail	Lack of detail or inconsistent detail
Answers the question directly	Asks for clarification of the question such as *'Where do you want me to start?'*
Immediately understands the context of the question	Does not know how much an innocent person would know. Thus asks clarification questions. *'How should I know that?'*
Gives truthful responses to questions where you already know the answers	Gives evasive or untruthful responses to questions to which you already know the answers

Open questions provide no template for deception

At this point the dishonest suspect will normally press for more clarification before responding, usually because he is concerned to find out how much you know. The innocent person is normally much more confident, not at risk and will just give his answers.

Always consider using open questions that focus on the subject's emotions, feelings and attitudes and which require him to consult with the subconscious monkey.

Example:
- 'What do you least like about yourself?'
- 'What is the worst thing you have ever done?'
- 'What were you *thinking* when you went to the post box?'
- 'What do you feel should happen to people who make false claims?'

Questions about feelings and attitudes get directly into the subject's subconscious, making it more likely that the truth or Freudian slips will emerge, or that by bringing unpalatable facts into focus, his anxiety will increase.

CLOSED AND LEADING QUESTIONS

Closed, or leading, questions can be answered by a simple binary: 'yes' or 'no'. The problem is that they often suggest the answer required and thus enable the subject to judge the extent of your knowledge.

Example:
- 'Did you go into the filing room?'
- 'Is this in your handwriting?'
- 'Did you speak to John Jones about this?'

Closed questions normally increase the pace of an interview and, if you change rapidly from one topic to another, the suspect may have great difficulty planning his responses and become anxious. You can tell a lot by how a subject answers binary questions (Table 7.5).

Table 7.5   Answers to binary questions

Reactions indicating innocence	Reactions indicating guilt
Committed 'yes' and 'no' answers	Avoidance of a 'yes' or 'no' answer Prevarication before saying 'yes' or 'no' or superfluous words following their use. For example, *'I would like to assure you the answer is yes'* or *'Yes, in truth it is'* Lack of commitment to the answer usually by words such as *'to the best of my recollection'*
Denial of a specific point, often in first person singular, past tense	No denial, limited denial or objection

Closed questions based on what is referred to as the '7WH mnemonic' of who, why, what, where, which, when and how are always useful. Closed questions do not usually result in a free-flowing dialogue, but should be used in Phases B and C to pin down detail on the mechanics of the suspected transgression. However, if the interview results in criminal proceedings, the suggestion may be made that responses to rapid-fire, closed questions were put into the mouth of the accused. Thus closed questions should be used carefully and corroborated by detail.

Closed questions increase anxiety especially when you jump from topic to topic

COMPLEX QUESTIONS

Normally questions should be simply constructed, so that there can be no misunderstanding about the answer. Complex questions have more than one element and cannot usually be answered by a single response.

THE ULTIMATE QUESTION

In the transcript of an interview, one question covered nearly eight pages of text and consisted of 1,200 words. At the end of it, the subject said, 'Would you please repeat the question?'

You must try to ask simple questions so that misunderstanding is minimized and the subject is committed to his answers.

Avoid complex questions

But before you get on to this, think about the themes you plan to concentrate on in the interview and how you will lead the suspect to the pivotal point. Planning an interview is again like a jigsaw puzzle, so make sure all of the pieces fit. Also remember that to get to the deep truth, the suspect has to trust you, so do nothing that marks you out as untrustworthy: this does not mean that you should not be unswerving in your quest for the truth

Important responses

BACKGROUND

The normal sequence of interviews is question – answer – question and so on. But there are a number of possible responses that displace this sequence and which you should consciously plan to deal with.

REFUSAL TO ANSWER QUESTIONS

Background

Even if the suspect appears ready, willing and able to take part in an interview, there is still a possibility that he will not answer some or all questions. If he does this you know that the answers would not be in his favour and you should proceed on that basis and persuade him to answer by using some or all of the following approaches.

If someone refuses to answer a question, you know it would not be in his favour. That is all you need to know

Types of and reasons for refusal

Refusal to answer questions, which is a very strong indication of guilt and the epitome of the flee in the 'fight or flight' decision, comes in two guises – overt (conscious) and covert (unconscious), as illustrated in Table 7.6.

Refusal to answer may apply to the interview as a whole or to a specific topic or question. Either way it is usually an acknowledgement by the subject that he has no defence and that by answering questions he can only make matters worse.

Table 7.6 Refusal to answer

Category Probable motivation	Examples
Overt refusal	
I cannot defend myself	*'I am not coming to see you'* *'I am saying nothing'* *'I am saying nothing unless my lawyer is there'*
I have had a bad experience before	*'I have already been interviewed by your colleagues and I am not going over it again'*
Subtle refusal	
I cannot defend myself but do not have the courage to refuse to answer your questions	Evasion Pseudo-denials Objections Emotional outbursts *'No comment'* *'You have already made up your mind and there is no point in my explaining'*

The soft approach

You may decide to take a soft, low-key approach to the suspect's refusal to answer:

- Concede his right to remain silent and point out your interpretation of his position.

> *Example*: 'I know you do not have to say anything and that is up to you. But this problem won't go away. I have been in this business for a long time and worked with lots of people in your position. In my experience, when people say what you have just said, they are afraid of something. Innocent people always demand the right to give their side of the story. Why don't you want to discuss this?'

- Try to build rapport and berate his decision to flee.

> *Example*: 'I understand how you feel and no one likes to feel they are under suspicion. I am very open-minded and we can call it a day now if you really feel that way. Do you want to give up now, or should we see how we get on, taking a step at a time? There are always two sides to every story and we should make sure that we get yours across. Shouldn't we?'

- If the suspect walks out of the interview you have lost nothing, but it is very unlikely that he will do so. If he stays, select the weakest piece of evidence you have or an unsubstantiated allegation and help him disprove it.

> *Example*: 'We know there are two sides to every story, so let's take an example. Someone said that you have just bought a villa in Spain for £100,000 in cash. This is not correct, is it? Shall we try to get this cleared up now?'

You should repeat this process, using the weakest evidence, until the suspect is talking freely: then turn quietly to the key points.

Don't allow a liar to escape by not giving an answer

The direct approach

You may adopt the role of a critical parent and deliberately increase the suspect's anxiety by making statements summarizing the evidence and your belief in his guilt to the point where he concludes that it is in his interest to offer an explanation:

- Concede his right to remain silent and point out your interpretation of his position.

Example: 'Of course you do not have to say anything. If that is your firm decision you will have to live with the consequences. But in fairness to you I am going to tell you what evidence we have, how the investigation will move forward and what will happen. You know this will not go away just because you say nothing.'

- Pull out your notebook.

Example: 'I am going to tell you what evidence we have and I will ask for your feelings about it. If you choose to sit there and say nothing, that's up to you, but I will note down how you react, including 'no comment' and your non-verbal reactions. Do you understand?'

- Ask questions starting with a piece of weak evidence or an unsubstantiated allegation, which you know he can disprove.
- If he gives an explanation, compliment him, move on to another piece of weak evidence and keep him talking.

Example: 'You see how things can get cleared up when you are prepared to discuss them? Let's move on.'

Once people start talking it is difficult for them to stop

It is possible that the suspect will refuse to talk under either approach when incriminating issues are raised. Again, everything depends on your persuasive powers, but don't give up too easily.

The dramatic approach

This approach should be considered only in extreme situations, but it sometimes works.

> *Example*: 'Of course you do not have to say anything, but I am going to ask the questions anyway. And as you may know, 80% of human communication is though body language, the way you move, swallow, blink, move your eyes, legs, arms, body, breathe, react etc. I am going to tell you out loud how I interpret your reaction to each question and write down what I observe. Do you understand that?' Then you ask the first question and write down and say out loud: 'To that statement, Mr Smith swallowed hard, his eyes dilated and he began to sweat'. Then continue: 'Did you have access to the computer on the day in question?' Again write down and announce what you have seen: 'To that he moved his right leg, very defensively, blinked and sweat appeared on his upper lip. He had a very sheepish look about him.'

Suspects on which the above technique has been tested have begun to give oral answers after the fifth or sixth question, but you should use the technique only as the last resort and never in criminal cases, unless you want your ass severely kicked.

The legalistic approach

This is a fairly high-risk strategy, but you may point out that the problem will not simply disappear and that by refusing to answer questions, the suspect is closing down the organization's options.

> *Example*: 'Bill, the company takes this very seriously and wants to give you the chance to explain. If you continue with the way you are going the company may be forced to take civil action against you. It could get an order to compel you to produce all of your bank accounts and other records and the truth will come out. Is this really necessary? Let's start with some simple issues that we can clear up quickly and see how we go.'

Alternatively, you may caution the subject.

> *Example:* 'Bill, I have to say I find your reaction incredible. I have never known an innocent person to refuse to answer questions. You give me no option but to tell you that you are not obliged to say anything and that anything you do say may be used in evidence.'

If all of these fail, the final option is to ask the suspect to produce a written narrative.

The written narrative

You should again acknowledge the suspect's right to remain silent, but suggest to him that he might like to write down his explanation, without interruption. If he asks what he should cover, say: 'Everything you believe is important'.

> *Example*: 'I can understand that you don't like the idea of answering questions. But your explanation is very important and this is not going to go away. Please take this paper and pen and write down – in your own time and words – exactly what happened.'

This is a much more effective approach than submitting a list of written questions as these may reveal what you already know and provide the liar with a template for deception.

DEALING WITH THE FACILE PHRASE 'NO COMMENT'

In a number of recent high-profile British cases (for example, the murders of Sarah Payne and Danielle Jones) the suspects, represented by lawyers, answered every question with the facile phrase 'no comment'. They were, nonetheless, convicted. Juries are not usually stupid and when they see videos of police interviews with suspects radiating non-verbal signs of guilt set against idiotic 'no comment' responses, they come to the right conclusion.

> *Good lawyers encourage their clients to answer questions.*
> *Bad lawyers get them to say 'no comment'*

The police approach in 'no comment' cases is usually absolutely correct in that they accumulate evidence through witnesses, forensic and other techniques, and go through the motion of asking questions, and video recording the responses. The rest is left to the wheels of justice.

In the business world the same approach is not usually possible and repeated 'no comment' responses must be dealt with as though they were pathetic refusals to reply. They are invariably an admission of guilt, based on very poor legal advice, low intelligence and a manifestation of the 'flee' response.

DEALING WITH EVASION, PSEUDO-DENIALS AND OTHER STUFF

Subconsciously, most liars cannot bring themselves to be committed to a firm denial, in the first person singular, past tense, but will produce pseudo-denials (such as *'Why should I do that?'*) or limited denials or objections (such as *'I could not have done it because I did not have the access codes'*). Even more significant are those cases where a suspect *should* fail to make a denial.

> *If a person does not make a spontaneous-committed denial, the chances are he is guilty*

Genuine denials are spontaneous, committed and can be in response to a vague allegation of responsibility or a direct accusation. *You should normally accept spontaneous-committed denials, especially when they are in the first person singular, past tense, as a sign of truthfulness.*

You can overcome psuedo-denials, evasions and other devices by emphasizing the strength of the evidence and pinning the suspect down to detail, thereby increasing his anxiety to levels at which he believes he can no longer succeed with deception. This usually calls for a professional and relentless approach, attention to the finest detail and focus on the suspect and the mechanics of what he has done.

DEALING WITH FREUDIAN SLIPS AND SPOONERISMS

Most times, people let Freudian slips, incomplete sentences, changes in direction within a sentence and spoonerisms pass without comment; this is an opportunity lost. Such slips result from thrashing between conscious and subconscious states and between memory and imagination. Immediately after making them the suspect is vulnerable to further disclosures. You should stop the suspect at the first opportunity, point out the error and ask what he really intended to say.

Freudian slips are direct from the subconscious and always have a meaning

DEALING WITH SUSPECTED LIES

Principles
From now on, challenge every bad lie because if you fail to do so, problems will only get worse. As a minimum, press for more detail and make the liar falsify.

Every falsification is a step towards finding the truth; every successful concealment lie is a step away

Making the right assumption
Although people tell lies for strange reasons, you should treat every provable lie, or failure to answer a relevant question, as though it were an admission of guilt. There will be occasions when this assumption is wrong, but it is the safe course to take.

There are two reasons why lies must be challenged. The first is that letting a subject succeed builds his confidence, reduces his anxiety and makes it less likely he will ever reach the pivotal point. The second is that it makes it more difficult for him to admit the truth later on, simply because he then has two problems to admit: the original transgression, and the fact that he lied to you.

Lies must be challenged

Dealing with most lies
The main options for dealing with lies are detailed in Table 7.7.

You should use the suspect's vulnerability immediately after being detected in a lie to ask an important question to which you do not know the answer or where evidence is weak.

> *Example*: 'Bill, I am going to ask you another important question, and in view of what has just happened I want you to be very careful how you answer. Now what … ?'

You should never, ever, whatever the circumstances call someone a 'liar' as it is a deep attack on his character and implies he never tells the truth. It is much better to attack the false or misleading statement (which is not a deep attack on his character) or specific action by saying something along the lines: 'Come on, Bill, you know that is not true.'

Attack the false statement and not the person making it

Dealing with the obdurate liar
There will be some occasions when the liar will take an unshakeable position and has no intention of telling the truth. If this happens, don't give up but take your time and pull out your

Table 7.7   Dealing with lies

Ways of dealing with a lie	Comments
Low-key	
Look away, up or down, pull your ear lobe, put your hand over your mouth, smile, or brush non-existent dust off your arm while the person is giving the false explanation	These are body language statements that tell the suspect that you do not believe him, without your uttering a word
Hold up your hand, like a traffic policeman	
Politely interrupt the lie by saying: *'I am having real difficulty understanding this. Help me understand and tell me why ...'*	This is a soft challenge
Point out that the suspect must have misunderstood the question and ask it again	This is a low-key approach, but achieves the objective of not allowing the person to escape with a lie
Interrupt the statement and say: *'Come on, Bill...'*	If he defers to this interruption, the chances are he is guilty and will confess
Say: *'That was not true, Mr Smith. I am going to ask the question again and please be very careful how you answer it ...'*	This raises the stakes. It will cause a liar to think carefully. An innocent person may object
Joke about the answer: *'Oh yes, and pigs fly ... now come on, Bill, what about...'*	This approach depends on the status of the subject, and his relationship with the interviewer. Don't try it on the chairman!
Say: *'Please stop right now. You are making things much worse'*	A statement along these lines should be delivered from the transactional role of a critical parent
Pull out your notebook and say something along the lines: *'That is absolutely incredible, Mr Smith ... I just cannot believe it is true. Please go over what you said again ...'*	This raises the stakes. It will cause a liar to think carefully. An innocent person may object
Direct challenges	

notepad and ask and repeat minutely detailed questions which lead the suspect into *barefaced*, foolish, unbelievable explanations, which even he may realize cannot be justified.

Depending on the nature of the case, you can also raise the pavement by saying something along the following lines.

Example: 'As you know, we will be relying totally on the truthfulness of your answers for [e.g. paying this claim]. You know it is a criminal offence to try to obtain money by deception, and if you are not sure about [the lie], now is the time to clear it up. It is not too late now, but next week it will be. Shall we clear this up now?'

In extreme cases you may say something along the lines: *'This is totally unbelievable, Bill. I would like you to make a written statement about this'* (or agree a note on this). You should take down a statement or note, with as much detail *(most of which will be false)* as possible. When the statement has been completed, you should ask: *'Are you sure you really want to sign this? Do you want us to start again?'* If the liar refuses, at worst, you have a damning deceitful statement, which he will find difficult to defend later on. If he changes his mind, chances are you *will* get to the deep truth.

Let the liar know his lies prove his guilt

DEALING WITH ADMITTED LIES

The suspect is brought nearer to the pivotal point every time he has to admit trying to mislead you, when he has to change a previous explanation or admit he has been less than frank. You should always press home your advantage by:

- Asking an important question where the answer is not already known or provable.

> *Example*: 'Tom, I am very disappointed that you tried to mislead me over this. I am going to ask you another very important question and I want you to think carefully before you answer it.'

- You should be prepared to compliment the suspect on an honest answer or admission along the lines:

> *Example*: 'Tom, it took courage to tell me that. Now let's deal with x.' (Another important topic.)

Reward truthful statements

DEALING WITH ANGER

Background

Genuine anger is the embodiment of 'fight' in the 'fight or flight' decision and may be directed at you, something you have done, or at a third party, and usually peaks and takes time to subside. Anger is an equal transaction between critical parents and rebellious children, but it is a very dangerous emotion for the subject for the following reasons:

- It opens a direct circuit to his subconscious (actually his limbic system), thus making it likely that he will make unplanned admissions or Freudian slips.
- A person who has gone overboard with an expression of anger usually becomes contrite and, thereafter, is vulnerable.

Thus you should always regard a suspect's anger – whether genuine or contrived – as a positive step forward in finding the truth. However, angry people do not make deep confessions, and so you must move the suspect to a less emotional position.

Angry people are exposed to making mistakes

Method of approach with genuine anger

Remember you have all of the advantages: you are not emotionally involved or at risk, while the subject is. You must tune the subject off his negative, emotional wavelength:

- Try to understand the cause of his anger and whether it is genuine or contrived. Ask yourself what the subject is hoping to achieve by his outburst.
- Stay emotionally detached, take nothing the subject says personally and let him know his anger will not deflect you.

> *Example*: 'Bill, I understand. It is a shame you are angry, but it is not going to make a scrap of difference to the way we resolve this. We can all get angry and that will get us nowhere. Now let's move on …'

- Turn to a nurturing parent role and state that you understand the subject's feelings, but do not concede the grounds for his anger. You may say you will review them later.
- Stress that you need to move beyond the present problem and try to resolve the larger issues.

> *Example*: 'I can understand how you feel, but I cannot comment on [the reasons for his anger], but I promise I will look into that later. All I know is that we should move forward and try to sort out this problem. Now, what about [ask about a *key point*]'

- Go back to a previous point in the interview when the subject was not angry, and move forward from there.

> *Example*: 'Bill, a few moments ago we were getting along fine and there is absolutely no reason why you and I should fall out. Now let's go back and start again …'

The key is for you to keep talking, to try to establish rapport with the subject and try to concede nothing. If this fails and genuine anger fails to dissipate, ask open questions.

> *Example*:
> - 'Let us go over what happened. Take me through the problem, step by step.'
> - 'Tell me, what can we do to resolve this?'
> - 'How can we make sure it does not happen again?'

Continue to ask open questions and, as soon as you can, return to the main focus of the interview.

Never test the water with both feet

Method of approach with falsified anger

False anger is usually employed as a device to distract you. If you believe anger is being fabricated, adopt the role of a critical parent and say something along the lines:

Example: 'Come on. Let's move onwards. This is getting you nowhere.'

Your aim is to shock the subject on to a sensible course. If the anger proves genuine, this approach may raise the temperature for a few moments, but will enable you to regain control. You may also consider taking notes of the subject's complaints.

Genuine and manufactured anger are totally different

DEALING WITH COUNTER-ATTACKS

This is one of the most difficult areas for the inexperienced interviewer, whose reaction is to panic when the suspect counter-attacks with statements such as:

Example:
- 'I am going to sue you.'
- 'My lawyer will be in touch.'
- 'Are you calling me a liar?'

If possible, you may pretend you have not heard the statement and carry on with the next question, regardless. If this does not work, you must stay cool and say something along the lines:

Example: 'I am not interested in that, Mr Jones, now what about ...'

If this approach fails, you should say:

Example: 'Let's leave that until later; I am trying to find the truth. Please tell me why ...'

It is vital that you do not get into an argument but ask the next question without hesitating. To the very common attack:

'Are you calling me a liar?'

you should respond:

'No, but it is obvious that you have not told me the truth: now what about …'

Only in exceptional circumstances should you back down or apologize. You must stay in control and move on to the next question without delay, as though it were the natural thing to do.

Stay cool in the face of counter-attacks

DEALING WITH DEPRESSION

People in a depressive state seldom confess, simply because they are so immersed in their internal conflicts that they are unprepared to face reality. You must try to find out why the person is depressed and to focus on the future and how the problem can be resolved. Also try to get the person to look upwards by holding an exhibit (not one that is too incriminating) above eye level or pinning it to the wall. Also, if you can get him to laugh or smile, you may jump-start him into a more positive frame of mind.

THE FAMOUS CASE OF ARTHUR

Arthur lived in South London and was a career conman. He gained employment, using false qualifications, as marketing director for a leading financial institution, which he then defrauded to the tune of £19 million. He initially refused to be interviewed by either the police or investigators employed by the victim company, but one morning investigators called at his house, without warning. Arthur, being a little short-sighted, mistook them for estate agents and let them in.

After more than a little prevarication he began to answer questions but when they turned to critical issues, Arthur threw himself on the floor and beat his hands, feet and head against it with considerable violence, saying: 'My life is in ruins: it has been destroyed. I am an unworthy father. I am going to kill myself.'

Investigators were not perturbed and gently placed exhibits under his prostrate figure and said, 'Come on, Arthur, what about this?' One eye furtively opened, then another and then further outbursts of sorrow and woe. 'I am going to jump out of the window, right now, and kill myself.' The investigators coolly pointed out that he was in his lounge which was on the ground floor and that he should stop 'fooling about'. Arthur burst into fits of uncontrolled laughter, cooled down and confessed. As the investigators were leaving he said: 'Do you know, I feel much better. Can you and your wives join my wife and me at a jazz dinner tomorrow? It should be a great night.' The offer was politely refused.

Try to get him to smile

DEALING WITH WAFFLE AND RAMBLING

These diversionary tactics are very popular, especially among politicians. You should remain consciously on the lookout and stop the rambler in his tracks by interjections such as 'That is extremely interesting, Bill, but can we get back to x', or 'Can we stop there. I have only ten minutes left so can you please summarize your position in that time.'

Stop waffle in its tracks

DEALING WITH SPONTANEOUS LOSSES OF MEMORY

Phrases such as 'I don't remember', when the person has made no attempt to access his memory, are signs of deception. Where you suspect deliberate deception, you should respond:

Example: 'How can you say that? You haven't given the question a single moment's thought. I am going to ask the question again, so please take a few moments and think carefully ...'

If this approach does not succeed, you should ask detailed questions about emotions and attitudes, or reverse questions (see page 208) and try to bring the suspect's memory to a conscious level. The liar will usually make no effort to latch on to the memory retrieval cues but will continue with an obdurate 'can't remember'. However, he *will* remember, and repression of memories will increase anxiety.

Don't accept the answer 'I don't remember'.
Try everything to make the suspect remember

DEALING WITH BODY LANGUAGE

Background
You must remain consciously aware of your own and the subject's non-verbal communications.

The subject's body language
Let the suspect know you have noticed his negative body language signals and deny him the comfort of manipulators. You can do this by looking closely at the offending movement or moving slowly and deliberately to mirror it. If you are in any doubt, or don't know what a particular non-verbal communication means, mime it and let the subject see you doing it.

Example: Any golfing reader who does not believe in the power of mimicry should, at a critical stage of a match, make an exaggerated copy of his opponent's putting stroke! Watch the very disturbing result. 'Do I really putt like that?' the gullible golfer says. 'Of course not,' you sincerely reply, smiling, but you know the seeds of doubt have been sown.

You may also get the subject to move from a negative posture (such as high, defensive crossing of his arms) by regularly handing him documents to read or by asking him to move to examine a chart on the wall.

Deny the suspect the comfort of manipulators

Similarly remain consciously alert to the way the subject uses his personal space. If he moves his chair away from you or leans back (both signs of withdrawal and possible deception), move your chair closer or get up and stand behind him. The object, again, is to deprive him of anxiety reduction positions.

Your own non-verbal communication

Your own body language should be driven by your subconscious and therefore consistent with your verbal statements, emotions and attitudes. However, in the following circumstances you may decide to take conscious control (Table 7.8).

If you don't believe in the power of non-verbal communications, next time you speak to your boss, pull your ear lobe or slowly place your hand up over your mouth while he is speaking. See what happens; but be prepared for a change of job.

Table 7.8 The interviewer's body language

Circumstances	Your body language
When the suspect does not tell the truth	• Pointing with the fingers • Looking away • Head moving slowly left to right • Leaning forward • Intruding on the suspect's personal space • Hand over mouth • Pull ear lobe • Brush lint off your clothing
When the suspect tells the truth	• Palms upward gestures with the hands • Looking at the suspect and smiling • Head moving slowly up and down • Leaning backward • Increasing the suspect's personal space
When the suspect uses a manipulator such as brushing dust off his clothes	• Look carefully at the movement • Mimic the movement (mirroring) • Ask if the question is worrying him
Critical balancing point	• Mimic the suspect's body language

DEALING WITH FISHING QUESTIONS

Sometimes a suspect will say something along the lines:

Example:
• 'You tell me what you know and I will give an answer.'
Or
• 'I am not prepared to answer general questions: let me see the evidence you have and I will answer it.'

In such cases, the suspect is simply trying to find out how much you know so that he can deal with it without giving anything else away.

Your response should be along the following lines:

> *Example*: 'I am trying to find out whether you are telling me the whole truth or not. It is a bit like being asked by Customs whether you have anything to declare. If you don't tell me the whole truth now, I have to draw my own conclusions that you are not being honest. Now please tell me everything, and I mean everything, about…'

A common fishing question is along the following lines at the pivotal point:

> *Example*: 'I did not do it, but as a matter of interest, what could happen? Would the person be fired or what?'

Great care has to be taken at this stage. Obviously you would not say:

> *Example*: 'The bastard would go to prison and they would throw the key away.'

On the other hand, you must not mislead anyone. The safe course is to say something along the lines:

> *Example*: 'I don't know, Bill, but I don't think telling the truth can make it any worse. Now why did all this start?'

Fishing questions are a step away from admissions

Introductory statements – Phase A

THE OPTIONS

Your choice of opening depends on the strength of the existing evidence and the level of certainty in the suspect's guilt.

You may merge or adapt the alternatives but, whichever one you choose, there are a number of common factors. We will deal with the options later.

FORMALITIES

You must get into an adult-to-adult or critical parent role as quickly as you can and take command. You must be totally committed in everything you say, how you say it and in your body language.

If you are not already known to the suspect, you should either introduce yourself and any colleague, or be introduced by a very senior manager who will emphasize the importance of the interview.

Example: 'Bill, this is Mr Jones, who is an HR adviser. We have asked him to investigate x and he has my full authority. He has worked on hundreds of cases around the world and has (list any impressive accomplishments). I am sure you will cooperate with him.' The manager should then leave the room.

You should always offer to shake hands and in the unlikely event that the offer is refused, look the suspect firmly in the eyes and say something along the lines of: *'That tells me all I need to know'*. Then continue, without pausing, to the opening. If he accepts the offer, make sure your handshake is not like a wet kipper: you must appear positive and committed.

USING NAMES

If you do not already know the suspect, the safe course is to address him as 'Mister' followed by his surname. However, with senior people, and to establish an equal adult-to-adult trans-actional role, you should use his first name. If you want to unbalance a pompous suspect you might call him by his first name but refer to his and your colleagues – many of whom will be junior to him – as 'Mister'.

Example: 'Bill, this is Mr Jones [the most junior member of HR]. I have spoken to Mr Smith [Bill's junior] and he will handle your calls for the next few hours, so would you please turn off your mobile telephone.'

You can further unbalance an overly important suspect if you start off calling him by his first name and later in the interview, when he is being deceptive, revert to 'Mister Smith' or start addressing him as 'Mister' and at the pivotal point use his first name. Small changes in the way you address the suspect will help you change roles from adult to critical parent and from critical to nurturing parent.

AVOIDING PADDING

The natural instinct of most interviewers is to prevaricate (in much the same way that suspects have problems in bringing themselves to address critical issues), ask irrelevant questions with which they feel comfortable or talk about the weather, a current event or even golf. This is always counter-productive, because it gives the suspect time to settle down.

Avoid any social chit-chat and only ask questions on how a process operates or what work the suspect does, if:

- The information is vital and the suspect is the only person who can give an explanation.
- It is essential to prove the suspect's knowledge of the process and to block off an untrue excuse later in the interview.
- The suspect can be enticed into giving an explanation which will later trap him.

In other cases, questions about responsibilities and processes tend to reduce the suspect's fear of detection and his opinion of you. So get straight to the point. If you need to prove a suspect's knowledge of a process, you can summarize it in your own words and ask for his agreement that it is correct. This approach may avoid endless questions and puts you in control.

Remember there are two interviews taking place and the suspect is trying to assess you

PREPARE FOR AN IMMEDIATE ATTACK

Even the best planning can be thrown off track if the suspect, or his lawyer, immediately takes a confrontational approach. Remember that attacks, especially at the start of an interview, are part of the liar's conscious fight or flight decision, and are most likely to be a deliberate attempt to gain control. Plan to deal with this as you would with any counter-attack (see page 187) and don't panic.

PLAN SAFE HAVENS

From time to time, the interview may go off course and it is wise to plan the safe points to which you will return in times of trouble. This may be a single-page schedule of a key point indicating the suspect's guilt.

THE SAFE HAVEN

At any point you can say: 'Forget about that, Bill, now let's come back to this.'

You should then move forward from that point.

OPTION 1: THE FACTUAL-TESTING OPENING

This is probably the safest option when the existing evidence is uncertain or where you are unsure of the suspect's guilt. You will use the first part of the interview to test his reaction to questions and to decide whether he is being truthful or not. Even when criminal prosecution is an objective, you technically do not have to administer a caution with this opening because you will use it only when the suspect's guilt is in doubt. If you are less than 50 per cent certain that the suspect is responsible for the problems concerned, consider using the elimination approach suggested in Chapter 11. Where responsibility is over 50 per cent and less than 80 per cent certain[1] the opening statement should include:

- who you are and what you do;
- what the suspicions are;
- how the investigation has been and will be conducted;
- confirmation that the organization has limitless time and resources and intends to find the truth;
- your wish to give the suspect the chance to explain.

For example, the opening – with a purchasing agent who may have taken bribes – may be along the following lines:

---

[1]   As best you can approximate

UNCERTAIN GUILT AND EVIDENCE

'I am Roger Jones from HR and I am investigating very serious allegations of corruption involving a number of vendors. The company takes this very seriously and will make every effort to find the truth. Investigations like this take time but I am sure you agree that bribery is a very big problem …' (pause and note reaction) '… and it is usually the purchasing agent that takes all of the blame as vendors run for cover and to protect their other businesses say that they were forced into paying and had no alternative. In my experience, this is seldom the case, but that's the way it always seems to go.

'Vendors know that we can take civil action to force them to produce their records or get the police involved. They also know that someone will always talk to save their own skin.' (Pause.) 'The facts always come out.

'We have got a lot of evidence already which we need to discuss. [To be fair with everyone involved and allow you to give your side of events, I have to tell you that you do not have to say anything unless *you* wish to do so and that anything you do say may be used in evidence.] I am particularly interested in AB Jones and Company Limited, what can you tell me about them?'

From this opening you can move into Phase B and ask more probing questions, if necessary increasing anxiety through Phase C until the suspect reaches the pivotal point. Alternatively, you may decide that the suspect is truthful and can be removed from suspicion. If this happens, don't end the interview too quickly, but try to encourage the subject as a witness or informant.

OPTION 2: BLOCKING QUESTIONS

You may choose this opening when you have good reason to believe the suspect is responsible, but that he may be able to produce a plausible excuse. The object is to give him the chance to volunteer potentially incriminating information and, if he fails to do so, to block a plausible but deceptive excuse later on. For example, in a price-fixing case the opening might be as follows:

'We have received a complaint that some of our salesmen have been fixing prices with retailers and this could cause very serious problems. The company is determined to find the truth and will leave no stone unturned to do so. I know that these things happen and that sales people, to make a sale, sometimes bend the rules. But now is the time for everyone to clear the air. It's not the end of the world, but we need to know.

- Do you understand the rules on price-fixing?
- Have you ever fixed prices with retailers?
- Have you ever had discussions with retailers or anyone else on fixing prices?
- Has anyone ever discussed price-fixing with you?
- What would you do if anyone ever asked you to fix prices?
- What would you do if you knew about anyone else fixing prices?
- Is there anything you know which could be relevant to our investigation?'

From this opening you should move on to a factual analysis of the evidence and Phase B.

OPTION 3: THE INTRODUCTORY STATEMENT

The introductory statement is very important and should be used where there are reasonable grounds for believing that the suspect is responsible and may be deceptive. You should write down the words you intend to use and rehearse them so that you do not have to refer to your notes. If criminal prosecution is an objective, you should include the caution in an introductory statement consisting of five main elements:

- who you are and what you do (if you have not already explained this);
- how the investigation has been and will be conducted, and administer a caution;
- indirect or soft accusation;
- bridging statement;
- rationalization.

For example, the introductory statement in an interview with an insurance company employee who is believed to have colluded with a gang making false claims might be along the following lines.

'I manage a team of four investigators who investigate frauds against the company and we travel the world. We handle around 200 cases a year and most are successful. In some we press for criminal prosecution and in others – where the people concerned have helped us – we can take a more sympathetic approach. [Caution] I want us to work together on this. It is in everyone's interest that we establish the truth. [Pause]

'Some people seem to think that making bad claims is a bit like saving on income tax, but this is not so. Ultimately, other policyholders pay, and making false claims is a very serious matter, which results in the loss of jobs and damage to our reputation. [Pause]

'We have been investigating a case in which false claims have been made to us for medical insurance. The people concerned have been claiming serious injuries, but we know that many are untrue. Thousands of pounds are involved and the company is taking the matter very seriously and will leave no stone unturned to find the truth. We believe that at least one employee has been dragged into this [Pause] and this is what we are currently investigating.

'Before we conduct interviews, we do a great deal of background research. We keep surveillance on policyholders who claim they have been injured, take videos of them running around, playing tennis and doing all sorts of things they say their injuries prevent them from doing. We interview neighbours, family members and so on and we build up the evidence until we are really sure of our facts.

'As far as employees are concerned, we audit the claims they have handled very carefully and look for patterns. We sometimes keep surveillance on them and see them meeting claimants. Sometimes we see money being handed over. In other cases we have observed them going to nightclubs together and doing other things that would make it clear to the employee that the claimed injuries are fraudulent. Sometimes, with the permission of top management, we will monitor the employee's office telephone, inspect his computer and check his files. We take great care to establish the facts. [Pause]

'Sometimes employees get pressurized into cooperating with false claims and, when this is the case, we will try to support them if they are honest with us. [Pause]

'In other cases, we find employees drift into these cases. Not because they are really bad people, but they just drift, often without realizing the seriousness of what is going on. But at the end of the day, the claimants blame the employees to save their own skins. They do this because they think they can embarrass us into not taking action. This is never the case. But I see lots of really good employees in serious trouble because of crooks.'

You should carefully monitor the suspect's reaction as this opening is delivered (Table 7.9).

Table 7.9   Most likely reactions to an opening statement

Reactions indicating innocence	Reactions indicating guilt
Listens carefully but does not appear threatened	Does not listen carefully
Relaxed body language	Moves body into a defensive position
Finds the story interesting or even boring	Nervous body language
May ask if you are accusing him	Unlikely to challenge the statement

If the suspect's reaction is indicative of guilt, you should plan to make a soft accusation.

Example: 'The trouble is that the employee involved may believe he can succeed by not telling the truth, and that the outsiders will cover for him. The fact is that this investigation will look into everything and we are determined to get to the truth. If the employee concerned is not prepared to tell the truth when we give him the chance, so be it. He must know that the game is up.'

If the suspect's reaction continues to be passive, you should continue with a bridging statement, which moves from an indirect accusation to the specific.

Example: 'The trouble is, Tom, I think you are involved in this and it is important that we work together to clear it up.'

The suspect will either move into an acceptance position (in which case plan your approach in line with page 224 or make a denial. In the worst case, you can continue, from any point, with a factual approach or revert to a safe haven (see page 193). If the suspect launches an attack, remain cool:

Example: 'Bill, I have been very fair with you and I have told you exactly what I believe the evidence shows. But I have an open mind, so please explain x [deal with one of the key points].'

OPTION 4: DIRECT CONFRONTATION

In rare cases, where the evidence is already overwhelming you may use an assumptive opening (i.e. that the suspect is guilty beyond doubt) and ambush him. This gives him minimal time to compose himself, although it may result in an angry outburst that you will have to control, probably by reverting to a safe haven.

The suspect should be kept waiting in the interview room and should ideally be seated. You should enter holding a file, stand within the suspect's personal space and deliver a direct accusation. For example, where the objective is criminal prosecution and the suspect is believed to have stolen a number of personal computers from the company, the opening might be as follows:

Example: 'Good morning, Mr Smith. I am Bill Jones from the Audit Department. We are investigating a case of theft of computers from the sales office. [Caution] The evidence we have makes it clear that you are responsible and I want to give you the chance to tell me about it and to work with me to get our property back.'

You should then sit down and wait for the suspect's response. From this point onwards, you are on your own, but remember the principles and the fact that you can always revert to a safe haven.

OPTION 5: THE FORMALITY

This approach can be used where the evidence is already overwhelming, and the main objective of the interview is to give the suspect the opportunity to give his explanation. This is usually essential if disciplinary proceedings are intended.

Example: 'Bill, we have been investigating an allegation that you have been taking kickbacks from vendors. I want to give you the chance of putting your side of the story. To be fair, and to enable you to give your side of the story, I have to advise you …[Caution].'

You then cover the key points, committing the suspect to detailed replies and more and more indefensible lies. You may, or may not, decide to try to reach the pivotal point and the turn.

THE BUSINESS MEETING

You eventually get Bill Smith off the golf course (continuing the saga from page 170), sit him down in a nice quiet room and then get into your introductory statement:

'Bill, as you know, we have been trying to see you for some weeks to get your explanation. My name is Tom Williams and I am a barrister and psychiatrist [but only if this is true!]. This is Jane Marshall and she is from Human Resources. The purpose of this interview is to give you the opportunity of explaining why you have been absent from work for so long, failed to appear when asked, abandoned your job …'

Bill tries to interrupt, but you continue: 'Please let me finish: abandoned your job and been less than frank with us in telling us that you were in hospital today when in fact you were playing golf. So that there can be no misunderstanding, we intend to get to the truth, however long it takes and costs. Why did you tell us you were in hospital today?'

With such an opening, Bill Smith is in a very unenviable position, from which he is unlikely to recover.

Probing and testing questions – Phase B

INTRODUCTION

The structure of this phase obviously depends on the success, or otherwise, of the opening but it is generally applicable when you are not certain whether the suspect is responsible or not and want to test his honesty. In effect you become a human polygraph machine. If you are already certain that the suspect is responsible, you may skip this stage, although it can be used to steadily increase anxiety.

   The following paragraphs describe the questions and possible responses, but you should always keep an open mind because there is an exception to every rule.

PROFILE OF DECEPTION QUESTIONS

Experience shows that the way liars answer questions can be profiled. For example, they tend to minimize the seriousness of the case, fail to make committed first person singular, past tense denials and use subjective truths and evasion. Questions based on these profiles are especially relevant to elimination interviews and are discussed in Chapter 11. You can adapt this approach for any interview when there are a number of suspects and you wish to eliminate the innocent and identify the guilty.

BLOCKING QUESTIONS

Blocking questions, which are usually asked early in an interview, are intended to 'block off' an exculpatory, but untrue, explanation later on. A suspect's denials, when given the opportunity to volunteer information, go towards proving his guilty intent. On the other hand, honest answers to blocking questions can quickly clear an innocent person of suspicion.

   Probably the most common blocking question of all is used by Customs Officers when you arrive in a country.

Example:

Question: 'Have you anything to declare?'

Answer: 'No, (because) I spent all of my money before I got to the duty free shop.'

Block: 'Have you read this notice which shows what you are allowed to import duty free?'

Answer: 'Yes, but obviously I have not read every word.' (Lack of commitment.)

Block: 'So you are telling me you have nothing with you in excess of those allowances.'

Answer: 'That's right. I never buy duty free stuff.' (Generalization.)

Block: 'And is there any possibility that you may have forgotten something you have bought while overseas?'

Answer: 'No, not unless Father Christmas got into my case.' (Misplaced humour.)

When the passenger's bags are subsequently searched and expensive jewellery and a credit card voucher for its purchase discovered, he is left with no plausible excuse. His answers have established guilty knowledge and pinned him into a corner.

You may use blocking questions to test to what extent the subject is going to volunteer information.

PRE-EMPLOYMENT
'Have you ever used narcotic drugs such as cocaine, crack or heroin?' 'No.' 'Or cannabis, LSD or ecstasy?' 'Not that I can recall.' 'But you have experimented with them?' 'Yes, but I did not inhale.' 'Then why didn't you volunteer that information when I first asked you?' 'Because you only asked about cocaine, crack and heroin.' 'I used the words narcotic drugs and gave them as an example to see how honest you were. I think you were playing on words. Now I want to ask you a very serious question about [important topic].'

You should consider using blocking questions when you have incriminating evidence, which – under the deception theory – the suspect may be able to explain with a plausible, but false, excuse. The suspect's responses to blocking questions are very important (Table 7.10).

Blocking questions should be asked in a low-key way so that you do not alert the suspect to their real significance. If he fails to volunteer the truth, this omission should be used later to increase his anxiety.

> *Example*: 'A few moments ago I asked you if you had ever claimed expenses to which you were not entitled and you said that you had not. I asked the question again and you gave the same reply. I am now going to show you this claim. It is false, isn't it?'

If the suspect admits to being less than open in response to a blocking question, you should press home your advantage by pointing out the seriousness of the attempted deception and then ask an important question to which the answer is not already known.

> *Example*: 'Your attempt to mislead me was very unfortunate. I am now going to give you the opportunity to tell me all about [another important topic]. Please take great care over this. You don't want to make the same mistake twice, do you?'

Blocking questions are very difficult for the liar

Table 7.10 Possible responses to blocking questions

Reactions indicating innocence	Reactions indicating guilt
Will usually make a full and honest disclosure and thereby clear himself of suspicion	Will fail to make an honest disclosure when given the opportunity May seek clarification of the question His response is most likely to avoid commitment

INVITE THE SUBJECT TO VOLUNTEER

Ask the suspect whether there is anything he would like to tell you, and that this is his opportunity to come forward with any honest explanation. Warn him if he does not take this opportunity, the evidence will come out and the fact that he has not offered the truth, when given this chance, will obviously add to his difficulties. The guilty person will be stretched by this question and will normally be very careful over the answer he gives (Table 7.11).

QUESTIONS TO WHICH THE ANSWERS ARE KNOWN

In addition to preparing visual summaries of the key points (see page 156) you should also make a special note of the evidence or intelligence that the suspect may not know you have. You can then pose questions, based on this knowledge, to test the accuracy of his replies (Table 7.12).

THE GOLFING HOLIDAY

For example, if you have conclusive evidence that the suspect went on an expensive golfing holiday paid for by a vendor, you may casually ask:

Interviewer:	'Have you ever been paid cash by a vendor?'
Suspect:	'No' *(Single word, binary answer: probably truthful)*
Interviewer:	'Been given cars, watches, expensive jewellery?'
Suspect:	'No' *(Single word, binary answer: probably truthful)*
Interviewer:	'Received any other direct or indirect benefit from a vendor?'
Suspect:	'No, except for a few golf balls' *(Note the qualified denial: untruthful)*
Interviewer:	'Had holidays paid for or anything like that?'
Suspect:	'No. Why should I do that?' *(Qualified denial with a question answered by a question and probably hiding responsibility)*

Dishonest replies must be challenged and the subject made to face the truth. You should immediately follow up all instances where the suspect has been caught in a lie or evasion with an important question to which the answer is not known.

Table 7.11   Most likely reactions to an opportunity to volunteer information

Reactions indicating innocence	Reactions indicating guilt
Volunteers facts, some of which may be against his self-interest (e.g. that he had made a mistake)	Prevarication and failure to volunteer information or *'What do you expect me to say?'*

THE TRIP TO PRAGUE

You know that the suspect downgraded his business-class ticket and took his girlfriend with him on an all-expenses paid trip to Prague. You have obtained a copy of the voucher from the travel agency. You do not know whether he did the same thing on a business trip to New York.

You ask:	'Did you travel by yourself to Prague?'
Suspect:	'Why are you asking that?' (*Question with a question: probably deceptive*)
You say:	'Because I want to know.'
Suspect:	'Yes. I always travel by myself.' (*Generalization: probably deceptive*)

You show him the voucher.

He responds:	'OK. I took Janet with me. So what? It did not cost the company any more money and everyone does it. I did nothing wrong.' (*Rationalization*)
You say:	'And you took her with you to New York in July?' (*Assumptive question*)
Suspect:	'Yes.'
You say:	'Now please be very careful answering this. On what other occasions have you downgraded your ticket, taken the cash or taken someone else with you on a business trip?'
Suspect:	'I have never taken cash.' (*Partial denial.*)
You say:	'OK, on how many other occasions has someone else travelled with you?'

Suspect hesitates while thrashing for an answer.

You interject:	'Twenty or thirty times?' (*Interjection*)
Suspect:	'No, less than that … Maybe five or ten times.' (*Admission*)

The suspect thinks and gives details of five other trips.

You say:	'Are you absolutely certain this is everything?'
Suspect:	'To the best of my recollection, yes it is.' (*Lack of commitment*)
You say:	'If you believed that you had done nothing wrong, why did you tell me that you always travelled by yourself?'

You continue to press the point and the suspect admits that he knew he was breaking the law. Now you turn to the deep truth and ask him to tell you who else does the same thing.

An answer that is already known can be used to test the subject's honesty

This sequence can be regarded as the 'naughty puppy rule': the suspect does not want to get immediately found out in another lie and is likely to answer honestly or, if he does not, he is likely to push his anxiety further up the scale.

> *Example*: 'Bill, we have got off to a bad start and you tried to mislead me over [x]. I am now going to ask you about [y] and I want you to think carefully before you try to answer it. Now what did you do with the money?'

Table 7.12   Most likely reactions to questions to which the answer is known

Reactions indicating innocence	Reactions indicating guilt
Answers that accord with known facts	Answers that do not accord with known facts

QUESTIONS ON THE KEY POINTS

You should ask questions on the key points and seek the subject's detailed responses to them. Specific indicators of guilt and deception – *in addition to those explained in Chapter 4* – are usually as follows (Table 7.13).

Table 7.13   Most likely reactions to questions based on key points

Reactions indicating innocence	Reactions indicating guilt
Clear answers with consistent detail	Evasion, subjective truths and inconsistent detail
Commitment	Lack of commitment
Quick responses	Slow, censored replies
Refusal to change an explanation in the light of new evidence	Changes story to fit emerging evidence
Positive non-verbal clues	Negative non-verbal clues

RELUCTANCE TO PROVIDE DETAIL

Ask control and relevant questions to test the subject's memory and recall of detail. Do not permit him to deceive you through concealment lies. When in doubt push for more and more detail and take your time (Table 7.14).

Table 7.14   Most likely reactions to requests for detail

Reactions indicating innocence	Reactions indicating guilt
Consistent, free-flowing detailed answers to both control and relevant questions	Evasion and inconsistent detail

UNWILLINGNESS TO COMMIT

Ask questions that require the suspect to commit to detailed, unambiguous answers and, for very important points, confirm this commitment with him (Table 7.15).

> *Example*: 'Bill, you have told me [x]. We both know this is a very important point. Are you absolutely sure. Is there any doubt in your mind?'

Table 7.15   Most likely reactions to a requirement to commit

Reactions indicating innocence	Reactions indicating guilt
Committed responses	Evasion, subjective truths and lack of commitment

ENTICEMENT QUESTIONS

Many suspects will tell you only what they believe you can already prove and will hold back damaging information if they can. You may do the same, obtain a denial or prevarication and then confront him with the contradictory evidence (Table 7.16).

Table 7.16   Most likely reactions to enticement questions

Reactions indicating innocence	Reactions indicating guilt
Will usually be reluctant to change an earlier explanation	May ask 'fishing questions' (see page 190) and then change his explanation to fit the new facts
May dispute the newly produced evidence	

The suspect's confidence is eroded every time he has to change an explanation or agree that he has not told you the whole truth. After such admissions, you should ask questions to which the answers are not known and press for detailed answers.

ASK HIM TO REPEAT

At appropriate times say: 'Would you please repeat that, I am not sure I heard you correctly.' Your tone should imply that you heard, but did not believe what was being said (Table 7.17).

Table 7.17   Most likely reactions to a request to repeat

Reactions indicating innocence	Reactions indicating guilt
Will repeat the answer with consistent levels of detail	More likely to prevaricate, feigned anger, reluctant to repeat

REPEAT IMPORTANT QUESTIONS

You may repeat important questions, each time pressing for more detail (Table 7.18).

Table 7.18   Most likely reactions to repeated questions

Reactions indicating innocence	Reactions indicating guilt
Will usually answer the question then point out you have asked it before	Will object to being asked the same question, but then may answer

ASK IF THERE IS ANY REASON

Ask the subject if there is any reason why the evidence makes it appear that he is responsible (Table 7.19).

Example: 'Tom, I have already explained some of the evidence to you and you have to admit it does not look good. Bill Jones, your manager agrees. What do you want to tell me about this?'

Table 7.19   Most likely reactions to strong evidence

Reactions indicating innocence	Reactions indicating guilt
Deny that the evidence points his way	May give a reason which is usually facile or say 'I don't know'

GET HIM TO HANDLE INCRIMINATING EVIDENCE

Hand the subject documents or other incriminating evidence and ask him to explain them: *'Can you explain this?'* (Table 7.20).

Table 7.20   Most likely reactions to incriminating evidence

Reactions indicating innocence	Reactions indicating guilt
May ask for clarification on what the documents mean	Will make abnormal assumptions and not ask for clarification
Will examine carefully and reply	May not examine carefully
Will retain the documents within his personal space	Will push the documents out of his personal space

ASK HOW HE WOULD HAVE DONE IT

Ask the suspect to tell you how he would have committed the act in question. Get him to go through exact details step by step, and watch for disclosure of facts that only the perpetrator would know. Then ask direct, admission-seeking questions (Table 7.21).

Table 7.21   Most likely reactions to possible commitment of the act

Reactions indicating innocence	Reactions indicating guilt
He would not commit the act	May explain May reveal detail known only to the perpetrator May suggest a stupid method as a diversionary tactic

The fact that a person will admit that he has considered the possibility of committing fraud is significant indication of guilt. You should remain on the lookout for obvious diversionary tactics. For example, the suspect may suggest a method that is obviously unworkable in the hope that he can demonstrate his ignorance of what actually happened.

ASK IF HE WOULD ADMIT

Ask the subject if he had done the act in question, whether he would admit it (Table 7.22).

Table 7.22   Most likely reactions to the possibility of admission

Reactions indicating innocence	Reactions indicating guilt
Pausing and then probably 'no' or 'would depend on the circumstances'	Most likely 'yes', but answered without thinking

RESPONSE TO ACCUSATIONS: FAILURE TO DENY

You should make a direct accusation (Table 7.23).

> *Example*: 'Tom, I think you did it for the following reasons.' Then explain the deception theory and key points.

Table 7.23   Most likely reactions to a direct accusation

Reactions indicating innocence	Reactions indicating guilt
Committed first person singular, past tense denial	Pseudo-denial (see page 88)
Anger	Feigned anger

RESPONSE TO REPEATED ALLEGATIONS

You should repeat the allegations throughout the interview (Table 7.24).

Table 7.24   Most likely reactions to repeated allegations

Reactions indicating innocence	Reactions indicating guilt
Denials increasing in strength	Pseudo-denials decreasing in strength

REASONS FOR LYING

If you believe the suspect is being deceptive, you should ask him if there are any reasons, other than the obvious, why he is not telling the truth (Table 7.25).

> *Example*: 'Joe, it is obvious to both of us that you are not telling the truth. I think it is because you [took the money], but is there any other reason why you are not being truthful with me?'

Table 7.25   Most likely reactions to being asked the reason for lying

Reactions indicating innocence	Reactions indicating guilt
Committed response that he is telling the truth	Hesitancy then a pseudo-denial that he is lying

PREVIOUS TROUBLE

Ask if the suspect has been in trouble before (Table 7.26).

Table 7.26   Most likely reactions to being asked about previous trouble

Reactions indicating innocence	Reactions indicating guilt
Will deny that he is in trouble	Probably 'yes' or 'no'

ASK WHOM HE CAN CLEAR OF SUSPICION

Ask the suspect to give the names of people he is sure are not responsible for the act in question (Table 7.27).

Table 7.27   Most likely reactions to being asked who is not responsible

Reactions indicating innocence	Reactions indicating guilt
Will immediately name himself	Will not immediately name himself

ASK TO PROVIDE ELIMINATION SAMPLES

In forgery cases, ask the subject to provide a specimen of his normal handwriting and ask him to copy the forged signature, 10 or 12 times (Table 7.28).

Table 7.28   Most likely reactions to being asked to provide elimination samples

Reactions indicating innocence	Reactions indicating guilt
Will look carefully at the forgery and make a genuine attempt to copy it	Will not look closely at the forgery and will make a poor attempt

The guilty subject may try to confuse the handwriting expert by giving poor samples and by making no attempt to copy the forged signature.

ASK IF HE WILL TAKE A LIE DETECTOR TEST

You may ask if the suspect would be prepared to take a lie detector test (Table 7.29).

Table 7.29   Most likely reactions to a possible lie detector test

Reactions indicating innocence	Reactions indicating guilt
May not agree	Will normally agree, but then prevaricate

If he agrees, ask if it can be done later the same day (Table 7.30):

Table 7.30   Most likely reactions to an imminent lie detector test

Reactions indicating innocence	Reactions indicating guilt
Will usually think and make a reasonable effort to get the matter cleared up	Without thinking, will find a reason why the test cannot take place (i.e. a typical 'stalling' routine)

ASK WHY THE PROBLEM OCCURRED

Ask the subject whether he believes the losses are the result of deliberate and premeditated theft (Table 7.31).

Table 7.31   Most likely reactions to being asked if the act was probably premeditated

Reactions indicating innocence	Reactions indicating guilt
Possibly 'yes' or 'I don't know'	Probably 'no'

SENSORY AND REVERSE QUESTIONS

These questions are useful in jogging a person's memory and for testing whether a reply is from memory (probably true) or imagination (probably false). Sensory questions can also be used to get a witness to examine his memory from an entirely different angle and access important information through another 'cue'.

For example, in a robbery, the witness might be asked:

Example: 'If you had been standing outside the bank looking in through the window what do you think you would have seen?' or 'Did the robber remind you of anyone you know?' or 'what smells did you notice?'

Reverse questions require the subject to recount an event from other than what he claims was the starting position.

Example: 'You say the robber ran out of the bank at around 2.03 pm. Starting from here, take me backwards through your memory to the point at which you first saw him come into the bank.'

Deceptive suspects have far greater difficulty in dealing with such questions and often make serious mistakes when recounting something in reverse order or starting halfway through a sequence.

Changing the order of events makes liars uncertain

PARAPHRASING AND SUMMARY STATEMENTS

Summary statements can be used throughout all interviews to reinforce earlier statements or admissions made by the subject and, where possible, should be supported by visual input covering the 'key points'.

Example:
- 'So far you have told me that ...'
- 'You have agreed that ...'
- 'Let's see if I have understood you correctly ...'

They can also be used to backtrack to a safe point if an interview goes off course. You may reinforce summary statements by agreeing and writing down bullet points with the subject.

Interviewer:	'You have told me:
	Point 1: That you were on duty at the time this happened. Is that correct?'
Subject:	'Yes'
Interviewer:	'Point 2: That the supervisor was asleep. Is that correct?'
Subject:	'Yes'

And so on.

The suspect's anxiety will increase as the process moves forward, again leading him towards the pivotal point.

DECISION POINT

At the end of this phase you will have reached a conclusion on whether the suspect is lying or not. If you believe he is being deceptive you must move on to Phase 4 and put the monkeys on his back. If you think he has told the truth, carry on with the interview, treating him as a potential witness.

Anxiety inducing questions – Phase C

INTRODUCTION

The objective of this phase is to increase the suspect's anxiety to the point where he loses confidence in his ability to succeed, thus bringing him to face reality at the pivotal point.

The suspect's anxiety will increase and the chatter from the two monkeys will become unbearable every time he has to:

- admit that he has not told the truth;
- admit he has done something wrong;
- falsify an answer (rather than to conceal);
- acknowledge that he tried to mislead you through a subjective truth or some other deception;
- change his story to fit new facts presented to him;
- make a denial.

It will also be increased every time he is confronted with evidence indicating his guilt, or discrepancies in his explanations. You should remember that anxiety becomes intolerable, usually not because of one knockout blow but through an accumulation of small points.

You should concentrate on the mechanics, or the 'how' of the case, and on minor wrongdoings; emphasize the evidence you believe you can get and adopt a professional, relentless and critical parent role. This phase has to raise the temperature but you can easily stay in control:

- remain totally committed in what you say and how you say it;
- don't panic in the face of counter-attacks but move on quickly to the next question.

If the interview goes off track, revert to a 'safe haven' and continue as seamlessly as possible.

TOPIC COVERAGE

In most interviews there will be a number of topics of interest, each with its own key points. *For example, you may have intelligence (and thus a deception theory) to suggest that the suspect took bribes, falsified his travel expenses, downloaded pornography from the Internet and so on. Each one can be regarded as a separate topic and you should summarize the key points for each one.* You may decide to deal with each topic in a self-contained portion of the interview, or you may deliberately decide to jump rapidly from one topic to another to make it more difficult for the suspect to plan ahead (Table 7.32).

Table 7.32   Most likely reactions to changes in topic

Reactions indicating innocence	Reactions indicating guilt
Will usually accept the change of topics without objection	The deceitful suspect will find topic changes difficult to handle and may object to them
Answers will be spontaneous	His delivery of responses is likely to be slow and cautious

Rapid switches from one topic to another are particularly relevant in Phases B and C to increase the suspect's anxiety.

The order in which you will deal with topics should also be carefully planned. You may leave the strongest until last, thus building up increasing anxiety throughout the interview, or hit him hard with it from the start. Your approach will be dictated by the circumstances, with the ultimate objective of bringing the suspect to the pivotal point on all topics.

SURPRISE QUESTIONS

Think of unusual questions that the suspect is unlikely to have anticipated and pop them in from time to time. For example, the suspect had given a brilliantly detailed description of a man he had seen supposedly running off with a bag of money and had an outstanding 'memory'[2] of the event.

LOOKING OUT OF THE WINDOW

Suspect:	'As I said, I was standing looking out of the window and saw this man ...'
Question:	'What was the window frame like, was it plastic or metal?'
Suspect:	'I don't know ... I can't remember.'
Question:	'Was the window a single pane or multiple?'
Suspect:	'I haven't the foggiest idea.'
Question:	'Was there anything on the window ledge, a pot, flower or anything?'
Suspect:	'I don't know.'
Statement:	'Given that your memory is so good in other areas, how come you don't remember any of this?'
Suspect:	[Silence]
Statement:	'It didn't happen that way, did it?'
Suspect:	[Long pause] 'I thought it had.'

He later went on to admit that his story was a sham and that he had taken the money.

Jump from topic to topic.
Ask surprise questions

---

[2]   It was actually far too good, suggesting rehearsal

EXPLAIN THE DECEPTION THEORY AND RESOLUTION PLAN

Explain the mechanics of the fraud exactly as you believe it happened, pointing out what evidence is available to prove the case. Confront the suspect with visual stimuli relating to the key points and keep incriminating evidence in his personal space. Explain how the investigation will be conducted – that there is limitless time and resources to do so and that cooperation will be forthcoming from third parties and witnesses. The guilty suspect is unlikely to interrupt and will listen closely to what you have to say. He is extremely unlikely to make committed FPSPT denials.

EXPLANATIONS OF INCRIMINATING EVIDENCE

Hand the suspect pieces of incriminating evidence (the key points) – documents, photographs and summary statements – and ask for his explanation. You may express an opinion that you believe they prove his guilt. Again the untruthful subject will try to avoid becoming committed to detail. His denials will usually become weaker when allegations are repeated (Table 7.33)

Table 7.33   Most likely reactions to key point evidence

Reactions indicating innocence	Reactions indicating guilt
The subject may ask for an explanation about the context in which the exhibits were produced and what they mean	The guilty person may make assumptions about the exhibits without asking questions about their context or meaning
He may examine the exhibits carefully and may retain them in his possession	After a cursory view he may push the exhibits away, wishing to distance himself from them

You can increase anxiety by repeatedly pushing the exhibits in front of the suspect and making him handle them. Generally, the more you can make him keep them within his personal space, the better.

MINOR TRANSGRESSIONS

Getting the subject to admit to breaches of company procedures and to small fiddles on his expenses is also important. Each admitted breach, and an acceptance of the potential censure involved, is a step nearer to a full confession on more important matters. You can point out that the small admissions he has made are sufficient to result in his dismissal and prosecution, and that he cannot worsen his situation by helping to resolve other matters.

REPROVING STATEMENTS

You should remain consciously alert to evasions, subjective truths, failures to volunteer etc. and chastise the subject for trying to mislead you.

Example:

Interviewer:	'Do you use narcotic drugs?'
Subject:	'I don't use drugs.' (Note the normal honest response would be a binary 'no'.)
Interviewer:	'But do you take them?'
Subject:	'Yes, sometimes, but I don't use them.'
Interviewer:	'Come on, Bill, you are playing with words. This is not the way we are going to clear this up. What drugs do you take?'

The subject's anxiety is increased every time he is caught out in this way. From time to time, you may plan to ask questions that give the subject the chance to use subjective truths and then chastise him for doing so or give him credit for precise, full answers.

INTERRUPTIONS AND AVOIDING DENIALS

Wherever possible you should try to intervene every time a suspect starts to tell a lie or wanders off the point. You can do this by oral statements.

Example:
- 'Hold on, Bill, that cannot be right, can it?'
- 'I think you should stop just there.'

Or by non-verbal intervention such as holding your hand up much like a traffic policeman and at the same time shaking your head left to right (Table 7.34).

Table 7.34   Most likely reactions to interventions

Reactions indicating innocence	Reactions indicating guilt
Will usually insist on completing his statement	Will usually defer to the interruption

There are obviously exceptions to every rule, but liars tend to be more passive, less assertive and less committed than truthful people. Stopping false explanations and challenging lies creates anxiety in the mind of the suspect.

An innocent person usually objects to being interrupted

ENTICEMENT QUESTIONS

The object of these questions is to get the suspect to change an explanation or alibi he has already given. They may be asked at any point in an interview, but should usually be asked when:

- the subject is committed to an untrue explanation, or deliberate concealment, probably through blocking questions;
- he can be confronted with a new and important piece of incriminating evidence;

- he has admitted to making an error in an explanation;
- he is at the pivotal point.

If you can get him to change his explanation, the chances are that a confession will follow. Even the approach, by itself, will increase his anxiety.

> *Example*: 'You have told me that you were not in the supermarket that day. As you know, the security office makes video recordings. Do you want to reconsider what you have told me?'

If the subject sticks to his explanation and adds detail to support it, you should add points to the list suggesting innocence.

Interviewing is not just about exposing the liar; it is also about clearing the innocent

ADMISSIONS OF LYING

Anxiety is greatly increased every time the suspect has to admit he has lied or concealed the truth. You must punish deception, taking the role of the critical parent and saying something along the lines:

> *Example*: 'I am very disappointed with you, Mr Smith. Please be very careful how you answer this question [Was Tom Jones involved in this?].'

NON-VERBAL COMMUNICATIONS

Observe the subject's body reactions generally and his eye contact in particular. You must deprive him of the comfort of manipulators. You can most easily do this by quietly mimicking them or looking closely at them. Either way, he will usually stop, again increasing anxiety.

INTERJECTIONS

Interjections are some of the most important tools for finding the truth. The right time to interject is when it is clear that the suspect's memory, imagination, conscious and subconscious states are in conflict and thrashing around trying to contrive a plausible response. At such points the liar is directly connected to his subconscious and memory monkeys and is thus vulnerable to making admissions, Freudian slips and other mistakes.

> *Example*:
> Question: 'Did you go to the office to collect the cheque?'
> Response: [Silence and deep thought by the suspect – looking down and to the right]
> Interjection: 'Have you been ten times in the last month or less than this?'
> Response: 'Well, no, not 10 times.'
> Question: 'Then what about 50 times in the last year?'

The key is to interject with an alternative every time the suspect's brain is thrashing for an answer.

In one case the managing director of a computer company, accused of pirating operating systems and exporting high technology to embargoed countries, made an angry outburst:

MD: 'I am really pissed off with your allegations that we have smuggled
                       thousands of boards and programs to the Soviet Union, inside jukeboxes.'

The investigator interjected:

                       'Well how many boards did you ship inside jukeboxes?'
MD: 'Well ... er.' [Pause for deep thought]
Investigator: 'Was it ten, a hundred, two hundred or what?'
MD: 'Not as many as a hundred.'
Investigator: 'But you did ship boards in jukeboxes?'
MD: [Silence. He could have bitten his tongue off and his lawyer glared at him]

In the cold light of day people find it incredible that suspects make such mistakes but fortunately they do. The reason simply is that the two monkeys are very dangerous creatures, especially when the suspect's anxiety is stimulated.

Interjections lead to unintentional admissions

REGRESSIVE QUESTIONS

Regressive questions, which return phrases from an answer parrot fashion, can be irritating and anxiety inducing.

Response: 'Then I threw the papers into the bin.'
Question: 'You threw the papers into the bin?'
Response: 'Yes.'
Question: 'Why?
Responses: 'Because I thought they were useless.'
Question: 'Because you thought they were useless, you threw the papers into the bin?'
Response: 'Yes.'
Question: 'Why did you think they were useless?'
Response: 'Because I just did.'
Question: 'Because you just did. You threw the papers into the bin because you
               thought they were useless?'

If you do not believe regressive questions generate emotion, try using them on your spouse or boss, but watch out! Consider using them at any phase in an interview with an overconfident subject to irritate and unbalance him.

LEVERS AND PROVING THE SUBJECT WRONG

Few people like to be proved wrong, even when the error is in relation to unimportant matters. Every error the subject has to admit to, forced changes to a previous explanation or lie exposed increases anxiety and is a step towards finding the truth. Thus, inconsistencies and untruths in the suspect's responses *must* be brought to his attention and detailed explanations sought.

> *Example*: 'I don't have to remind you, Bill, that you have just admitted to trying to mislead me and I am not happy about that. Now I want you to take your time and think very carefully about the next question.'

He can also be asked enticement questions, but it is important to press home the advantage you have obtained because after being caught out in a lie, the suspect is very vulnerable.

A liar is vulnerable when he has been caught in a lie

WEAKNESSES WITH CONSPIRATORS

It may be possible to drive a wedge between a suspect and his co-conspirators; point out that they will not protect him.

> *Example*: 'Bill, you know my colleagues are interviewing x and y at this very moment. You know they're going to save their own skins, don't you?'

I KNOW WHAT YOU ARE THINKING

This statement is always worth a try. Some suspects seem to react very strongly to it and it definitely makes them anxious, while others ignore it.

MORE ON ARTHUR

Arthur, whose exploits were partly described on page 188, was initially extremely confident and domineering until the interviewer said: 'Arthur, I know exactly what you are thinking.' Arthur responded: 'There is no bloody way you know what I am thinking: my mind is my own. You cannot possibly know. You cannot f******* know.'

The interviewer responded: 'I knew you were going to say something like that. I can read you like a book. Your body language keeps giving the game away. You know you cannot go through with this. You made a mistake, OK, now tell me how this all started.' This is precisely what Arthur did.

'WHY', FEELINGS AND REASONS QUESTIONS

These open or closed questions focus on the suspect's emotions, feelings and the reasons why certain things happened or did not happen. They are especially relevant when you believe the suspect is delivering a prepared, deceptive answer.

MISSING FEELINGS

Interviewer:	'You have told me that Mr Smith told you to complete the form the way you did. Is that correct?'
Suspect:	'Yes.'
Interviewer:	'But you knew it was misleading, wrong or false?'
Suspect:	'Not false, no.'
Interviewer:	'But misleading?'
Suspect:	'Yes, a little, but he was my boss.'
Interviewer:	'How did you feel when he told you to do this?'
Suspect:	'What do you mean?'
Interviewer:	'How did you feel about your boss asking you to complete a false form?'
Suspect:	'Well, to be absolutely truthful, I do not remember feeling anything. He was my boss.'
Interviewer:	'Didn't you feel really worried, concerned or upset that he was telling you to do something you knew was wrong, if not criminal?'
Suspect:	'Not that I remember.'
Interviewer:	'I think if he had told you to do this, you would have been very angry, wouldn't you?'
Suspect:	'Possibly.'
Interviewer:	'But you were not angry, were you?'
Suspect:	'Not that I recall, no.'
Interviewer:	'But you would remember being angry, wouldn't you?'
Suspect	'Probably.'
Interviewer	'I have to tell you, Mr Jones, that I think you are mistaken. Maybe you are confusing this incident with another occasion and that you completed this form by yourself. Isn't that correct?'
Suspect	'Maybe.'
Interviewer:	'And that your boss was not involved at all.'
Suspect:	[Silence] (The pivotal point)

Again, the exchange proves nothing, but it has forced the subject to change his prepared story, and thus increases his anxiety and takes him a step further towards the pivotal point.

Truthful people are more likely to admit their emotions

FUTILITY OF ENDGAME STATEMENTS

Most liars do not plan their endgame, possibly assuming that the consequences of their dishonesty will naturally go away. Thus some questions and statements should be directed towards this vulnerability.

Example: 'Mr Jones, you know that this is a very serious matter and that we will find the truth. How did you expect all of this to come to an end? You didn't think this through, did you?'

The responses to such a question are likely to be along the lines shown in Table 7.35.

Table 7.35   Most likely reactions to endgame questions

Reactions indicating innocence	Reactions indicating guilt
The question is irrelevant	Delayed response and careful thought
Committed denial	'I don't know'
Possible anger at an implied accusation	

Exploring the endgame weaknesses is likely to increase anxiety with a guilty suspect.

Talking about the endgame forces the liar to face reality

SILENCE

Misconceptions
The steely eyed television detective who stares down the silent suspect would be a failure in real life and silence has to be very carefully handled because it can increase anxiety for both the suspect and the interviewer.

Causes of silence in an interview
Silence can be the result of a number of factors:

- Created by you:
  - deliberately introduced to increase the suspect's anxiety either in relation to a relevant question or at the pivotal point;
  - while preparing for your next question or considering an earlier reply.
- Created by the suspect:
  - after a question to give him time to plan the next response;
  - at the pivotal point when he is considering whether or not to make an admission;
  - generally, such as by crying or through any other emotional collapse, in the hope that the interview will be terminated.

In all cases plan your response to silence and make sure you deal with it effectively.

Silence is not golden

Deliberately creating a silence
You may deliberately induce an anxious silence by saying something along the lines of:

Example: 'I want you to pause for a minute and think very carefully about the next question. If you are not prepared to tell me the truth, I suggest we stop the interview, right now.'

If you use this approach you *must* wait for the subject to respond and under no circumstances should you break the silence. It is unheard of for a suspect to walk out at this point: the reason being that it requires a very high level of commitment to do so.

Silence created by the subject

Silence by the suspect in response to a relevant question usually means the following (Table 7.36).

Table 7.36   The sound of silence

Meaning of the silence	Your reaction, depending on the context and the phase of the interview
He is deciding whether to fight or flee	You should present him with the most detailed evidence you have and require him to commit himself to responses
He is playing for time to prepare an answer *(and fighting the two monkeys on his back)*	Assume the silence is an admission. *Interject* with a phrase such as: 'This is too much, Joe, isn't it?'
He is confronting himself with the critical decision whether or not to tell the truth: *the pivotal point*	

An important fact to remember is that when the subject has created a silence to give him time to plan his next response, you must interject (see page 213).

WRITING IT ALL DOWN

As Spot kindly mentioned in the preface to this book, it was one thing Mr Staples saying something nice about the elderly ex-guru and quite another committing it to writing. This is true in both trivial and serious cases of deception. If you cannot understand an explanation or don't believe it, consider asking the subject to write down the important facts on a single sheet of paper. Liars don't like doing this because it commits them to barefaced lies.

THE FIRE EXTINGUISHERS

An accountant, working for a small company, asked the managing director to approve a purchase order (of £10,000 addressed to X Limited) for fire extinguishers, which he said were urgently needed to conform with new fire regulations. The MD believed his company already complied fully with all regulations, but his questions were answered with a load of technical waffle and evasion, which concluded with 'Believe me, we will be in trouble if we don't buy this stuff this week'. The MD said, 'Well we have a few days, so put your case down on a single sheet of paper and tell me all you know about X Limited.'

A few days later, the MD bumped into the accountant and asked him what was happening. 'Oh,' said the accountant, 'I checked and found we were OK, after all.' What he did not admit, as the MD subsequently found out, was that his son-in-law owned X Limited.

When in doubt, get it in writing

THE ULTIMATE STATEMENT

If you believe the liar has no intention of telling the truth, you may seriously excite the subconscious monkey by making a statement along the lines:

> *Example*: 'Bill, you have told me x and I have explained to you that I do not believe you. I want you to confirm that there can be no misunderstanding about this. If what you have told me is untrue, it must be a barefaced lie, mustn't it? You can have no excuse whatsoever, can you?'

Experience shows that liars hate this question because it commits them to a barefaced lie (Table 7.37):

Table 7.37   Most likely reactions to the ultimate statement

Reactions indicating innocence	Reactions indicating guilt
A direct, short and committed answer such as 'no'	The liar will try to reduce the anxiety within his response by softening the 'no' with additional and unnecessary words
Becomes angry	Becomes cautious
	Asks for clarification

Questions of this nature can be asked at any point in an interview, but are particularly relevant in Phases C and D (probing and raising the pavement). In over 40 years of dealing with liars, we have never once known a person whose guilt was subsequently proven to simply say 'no'.

RIDICULOUS LIES

If the suspect is totally determined not to tell the truth, no matter what, ask detailed questions then explain how his answers can be disproved. If the suspect continues to deceive, he should be asked to sign a witness statement containing all of his lies in the finest detail. Subsequently, these will act against him. After the statement has been completed, you may point out that it is obviously untrue, makes the suspect look foolish and ask him if he wishes to change it. If he does, keep the original.

Accusatory questions and statements – Phase C

INTRODUCTION

It is critical in all interviews with people suspected of deception that you tell them precisely what you believe to be the truth based on your deception theory, i.e. that they did it. However, a statement such as: *'I know you stole the cash, you cheating ratbag,'* is likely to result in a denial, stalemate or worse. You must always treat even the nastiest villain with respect and carefully plan the way in which you make the first accusation:

- a suitable war story, or drawing a parallel in a current news event;
- assumptive questions;
- hypothetical questions;
- a direct accusation prefaced or followed immediately by a rationalization statement.

These questions and statements are particularly relevant in Phases C and D.

You must politely accuse the liar

WAR STORIES AND GOLDEN NUGGETS

War stories (akin to Biblical parables!) are especially useful in making soft accusations.

Example: 'There was a case just like this a few years ago, involving a senior manager just like you. He got caught up in something and got into trouble over his head. He had been a good employee for many years but all of a sudden, through no fault of his own, it all got too much and he took money, which I am sure he intended to repay. Then things went from bad to worse – do you know what happened to him?'

The subject's reaction to a story such as this can be very revealing (see Table 7.38).

Table 7.38   Most likely reactions to war stories

Reactions indicating innocence	Reactions indicating guilt
Will listen carefully, but will not hear the story as being applicable to him	Will normally take the story very personally
Will usually appear relaxed and show a confident interest	May show non-verbal signs of anxiety
	May ask: *'Are you accusing me?'*

If the subject's reaction is indicative of guilt, you may make a direct accusation.

Example: 'The problem is, I believe the same thing is happening to you.'

When planning tough interviews, you may wish to consider developing one or more war stories to fit important elements of the deception theory.

People like stories and relate to them

ASSUMPTIVE QUESTIONS OR CLOSED ALTERNATIVES

These, which can be open or closed, are constructed around an assumption which you may or may not be able to prove (Table 7.39).

In planning tough interviews, you should review the deception theory and list the main assumptions and plan questions to cover them. These can be asked at any stage, but are particularly relevant when the subject is at or near the pivotal point. Wherever possible try to phrase assumptive questions with one soft alternative.

Example: 'Did you accept a personal payment from ABC Limited because you believed you had earned it, or was there some other reason?'

Guilty people are more likely to accept assumptions

Table 7.39   Examples of assumptive questions

Example of assumptive question or alternative	Assumption that could result in a denial if posed in an open question
'When did you stop beating your wife?'	That he beat his wife
'How much money did you make from this?'	He did 'this' and made money
'Did this all start because you needed money for your wife or for some other reason?'	That this started
'What time did you leave the office with Bill?'	That he was with Bill
'Did this start because you were short of money or because you saw everyone else getting away with it?'	That this started; everyone is doing it

HYPOTHETICAL QUESTIONS

These can be used to challenge, accuse or to deal with any other significant matter where you do not want to confront the suspect directly.

> *Example*:
> * 'If someone said you had taken the money, how would you feel?'
> * 'If I could prove to you that what you just said is not true, what would you say?'
> * 'If you had taken the money, do you think we could prove it?'

The suspect's reaction should be carefully monitored (Table 7.40).

Table 7.40   Most likely reactions to hypothetical questions

Reactions indicating innocence	Reactions indicating guilt
Will not normally see the question as applying to him	Will take the question personally
Will not normally enter into conjecture or may take a hard, judgemental line	Will discuss the possibilities but will normally take a non-judgemental line
Will take a strong committed position	May challenge your proof or evidence with statements such as: *'If you can prove it, then I will have to go to prison'*

The bottom line is that guilty suspects and liars are usually much more prepared to consider hypothetical questions: possibly because they do not understand how an honest person would react.

DIRECT ACCUSATIONS

There is no legal or other reason why you cannot simply say what you believe the subject has done. On the contrary, from a technical, truth-finding standpoint you must say this and repeat it. For example, 'I believe you have taken bribes and passed business to X Limited', or, 'you have told me that your product turns water into wine and I don't believe you'.

You may soften the accusation through a rationalization statement.

Example:
- 'I can understand why this happened and we must sort it out together, but there is no doubt that you ...'
- 'The evidence is overwhelming that you took the money: I can understand how it happened, but it has now got out of control and we have to sort it out.'

There is no doubt that accusations stir up anxiety, and the reaction to them tells you a great deal. If they are not denied with a strong negative response or a first person singular, past tense denial (see page 88), the chances are you are correct and you should proceed on that basis. When accusations are repeated, the reaction of the guilty suspect will usually soften, whereas that of an innocent person will stay consistently strong or harden (see Chapter 10).

Reactions to accusations are critical

INNOCENCE, BARGAINING AND ACCEPTANCE

If Phase C has gone to plan, you will either have concluded that the suspect is innocent or brought him to the pivotal point. If you are convinced of his innocence, you should say so and, if necessary, apologize. You should explain why it was necessary to ask probing and difficult questions. In most cases, the subject will understand and accept the apology and no permanent harm will have been done, especially if you ask him out for a game of golf.

It is much more likely that the suspect will be brought to the pivotal point where he is deciding whether or not to tell some or all of the truth. He will usually:

- become passive, very thoughtful and possibly tearful;
- will look downwards, with closed or fluttering eyes;
- sigh deeply;
- slump in his chair, possible in a foetal position;
- his legs may move forward, away from his chair;
- often appear to get smaller.

He may ask questions such as:

- 'I didn't do this, but if I admit it, can we get this over ...?'
- 'Can we speak off the record?'
- 'What would happen if ...?'
- 'Would it be possible for me just to resign ...?'
- 'Couldn't I just withdraw the claim ...?'
- 'Would the police have to be involved ...?'

These are all acceptance signals and you know the suspect is at the pivotal point (see Figure 7.2). *You must then switch to the transactional role of a nurturing parent.*

Empathetic questions – Phases D and E

PRINCIPLES

People usually confess because they cannot continue with the anxiety caused by deception: in short, because they have internalized that 'the game is up' (see Chapter 3, page 65). At this stage, which will be repeated throughout a 'tough' interview, the suspect is faced with what are usually unbearable conflicting pressures. The first is that he has recognized the futility of further deception; lost confidence in his ability to succeed and wants to confess. The second is that he is fearful of the *immediate* consequences of telling the truth. The monkeys are really on his back.

THE PIVOTAL POINT

The suspect was at the pivotal point and had gone very quiet. He was considering a confession and asked: 'What could happen over this?' The interviewer replied: 'You will go to prison for eight years, you bastard'. Unsurprisingly, there was no confession.

Your approach is to work *with* the suspect to help him resolve this dilemma by:

1 *Stressing his inability to succeed with deception –*
   • the absolute *inevitability* that the facts will be established;
   • that you have *limitless time* and resources to find the truth;
   • the *weaknesses* in and hopelessness of his explanations.
2 *Stressing that the consequences are tolerable –*
   • how *you and he* can resolve the problem together and what the future could hold;
   • *why* the problem occurred and a rationalization for it.

This stage is likely to be emotional and you must take your time. You must make a conscious move to adopt the transactional role of a nurturing parent. In the cold light of day, the sug-

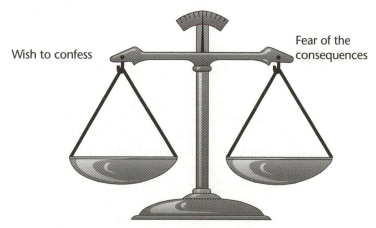

Figure 7.2 The pivotal point

gested approach may sound trite,[3] but it works simply because at this stage the guilty subject is overburdened by anxiety in a world that has closed in around him.

CONSCIOUSLY BECOME A NURTURING PARENT

Push incriminating and other exhibits to one side, implying that the formal interview is over. Address the suspect by his first name, reduce the tone, speed and volume of your voice and:

- if you have been sitting behind a desk move slowly around to sit alongside him within arm's length and to his left;
- address him by his first name;
- as far as possible, mirror his posture and eye movements;
- use slow, positive palms upwards demonstrators;
- talk about his feelings ('I know how you feel');
- emphasize the word 'we' and how the problem can be resolved;
- drop the tone, volume and speed of your speech;
- avoid being judgemental: 'No one could say how they would have reacted in your circumstances.'

However, under no circumstances make promises you cannot keep, and do not mislead the suspect. You must genuinely feel for him and try to put yourself in his place.

To move into the role of a nurturing parent imagine you are speaking to a loved child who is unwell

EMPATHY AND WORDS OF CAUTION

One of the most common failings is that interviewers do not understand that crooks and liars don't share the same values as honest folk. Most have seriously distorted values, so don't go overboard on suggesting that someone that you know is a right villain is really an angel of unconditional virtue who has just temporarily strayed from the heavenly path. For what it is worth, most liars are self-centred and selfish and, at the end of the day, confess because it suits them. So forget about rationalizations like: 'You owe it to your boss' or 'to the company', as these will not work. Very few crooks say they are sorry for what they have done, though many are sorry that they have been caught.

Suggest highly moralistic or religious rationalizations and the suspect will regard you as a gerbil and you will fail. You must put yourself in his shoes and try to hit the right empathetic buttons. Does he seem responsive to the rationalization that he did what he did by accident, because he had been unfairly treated, wanted better things for his family, or because he was in serious financial trouble? You can identify the right 'hot buttons' through trial and error. But, again, take care. For example, if the suspect is a serial philanderer, rationalizations about his wife and family may not go down too well. This is where your background research – and knowing what makes the suspect tick – should pay dividends.

---

[3]   This may be why academics are so reluctant to address the solutions!

RATIONALIZATION STATEMENTS

You should never, ever attack or criticize a suspect's character by, for example, calling him a 'liar' or a 'crook'; it is always important to allow him to save face, possibly by suggesting a reason why he wandered from the path of honesty.

A TYPICAL RATIONALIZATION STATEMENT	
'Bill, I know this is very difficult for you and that you are, at heart, a decent person. We all make mistakes and can get over them.	Let's try to work this out. Now why did all of this start?'

You can often identify the right rationalization button by carefully listening to what the suspect says and testing his reaction to a menu of options.

> *Example*:
> * *Financial pressure*: 'I can understand when people get so financially stretched, they are tempted. Probably you thought you could pay it back. Am I right?'
> * *Family problems*: 'I know you have worked hard for your kids, but sometimes hard work is not enough. Am I right?'
> * *Being treated unfairly*: 'I know things have been tough at work and have gone against you. Maybe you thought this would solve your problems, but you know it won't. Am I right?'
> * *Everybody else is doing it*: 'Everyone seems to have to fight for every penny these days and it is easy to overstep the line. Am I right?'
> * *Blaming the victim*: 'Sometimes [the victim company] does not seem to care and leaves temptation in the way of people. That's how it all starts. Am I right?'
> * *Any other reason you think might be appropriate*: '... am I right?'

If the suspect shows an interest, the rationalization offered should be developed and repeated (Table 7.41).

Generally, all rationalization statements should be delivered from the position of a nurturing parent and through an emotional channel of communication.

Guilty people like rationalizations

Table 7.41 Most likely reactions to rationalization statements

Reactions indicating innocence	Reactions indicating guilt
Will normally hear the rationalization as an accusation: may interject	Will usually listen carefully without interruption
Will usually dismiss the rationalization as being inappropriate and may become genuinely angry	May dismiss inapplicable rationalizations, but usually in a low-key way
	May accept the rationalization

COMPLIMENTS

You should be prepared to compliment the subject when he makes an admission.

> *Example*: 'Sam, it took real courage to admit that. Let's see if we can clear up [another important topic].'

You may use positive hand and body movements to reinforce a nurturing parent role.

Small compliments reward the liar for telling the truth

ASK WHY AND GIVE AN ACCEPTABLE ALTERNATIVE

Ask the suspect why he committed the crime, but give him at least one acceptable alternative.

> *Example*:
> - 'Did this start by accident, or did you feel you had no alternative?'
> - 'This started on the spur of the moment, didn't it? I am sure you didn't plan for it to turn out like this, did you?'

Again, the principle is to allow the suspect to save face.

POINT OUT THE CONFLICT YOU KNOW THE SUSPECT IS FACING

Point out that you know the conflict that the suspect is facing.

> *Example*: 'I have seen many cases like this and I know that it calls for enormous courage to admit you have gone off the rails. People sometimes believe that they can escape by being evasive, but this is never the case. The evidence in this case is overwhelming – you know that – and the facts will come out anyway. Let's try to clear this up now.'

LOOK TO THE FUTURE

Describe the advantages of telling the truth and focus on the future.

> *Example*:
> - 'Everyone deserves a second chance, but let's see if we can sort out …'
> - 'This is not the end of the world. With all of this behind you, you can get off to a new start, but first we have to sort out …'
> - 'This is a temporary setback, but you have the rest of your life before you. But first we have to sort out …'
> - 'If we can get most of the money back, the problem will not be as bad. Am I right?'

You should also remember that the suspect is probably thinking about two immediate concerns. The first is his wrongdoing and the second having to tell his family and pals that he has admitted to it. Often the second it more important than the first.

> *Example*: 'It takes real courage to admit we have done something wrong ... but people will think better of you if you help.'

OFFER THE SUSPECT YOUR ASSISTANCE

Offer the suspect your assistance. Tell him you are independent and, like a doctor, used to hearing about the mistakes people have made and that you have seen it all before. Suggest that you can solve the problem by working together.

> *Example*: 'There are things we all would have done differently, and until you are in that position, you never know how you will react. I can understand why this happened. Now can *we* clear it up?'

ASK WHAT IS HOLDING HIM BACK FROM TELLING THE TRUTH

Ask the suspect what is holding back his admitting the truth. Establish what his fear is. Downplay the motives for the crime, suggesting that it may have started off as borrowing or as a practical joke.

> *Example*: 'You are a sensible bloke, you know this is all going to come out. What is holding you back from getting this sorted out now?'

Also point out that it does not matter to you whether he tells the whole truth or not. Explain the resolution plan, how evidence will be obtained and that his refusal to accept reality may force the company to take legal action.[4]

NOTHING TO LOSE

If the suspect has admitted to minor violations (or they can be proven), you may suggest:

> *Example*: 'Geoff, you know that if the company wants to throw the book at you for [the minor offence] they can. If we can help them sort out this [more serious matter] I am sure that will influence any decisions they take. You know you have nothing to lose by getting all this out of the way, don't you?'

THE LIMITED WINDOW

Emphasize that the suspect does not have unlimited time.

---

[4]   But don't make threats or promises you cannot keep

> *Example*: 'Our investigations will be completed in a couple of days and I will not be able to see you again. This is your best chance of getting this sorted out now … so how can we get some of the money back?'

DEALING WITH ADMISSIONS AND CONFESSIONS

Now comes the really tricky bit. Your initial reaction to an admission of a deep truth may be one bordering on euphoria, but this is the last thing you should show. You must treat even the most damning or dreadful admissions and confessions in a low-key and unemotional way and then probe, as a nurturing parent, for corroborating detail. The more detail you can get, the less likely it is the confession will be withdrawn or that you will be attacked in the witness box, or elsewhere, for giving a misleading account of what was said. Corroborating detail may include why the person did something one way rather than another; how he felt at the time; by recovering tangible evidence; or by noting something known only to the perpetrator. You must take your time obtaining this detail and getting to the deep truth. It is always time well spent.

Always probe for more detail of the worst case

You may also invite the suspect to make a written statement, apologize to his manager, or write a letter: again this will serve as corroboration of his confession. Finally, you must handle the suspect fairly. He has placed a great deal of trust in you by telling you the truth and you must not betray it.

Getting to the deep truth – Phase F

PRINCIPLES

This phase is where the really good interviewers earn the pittances they are paid. It is all about getting to the deep truth and finding out everything that could be relevant. Both you and the suspect should be totally on the same wavelength and you must take limitless time.[5] You have three objectives:

- to obtain a detailed, accurate confession which the suspect will find impossible to retract;
- to find out about other matters;
- to identify ways of getting your money back.

It is critical that you do not rush or become judgemental or assertive. You are now in the role of a nurturing parent and the suspect an adaptive child and you must really believe this and become totally empathetic.

CONFIRMING THE CONFESSION

There is no doubt that some people (although it is fairly rare) confess to things they did not do. There are various reasons for this including attention-seeking, the Freudian *thatanos* death

---

[5]   If criminal prosecution is an objective and you have not already cautioned the suspect it is far too late, you have destroyed the case and your only option is to apply to become an accountant

wish, bravado etc., but the most dangerous and unfair is where a false confession is made simply to bring a fear-ridden interview to a close. Thus you should make every effort to confirm every aspect of the confession by:

- trying to identify and recover documentary and other corroborative evidence;
- trying to confirm information known only to the perpetrator;
- establishing how the suspect felt at the time the offences were committed and his motivation;
- any other detail that supports the confession.

If you have even the remotest suspicion that the confession is untrue, you must discuss this in depth with the suspect. This is a very rare and difficult position and you must balance the possibility of encouraging a guilty suspect to withdraw a true confession with the interests of justice. Any doubt should be in favour of the suspect.

HELPING THE SUSPECT

In this phase it is not unusual for the suspect to ask what might happen to him. This is a very serious and important question which you must answer truthfully. You should list the options and (hopefully, you may genuinely feel this way) say something along the lines of:

> *Example*: 'I don't know what will happen. We both know this is a serious matter, but I can see why and how it happened. It is difficult to see how facing up to your responsibilities can make matters worse and you have been brave enough to do this. I am quite prepared to state on your behalf that you have been frank with me and have genuinely tried to minimize the company's losses, but I need to know x.'

You should continue with any outstanding matters and, in due course, bring the interview to a natural close. You must stick to your word.

AGREE THE SIZE OF THE PROBLEM

In general and very low-key conversation, ask the suspect to:

- agree to when the offences started;
- agree to the average frequency of the fraud;
- agree to where the fraud started;
- agree to the average amount stolen each time.

You should also try to establish detail that only the guilty person would know.

LETTER OF APOLOGY

Consider asking the suspect if he would like to write a letter of apology to his manager. This makes withdrawal of the confession less likely.

OFFER THE CHANCE OF MAKING A WRITTEN STATEMENT

When all aspects of the fraud have been covered, ask the suspect if he would like to make a written statement. You may say: 'To avoid any misunderstanding over what you have told me, I would like to record the main points in writing. Would you like to make a written statement?' The statement should then be taken down at the suspect's dictation; he should not be prompted, although questions to remove any ambiguities may be asked. He should be asked to read through the statement and should initial all alterations.

The suspect should write and sign the following declaration at the end of the statement: 'I have read the above statement and I have been told that I can correct, alter or add anything I wish. This statement is true, I have made it of my own free will.'

If the suspect refuses to sign this declaration, a note should be made of the circumstances surrounding the refusal. The note should be signed by you and by any witnesses to the interview.

OPEN QUESTION ON ANYTHING ELSE

Compliment the suspect on his courage in admitting to his mistakes, then ask:

'Is there anything else that we should get cleared up now?'

Emphasize that all sympathy for the suspect will be lost if he is not totally honest.

FURTHER INTERVIEWS

You should plan to close the interview with an agreement that you might wish to see the suspect again.

> *Example*: 'Bill, I know this has been very difficult and I appreciate your being frank with me. I have to check out some of the things you have told me and we may need to meet again. Will that be OK? You can also telephone me at any time if there is anything else you want to say or if you have problems.'

This sort of agreement will make it less likely that the suspect will refuse to see you later on. Also, always try to leave the suspect some small task to do, like finding papers, or returning property. This will provide a good reason for keeping your communications channels open.

Things to avoid at all costs

INTRODUCTION

There are a number of things that you must avoid at all costs. There are two reasons for this. The first is that they are improper and may lead to the creation of fear and false admissions. The second is that you will not be able to defend them honestly if the case comes to court.

THREATS, BLACKMAIL, PROMISES AND AMNESTIES

It is critical that no threats or promises are made which could render admissions and confessions improper and thus inadmissible. Ultimately, a trial judge may decide what is fair and what is not, but statements and questions such as the following are dreadful.[6]

- 'If you don't tell the truth you will go to hell and your soul will be forever damned.'
- 'I suggest you get down on your knees and pray to God for forgiveness.'
- 'If you don't tell the truth, I will give you a good spanking.'
- 'Tell me the truth and we can then forget it.'

They and statements like them must be avoided at all costs. The rule is 'if you have the slightest inkling that what you are thinking of doing could not be admitted without fear in the highest court in the land: don't do it.' This still leaves all of the techniques described in this book at your disposal, and even if you apply them fairly and honestly, you must still anticipate getting your ass kicked in court: this is life (see Chapter 11).

WINGERS AND VERBALS

These are admissions and confessions falsely attributed to the suspect by a dishonest interviewer. In days gone by, 'wingers' and 'verbals' were far too common for comfort, especially in criminal prosecutions. Most times they varied from the totally unsubtle, such as: 'It's down to me, Mr Smith. I was the one what did it and you are the only person clever enough to catch me. You should get a pay rise for this', to the case where a bank robber, who, during a five-hour interrogation, denied everything, was reported as saying: 'I have told you I did not do it. But if I am picked out at an identity parade, I will grass on the others'.

Today the pendulum has swung towards rampant suspicion and opposing barristers will challenge (quite rightly) any alleged admissions by their clients, possibly arguing that they have been 'winged' or 'verballed'. They overlook the fact that people regularly confess and find their bursts of honesty cathartic.

THE FORGIVENESS COMPUTER

Professor Greg Harvey from Concordia University, Montreal, has developed an interactive computer called the 'Automatic Confession Machine' which can replace the more conventional confessional. The not-for-profit system requires the penitent to type in the customary 'Bless me father for I have sinned'. It responds by getting details and then churns out the penance.

The bottom line is to ensure that all interviews are professionally conducted, accurately recorded, and that evidence of them is given honestly and openly. If, by chance, someone does confess by saying: 'It's down to me, Mr Smith. I was the one what did it and you are the only person clever enough to catch me. You should get a pay rise for this', best get some ass protection as no one will believe you.

---

[6] Believe it or not these statements were made and given in evidence

Rehearsing the interview

You should carry out a practice run with a colleague acting as the suspect. In a second trial, you should take the role of the suspect. Often the rehearsal in which you *play the role of the suspect* is the most important. You will understand where the evidence is the strongest; you will be able to anticipate, and then defeat, false excuses. Rehearsal will make you more confident. When an interpreter is to be used, he must be involved in the rehearsals.

Conducting the interview

If your planning and rehearsal have been completed properly, conducting the interview should be a cinch but:

- Have a good night's sleep before the interview is due to take place: keep off alcohol and vindaloos and, ideally, remain celibate.[7]
- Make sure you dress professionally and settle in the interview room before the suspect arrives. Check everything.

Stick to your plan and don't panic. You can overcome any nervousness (which is entirely justified in important cases) by taking a few deep breaths before the interview starts and by really concentrating on the suspect throughout. He has far more to lose than you have and the cards are stacked in your favour.

When you are feeling nervous concentrate on someone else

Follow-up – Phase G

As soon as possible after each interview, complete your notes and secure all of the other evidence. Update the resolution plan, diary of events and deception theory and carry out further investigations and interviews as quickly as you can. In the days and weeks following the interview you should keep in regular contact with the suspect until asked to do otherwise.

Before the case goes to court, it is possible that the suspect's attitude towards you will become hostile: this should not affect your position. You should continue to deal properly with him and be abundantly fair in the way you act and give your evidence. Always remember that what goes round, comes round.

Checking your performance

Tiger Woods says he only hits one good shot a round, but he analyses every one and learns from his mistakes. We can do the same with interviews: think what you did well and what went badly and learn your lessons.

---

[7]   This is why elderly investigators are to be preferred because they no longer bother with such trivia

Some investigators have 40 years' experience: others have one year's experience repeated 40 times

Conclusion

Despite what the smelly-socks say, even the worst of malodorous villains confess, as do a lot of basically good people and both types feel better for it afterwards. If an interview with an obviously guilty suspect fails (and in reality not many do) you must go back to basics and try to prove the case by other means, through witnesses, documentary, forensic, technical and other evidence. But remember, a clear confession speeds up the wheels of justice and saves taxpayers' money.

Never give up.
The last person left standing is the winner, or his lawyer

'WELL, MR JONES, THE MANUSCRIPT IS GOOD, BUT AN ADVANCE ON ROYALTIES IS OUT OF THE QUESTION'

8 *Forms*

The easiest way to predict the future is to invent it

Background

All organizations rely on forms,[1] for doing such things as recruiting employees, appointing customers, controlling processes or establishing ownership. They are a primary carrier of deception, yet few organizations pay sufficient attention to them or the security and control issues involved.

SOCIAL SECURITY CASES

The UK Social Security Services pay out hundreds of millions (if not billions) in benefits to people who are not entitled to them. Many frauds result from people who claim false identities ('identity theft'). As we will see later, the majority of such cases are preventable by effective forms design.

Effectively designed forms should ensure we:

- obtain the facts necessary to make the right decisions;
- deter dishonest applicants by the design of the form;
- act in compliance with the law, especially the Data Protection Act and human rights convention;
- are able to prove that we have acted prudently if our judgment is questioned after the event.

The purpose of this chapter is to encourage you to review the forms you use in your organization and to make sure their control benefits are optimized.

Forms are important

TYPES OF FORMS

Forms are used to collect and process information, and they can be categorized as follows:

---

[1] Defined as: 'Printed or electronic documents which set out questions in a structured way, leaving spaces for the entry of information'

- for *internal use* only, when the image it presents of your organization is not critical;
- for *external use*, where the image created of the organization is important;
- forms *provided by others* for our completion.

The categories can be further divided according to their purpose:

- *Decision-related*. This may be a binary 'yes' or 'no' decision, or graded to the extent that successful applications are put in order of priority. *Examples include job application and bid evaluation forms.*
- *Process control*. When a form is used to direct or monitor an accounting or other operation. *Examples include electronic payment instructions, data entry forms and journal vouchers.*
- *Informational*, or with intrinsic financial value – when the form is used to collect and preserve information or to establish *legal* ownership, value or agreement. *Examples include: share certificates, certificates of deposit, contracts, custodial receipts, agreements and tax deduction statements.*

These categories frequently overlap and some forms may serve more than one purpose (Table 8.1).

Table 8.1   Examples of categories of forms

Examples of form Internal External	Decision-related *Applications and claims*		Process control Action required *Financial or other*	Informational *Minimal action required*
	Absolute	Graded or ranked		
Objectives of the form	Used as the basis for making an absolute, 'yes or no' decision	Used as the basis for ranking applications in order of priority	Used for processing transactions, proving value or title	Used for record keeping or archiving purposes
Application for employment and prepared biographies	**Yes** *The applicant is either accepted or rejected*	**Probably** *Accepted applicants are ranked in order*	**Possibly** *Used to set up master file entries and payroll*	**Possibly** *Used for tax and insurance purposes*
Mortgage applications	**Yes** *The applicant is either accepted or rejected*	**Yes** *The amount and other terms are decided*	**Yes** *Accounts are established and bank mandates obtained*	**Possibly** *Tax deduction certificates are processed*
Car insurance claims	**Yes**	**Possibly**	**Possibly**	**Partly** Archived records
Blank letter of credit form	**No** *Has intrinsic financial value when blank*		**Yes** *Financial instrument*	**Yes**
Electronic purchase order	**Yes**	**No**	**Yes**	**No**

Deception is more common on decision-related forms (columns 2 and 3), but the careful design of process control and informational forms is also justified, especially when they have a legal or monetary significance.

Some forms contain confidential information, but are usually sensitive only after they have been completed (*e.g. staff appraisal reports*). Forms may be submitted on paper or, more frequently these days, electronically through the Internet, intranet or a computer terminal. The permutations are almost limitless but most forms can make a much greater contribution to control than most organizations realize.

Effective form design can prevent deception

CATEGORIES OF DECEPTION

The type and nature of the form will determine its value and the way in which it can be corrupted by deception. Liars will often falsify or conceal derogatory information about themselves (Table 8.2).

In most cases important answers can be corroborated by supporting data (for example by examining the applicant's birth certificate) or verified externally (for example by taking references from a credit agency or comparing information from sources that are not normally related) and supported by an interview when the key facts can be confirmed by the way the subject responds to questions.

PENSIONS

In 2002, District Audit ran a programme comparing death records against the current roll of pensioners. They discovered thousands of cases where pensions were being claimed by people who had died years ago.

Notwithstanding these corroborative and reactive controls, liars should be primarily deterred by the design of the form itself.

The design of the form should deter liars by hitting their subconscious: hard

Table 8.2   Examples of types of deception

Factor which is falsified	Examples
Identity	False names and addresses to claim social security benefits
Other personal attributes	False health record to obtain life insurance
Track record	False educational qualifications
Level of authority	False employment record or present status
Nature of the transaction concerned	False accounts or financial results
Future intentions	False business plans

A VITAL PRINCIPLE

It is obvious that any person who puts down deceptive information on a form does so in bad faith and cannot be trusted thereafter. Thus, many forms have a dual purpose:

- To provide the information needed to make a decision. These are referred to as 'relevant questions'. *An unsuitable applicant either has to admit the truth to a relevant question or respond deceptively.*
- To provide information which may not be directly relevant to a decision, but which can be used to test generally whether the applicant is honest and acting in good faith or not. These are referred to as 'control questions' and they provide a baseline for determining the likely accuracy of answers to relevant questions and the applicant's overall honesty.

> *Any deception on an application form should immediately debar the applicant from consideration*

Control questions may be historical or they may relate to the applicant's future intentions or attitudes and, either way, they are very important. Experience shows that liars struggle with control questions because they do not understand their significance or how an honest person would answer them.

Insurance claims

For example, an insurance claim form may contain the following questions relating to an accident at work (see Table 8.3).

One of the biggest sucker punches on open questions has been:

HOW HONEST	
On a scale of 0 to 100, how accurate do you believe your answers to be? Experience shows that honest, committed people ask which way the scale runs and then	tick '100': liars usually don't ask for clarification and frequently enter their response halfway down the scale. Believe it: it happens and results from a lack of commitment.

Table 8.3   Examples of control and relevant questions

Relevant question	Control question
How was your injury sustained?	Tell me everything important about your injury. *The genuinely injured person will usually explain the intricacies of his operation, the symptoms and present status. The liar will usually focus on how the injury allegedly happened*
State the precise nature of your injury	What were you thinking about at the time the accident occurred?
Please give the name and address of the doctor who first treated you	Sometimes people falsify claims. What do you think about this and in what circumstances would you consider making a false claim justified?

To succeed with a false claim, the liar must answer the relevant questions untruthfully, whereas with control questions he has the option to claim poor memory, or in other ways avoid committing himself to a falsification.

From the liar's position, deception in response to relevant questions is compulsory but it appears optional for control questions. Inconsistencies in the responses between the two types are a strong indication of deception.

THE FALLACY OF HISTORICAL PERFORMANCE

Historical information – usually based on relevant questions – is often used to decide whether a person or organization can be trusted in the future. This is not necessarily a reliable indicator, and there are four important reasons for this:

- The fact that a person's record suggests that he has behaved properly in the past is by no means an assurance of future reliability. *For example, some employers allow fraudsters to resign and even go to the lengths of providing them with good references. Other employers prosecute. Thus it is purely by chance whether a crook gets a criminal conviction, bad reference or not.*
- Most large frauds were committed by people who appeared to have generally satisfactory track records at the time they were recruited into positions of trust. However, there are usually small indications of unreliability (discussed in Chapter 10, page 294).
- The fact that a person has behaved improperly in the past does not necessarily mean he will act dishonestly in the future. However, experience shows that there are two important considerations: the previous problems must have been exposed and resolved, and the person concerned must have been open about them when applying for a job.
- When a person has been dishonest and has either escaped without exposure or has concealed the truth when trying to establish a future relationship, fraud is almost inevitable.

The bottom line is that historical data has limited value in assessing future performance, although it is still important.

LEGALITY OF QUESTIONS

In many parts of the world, questions which might discriminate against someone on grounds of race, religion or sex or which could invade his right to privacy or contravene the data protection laws have to be drafted with care.

Besides these legal issues, if forms are too intrusive they can deter good applicants or create a negative image of the organization concerned. The balance between illegality, intrusion and effectiveness is critical (Figure 8.1).

In most organizations the balance is nearly always in favour of image over possible intrusion and this is a mistake.

You have the right to ask questions to keep out the bad guys

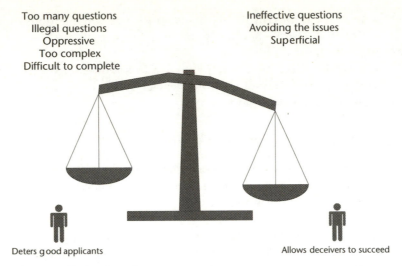

Too many questions
Illegal questions
Oppressive
Too complex
Difficult to complete

Ineffective questions
Avoiding the issues
Superficial

Deters good applicants

Allows deceivers to succeed

Figure 8.1   The critical balance on forms

GETTING INTO THE MIND OF THE APPLICANT

Most forms never take the psychology of deception into account (see Chapter 3 *ad nauseam*) or evaluate questions in terms of their impact on the liar's subconscious. For example, forms can play into the liar's hands by asking closed questions which suggest the answers required.

Open questions, on the other hand, call for freestyle explanations which are usually much more revealing. For example, an application form might ask:

> *Example*: 'Is there anything further you believe we might consider is relevant to your application? Please explain your answer, whether it is "yes" or "no".'
>
> *'If we found that your answers were not true and complete, please explain what your reaction would be and why'*

Obviously such questions would be used only in exceptional cases, but they are likely to throw a liar off track far more dramatically than they would a truthful applicant. The liar has to draw details from his memory, determine how much he has to reveal to succeed, and format answers in his own words.

These may reveal his attitude and hidden emotions, and he has the choice of either answering accurately or repressing the truth.

Effectively designed forms make liars uncertain

SUBJECTIVE AND ERRATIC DECISIONS

Many forms are intended to provide the foundations on which decisions are taken, but these are often made on a subjective, case-by-case basis. For example:

A SIMPLE TEST

If a good candidate declared that his last job had been as marketing director with a 'total package' of £200,000 pa and you discovered he had been marketing manager at a salary of £150,000, would you employ him? We suggest you should give him the chance to explain and, if there is not a sound reason for the discrepancy, reject him.

Decisions – whether absolute or graded – should be based on a pre-determined matrix of evaluation criteria. For example, it might state that anyone who deliberately falsified his earnings with a previous employer would be disregarded, or any potential customer whose assets have been secured by another creditor will be rejected.

For every decision-related form, there should be an associated template

Where a ranked decision is to be taken (for example putting bids in order of priority) the matrix should be based on the Kepner-Tregoe system of evaluating 'needs' and 'wants'. Appendix 2 sets out an example of an evaluation matrix that is used for grading potential vendors and a blank form can be downloaded from www.kepner-tregoe.com. A Kepner-Tregoe matrix enables decisions to be made consistently and transparently and establishes a clear audit trail. A matrix also reduces the risks of a decision being improperly influenced (for example by bribery) and allows vendors to be effectively debriefed after a contract has been awarded.

UNOFFICIAL FORMS

Sometimes employees introduce unofficial forms, and these can be dangerous for several reasons. They create deviations from approved procedures, resulting in inconsistencies and uncertainty. Further, in contested litigation, the victim may be unable to prove what procedure applied, during what period and to whom. Perhaps even more importantly, unauthorized forms and processes which have not been followed can be used in litigation to prove that the organization was negligent in not doing what it said it would.

It is more dangerous to have forms and procedures which are not followed than to have none

All forms should be properly authorized through a formal process and preferably a corporate policy: few organizations do this. More usually, forms are inconsistent and poorly designed. Archive copies are not retained, and thus users are unable to say which form or procedure applied at a specific time. This may be very important in both criminal and civil cases.

The title or code number and the date of printing should be shown on the face of all forms. Ideally they should also refer to any related procedure and the dates on which it was operable. A simple records retention programme is recommended for every organization (see Chapter 9, page 346).

ELECTRONIC FORMS

Increasingly, data traditionally collected on written forms is now entered electronically. This provides considerable advantages. For example:

MEDICAL CLAIM FORMS

One insurance company asks for claimants to enter details directly into a personal computer. If they cannot use a keyboard themselves, a trained operator makes entries, at the speed and in the order dictated by the claimant. The computer assesses the time taken to answer each question, the number of words used, answers which have been entered and subsequently altered and other criteria to highlight deception. The initial trials look promising.

In future, the most efficient organizations will use neural networks and other technology to uncover deception on such things as credit applications and insurance claims.

Psychology of deception

THE IMPORTANCE OF DETAIL

Few people like completing forms, although some forms (such as those for claiming lottery wins) are much more satisfying than others (such as tax returns). Form designers have to accept this, and should balance ease of completion against the risks of not asking for sufficient detail.

From a control point of view, the more detail the applicant is asked to submit, the better

ATTITUDES TO WARNINGS AND VERIFICATIONS

Honest people will not usually be worried by warnings on forms about the penalties for providing incorrect information. Neither are they afraid of committing themselves to the accuracy of their answers and are willing to provide corroborative detail, such as original copies of their educational certificates. Liars may be deterred by warning notices and because of this fail to pursue their applications: this is all to the good.

The objective is to deter liars

Also, honest people assume their replies will be verified and are not usually concerned about the methods and sources that might be used. They will usually unhesitatingly provide a release for references to be checked from past employers, bankers and so on.

On the other hand, liars are usually very concerned that their untruthfulness will be uncovered and may be disinclined to provide releases for external references to be obtained. They are more likely to give the names of referees they know cannot be checked, such as supposed previous employers whom they know have gone out of business or teachers or supervisors that they know have died. They may falsely list the telephone number of a friend or relative as the genuine contact point of a previous employer or educational establishment.

Information that cannot be verified is a profile of deception

The liar's confidence may also be shaken by any indication on the form which suggests that it will be extensively checked. As an extreme example, a block on a credit card application might appear as shown in Figure 8.2.

For Official Use Only					
Source	Polygraph	Fingerprints	DNA	Police	MI5
Residence	NSY	CIA	FBI	GCHQ	
Score					

Figure 8.2   Showing the checks and balances

This block creates the impression that extensive checks will be made (in the above case with the FBI, CIA[2] etc.) and serves as a strong deterrent to potentially deceptive applicants. *They will often refuse to submit the form, ask for an explanation, or hide their fears with misplaced humour.*

FALSE IDENTIFICATION AND FINGERPRINTING

Some liars go to great lengths to conceal their true identity, and this is made slightly more difficult when they are required to produce official documents such as passports or driving licences. However, these documents are easily falsified and the only way a person can be positively identified is through his fingerprints or DNA. Obviously, it would be unacceptable to fingerprint all applicants, and even less acceptable to draw their blood, but if it can be made clear to a dishonest applicant that his fingerprints will be obtained *covertly*, he may be deterred.

For example:

COVERT FINGERPRINTING AND PSYCHOLOGICAL DETERRENTS

Applicants are required to complete a short form under *supervision* of a representative of the company. The form is laid out as illustrated in Figure 8.3.

The form, which is enclosed unfolded in an A4 envelope, is handed to the applicant, and the desk on which he has to fill it in is shiny. To complete the form he has to hold it down (probably with his fingers on the glossy edges). It would be obvious to anyone who wished to avoid being identified that fingerprints would be captured on the blank edges. Innocent applicants do not appear to notice the significance of the glossy edges or the sealed envelope. In some cases, applicants have walked out, taking the partly completed form with them: others have tried filling it in with their gloves on. Both show dishonest intent, and if a deceptive applicant does complete the form, there is every chance that his true identity can be established if it subsequently becomes necessary to do so.

Identity theft is also very common when medical, driving or other examinations have to be carried out and it is not uncommon for an unsuitable applicant to ask a friend to take the

---

[2]   This is for illustrative purposes and not serious

Fingerprint sensitive edge

Figure 8.3   Form to covertly obtain fingerprints

tests on his behalf. For this reason, the identity of any applicant attending an examination or test should be positively confirmed and the details retained.

WIFE'S FRAUD TO IMPROVE HER LOVE LIFE

'A woman has been convicted of fraud for persuading her lover to pose as her husband to receive impotence surgery on his medical insurance. Jeane Lewis, 42, introduced Andre Dovilas as her husband to Brian Stone, a urologist at the New York hospital where she worked. Dovilas, 45, who works in a shop selling voodoo and black magic items, was prescribed Viagra but the couple returned because he was unhappy with the results. Dr Stone then suggested injections of phentolamine, alprostadil and papaverine, which Dovilas took along with Viagra. He was taken to hospital after spending 24 hours in a constant state of arousal. He then had two inflatable rubber cylinders implanted. Steven Lewis discovered his wife's infidelity when he received a letter for a "further appointment".

'Mrs Lewis faces up to seven years in jail, despite Dovilas fleeing to Haiti with the main prosecution exhibit: i.e. his todger.'

Daily Telegraph, 4 May 2000

Identity theft is a serious problem

SIGNATURES

From time immemorial, signatures have been used for identification purposes and while they are better than nothing, their control value is very limited.

THE HILL SAMUEL CASE

Hill Samuel is a leading merchant bank, based in the City of London. Various trading departments generate transactions which require settlement. These departments prepare forms authorizing payments under the signature of two employees. After authorization, the forms are sent via internal mail to the cables room, where relatively junior employees compare the signatures against specimens. If the signature on the payment form compares favourably with the specimen, the transaction is processed. One day, someone put 13 false payment instructions into the system: these were processed and £100 million paid out. Fortunately, Hill Samuel's reconciliation procedures were such that most of the money was recovered. But it was lucky; most victims are not.

The same sort of scam has been repeated hundreds, if not thousands, of times, and most organizations are vulnerable because they place too much reliance on signatures. They illustrate the need, especially on process control forms, to use secure authentication methods such as encryption, message authentication or biometrics.

From a control point of view, signatures are virtually valueless

CONCLUSIONS

Effective forms design can seize the initiative from crooks and put them on the defensive. If they foolishly decide to continue with their deception, they will be left exposed and without a plausible excuse.

Examples of deception on forms

INTRODUCTION AND EXAMPLES OF DECEPTION

The following paragraphs discuss some of the problems with commonly used forms. Pages 250 ff. make recommendations for improving controls.

APPLICATION FORMS

Introduction

Application forms normally result in an absolute or a graded decision and in all cases are exposed to deception.

Job application forms

It is reliably estimated that over 70 per cent of all job applications contain misleading information, and that if the potential employers knew the truth, in half of these cases the candidates
would have been rejected. The level of deception on prepared biographies is probably even
higher. Pages 294–326 set out a recommended procedure for screening job applicants.

Don't rely on prepared biographies

Mortgage applications

Over the past 20 years, mortgage frauds have spiralled out of control and are now estimated
to run at £4 billion per annum in the UK alone. The problems can usually be traced to the
fact that the lenders advanced funds without performing adequate checks on the honesty
of the borrowers, and especially their identity, financial standing and credit record. Lenders
also failed to ensure that the properties actually existed and were not the subject of other
mortgages.

These profiles make it important that:

- the identity and financial capacity of an applicant is confirmed;
- there are no duplicate applications running in parallel, possibly with other lenders;
- corroborating data, especially valuations, are confirmed;
- experts – such as surveyors, solicitors and valuers – are independent and warrant the accuracy of their opinions;
- the applicant and those with whom he is associated have not been involved in previous false
  applications.

Thus, most mortgage frauds can be prevented by the use of effective forms, basic verifications
and effective interviewing.

Look for patterns of repeated dishonesty

Welfare applications

The Department of Social Security (DSS) estimates that over £7 billion is lost annually to false
or inflated housing benefit claims.[3] The main frauds are committed by applicants for benefit
and by the owners of properties which they claim to occupy, and centre on:

- false identification and financial or political standing of the claimants;
- concealed income, assets and other benefits;
- falsification of dependent relatives;
- totally false claims by property owners, who make multiple or totally fictitious claims.

Many of these frauds could be prevented by making it clear – before the event – to the dishonest applicant that he will be positively identified, and prosecuted.

Design forms to deter the dishonest applicant

---

[3]   Intended to help people in receipt of state benefit pay their rent or mortgage

CLAIM FORMS

Introduction
Most claim forms are exposed to risks of deception, normally involving falsification rather than concealment. For this reason, detail is critically important.

Expense statements
Claims for reimbursement of business expenses are routinely falsified, including:

- fictitious expenses, such as misdescribing private entertaining as a business necessity;
- inflated amounts, such as altering taxi receipts or claiming for airline tickets at a higher class than travelled;
- duplicate claims, such as claiming the same expense in overlapping periods;
- incorrect currency conversions, such as claiming dollars instead of lira;
- personal items claimed as a business expense, such as claiming for petrol used on private journeys;
- alteration of amounts after authorization, such as altering an authorized amount from '£112.57' to '£712.57'.

Deception is made easier by the fact that most expense claim forms do not call for detailed information or corroborative vouchers.

DUFF EXPENSES

A senior salesman submitted his travelling expenses to his manager for authorization. After signature, he would collect them from his manager's out-tray, and alter amounts from £10 to £100 or from £40 to £400, and adjust the supporting vouchers accordingly.

He escaped with over £50,000 over a period of three years. Investigations established that he had pulled similar scams on two previous employers, both of whom had asked him to resign.

The risks of being deceived can be reduced by asking for detail and, from time to time, verifying it.

The deeper you dig, the more dishonesty is discovered

Sickness and other absence forms
Malingering is a serious problem, and avoiding work through feigned sickness is a significant cost for all employers, and may run at over 10 per cent of payroll costs per annum. Even the police service is hit by malingering. Some organizations fail to require corroboration of the supposed illness by a doctor, and most do not ask for detail that might deter malingerers.

MONDAYS AND FRIDAYS

The worst abuses occur on Mondays and Fridays, or immediately before and after public holidays such as Christmas and Easter, providing the malingerer with an extended vacation.

Open questions, asking for detailed responses, would make life much more difficult for the malingerer:

- While you were away from work sick did you leave your house? Please give details.
- How many days have you taken off from work in the past two years?
- Do you think your sickness record will be better or worse over the next twelve months?

A malingerer will be anxious about such questions, perhaps suspecting that he has been kept under surveillance. The questions will certainly make him think again before reporting sick to play golf. He is also more likely to say that he expects the next 12 months to be better whereas a person who is genuinely ill will not know.

Similar abuse takes place with annual holidays; employees take days off but do not submit the appropriate request, overstate their entitlement (often by bringing forward the balance from a previous period) or destroy the form after it has been authorized.

The dangers can be reduced by the use of a form which shows:

- the dates on which leave is requested and the number of work days involved;
- the employee's annual entitlement;
- any carried forward entitlement;
- the days taken so far and the balance remaining;
- the address at which the vacation will be taken and the telephone numbers.

A FREE HOLIDAY

In one case a purchasing agent put down the telephone number of a vendor's villa in Spain where he was discovered to be staying free of charge. Another agent entered the telephone number of a hotel but when a call was made, the employer found that he too was staying in the vendor's villa. Big villa: important vendor.

The absence form (which should be in duplicate) should incorporate a certificate to the effect that 'I have checked my entitlement and the balance of vacation. I certify that the above are true and correct.' The duplicate copy should be marked: 'Please retain this copy for your own records'. A related process should log each employee's absences, and an annual declaration (see page 327) may be used to confirm its accuracy.

CALL REPORTS

Most banks keep 'call reports', summarizing details of the conversations they have had with customers. When a customer defaults, banks, unsurprisingly, go into a flat spin to get their money back and refer to call reports to see whether there are any clues as to where the customer's assets may have been hidden. Banks could make much greater use of call reports by training their employees (while the customer is solvent, bright-eyed and bushy-tailed) so that they get all possible details that could be useful if recovery becomes necessary. Few do this (see Dealing with Conmen: Chapter 10, page 356).

MISCELLANEOUS FORMS

Introduction

Organizations use an array of miscellaneous forms and rely on some produced by others. Of these, birth certificates are among the most unreliable.

Birth certificates

Most people will remember the film *The Day of the Jackal,* in which the anti-hero played by Edward Fox obtained the birth certificates of babies who had died soon after birth and used their names to create a number of false identities. The same method is true today and has become something of a science among the criminal fraternity.

THE WEST AFRICAN SCAMS

The West African groups, which rely on false identification for many of their scams, covertly mark the birth records at the UK's central registry, to let other gangs know that the certificate has already been used. Who says there is no honour among thieves?

In some countries the issue of birth certificates is barely controlled at all and duplicate documents can be obtained by anyone, almost at any time. The fact is that no organization should rely on a birth certificate as proof of identity.

AUTHORIZATION FORMS

Introduction

An array of forms is used for authorizing transactions and to provide an audit trail after the event. They are all exposed to alteration, concealment and falsification, including:

- purchase orders;
- contracts;
- credit notes;
- discount approvals and price adjustments;
- payment instructions;
- travelling expenses;
- journal vouchers.

The forms used in such processes vary from simple unnumbered documents through to sophisticated entries via a computer terminal. They may be controlled by authentication tokens, passwords, dual entry, triangulation and separate levels for entry, confirmation and release.

Main problems

The main problems are that:

- inadequate corroborating data is available at the time of authorization;
- limits are defeated by dividing the transaction into slices which are within the crook's own authority;

- where dual signatures are required, one signatory signs a block of blank documents in advance;
- transactions are duplicated;
- the authorizer is overwhelmed and does not have time to check;
- signatures are forged;
- documents are not invalidated – to prevent reuse – after authorization;
- after authorization, the documents are returned to the initiator, thus providing him with the opportunity to alter them.

Often a signature is the only evidence that a transaction has been authorized, and this is a very weak control.

Control considerations

PRINCIPLES

The most important principle is that forms achieve their intended objective. This may vary from providing the information necessary to make good decisions, to assuring the accuracy of a process or protecting evidence of value or ownership. There are a number of important control principles.

FORM DESIGN

Standard information
Every form should show:

- an identifying label, title or code;
- the date of printing, its retention period and destruction date;
- a copyright notice and security classification (e.g. 'confidential' or 'private');
- colour coding (e.g. all forms used by and destined for audit might be coloured red);[4]
- extracts of the relevant process, or a reference to where explanatory information can be found.

Ideally all forms should be consistently designed, using common layouts and fonts. Forms for external use[5] should incorporate the company's logo, contact addresses (including website and email), telephone and VAT numbers and, where appropriate, a summary of the terms and conditions of business, policies on business ethics, reporting of incidents, data protection and other releases.

The immediate impact of the form
The initial impression created by a form is very important, especially when it has to be completed by customers and other third parties. Factors that should be considered include:

---

4 This makes misplaced forms easy to identify
5 These should be a marketing tool

- the size and length of the form: generally forms are too small;
- the size of the spaces allowed for data entry: generally these are too cramped;
- the overall layout and structure;
- the use of graphics: these have a significant impact on the readers' subconscious, but they must be professionally designed;
- the size and colour of print: warnings should be in red and emboldened to create the maximum right hemisphere impact;
- the colour and quality of the paper.

A cramped form, in which the user has insufficient space to enter data, gives the impression that it is not important. This is a fatal failing. The size of the form should be dictated by the information it is required to provide, not by cost considerations.

Raising the pavement

Important forms used for decision making should, by their design, make it clear that:

- deception will be detected and punished, possibly by criminal prosecution;
- answers will be verified.

By having to commit to a deliberate falsification, many otherwise deceptive applicants will be deterred. The pavement can be raised by:

- the visual impact the form has on the applicant, such as layout and colour, with boxes for official use;
- warnings on the consequences of false declarations;
- clear or chemically impregnated edges to capture fingerprints;
- an explanation of how the form will be checked, the corroborative data that will be required and the process generally.[6]

Ways in which a deterrent to deception can be achieved on job application forms are explained at page 304.

Classification and retention

The financial, privacy or other sensitivity of the form should be evaluated based on the information it contains, or will contain, and its possible exposure to misuse – both when completed and in blank. For example, job application forms should be pre-printed with the classification[7] of *'private'*, whereas blank 'letters of credit' forms might be preprinted with a sequential number and the words: *'financially sensitive'*. Processes should ensure that such classifications lead to consistent protection in terms of secure filing, dissemination, transmission and destruction.

In some cases it is also prudent to mark forms with their retention period. This may be by preprinted wording, such as *'retain permanently'*, or in the case of financial records (which by UK law must be retained for six years) 'Do not destroy before xxxx'.

---

[6] An explanation of the related process is advised by the Information Commissioner (see Chapter 10): it is also a good way of raising the pavement

[7] Every organization should have a process for classifying and protecting sensitive information

Welcoming address or explanation

Where appropriate, forms should explain why they are required and their importance. The introduction should also alert the user to the information he will need to collect and possibly attach.

For example, a form to be completed for pre-qualification by potential vendors might state:

WORDING FOR PRE-QUALIFICATION OF VENDORS

'This form is very important. It will be used to establish the basis of our trading relationship. We are committed to excellence for our customers and if your application is successful you will become an important member of our team. It is vital there are no surprises. So please take care over the completion of the form; if any information you provide is found to be inaccurate, our relationship will be terminated.

To complete this form you will need:

- a copy of your last year's accounts;
- a copy of your company incorporation certificate and VAT registration documents;
- details of your directors and shareholders;
- references from three existing customers and their telephone numbers;
- a copy of your current price list and product catalogue.

If at any time you have any complaints over aspects of our relationship, please contact our compliance manager on telephone number xxxxx or by email on xxxx. If your application is approved, you will be required to comply with our code of conduct, security and other procedures, copies of which will be provided at the appropriate time. We look forward to working with you.'

Such introductions create a common framework and raise the pavement, making deception less likely and less defensible, if detected.

Coverage and relevance of questions

Basic principles

The questions asked must be legal and should concentrate on the key issues. But control questions may be included to evaluate the applicant's general accuracy, attitude and approach.

Legality of questions

The questions that can be asked for personal applicants are becoming more and more limited on the grounds that merely asking about any of the following can result in claims of unfair discrimination:

- race or colour;
- sex;
- age;
- religion;
- marital status;

- nationality or citizenship;
- health, physical and mental disabilities.

Thus legal advice should be obtained before the application form is finalized.

Releases and undertakings

On most decision-related applications, it is prudent to obtain the applicant's release to check references and to confirm his understanding that:

- Data provided may be used for loss prevention purposes (to comply with data protection legislation). For example:

PERSONAL DATA

'Personal and other information provided on this form will be used for: [x]. It may also be used for the prevention and detection of fraud and for security purposes may be released to government agencies. If you object to this use, please tick here.' The response to such warnings and releases may tell you a lot about the applicant!

- Communication, computer and other systems provided by the organization may be used for reasonable private purposes, but such use does not give any expectation to rights of privacy when fraud or abuse is suspected (to comply with the human rights legislation). The form of wording used by one British company is:

COMMUNICATIONS MONITORING RELEASE

'Employees are permitted to use computer systems, telephones and other equipment for occasional non-business purposes. Nevertheless, the employee has no right of privacy as to any information or file maintained in, on, transmitted or stored on the company's computer or telecommunications systems, voice mail, email … employees are permitted to use their own laptops for company business on the clear understanding that they may be subject to audit at any time.'

- He will comply with all of the organization's policies and procedures relating to loss control and will cooperate in any investigation when requested to do so. The form of wording used by one European company states:

SECURITY POLICY

'If employed, the candidate undertakes as a condition of continued employment to comply with all of the company's policies and procedures, specifically those relating to audit, security and control, and will report errors, discrepancies and malpractice without delay, assist in investigations and recoveries including, if necessary, permitting any personal property on company premises to be searched or examined.'

- He will give immediate notification of any change in his personal circumstances that could have an impact on the facts disclosed in the application.

Finally, the applicant should give an undertaking that he will advise you of any material changes to his circumstances both before and after his application has been accepted.

Corroborating data

Corroborating data should be required to support key questions on all application forms. For example, this might include for vendors:

- certificate of incorporation;
- annual accounts for the past three years;
- biographies of directors;
- tax certificate, etc.

On process control forms, corroborating data might include a copy of any relative transaction *(e.g. on a form to approve a credit note, it might be necessary to attach the original sales invoice)*. For personal expense claims, a box should be provided for the mileometer reading on the company car or a copy of the employee's credit card statement, rather than just the individual vouchers.

Always consider corroborating data

Closing declarations and warrantees

Where appropriate, applicants should be required to warrant the accuracy and completeness of the answers they have given. On a vendor application form this might be:

ON VENDOR APPLICATION FORMS

'I certify that the answers I have given are true, complete and correct. I understand that this form will be used as the basis of any future contract between me and x and that any incorrect, incomplete or inaccurate answers will result in my removal for consideration or immediate termination of any contract. I undertake to advise x of any changes in my circumstances which could affect this application, any future relationship or contract. I also undertake to advise x of any changes in my personal, financial and business circumstances which in any way could influence this application or, if engaged, my continued engagement.'
Signed …

Besides providing the organization with powerful rights of redress, the need to enter into such undertakings is likely to deter a deceptive applicant.

SECURITY AND CONTROL FEATURES

Depending on its type and importance, a number of security features can be incorporated into the form, for example including:

- anti-counterfeiting measures such as holograms and security printing;
- sequential numbering and check digits to prevent alteration and detect omissions;
- authorization codes and test keys (rather than signatures);

- blocked fields to prevent the entry of data other than by authorized people;
- colour coding.

Cobasco's website (www.cobasco.com) contains an annotated list of control tools for both forms and their associated processes.

RELATED PROCESSES

General
Forms should be supported by specified processes which state how they should be used. Processes may be specified in operating manuals, on the reverse of forms, on an intranet or elsewhere. The object in all cases is to make it clear what action should be taken, when and by whom.

Library
Sets of blank forms should be retained in a library, intranet site or central computer. For example, programs such as Omnipage are excellent for designing forms and for retaining copies for use by anyone connected to an internal network, intranet or Internet. The processes that support them should also be available on an intranet or other easily accessible source.

Decision matrices
For every decision-related form there must be an appropriate matrix which will be used to make absolute or graded decisions. The matrix for absolute decisions can vary in complexity from a simple checklist through to a sophisticated neural network. Either way:

- the matrix should be unambiguous;
- it should be applied consistently;
- a copy of the completed matrix should be filed with the form concerned;
- the effectiveness of the matrix should be reviewed from time to time.

For graded decisions, the template should be prepared on a Kepner-Tregoe or similar basis that identifies absolute requirements (called 'needs') and desirable attributes (called 'wants'). An example in the procurement screening area is in Appendix 2.

Receipt and evaluation of the form
Experience shows that most important application forms are best reviewed by at least two people in brief brainstorming sessions. In this way, deception is more likely to be uncovered.

Examination of corroborating data
A consistent process should be established to ensure that corroborating data is properly examined and validated, before decisions are taken. For example, on educational certificates the bona fides of the school or university should be confirmed, as should the day on which the certificate was issued.

> *Example*: In one case a false certificate was issued during a national holiday, another outside the school term and in one case on Christmas Day.

Copies of corroborating data should be filed securely with the associated application form.

Depending on the circumstances, applicants may be required to attend special tests or medical examinations, and in such cases it is critical that their identity is positively confirmed and recorded.

External verification

On most decision-related forms, a process should be specified and responsibilities allocated to verify key data with external sources. This should be part of a formal due diligence and integrity validation process (see Chapter 9, page 293).

Clearance interviews

In some cases, the detail provided on application forms should be corroborated by independent and externally verified data. Based on the findings, the applicant may be invited to attend an interview. Here the objective is to expand on and test the accuracy of the application form. See page 419 ff.

The decision process

At some point in the life of all forms, decisions will be made or actions taken based on the information they provide. In important and appropriate cases, the reasons behind the decisions reached or action planned should be documented.

Trial periods

In some cases (employment is a good example), it is prudent to make a commitment based on the successful completion of a trial period. In this time, performance can be monitored.

Secure authorization

The process for authorizing and transmitting financially sensitive and process control forms should be reviewed and improved where reliance is placed on a signature. The options include test keys, message authentication codes, sequence numbers, encryption and triangulation. Whichever one is used, it is critical that forms are not returned to the initiator after they have been authorized.

REVIEW OF PAST DECISIONS

From time to time, it is important to review the success and failure rate of all decision-related forms. Such reviews will identify areas for improvement, and especially the accuracy of evaluation templates.

Decisions may be divided into four categories (Table 8.4).

Table 8.4 Potential decisions

Example of form	Positive Application or claim approved		Negative Application or claim rejected	
	Valid	Invalid	Valid	Invalid
Employment application	Effective employee recruited	**Ineffective employee recruited**	Ineffective employee rejected	**Effective employee rejected**
Insurance claim	Valid claim settled	**Invalid claim settled**	Invalid claim rejected	**Valid claim rejected**

Organizations tend to monitor valid and invalid positive decisions, but do not analyse invalid negative decisions. These are shown in Table 8.4 in bold type. For example, in vendor selection the result of a positive decision is obvious from subsequent performance. But what of rejected candidates? To validate a decision matrix, occasional reviews should be made of the subsequent progress of rejected candidates. If they have been outstandingly successful, the decision matrix should be reviewed and improved criteria incorporated.

Reviewing your forms

THE STARTING POINT

If you have not reviewed the forms used in your organization, now may be the time to do so. Why not consider setting up a small project team to get the review underway or perhaps evaluate the forms in the area for which you are responsible. The results will be improved control and much better decisions.

The starting point is to decide on the extent of the review; for example, whether all forms in a company or department will be included or whether it will be limited to a process or even a single form. We recommend not dealing with forms individually, but reviewing them in sets for related departments or processes.

CATALOGUE OF THE FORMS AND PROCESSES IN USE

The starting point is to prepare a catalogue of approved and unofficial forms in use:

- in the organization as a whole;
- covering a discrete process, such as sales accounting;
- in a specific department.

A sample catalogue can be downloaded from www.cobasco.com.

Table 8.5   Simplified example of a catalogue

Description of form Internal or external use Completed by	Type (decision-related, process control, informational)	Ref no. or code	Owner and date taken into use Procedure manual	Objectives and key factors on which decisions will be based
PRE-QUALIFICATION OF VENDORS External: Decision Potential vendors	Info Decis	PQV1	Purchasing 1 May 1997 PURCHASING MANUAL SECTION 3.3	To obtain background information on the reliability and quality of potential vendors. There is no template and decisions whether or not to place a vendor on the pre-qualified list are taken on a subjective basis by members of purchasing
VENDOR'S BANK ACCOUNT DETAILS External: Informational Approved vendors	Fin Info	BA1	Purchasing 1 May 1997 PURCHASING MANUAL SECTION 3.3	Used to process payments to vendors
EMPLOYEES' EXPENSE STATEMENTS Internal: Financial process Employees	Fin	EE1	Personnel 1 June 1995 PERSONNEL MANUAL SECTION 2	To reimburse employees for expenses genuinely incurred on company business
PAYMENT AUTHORIZATION FORM External: Financial process FX trading Commodities Other Line manager	Fin Proces	PAY 1	Treasurers Department 1 October 1997 NONE; Informal	Serves as the authority for the Cable Room to pay funds

It is important to determine the ownership of each form and the related process. This might be a department or an individual but, either way, every form should have a designated owner who has the authority for control and who carries responsibility for failure. Also the coding system used should be easy to understand or forms should be consistently referred to by their title e.g. 'Vendor approval form'.

DETAILED ANALYSIS OF FORMS

Risk identification

A copy of the form should be obtained and a flow chart prepared summarizing the way it is processed. In a *brainstorming session*, the following aspects should be considered:

- the type of form, i.e. decision-related, process or informational;
- the key information or data elements it is meant to handle;
- how the key information is corroborated;
- past experience and especially any problems;
- the existing processes and control features.

The exposure to error, fraud or unauthorized disclosure should be considered, including:

- External counterfeiting.
- Misuse of blank forms.
- False information:
  - concealment, failure to submit a form and destruction,
  - insufficient or inaccurate external corroborative information,
  - insufficient or inaccurate historical record of previous decisions.
- Improper processing:
  - concealment or destruction,
  - duplicate processing.
- Fraudulent processing.
- Data entry:
  - validation,
  - authorization,
  - signature verification,
  - fraudulent authorization.
- Post processing alteration or destruction.

The result should be a catalogue of risks relating to each form and the data elements that are exposed to deception.

Evaluation and recommendations

Based on the review of the form itself and its related process, aspects that require improvement will emerge.

REVIEWS OF RELATED PROCESSES

The procedures relating to each form should also be analysed:

- Are they compatible with the current use of the form?
- Do they explain its use?

- Have important extracts from the procedure been summarized on the form?
- Are the procedures easily accessible, but only to those people who need to know?

Particular attention should be paid to unofficial forms where there is not a related specified procedure.

Conclusions

The review suggested in this chapter can significantly improve your security and control. We hope you will give it a try.

Solutions to HR Problems

THE 'TONE' AT THE TOP

9 HR Procedures

Who laughs last, thinks slowest

About this chapter

It is axiomatic that every asset and every process is secure if the only people allowed access to them are honest. This chapter explains:

- The legal and other standards that directors and employees must maintain to discharge their responsibilities: these are worrying and becoming increasingly more onerous. Failure can result in swingeing personal liabilities.
- The policies and processes needed to motivate humans (and especially employees) to behave honestly.

It also enables you to benchmark critical control-related personnel policies and procedures such as:

- business ethics;
- due diligence, integrity validation and pre-employment screening;
- HR control-related policies and procedures;
- reporting of incidents, hotlines and whistle-blowing;
- investigatory policies and procedures;
- other control-related policies and procedures.

This is a long and technical chapter but it is important because, unless you have the right policies and procedures in place, you will be unable to deal effectively with deception at work.

In the final analysis, the success of many policies and procedures comes down to effective interviewing and asking the right questions at the right time including:

- recruitment;
- annual appraisals;
- termination of employment;
- pre-qualification of vendors;
- business meetings and negotiations.

The cunning plan, described in Chapter 5, can be applied to these interviews which will be far more effective if the right policies and procedures are in place.

The importance of honest humans

In 1997 the Economic Policy Institute of Washington DC (www.epinet.org) stated what has since become glaringly obvious, and that is that the market value of businesses depends more upon their intellectual capital, and especially their human resources, than it does on conventional assets. What has not been equally recognized, however, are the liabilities arising from negative intellectual capital, especially from greedy or dictatorial directors, dishonest senior managers and unethical employees.

Catastrophic cases, ranging from BCCI through to Enron and WorldCom, demonstrate that an organization's ambivalent approach to honesty by the people on whom it relies can be its biggest liability. On the other hand, an honest, strongly motivated workforce is an organization's greatest asset.

Honest people are the key to success.
Human relations are critically important

The principles of control

THE BASICS

A control is defined as anything that assures the performance or integrity of something else and includes such things as:

- *perception and values*, which define the culture and ethics of the organization and the way it is viewed by others:
  - statements of the company's values, visions and goals,
  - leadership and setting the tone from the top;
- *effective supervision*, which ensures responsibilities are assigned and enforced;
- *education and training*, which ensures employees appreciate risks and understand their responsibilities;
- *policy*, which sets out management's intentions and standards of control;
- *standards and procedures*, which specify the standards to be maintained:
  - for assets and hardware used by the organization,
  - for specified processes, such as accounting, HR, security, IT etc.

Contrary to popular misconception, controls, when properly applied, do not restrict entrepreneurial flair nor flexibility but should, in fact, support them and provide the foundation for success.

Effective control leads to opportunities

Inadequate control can lead to performance compromises, to losses and, increasingly, to personal liabilities for managers and employees.

Poor control results in problems: the chickens always come home to roost

This chapter discusses controls in the categories shown in Table 9.1.

Table 9.1 Control categories

The control is applied to	Examples of control			
	Intelligence	Preventive	Reactive	Reconstructive
Environmental	Values, visions, ethical standards			
Specific processes	Business intelligence	Accounting procedures	Monitoring software	Fidelity insurance
Specific hardware	CCTV	Access controls	Alarms	Standby centres
Human resources	Hot lines	Screening contracts	Appraisals	Replacement charts

As far as possible, controls should be commensurate with the risk and should be sufficient to meet the organization's legal and compliance requirements (Figure 9.1).

Achieving this balance is easier said than done because risks vary dramatically over time and compliance requirements change almost daily. The two critical balancing factors are good intelligence and effective reactive controls. If you have these in place, the chances are you will not go far wrong.

The reason why fraud can be disastrous is because victims don't understand their risks and react ineffectively when suspicions first surface

Each organization is unique and controls have to be tailored to its specific risks. There are few standard solutions but two critical principles apply. The first is that profitability and risks are usually symbiotic: the greater the potential reward, the greater the risk and thus the need for control. The second principle is that risks and controls do not align on a one-to-one

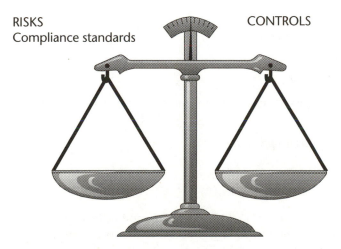

Figure 9.1 Balance of risks and controls

basis. The relationship between them is 'many to many' where an array of risks can only be countered by an array of controls. This calls for defence in depth.

OBJECTIVES OF CONTROL

There are three primary objectives of control:

- To *optimize profits* and business continuity by reducing risks and to comply with regulatory standards.
- To have *fail-safe procedures* and resources in place so that potential problems are quickly detected and corrected.
- To be *able to demonstrate*, after the event, that the company acted prudently and made every reasonable attempt to comply with laws, rules and regulations.

Often this third consideration is overlooked, but it is vitally important, because in the final analysis such proof might mitigate the personal liabilities of good managers (see page 272 ff.).

ENVIRONMENTAL CONTROLS

Some controls positively influence the environment in which the organization operates. For example, most HR processes (such as pre-employment screening, conflicts of interest etc.), and security, audit and accounting procedures are environmental in their nature and should apply consistently to every part of the organization.

The most important environmental controls are those concerning the organization's values, visions, business ethics and leadership style, because there is no question that the tone is set at the top.

Conversely, criminal behaviour is learned. It is both corrosive and contagious and senior managers who break, or pay little regard to, the law and ethical standards, encourage others to follow. The art is to promote policies, processes and practices which set the tone of the organization as both an exemplary corporate citizen and a very hard target that will stand no nonsense.

Become an exemplary citizen and a hard target

SPECIFIC CONTROLS

Environmental controls should be supplemented by others applied to specific 'elements', which are either:

- assets;
- processes;
- people.

Specific controls should function within a secure and ethical environment and should be specified for all important and commonly used elements including hardware: such as personal computers, photocopiers, computer networks or processes; such as employee screening, accounts payable or credit reporting. Specific controls are implemented through hardware standards and specified procedures.

CATEGORIES OF CONTROL

Introduction
There are divisions within the categories of environmental and specific controls: these are described below.

Intelligence and risk analysis
Accurate intelligence, and an understanding, and thus a forewarning, of risks, enables problems to be anticipated and avoided. When it comes to dishonesty, most organizations are woefully unaware of the potential dangers and have no reliable process for evaluating their risks.

FAMILIAR AND UNFAMILIAR RISKS

As we have seen, the human brain is a weird and complex organism. It tends to be more concerned with esoteric and improbable risks, while overlooking obvious perils in routine life. It is also true that the perception of risks varies directly with intelligence. This is probably a reflection of the evolutionary process since the more intelligent animals dealt more effectively with risks and thus had a greater chance of survival.

Ironically, in the commercial world, the perception of risk seems to vary inversely with rank. This simply means that the more senior you are, the more divorced from reality you become, but don't tell your boss this.

The perception of risk varies directly with intelligence and inversely with rank

Intelligence on, and evaluation of, risks should be provided by the corporate security or internal audit department or by external advisers.

Every organization should have a source of intelligence on risks

Preventive controls
Preventive controls are essentially 'before the event' and are intended to restrict access, pin down accountability and provide a deterrent against malpractice. Locks, physical security barriers or processes such as authority tables and separation of responsibilities can all be classed as preventive controls. They are normally related to a specific hardware element or specified process.

Preventive controls can also be covert or subliminal to the extent that they impact on the subconscious of the potential opponent and deter or deflect him. At a basic level, things like dummy television cameras or alarm boxes, or Percy the poodle who would bite any burglar, can be regarded as perceptual controls. But more advanced techniques, such as the covert collection of fingerprints (pages 243–4) and building designs based on controlled space planning or 'crime prevention through environmental design' (CPTED), have a role to play in preventing crime and dishonesty, by hitting the villain's subconscious.

Reactive controls

Not all risks can be prevented and thus reactive controls monitor performance, detecting deviations from the norm that may be symptomatic of fraud. Burglar alarms or processes such as reporting of incidents procedures are examples of specific reactive controls. They are mainly after-the-fact, but are extremely important. Knowledge of their existence may also deter potential opponents.

Reconstructive controls

Not all risks can be prevented or detected quickly. Thus, controls in a third layer are classed as 'reconstructive' and enable the organization to recover quickly from an adverse event. Contingency planning, replacement tables for key employees, insurance and computer back-up are examples of reconstructive controls. It is vital that they are simple and fail-safe and work effectively when needed.

The important balance

Generally, preventive controls are expensive to maintain; they usually inconvenience honest people and can quickly fall into disuse.

AUTHORITY TABLES

For example, if five signatures are required to authorize a purchase invoice over £500 in value, junior employees will collude with vendors to get multiple invoices, for amounts that fall within their authority levels. The control is thus useless.

Ideally, an organization's control strategy should be based on good intelligence, effective environmental controls with minimal preventive elements and highly effective reactive and reconstructive controls. This approach improves flexibility and provides cost-effective solutions.

THE PRINCIPLE OF OWNERSHIP

Each element in the extended enterprise should have a designated owner, who has the authority to ensure controls are effective and who should carry the responsibility for failure. The balance between authority and responsibility is critical to effective control (Figure 9.2).

Ownership should be established through contracts, organizational charts, asset listings, policies, procedures and, most importantly, through job descriptions, leadership and effective supervision. Ownership rights and responsibilities must be assigned so that every asset and process has a designated owner and every person a supervisor to whom he is accountable for control.

AUTHORITY   RESPONSIBILITY

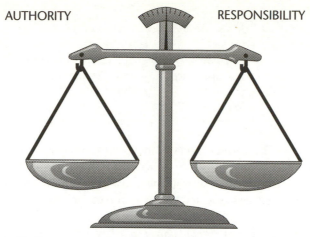

Figure 9.2 The critical balance

TURN TO PAGE 252

Consultants were retained by a major international company to review and improve its IT security. They were told not to write a big report as: 'our people are too busy to read them'; 'don't try to rush around the world making presentations and forget about making any sort of gimmicky video'. This was a tough brief, but the consultants identified serious problems, mainly caused by a total lack of ownership, with senior managers who had the power and authority to improve controls doing nothing because they knew they could blame their subordinates for any failure.

The consultants wrote a very large book, entitled *Information Security Standards*. The first page gave a brief introduction and said:

'If you want to improve controls over the resources for which you are responsible, please turn to page 2'. This contained the start of a checklist. The introduction also said: 'If you believe everything is fine and you do not need to make any improvements, please turn to page 252'. This page said: 'Please complete and sign the following letter addressed to the managing director'. The letter said: 'I have received the Standards on IT Security and I am totally satisfied that everything is fine and that nothing can go wrong. If it does, I will resign without question and pay back anything that has been lost'. The page also contained a postscript which said: 'If you won't want to sign this letter, please turn back to page 2'. Most people did and things improved.

The cow grows fat under the eyes of the owner

In organizations that operate on a matrix management structure, the control reporting lines must be singular and unambiguous.

NICK LEESON

Mr Leeson was able to succeed in his scam for so long because, under a matrix management system, he had one reporting line to Singapore and another to the product group in London. Rivalry, and a lack of communication between his bosses, enabled him to say one thing to some and a totally different thing to others. No one had ownership.

Since most owners will be line managers, who have limited security and control expertise, specialists – such as internal audit or corporate security – must provide assistance by identifying risks and specifying the baseline controls that must be maintained by owners, monitoring their compliance, investigating suspected breaches and enforcement.

Internal audit or corporate security should provide a safety net

RELATIONSHIPS OF VALUES, POLICIES, PROCEDURES AND STANDARDS

In theory, the tone, set at the top, and other environmental controls spread throughout the organization in a continuous flow to the lowest levels and outer reaches of the extended enterprise (Figure 9.3).

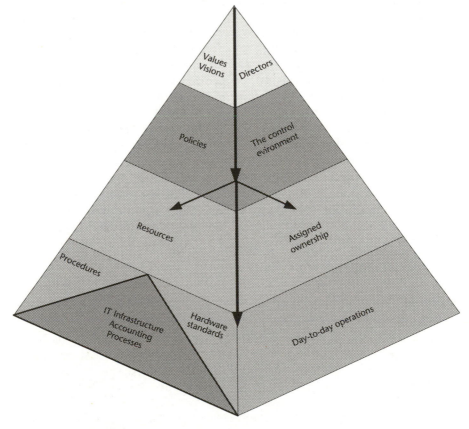

Figure 9.3 Critical relationships

The connection between values and baseline procedures in Figure 9.3 appears as a hierarchy, but it is more in the nature of a chain, with each link being dependent on another. Thus, statements on values and visions as well as policies must be linked to detailed procedures and operating standards.

REASONS FOR CONTROL FAILURES

The most common reasons for control failures are:

- risks were not understood;
- the culture of the organization (or important departments within it) was control averse, usually believing it could never happen to them;
- controls were not specified nor allocated to an owner who had the authority and responsibility for maintaining them, thus people did not know what was expected of them;
- controls did not function in the way they were specified, thus although people knew what they should do, they ignored it.

All of these faults can be corrected with a little planning and for minimal cost and, if they are not, can lead to serious consequences for the organization and for its managers, personally.

The art of effective control is to be wise before the event

The standards expected

BASIC POSITIONS

In companies, liability is only limited for shareholders, and a director or employee who is found to have acted negligently faces the prospect of unlimited personal liability. If this is not a reason for careful control from the top, nothing is.

Increasingly, alleged corporate misdeeds result in personal liabilities

Companies may be held criminally and civilly liable for the tortuous acts of their employees, even when they have acted outside the scope of their authority. Directors may be responsible for *ultra vires* acts of their companies if they did not vote against them. The reverse of this coin can be found in some American cases, where the collective knowledge of employees has resulted in liabilities for their employer.

COLLECTIVE KNOWLEDGE

In the case of US v Bank of New England (1st Cir. 1987), an employee received cash deposits from a customer for more than $10,000 which under the Currency Reporting Transaction Act he should have reported. He did not know the law. His superiors knew the law, but not about the transactions and the bank was penalized under the 'collective knowledge' rule.

In the UK, a director need not exhibit in the performance of his duties a greater degree of skill than may reasonably be expected from a person with his knowledge and experience. Thus a truck driver who is promoted to become chairman is only required to exercise the skills of a truck driver. In the US, a chairman must act like one, whatever his background and experience.

In the UK the duty of care for a manager or an employee requires him to:

- exercise reasonable skill and competence in the areas in which he holds himself out as skilled to undertake;
- indemnify the employer against liabilities to third parties by reason of his failure to exercise his skills or to take reasonable care.

The same standards are required of a director who also works as an employee. Courts decide, on a case-by-case basis, whether a person's performance was sufficient to discharge his responsibilities. Directors act as agents of the company and must not let their personal interests prevail. Thus, a director who conceals a bad decision to protect his job, or to gain promotion, could be in breach of his obligations as an agent of his employer.

DEFECTIONS

It is not at all uncommon for employees who are thinking of leaving their employer – maybe to start a rival business – to discuss plans among themselves. They don't realize that such discussions are illegal and that their fiduciary duties require proper disclosure to their employer.

Normally, employees only become liable under the criminal law when they have acted with specific intent, but a number of American courts have ruled that 'wilful blindness' is just as bad.

REGULATIONS

Background

Laws and regulations vary from country to country, but there are some common patterns which can be identified by examining the regulatory framework in the US and UK. In many respects US laws are crucially important, because they apply to any 'domestic concern', which includes any business with a base, branch, office or connection in the US and companies publicly listed in the US. Thus, many European companies are bound in all of their worldwide operations by such laws as the Foreign Corrupt Practices Act, the Sherman Act (anti-trust and price fixing) and by the newly passed Public Company Accounting Reform and Investor Protection Act.

Regulations in the US

Basic positions
Over recent years the legislative branch has been especially active in the white collar crime area. Overtly, the intent has been to deter 'fraud in the suites and suits', but it is no coincidence

that the laws have resulted in very significant revenues being collected. Cases such as Drexell, Burnham and Lambert, where penalties and fines exceeded one billion dollars, did no harm to the Treasury.

The US courts have also claimed extra-territorial jurisdiction (see the case of Leasco v Maxwell, 2nd Cir. 1972) over companies operating outside the US where their conduct has a significant effect on the domestic market or where it causes injury within the US (see Laker Airways v SABENA, DC Cir. 1984). This trend has been reinforced by a number of criminal and civil actions. They have ruled that directors will be civilly and possibly criminally liable if they respond improperly to the symptoms of fraud.

The case of Smith v Van Gorkom (Del. 1985) determined that directors must:

- take all due care to investigate allegations of wrongdoing;
- keep themselves informed of the facts;
- seek appropriate professional advice;
- take time to consider the options;
- take appropriate action.

They must also keep the full board of directors updated.

Also US courts have generally determined that they have jurisdiction over all companies which have any connection with the US and have been forceful in asserting rights to discover evidence from overseas and demand the attendance of witnesses.

RECORDS PRODUCTION

In the case brought by the Grand Jury against the Bank of Nova Scotia (11th Cir. 1984), the court ruled that the bank had to produce records that were held by one of its overseas subsidiaries, on the basis that the company could not 'expect to avail itself of the benefits of doing business in the US without accepting the concomitant obligations'. The test for the production of documents is one of control rather than location.

Failure to comply with demands to produce documents and witnesses can result in a company's debarment from doing business in the US, daily fines and other sanctions.

Federal Sentencing Guidelines

The Federal Sentencing Guidelines ('FSG') became effective on 1 November 1991 and are intended to provide just punishment, adequate deterrents and incentives for organizations to maintain internal mechanisms for preventing, detecting and reporting criminal conduct. It is a very important Act, and for the first and probably last time sets out the framework of what regulators regard as an effective compliance programme.

The act takes a base penalty that could be applied under any statute, which can be in the range of US\$5,000 to US\$72,500,000, and modifies it by two factors: a culpability score and a mitigation score.[1] The culpability score increases the base penalty, according to various formulae, and takes into account such factors as:

---

[1] This is not a literal interpretation of the Act. The mitigation score is in fact a reduction of the culpability score

- the size of the organization;
- aggravating circumstances;
- the seniority of management involved in the offences;
- the offender's record of previous offences;
- any obstruction of justice.

Regulators take a dim view of 'wilful or deliberate ignorance', 'conscious disregard' or 'unwarranted obliviousness' and companies that fail to investigate their suspicions can expect little sympathy. So too can companies that route bribes through agents and close their eyes to the consequences.

Mitigating factors, which reduce the culpability score, include:

- whether or not the offences were voluntarily disclosed;
- the level of cooperation afforded the regulators;
- acceptance of responsibility.

Two other factors are taken into account in mitigating penalties. The first is whether or not the company had an effective programme to detect and prevent violations. The second is that it was open when problems were first detected. An effective programme should include the following seven principles:

- having *compliance standards* and procedures that are reasonably capable of reducing criminal conduct;
- specifically designating *high-level officials* to oversee the programme;
- exercising due care not to delegate major authority to a person known to have *criminal tendencies*;
- developing a method of *communicating the policies* and procedures to all employees and other agents, either with ethics training or practical publications which explain the programme;
- taking reasonable steps to *achieve compliance*, by using auditing and monitoring systems designed to detect criminal conduct by employees and having in place and publicizing a reporting system through which employees can report criminal conduct by others without fear of retribution;
- consistently *enforcing the standards* through appropriate disciplinary mechanisms;
- taking steps to prevent any similar occurrences in the *future*.

The precise standards that are required in a particular case depends on a number of factors including:

- the size of the company and the degree of formality necessary;
- the risks that arise because of the nature of its business and the countries in which it operates;
- its history of previous problems.

The failure of a company to follow normal industry standards or professional guidelines will act to its disfavour.

To readers outside the US, the FCPA and FSG may appear irrelevant and the possibility of being the target of a Justice Department investigation remote. This is not the case and compliance systems should be developed now: it will be too late after the event.

Public Accounting Reform and Investor Protection Act 2002 (Sarbanes–Oxley)

In July 2002, in an effort to restore public confidence in financial markets following the Enron and WorldCom collapse, President Bush signed a law (often referred to as the Sarbanes–Oxley Act) which imposes stiffer penalties on frauds by publicly listed companies. The act:

- improves the quality and transparency of financial reporting;
- creates a Public Accounting Oversight Board to monitor auditing standards and enforce the independence of auditors;
- forbids auditing firms from providing consulting services to the companies they audit;
- ensures the objectivity of security analysts who work for banks;
- increases the resources of the SEC.

One of the most important aspects of the act is to require CEOs of publicly listed companies to personally vouch for the accuracy and fairness of their companies' disclosures. This requirement will spread to Europe and other parts of the world.

Money laundering

The US has led the way in anti-money-laundering enforcement, setting standards that require virtually all businesses to check the backgrounds of customers ('know your customer'), to monitor and report suspicions of transactions and to assist in investigations. These laws subrogate everything on bank confidentiality, privacy, data protection and human rights.

Ironically, there is no requirement to 'know your employee' which is a nonsense when intelligence shows that organized criminal groups routinely corrupt or subvert bank officers or infiltrate their members on to the bank's payroll.

On the contrary, privacy and other laws have made it far more difficult for employers to check the backgrounds and monitor the performance of employees. Such confused thinking and double standards are common in the regulatory framework of most countries, and especially those in Europe.

Regulations in the UK

Basic positions

If the laws and regulations in the US are difficult, the UK is a nightmare, bound by its own laws, extra-territorial obligations to the US, to the European Union and the Commonwealth.

Examples of double standards

The English anti-corruption laws date from the period between 1889 and 1916 and relate to varying standards of naughtiness in the private and public sectors. In March 1998 the Law Commission was scathing about the archaic state of these defective laws, proposed a comprehensive change and submitted a draft bill. One of the problems with this eminently sensible proposal was that, for the first time, it would lead to criminalizing corruption by Members of Parliament. Unsurprisingly the prospect, like asking Dracula to give up blood, was not greeted with roaring enthusiasm by the MPs concerned. The legislation faltered despite the fact that successive governments (of course, comprising mainly MPs) promised new comprehensive laws to deal with the appalling behaviour of some of their colleagues.

No doubt nothing would have happened had it not been for pressure from the US and the Organization for Economic Cooperation and Development (OECD). Since 1977, the US has complained – if not whinged – that its Foreign Corrupt Practices Act (FCPA) put American corporations at a disadvantage when competing for international business. The argument was that the FCPA criminalized corruption of overseas government agents and thereby imposed the potential for punishment of American corporations and citizens based in the US.

In truth there have been very few prosecutions under the FCPA and for most observers it is more of a cosmetic than a deterrent. This view is supported by the 1988 amendment to the FCPA which permitted American companies to bribe overseas government officials providing it was not to get business and simply to grease the wheels. Such payments are specifically referred to as 'grease payments', and cover such things as paying small bribes to get goods cleared through Customs, to obtain a licence etc. and under the FCPA they are permitted. This goes to prove that you can be acceptably corrupt.

The OECD produced a convention on corruption which the UK ratified in 1999 but did absolutely nothing to implement. Politicians did this by following the rule that to do nothing it is best to set up a commission or a committee and the UK did lots of this, but nothing else.

A central feature of the OECD convention was that members should make it a domestic criminal offence (i.e. prosecutable in the UK) for its companies and citizens to corrupt overseas government officials. The idea was that the UK laws would replicate the FCPA. The convention is predicated on the smelly-socks belief that innocent, bordering on virginal, overseas officials (in such places as Nigeria, India, Indonesia and Pakistan, called 'demand-side' countries) were being led off the heavenly path by unscrupulous Western businessmen (from what was referred to as 'supply-side' countries). To anyone with experience this is more than a slight oversimplification.

Despite the UK government's inclination to do nothing, pressure from the European Union, the OECD and the US resulted in limited action. But rather than introduce the all-embracing and sensible recommendations of the Law Commission, Parliament spun cosmetic changes in the corruption laws into the Anti-Terrorism Crime and Security Act (ATCSA) 2000. There are two points to note. The first is that ATCSA took what everyone recognized as the hopelessly defective laws of 1889, 1906 and 1916 and incorporated them verbatim.

The result is that it is illegal for British companies to make payments of any sort to overseas government officials. If they do, the companies and their employees can be prosecuted and imprisoned in the UK.

JAKARTA AIRPORT

You arrive at Jakarta Airport travelling with an American competitor to bid for a vital contract. The smiling Immigration Officer pulls you both to one side and says, 'Passport not in order, mister. You pay me twenty dollars or you on next plane out of here'.

The American citizen pays over the 'grease payment' as he is allowed to, but you refuse because you are an honest man and don't want to break the ATCSA laws. The American gets the contract, while you are back in the UK telling your boss how honest you have been.

When the disparity was pointed out at the DTI conference launching a great anti-corruption 'initiative', a representative from the Crown Prosecuting Service (CPS) said it would be very unlikely to prosecute in such cases. If this is true, why pass the law?

The second point to note is that there is no practical connection between terrorism and corporate corruption and the British government's dervish-like spinning to prove the negative is facile, to say the least. In truth, ATCSA was chosen as a suitable vehicle to bury the bad news on corruption by MPs and to get the government off the hook with the OECD. It is a stupid law and unfortunately there are too many like it.

CADBURY, TURNBULL AND WHO NEXT?

In the UK, under successive codes of practice, the standards expected of directors, managers and employees have been, and are continuing to be, raised. Currently, under the Turnbull Report (see http://www.cabinet-office.gov.uk/risk/Corporate_Governance_Folder/turnbul.pdf) and the UK's Stock Exchange Listing Rules:

- the board of directors should maintain a sound system of internal control;
- the directors should, at least annually, review the effectiveness of the company's system of internal control and risk management;
- internal control systems should be embedded in the operations of the company and not treated as a separate exercise;
- the system should be capable of responding to changing risks both within and outside the company and should include procedures for reporting any significant control findings or weaknesses.

In addition, directors are required to state in the annual company report that the company has complied fully with the code. The code also makes it clear that directors will be held personally liable for misstatements

THE CIVIL LAWS

Companies, and their directors and officers, are also exposed to risks of civil litigation if someone, somewhere happens to believe it would be in their interest to allege that they have failed in their duties. Although the creativity of litigators is without limit, the most likely exposures are shown in Table 9.2.

Claims may be supported by orders freezing the company's, or the employee's, assets or requiring them to hand over evidence or to attend as witnesses. Other orders may restrain them from doing specified things or insist that they do them. Writs may be issued in the courts of one country and enforced in another. Actions may be started in any country, including European Union tribunals and courts. They can be started individually or in parallel. The hearings may be in private or open to the public and often the resulting publicity, disruption, legal costs and wasted management time are more damaging than the underlying action and any final penalties.

It is therefore a very good idea for companies to develop a plan for dealing with litigation, regulatory action and other troubles. These days it is a major non-entrepreneurial risk.

THE BOTTOM LINE

Although the above discussion is far from complete, it should really worry you, so get the old amygdala pumping away because:

Table 9.2   Examples of civil actions

Possible action by	Examples and comments
Fidelity insurance companies	Under the subrogation clauses, insurers can take action for the recovery of any amounts they have paid out. Claims, which are effectively derivative actions, may be against the external or internal auditors, bankers, etc. or the directors and officers of the insured company
Competitors	Allegations of price-fixing or unfair competition, including bribery of customers or foreign agents
Liquidators and receivers	Against past and present directors and officers
Customers and suppliers	Fraud and breach of contract
Shareholders *Class actions*	Fraud or breach of fiduciary duty. The actions may be direct in the names of the shareholders or derivative when they are taken ostensibly by the company against its own directors and officers
Consumer groups	Environmental and safety breaches Product liability actions
Employees and ex-employees	Unfair dismissal
Other groups	Class actions, taken by a group of people with a common interest: these may allege fraud, breach of duties etc.

- The legal and regulatory framework in relation to fraud is a mess.
- Standards demanded of directors and officers are becoming higher by the day. They are increasingly complex and difficult to track. Most organizations do not understand the regulations by which they are bound, especially those operating extra-territorially from the US.
- Breaches of even apparently esoteric rules and guidelines can lead to criminal prosecution and civil liabilities.
- Penalties are increasing and becoming more personal; the separation between company and individual is disappearing. Employees carry the responsibility for company violations and vice versa.
- Ignorance or wilful disregard of the rules are not defences.
- All directors and officers face the risk of debilitating civil litigation.

On the other hand, the world is not run by regulators nor lawyers and if it were, no one would ever get out of bed: life goes on and all anyone can do is their honest best. There is often a massive moral gap between what is right and what lawyers advise should be done.

REFERENCES

The typical legal advice when a new employer asks for a reference on someone dismissed for fraud is to say nothing or something neutral so that the crook cannot sue for defamation. This just passes the problem on to someone else and if everyone does the same, God help us.

The solution is to work on principles that surpass any reasonable regulatory requirement. The starting point is setting corporate values and the tone from the top.

The culture and tone

THE DEMAND FOR POLICIES ON ETHICS

Unsurprisingly, against the legal chaos touched on above, business ethics have become flavour of the decade with companies and managers self-flagellating and exposing massive guilt complexes.

The hard fact is that most of the stuff on ethics seems to overlook the basic point that businesses exist to make money. The principle that they should do it fairly is without question, but the way of achieving this against a hyperventilated ethical backlash is far less obvious.

The second thing to note about all this ethical stuff is that standards do not spread automatically throughout the organization by magical osmosis, but have to be worked at. Even in good companies there are unethical pockets and groups.

Business ethics have to be worked at

MYTHS ABOUT ETHICS AND CULTURE

Perceptions of corruption

There is a great deal of nonsense spoken and published about business ethics and the absence of them. For example, Transparency International (TI), a non-governmental organization intent on stamping out some (but, apparently, not all) forms of corruption, publishes an annual survey called *The Bribe Payer's Index* based on a poll of people doing business with the countries concerned. The 2002 edition states that the most ethical countries are Australia, Sweden and Switzerland, with the UK in eighth position. TI does not mention the fact that the Gulf States, such as Saudi Arabia, Kuwait, UAE (in which there is very heavy Western investment and massive corruption) are not rated. Why is this?

Equally TI does not refer to the list produced by the World Bank Organization which shows that of 71 companies it has banned from doing business, 36 are British and 8 Swedish. So much for perceptions of corruption.

Ethics and increased profits

Possibly one of the worst myths is that the companies with the highest ethical standards are the most successful financially (see, for example, *Business Ethics* magazine Volume 16 March 2002 – www.business-ethics.com/back.htm). This is total nonsense, and no more than a dissembling of the truth to encourage companies to go overboard on the ethical surfboard.

Detailed analysis of the *Fortune* worldwide statistics (www.fortune.com) shows that those companies that have the highest profits, greatest return on assets and fastest growth tend to take a low profile in the ethical stakes, i.e. they say nothing. On the other hand, companies that have lost their pants through poor performance (such as Nortel, Vodafone, Lucent, etc. (www.fortune.com/lists/G500/losers) took a high ethical stand with policies and large internal audit, compliance and security departments.

Little can be concluded from this, other than that financial success appears to be more reliant on the business sector in which the company operates rather than on some mystical ethical code. But the bottom line is that ethical programmes are important because it is the right thing to do and they can establish the tone from the top. But don't expect them to suddenly produce windfall profits, because they won't.

WHAT THE BETTER COMPANIES DO

The better companies (and, believe it or not, they are in the vast majority) have worked hard to put statements on values and visions in place that really get into the bloodstream. For example, Boeing (see www.boeing.com/companyoffices/aboutus/ethics/) has avoided serious ethical problems while operating internationally in a very hard sector. The Conference Board (www.conference-board.org) also publishes very interesting papers on ethics.

WHAT VALUES AND ETHICAL POLICIES ACHIEVE

Carter McNamara (see www.authenticityconsulting.com) has been involved in ethical programmes for many years and he seems to take a sensible, practical view. He states that:

- business ethics programmes have substantially improved society;
- they help maintain a moral course in turbulent times and influence the behaviour of those involved in them;
- they cultivate strong teamwork and productivity and support employee growth and meaning;
- they are an insurance policy – they help ensure that operations are legal and that inadvertent breaches can be defended after the event;
- they help avoid criminal acts and can mitigate penalties;
- they help managers take honest decisions and legitimize them;
- they promote a positive public image (and increase revenues);
- they provide a benchmark against which performance of the organization and employees can be assessed

Mr McNamara concludes that: 'Ethical compliance cannot be achieved in a vacuum. The most ethical business is one that does not exist or which has closed its doors. Thus a balance has to be struck between commercial reality and ethics.'

WHAT MAKES AN EFFECTIVE ETHICAL PROGRAMME?

Effective ethical programmes contain a number of elements:

- Their tone is set from the top, by directors who believe in them (that is, they are not cosmetic).
- A senior person, with direct access to the board, is put in charge.
- The clearest statement possible is made of the organization's values, goals and objectives.

- This statement is translated and disseminated through specified procedures, training programmes, bulletins, screensavers, log on banners, online e-training programmes etc., made available to all of the people potentially concerned. Ethics must be given a very high profile.
- The need to adhere to ethical policies is specifically set out in job descriptions and contracts: disciplinary codes must make ethical breaches dismissible offences.
- Employees and others must be required to report suspected violations: if necessary, anonymously through a hotline.
- People subject to the ethics programme (particularly employees, agents and trading partners) should make annual declarations of compliance as part of their annual performance reviews.
- The programme as a whole should be subject to review by the audit committee and board of directors.

General Electric publishes an excellent booklet, called *The Spirit and Letter of Our Commitment*, and there are many other publications on the Web that can be used to get your programme on ethics underway or to benchmark what you already do.

Review your ethical programmes

EMPHASIZING THE POSITIVE

One of the problems with crime prevention, the criminal justice system as a whole and business practices is that they work only by punishing offenders and do little to encourage good people. As we know, in most aspects of life, a 'stick and carrot' approach with emphasis on the latter works best. Thus effective personnel control processes should build on positive motivational factors including, in alphabetical order, those listed in Table 9.3.

Finally, please remember that if liars and crooks are not dealt with, the morale of honest employees will suffer.

Small things make a difference

The fraud policy

INTRODUCTION

A fraud policy, and its associated investigatory procedures, ensures that assets and processes are controlled by their owners, and that suspicions of dishonesty are resolved quickly and effectively. The policy also ensures that recent and other legislation (such as the Human Rights Act and the Data Protection Act) does not unnecessarily impede investigative and recovery options.

Table 9.3 Possible positive measures

Feature	Comments and how achieved
Aspirations Research shows that people are more inclined to commit fraud and other wrongful acts when they perceive that they have been unfairly treated or that artificial barriers are impeding their progress. The theory of *anomie* suggests that problems breed in the gap between opportunity and aspiration	The aspirations of all employees should be considered and addressed openly in annual appraisals, with no false promises. The objective is to let the employee know that his contribution is appreciated and to set out a realistic career path. In cases where an employee's aspirations surpass his abilities or the opportunities genuinely available to him, he should be told and, if possible, alternatives suggested to keep him motivated
Authority Employees like to be appreciated, believe that they are trusted and want to have the authority to do their jobs without reference to their manager for every decision	Authority tables, job descriptions etc. should give employees the powers necessary to do their jobs. Reactive controls, including positive supervision, should ensure that problems are quickly identified so that the employee's decision-making process can be guided in the future
Awareness Honest employees can make a positive contribution to the prevention and detection of fraud and other problems. They have to be trained in what to look for and how to report it	Introduce processes to increase the awareness of employees to risks and their compliance requirements: Educational programmes Staff handbooks Intranet sites Control self-assessment (see page 292) Think about a byline or mnemonic to summarize the programme
Bad apples Bad apples corrupt others. If employees see that bad behaviour is tolerated they may be tempted to do the same	Make sure that disruptive employees are dealt with and, if necessary, dismissed. Management's failure to address problems has a negative effect on honest employees
Chairman's annual email The chairman should consider sending an annual email to all employees, updating them on the company's performance and inviting them to contact him directly if they are aware of any serious problems	This has proven to be a very useful tool
Change management Changes can make employees uncertain and, in some case, trigger dishonesty	All changes should be sensitively handled and employees kept fully informed. Ideally employee groups should be consulted before important changes are made
Consistency and precedents Inconsistent decisions affect the motivation of employees	Employees should be advised why decisions affecting them have been made (ideally before the event). Those which run contrary to precedent (or which could establish a precedent) require even greater care

Feature	Comments and how achieved
Control self-assessment Get employees involved in assessing risks and improving controls	See page 292. CSA is a very important tool which keeps employees involved in controls
Cost cutting Any idiot can cut costs. The art is to do so sensibly	Consider the effect cost cutting has on employees. Make sure cutting costs makes a useful contribution and is not simply cosmetic. Explain the reasons to employees and ask for their suggestions and support
Discipline Breakdowns in disciplinary codes are corrosive	Managers should lead by positive example. If the supervisor ignores the rules, subordinates will do the same. The tone is definitely set from the top
Family gatherings Social events, involving employees' families help build a good team spirit	Consider holding team and company social events, especially involving employees' children
Fairness Employees who believe they have been unfairly treated usually cause problems	Encourage managers to take decisions on principle, to be honest and transparent and to treat others fairly
Fast tracking The fast tracking of some employees can cause resentment in others (the theory of *anomie*, in practice)	Employees should understand the process and why they have not been selected. Fast tracked employees must behave sensitively towards their colleagues: arrogance causes resentment
Financial results Concealing bad results will be discovered and will demotivate employees	Let employees know how the company is performing and if it is badly, explain what measures are being taken and how they can help. Treat employees as adults
Grey hairs Early retirement programmes can result in the loss of both experience and balance	Keep a few 'grey hairs' scattered throughout the organization
Job candidates Don't let bad apples on to the workforce	Introduce effective pre-employment screening programmes. Also consider letting junior employees meet job candidates and give their opinions
Ombudsman Give employees an independent release valve to express their grievances	Consider appointing management and employee representatives as ombudsmen (but not too many!)
Open days Get people involved	Consider having at least one open day, when family members, customers and suppliers are entertained on company premises
Leadership Good leaders make all the difference to controls	Train supervisors to be creative, flexible leaders who enjoy their work and encourage others to do the same. Try to avoid bureaucracy
Charitable donations	Consider making donations to a local charity on behalf of the employee who makes the best suggestion for control improvements. Give this the maximum publicity

Feature	Comments and how achieved
Personal support	Develop an involved leadership style which inspires confidence in employees that they will be supported when they have personal problems
Processes Tell employees what they are supposed to do	Specify all important processes (see page 290) and train employees in their use. Give them confidence that they know how to do their jobs effectively
Rotation Let in fresh air... break down inward-looking and collusive groups	Introduce processes that rotate the duties of some employees. This is especially important for employees who have not been 'fast tracked' or have no clear progression path
Right to manage Empower employees	Every job is easy for the person who does not have to do it. Introduce training programmes, mentoring and other processes that encourage employees to manage and take decisions on principle
Salary	Make sure salary policies are fair and ideally transparent
Share options	Consider introducing share option schemes for all employees after they have completed one or two years' service
Shared successes Let people know the good news	Consider an employee newsletter or intranet site emphasizing the achievements of the organization
Smoking It is a fact of life that smokers are high achievers and have no intention of giving up. In many organizations they are treated as pariahs: this is bad news	Consider your policy on smoking. Under no circumstances allow directors and others to smoke while banning others. Ideally provide one of two air-conditioned meeting rooms where smoking is allowed
Suggestion box Keep employees involved	Introduce a process where employees can make suggestions for control and other improvements. Consider paying rewards (possibly to a local charity)
Temporary employees Don't create resentment	Don't treat temporary employees as second-class citizens
Training	Make sure that employees are properly trained: cuts in a training budget are the first sign that the organization is heading south!
Work environment	Make sure the work environment is one in which employees can take pride
Values	Do everything possible to promote ethical values throughout the organization

RIPA

Under the Regulation of Investigatory Powers Act (RIPA) companies are permitted to intercept the data and voice communication lines of employees (for example if they suspect they are downloading porn or engaged in fraud), providing the permission of the communications controller is obtained and under the business rule that 'every reasonable effort has been made to advise employees that such interception might take place'.

If a company has not made such a general statement and then suspects serious fraud, it faces a crucial dilemma. Does it quickly issue a policy statement and thus alert the suspects concerned or does it take a chance and intercept anyway?[2]

There are similar problems under the Data Protection Act, Human Rights Act etc. and it is best to resolve these in advance by clear policy statements and specified procedures.

POLICY STATEMENT EXAMPLES

All processes and forms (see Chapter 8) should be reviewed for compliance with Data Protection and Human Rights legislation and the Regulation of Investigatory Powers Act. Wherever possible, appropriate warnings, releases and instructions should be highlighted to *raise the pavement*, deter deception and to provide the legal basis for using potentially contentious investigation procedures such as the interception of communications and the use of personnel information to prevent and detect crime. The organization should also take a very open policy position on its approach to human rights.

Also the company's Data Protection Act registration should be reviewed and, if necessary, amended to allow it to receive, store and process confidential personal information and to exchange data with banks, credit card companies and communications providers for the prevention and detection of crime. It should also ensure that organizations with which it might want to share data have equivalent registrations. Great care should be taken to make certain that all aspects are addressed, including the use of closed circuit television, email, mail boxes, and other forms of computer and structured manual systems.

The company should then set out its policy on fraud, possibly along the following lines.

---

[2] The answer is it takes specific legal advice which is likely to be to the effect that it should go ahead with the interception (providing such action is proportionate to the seriousness of the case) and once it has been completed send a general announcement to employees

FUNDAMENTAL PRINCIPLES

The values that govern all aspects of [your company's] operations are set out in staff handbooks, training programmes and elsewhere, and include the following:

- The company intends to maintain its reputation as an exemplary corporate citizen and to support its position as a respected member of the international business community.
- Its ethical values will always take priority over short-term financial gain and all employees are expected to take decisions based on principle.
- As far as practicable, every process, procedure or task and every asset will be under the control of a designated employee who is regarded as its 'owner'. Owners have the authority to apply appropriate safeguards and will bear responsibility if they fail.
- The company will make every effort to control all aspects of its business in accordance with the law and commercial best practice. Wherever possible, the controls which employees are expected to maintain will be specified in writing and they will be given every possible assistance in maintaining them.

PRINCIPLES IN RELATION TO FRAUD

Employees are not expected to guarantee that fraud will never take place in operations under their control. They are, however, expected to react effectively when suspicions are aroused and dishonesty will not be tolerated:

- The company will support employees and others wrongly accused of impropriety and will investigate, based on a presumption of innocence.
- All employees (and others granted equivalent rights) are required to report suspected dishonesty and control weaknesses to [name and contact numbers] without delay.
- The responsibility for investigation will be taken out of the management line and into the hands of the audit and legal departments as quickly as possible.
- Employees who report suspected dishonesty in good faith will be protected, and any person who attempts to impede or sanction them will be subject to immediate dismissal.
- The company will thoroughly investigate to establish the facts, prosecute and take other appropriate action against any person or organization whom it suspects of dishonesty.
- The company will not stand passively by when it sees other people or organizations being defrauded. It will report suspicions without delay and make every reasonable effort to assist the victim.
- The company will provide assistance to law enforcement and other regulatory authorities in their fight against crime.

HUMAN RIGHTS AND DATA PROTECTION

Company standards

The company will comply with all relevant legislation, while asserting its rights to protect the interests of honest employees, customers, suppliers, investors and others.

Rights to privacy

Employees and others are permitted to use company premises, telephones, computer systems, communications networks, postal, courier and other facilities on the specific understanding that there is no guaranteed right of privacy.

Any item on company premises or in any vehicle or craft owned by the company is subject to search for security purposes.

Personal information provided by employees and others may be used for data matching and other fraud prevention or investigation purposes and may be released to other organizations involved and public authorities.

Use of privately owned computers etc.

Employees are allowed to use personal computers on company premises, to download, process and upload data and programs on the basis that they will secure such data or programs and will permit inspection by the company at any time.

Registration of encryption keys

Employees using encryption or other security packages on company or their own computers for company work must register the keys or other devices with the IT manager and permit inspection at any time. If the key or other security feature has not been previously registered, the employee will immediately make it available on request by [state name and contact details]. Failure to comply will result in disciplinary action.

The policy should be made available to every employee and any other person that might be affected. It should be summarized on appropriate forms, staff handbooks and instruction manuals. A complete 48-page version of a fraud policy can be downloaded, free of charge from www.cobasco.com.

Organization of control resources

LINE MANAGEMENT

The principle is that line managers must be given the authority to maintain controls for the assets and processes in their domains and held responsible for failure. This can be achieved through organization charts, job descriptions, contracts, specified processes and supervision and enforcement.

INTERNAL AUDIT

Internal audit is a key department, yet its normal contribution to fraud prevention and investigation is limited, often based on the dreadful statement: 'Auditors are watchdogs and not bloodhounds.' In fact, far too many auditors, if they are dogs at all, are poodles that run after lots of balls thrown down by managers: they should be Rottweilers.

There is often a large gap between the expectations of management – which believes internal audit has fraud under control – and the auditors themselves who abrogate responsibilities in the fraud area. In modern organizations, internal audit is a key department with representation at, or immediately below, board level.

Internal audit is a vital department and must be empowered

Salaries and status should encourage the development of career auditors. These are the sorts of men and women who, when they die, will take their audit manuals and fraud detection software with them.

Internal audit should provide the safety net for the organization and its managers should take on fraud prevention, risk analysis and detection and investigation responsibilities (accounting for up to 15 per cent of departmental resources) under the authority of an audit charter.

Internal audit provides the safety net for good managers

HUMAN RESOURCES

There is usually a natural tension between HR, audit and corporate security, often brought about by the fact that the latter see the worst in people and the former the best. This is life and it is all fuelled by left or right hemisphere domination. The fact is that a powerful HR department is essential to good control. It should be the owner of a number of important policies and procedures (see Table 9.4).

Table 9.4   HR policies and procedures

Procedures owned by HR department	Examples of specified company-wide controls
Annual declarations, letters of representation and annual appraisals for all employees	On compliance with values, visions and procedures
Conflicts of interest	Initial declarations Annual declarations
Data protection and privacy releases	Permitting the company to use personal data to carry out automated fraud detection tests Permitting the company to monitor emails and telephone lines
Disciplinary procedures	Linked to procedures for conducting investigations Rights to legal and other representation
Drugs testing	A part of the pre-employment screening medical to ensure that new employees, part-time and agency staff are not addicted to narcotic drugs. The procedure may also be extended to annual medical examinations

Procedures owned by HR department	Examples of specified company-wide controls
Employment of temporary staff	Clearance of agencies (in conjunction with security) Screening of agency staff Specification of posts in which temporary employees may be engaged
Exit interviews	To ensure that employees on termination of employment or transfer to another location are interviewed, by other than their line managers, to make a closing declaration of compliance and to make recommendations for control improvements
Identification	To ensure that employees are provided with secure means of identification
Internal reporting	To ensure that problems that come to notice in an employee's private life and which could have an impact on their job performance are reported to audit and legal
Job descriptions and contracts of employment	Incorporating principles of ownership etc. Agreement to assist in investigations
Recruitment and pre-employment screening	Approval and legality of procedures Design of forms Specification of acceptance and rejection criteria Interview processes Verification procedures Analysis of results
References	HR should be the department authorized to give references on behalf of the company. Procedures should be specified to this effect
Special agreements	Agreements on confidentiality, assignment of patent and other intellectual property rights
Staff handbook	Incorporating important security controls
Training	On all aspects, including security
Termination procedures	Withdrawal of access and other rights Undertakings on confidentiality and undertakings not to unfairly compete

The investigatory procedures that form part of the fraud policy (see page 281) should ensure that HR releases personnel and other files when requested and also specify the roles, if any, that HR should play in disciplinary interviews.

LEGAL

The closest cooperation between corporate security, legal and internal audit departments is essential and they should work together to ensure that procedures are developed in the following areas (Table 9.5).

Table 9.5   Legal procedures

Procedures owned by legal department	Examples of specified company-wide controls
Compliance standards	Laws, rules and regulations with which the organization must comply
Contracts and agreements	Warranties on the accuracy of forms Incorporating audit rights Alternative dispute resolution
Application and other forms	Legality of questions Privacy and data protection issues and releases Linkage with formal contracts Warranties and undertakings
Appointment of external litigators	As part of the procedure for conducting investigations

The legal adviser should review policies and procedures in other areas and provide advice generally. However, unless he is an experienced litigator, he should not be directly involved in investigations. This critical task should be contracted out to external litigators.

CORPORATE SECURITY

Organizations with more than 2000 employees should have at least one dedicated, professional security adviser, operating company-wide and internationally. Called the 'head of security' or 'security adviser', he should have a background in law enforcement or intelligence and, ideally, should have previous experience in the commercial world.

The security function should be the designated owner of the following procedures (Table 9.6).

An annotated checklist setting out the background and recommended responsibilities of a modern corporate security department can be downloaded from www.cobasco.com.

Processes

HOW CONTROLS ARE MADE EFFECTIVE

Controls must be specified in writing, so that employees and others know what is expected of them, for example, in:

- procedure manuals (printed or electronic);
- flow charts;
- on forms and screen input prompts;
- automatically through data entry and editing screens;
- on an intranet (this is by far the best option).

To be effective, controls must function as specified and assurance that this is the case can be achieved through exception reporting, good supervision and effective internal audit.

Table 9.6   Specified security procedures

Procedures owned by security	Examples of specified company-wide controls
Contingency planning	Procedures for dealing with bombs and bomb threats
Due diligence reviews	On all entities and people with which the company intends to deal Routine and surprise monitoring
Executive protection	Protection and recovery plans for key executives world-wide and especially in hostile countries
Fidelity and computer crime insurance	Ensuring that coverage is maintained
Fraud detection	In conjunction with audit Automated fraud detection programs Development of informants
Information classification	Identifying sensitive information and vital records Specifying minimum standards of protection Routine checking
Debugging and counter-measures sweeps	
Reporting of incidents	Routine procedures for all employees in the extended enterprise Hotline
Security education programmes	Video packages Instruction booklets Induction programmes Senior management meetings Intelligence digests and internal bulletins
Security equipment	Specification of suitable products Negotiation of discounts Control of maintenance agreements Specifying related procedures
Control self-assessment	Company-wide risk analysis (See page 292), probably in conjunction with internal audit
Conduct of investigations	Basic procedures Responsibilities and special task forces Reporting to police and prosecution
Security guards and hardware selection	Selection and approved contractors Negotiating national and local contracts Assignment instructions
Telephone call logging	Enabling APBX equipment Records retention programme Maintaining logs

FORMAT AND DISSEMINATION OF INSTRUCTIONS

Procedures may be specified as guidelines – containing advice which may or may not be taken – or mandatory standards which must be followed. Generally, in the control area, guidelines are ineffective and all organizations should specify minimum or baseline standards.

Guidelines are generally useless unless they are additional to mandatory standards

Organizations sometimes fail to consider carefully enough how, and in what form, procedures should be issued. For example, they produce bulky manuals that are issued to everyone who might have a need to refer to them. This is a security breach, because it discloses controls in areas outside the reader's domain and which he does not need to know.

Manuals should be issued in a modular form to cover the specific responsibilities of the department or person concerned. Also, manuals are often segmented into the types of controls or in some other arbitrary way. For example, in the computer security area, control manuals might be separated into hardware, software and systems development etc. Thus, a reader who wishes to establish what controls he is expected to maintain must read all the manual and select those bits which he believes apply to him. He could be wrong, leave some out and put others in.

It is much better to write manuals so that they are job specific. For example, with segments applicable to programmers, data entry clerks, engineers etc. In this way, there can be little ambiguity over the controls each person or department is expected to maintain and segmentation complies with the principle of 'need to know'.

PROCEDURES ON THE INTRANET

When procedure manuals are loaded on to an intranet, access to segregated modules can be enforced by user names and passwords. Checklists and flow charts are usually much more effective than large blocks of text.

Finally, extracts of procedures should be summarized on related forms or screen layouts to remind users continuously of their responsibilities.

Control self-assessment

Security and internal audit should be the joint owners of a company-wide control self-assessment (CSA) process which requires owners – usually on an annual basis – to review risks and controls in the areas for which they are responsible. The process is simple:

- meet annually;
- review risks in brainstorming sessions, usually under the guidance of an experienced mentor;
- catalogue risks and control weaknesses;
- identify improvements and an action plan for implementation.

CSA is consistent with empowerment and the principle of ownership and is especially useful in technical and complex operations in which risks can be difficult to identify by conventional means. CSA also frees audit resources for other work, such as fraud detection, investigations and recovery. An excellent summary of CSA resources can be found on www.auditnet.com.

Integrity validation and due diligence

Processes should be specified to confirm the reliability of people and other third parties in which the organization intends to place trust. In large organizations responsibility for integrity validation processes should be assigned to corporate security or some other specialist team (rather than be dispersed through a number of different departments such as credit control, human resources, business development etc.) and should apply to the following (see Table 9.7).

Table 9.7   Integrated due diligence and keeping out the bad guys

People or organizations whose integrity should be validated	Time when integrity should be validated	Suggested OWNER of the process and *depth of verification*
Senior managers	Prior to appointment Annual declarations of compliance Prior to promotion or transfer overseas Annual validation of senior managers employed overseas Exit interviews	HUMAN RESOURCES *See page 288*
Employees – including members of the extended enterprise (which consists of outsourcers, suppliers, customers etc.) who have access rights and authority equivalent to employees	Prior to appointment Annual declarations of compliance Prior to promotion or transfer overseas Exit interviews	
Agencies providing part-time employees	Prior to appointment of the agency	
Part-time and temporary employees	Prior to appointment Annual declarations of compliance Prior to promotion or transfer overseas Exit interviews	
Consultants	Prior to appointment Annual declarations of compliance Prior to promotion or transfer overseas Exit interviews	

continued

People or organizations whose integrity should be validated	Time when integrity should be validated	Suggested OWNER of the process and *depth of verification*
Customers, brokers, agents and distributors	Prior to commitment Annual declarations of compliance	PURCHASING OR CREDIT CONTROL *Entity verification* *Credit history* *Financial stability*
Suppliers	Prior to commitment Annual declaration of compliance	PURCHASING *Entity verification* *Credit history* *Financial stability*
Businesses considered suitable for acquisition	Prior to commitment	INTERNAL AUDIT *Full due diligence review*
	Post-acquisition (within warranty periods)	*Fraud profile analysis* *Security review*

The amount of information available on any subject varies inversely with the importance of the decision

The typical reaction of managers to suggestions of such detailed verification is normally one of shock-horror and indignant responses such as: 'We are not the CIA', 'We trust our customers', or 'We cannot afford to do it'. They are, of course, wrong and the penalties for inadequate due diligence can be serious if not disastrous, including those listed in Table 9.8.

Obviously a reasonable balance has to be struck between the costs and delays involved in checking too deeply and the potential losses when checks are not made at all. This balance can usually be determined by control self-assessment.

Post September 11, all organizations are strongly advised to check out existing and planned business contacts against the US/UK lists of prohibited organizations.[3]

Pre-employment screening

BACKGROUND

Confirmation of the integrity and good intentions of people and organizations before allowing them into positions of trust is critical and should be part of a wider integrity validation and due diligence process.

LITTLE CLUES

In the Barings case, had Nick Leeson's background been subject to annual review, a serious record of bad debts would have been revealed. This should have been sufficient to sound the warning bells and thus to have saved Barings £400 million.

---

[3] See www.www.state.gov/s/ct/rls/pgtrpt/2001/html/10252.htm and www.fco.gov.uk/servlet/Front?pagename=OpenMarket/Xcelerate/ShowPage&c=Page&cid=1007029391629&a=KArticle&aid=1013618409426.

Table 9.8 Possible consequences of inadequate validation

Person or organization whose integrity should be validated	Consequences of inadequate validation *(Examples)*	Average cost of loss or liability (per case)	Losses and liabilities ACTION BROUGHT BY
Senior managers	Financial loss	£300,000	Company is the prime victim
Employees	Cost of poor recruitment Harm caused to others	£25,000 to £1 million	Consequential liabilities to other victims
Agencies providing part-time employees	*(violence, sexual harassment etc.)*		VICTIMIZED EMPLOYEES THIRD PARTIES
Part-time and temporary employees	Entry of drugs into the workplace Breaches of money		INSURANCE COMPANIES POLICE
Consultants	laundering regulations		REGULATORS LITIGANTS INSURANCE COMPANIES OTHERS
Customers	Financial loss Product liability issues Credit exposures Counterfeiting Parallel trading	£300,000 on average	
Suppliers	Financial loss Product liability issues Continuity problems Loss of intellectual capital		
Brokers, agents, distributors etc.			
Acquisitions	Financial loss through deceptive accounting and fraud Dishonest employees who have not been screened	Virtually limitless. It is suggested that the majority of acquisitions are less beneficial than anticipated	

Possibly more important than protecting the organization from financial loss is the potential harm to other employees if backgrounds are not thoroughly checked. There are a number of cases where psychopaths have been unknowingly employed who then went on to kill their colleagues and customers.

Too many people (including the Information Commissioner, see page 299) concentrate on the rights of the job applicant and forget about the rights of existing employees. It should be remembered that one person's freedom is another's restraint: a fair balance has to be struck with any benefit of the doubt going to existing employees and the organization.

The greater the trust to be placed in someone, the more assured you should be about their integrity

The scale of the problem
The scale of dishonesty in all countries is appalling:

- In the UK, 35 per cent of all males and 8 per cent of all females will be *convicted of a standard list criminal offence by the age of 35*. (Source: *HO Digest of Information on the Criminal Justice System 1993*)
- *Employee theft* accounts for 27 per cent of all retail losses. (Source: *Retail Crime Institute Survey 1994*)
- One in 50 doctors in the US is practising medicine with *bogus or fraudulent credentials*. This means 12,000 dishonest people are operating in a profession in which others have implicit trust.
- The annual cost to British industry from *malingering* and poor performance as a result of drug and alcohol abuse is estimated at being in excess of £16 billion a year.
- Correcting employment mistakes costs American industry an estimated $11 billion annually.
- According to the US Department of Justice, almost *1 million violent crimes* are committed in the workplace annually – costing employers $4.2 billion.
- It is estimated that *'virtual employees'*, working for vendors, customers or others as members of integrated supply chains, already make up more than 25 per cent of a typical workforce.
- In 1998, Trusted Health Resources Inc. of Brockton, Massachusetts, had to pay $26 million to the family of a man stabbed to death by one of their healthcare professionals because *its screening process had not been in sufficient depth* to uncover his criminal past. There are hundreds of similar cases.
- Operation Ore, recently carried out by the FBI into credit card customers who accessed a paedophile site in the US, exposed more than 10,000 people who dealt in child pornography. This allegedly included two British police officers who had been involved in the investigation of the abduction and murder of Jessica Wells and Holly Chapman, judges, civil servants and senior businessmen.

Fake certificates for UK universities can be bought on the Internet for as little as £30. Dealers in these bogus qualifications claim that the certificates can fool anyone and transcripts of attendance records can also be provided as optional extras. See www.iccwbo.org/ccs/news_archives/2000/fake_degrees.asp.

The US educational authorities recently reported that more than 20 Internet sites were offering false degrees, including:

- Bogusphd.com
- Cooldegree.com
- Degrees-r-us.com
- Diplomamakers.com
- Fakedegree.co.uk
- Fakedegrees.com
- Fakediplomas.com
- Replacementdiplmas.com
- Secretknowledge.com

The British and other governments have always based their own security on vetting the backgrounds of people allowed into positions of trust and have gone so far as to publish a

British Standard (7858:1996) on the subject. However, the Information Commissioner appears opposed to such vetting, except in extreme cases (see pages 298–9), again highlighting government duplicity in the standards expected.

Types of falsification

Although some candidates falsify information, the main problem is one of concealment. Job applicants simply do not tell you everything they should, including:

- the candidate's true identity;
- abysmal work records, including dismissals, violence, absenteeism, insubordination and disruption;
- drug, gambling or alcohol abuse;
- poor medical history coupled with extended absences and malingering;
- incomplete professional or academic qualifications resulting in the candidate being unable to do the job effectively;
- financial distress, including court judgements and bankruptcies;
- pending litigation;
- obviously conflicting interests, involving themselves or close family members.

MISSING DETAIL

Derogatory information is habitually concealed by omitting details of the period in which the problems occurred, including obvious gaps in an employment record or home address; his claiming to have worked for a company which has since gone out of business and cannot be traced; extended overseas travel; private studies or periods of self-employment. Every month in a candidate's history should be accounted for.

In all cases, the potential for falsification, misrepresentation and concealment makes it imperative that job applications ask detailed questions, and that the given answers are carefully checked.

DEGREE MILLS

In addition to the crooks who have set up dummy universities, others offer 'a degree replacement service'. If you contact them and say you obtained a PhD from Harvard on such and such a date they will issue a replacement. One of the most notorious British degree mills is the Sussex College of Technology, which operates from a private house in the wilds of East Sussex and from whom you can obtain a degree for less than £100 in ten minutes. A recent search of the Internet reveals a number of apparently respectable businessmen and doctors who claim qualifications from this university.

Currently there are more than 30 active degree mills in the UK, including one called the 'London Institute of Applied Research' (with the humorous acronym LIAR). Few HR departments check to see that qualifications claimed are from a genuine university. For example, do you know whether the following universities are genuine or not?

- Cromwell University;
- Faraday College;
- London College of Psychology;
- Newcastle University;
- University of London;
- University of Coventry;
- West London College of Technology.

If you don't have a process for checking which college is genuine and which is not, you are likely to become a victim of fake degrees.

Liabilities

Whatever people might argue, employers who recruit unsuitable candidates can be held liable for the consequences. So far, the major actions for negligence have been confined the US, but it will not be long before other parts of the world follow.

PIZZA DELIVERY BOYS

In the US there have been a number of cases in which the backgrounds of part-time employees used to deliver fast foods (such as pizzas) have not been checked and where they have subsequently raped, attacked or murdered customers. In some cases, very substantial damages have been awarded against the employer for lack of due diligence in their selection process. The bottom line is that if criminal convictions are not discovered, an employer could face serious liabilities.

When a pizza delivery man raped a customer, the jury awarded the victim $6 million of his employer's money. The firm had failed to perform a background check that would have disclosed the man's previous sex-offence record.

According to the Department of Justice, almost 1 million violent crimes are perpetrated in the workplace annually – costing employers $4.2 billion.

In addition, most fidelity insurance policies operate on the basis that the backgrounds of job applicants will be checked and that details of the vetting process will be retained to prove the point if a claim is made. This requirement conflicts with the guidelines put out by the Information Commissioner (page 298). Further, most policies have an exclusion clause that kicks in if the insurer has not been advised of any prior dishonesty by the employee in respect of whom a fidelity claim is made.

The bottom line is that every prudent organization should have an effective, fail-safe process for validating the integrity of those in whom it intends to place trust and should have compliance systems in place to assure their future performance.

The Information Commissioner's Employment Code

In March 2002, the Information Commissioner published *The Employment Practices DP Code* (see http://www.evh.org.uk/uploaded/members/Dataparttwo.pdf) which, by any measure, is an extreme example of guidelines running well ahead of the law. At present the code is only in draft form and will not become effective until three other parts have been published. As the commissioner says:

> 'Each of the four parts of the Code will be posted on this website as soon as they are finished. However, they will not be formally published until all four booklets have been completed. The Information Commissioner does not intend to change the substantive content of the Code prior to its formal publication. She believes, therefore, that the pre-publication version of the Code that appears on her website will be of use to everyone with an interest in or responsibility for data protection in the workplace.'

The code's introduction makes it appear that it is backed by the power of the law and threatens immediate calamity on any organization with the temerity to question it. This seems to be a common feature of many government 'guidelines' and interpretive documents and is a sign of the creeping erosion of victims' rights.

A BAD APPLE

Psychology students at Lambeth College had an unpleasant shock when a lecturer was imprisoned for life at the Old Bailey for attempting to murder one of them. In a horrifying example of the results of inadequate or non-existent due diligence processes, Richard Gash was able to obtain a teaching post at the college despite a terrible criminal record, including six convictions for violent attacks on women, and being on bail while awaiting sentence for molesting a five-year-old girl. He actually gained his teaching qualifications whilst in prison. He became obsessed with Nicholene Vassall and, when she put the phone down on him, burst into her house and stabbed her 40 times.

There is no doubt that the commissioner is trying to do a good job and that she is dreadfully committed to her cause, whatever it is, but she seems to have fallen into the trap of believing that the world centres on the Data Protection Act and that it is more important than life itself or even golf. We all know that this is not true.

The Information Commissioner states that the objective of the code is 'to strike a balance between a worker's legitimate right to *respect for his private life* and an employer's legitimate right to run its business.' This is a very revealing statement and suggests that the Information Commissioner has, without any apparent authority, extended her role to become a defender of the Human Rights Convention and being responsible for the moral tone of the nation. This is not her role and the statement conflicts with the stern website where she says that *'it will be of use to everyone with an interest in or responsibility for data protection in the workplace'.*

Although some people, who interpret human rights legislation as an all-embracing privacy act (which it is definitely not), would applaud the commissioner, her interpretations on such matters as a person's right to private life at work should not be accepted as gospel. Even the most worthy judges in the European Court of Justice have never defined to what extent an individual's rights to a private life are protected at work. They have deftly avoided making a definitive judgement of Article 8 (2) of the Convention and it is rare to see any mention of judgements that go against the liberal flow. For example, in the case of Ludi v Switzerland, the European Court ruled that once people engage in a course of criminal conduct, their rights to a private life go down the tubes. This, of course, was not the exact phrase used by the judges, but it accurately summarizes the position.

The code also promises that the Information Commissioner will issue further guidelines in three additional areas: the maintenance of employment records, monitoring the use of employees' emails and telephones at work and medical information including occupational health, medical testing, drug and genetic screening. Let us hope that she does not confuse any further the rules for intercepting communications, already in a mess with the Regulation of Investigatory Powers Act (see page 285) and the business regulations based upon it.

There are plenty of statements in the Code to which sensible people, with real-life experience, would object. These are mainly that the Information Commissioner seems to have:

- Totally disregarded the potential liabilities of companies that recruit criminals, especially if they are violent towards members of the public or other employees.
- Overlooked the requirement of most fidelity insurance policies that the background of people placed in positions of trust should be vetted.
- Forgotten the requirement of the Turnbull Report that directors should warrant the adequacy of their systems of control: they cannot do this if they have to let in people willy-nilly.
- Acted in blind ignorance of the American extra-territorial laws (especially the Federal Sentencing Guidelines) which require that companies check the backgrounds of employees.
- Fallen into the trap of the anti-money-laundering lobby, by failing to appreciate that the 'know your customer' principle is ineffective if crooks subvert or infiltrate the workplace.

Chances are that if the Information Commission ever reads the above, two things will happen. The first is that she will be slightly miffed and give her dog, Rover, a kicking; the second is that the authors can expect a dawn raid. However, the commissioner should be pleased to learn that the code can be implemented and, in fact, used to deter liars in the ways explained later.

Access to UK criminal records

The Data Protection Act 1998 (www.dataprotection.gov.uk) opened up a Pandora's box on the matter of access to criminal records. Historically, employers had been unable to obtain any information about a candidate's criminal convictions. Section 122, which ironically was included to comply with the subject access rights of the Data Protection Act, enabled anyone to ask for a Criminal Convictions certificate. Some employers made the production of such certificates a condition of employment, but this did not please the great unwashed who condemned it as 'enforced subject access' and a definite no-no.

The result was that Section 56 of the Data Protection Act 1998 makes it a criminal offence for a person to require a data subject to supply a relevant record (i.e. from the Criminal Records Office) in connection with his employment, continued employment or the provision of services unless it is in the public interest to do so. Section 56 (4) specifically states that: 'Requiring the production of certificates of criminal records is not justified in the public interest on the grounds that it would assist in the prevention or detection of crime'.

Thus, in a stroke, the legislators took away from employers some useful tools that had only just been given to them. Then the government announced yet another 'initiative' with the creation in 1997 of the Criminal Records Bureau (CRB), which is an 'executive agency of the Home Office' and not just any old 'agency'.

The CRB's objectives are stated as being 'to help organizations make safer recruitment decisions. By providing wider access to criminal record information, the CRB will help employers in the public, private and voluntary sectors identify candidates who may be unsuitable for certain work, especially that involving contact with children or other vulnerable members of society.' The CRB will help protect the public through a new service called 'disclosure'.

There are two higher levels of disclosures, referred to below, which can be obtained by registered persons[4] and umbrella bodies:

- Enhanced Disclosure – the highest level, principally available to anyone involved in regularly caring for, training, supervising or being in sole charge of children or vulnerable adults. Enhanced Disclosures show current and spent convictions, cautions, reprimands and warnings, as well as other relevant information held by local police forces. If the post involves working with children, lists held by the Department of Health and Department for Education and Skills will also be checked for those considered unsuitable to work with children.
- Standard Disclosure – available for jobs that involve working with children and vulnerable adults but do not qualify for Enhanced Disclosures, as well as certain other occupations and professions. This check details any convictions, spent or unspent, which are held at national level on the Police National Computer.

In addition, there are Basic Disclosures (under section 112 of the Police Act 1997) which can be requested by the data subject. These set out details of any convictions held on central police records which are not spent under the terms of the Rehabilitation of Offenders Act 1974.

Following a public outcry in the summer of 2002, the CRB had to admit that it was months behind in screening teachers and others in charge of children and vulnerable adults and had not even thought about 'Basic Disclosures' for ordinary employers.

Objectives of a pre-employment screening process

The objectives of a pre-employment screening process are to:

- provide a safe working environment for existing employees;
- ensure the recruitment of the most suitable candidates;
- deter and reject rogues, villains and other bad apples;
- be able to demonstrate, after the event, that the organization took all reasonable steps to act prudently;
- to comply with legal, insurance and regulatory requirements.

These objectives can be achieved, within the law, by:

- Deciding in advance – *as a specified matrix* – what elements in any candidate's background would disqualify him from consideration. You have to make sure that none of these break the law by discriminating on grounds of age, sex, religion, colour and so on but you are perfectly free, for example, to decide that you will not *employ anyone* who has served a term of imprisonment, takes drugs, has a record of violence or wears smelly socks. *The critical*

---

[4] Basically organizations that the CRB accepts have a legitimate need to check and umbrella bodies which represent associations of employers

factor is that you should never employ anyone who attempts to deceive you during the recruitment process as this demonstrates mal-intent.

- *Making sure you ask questions* – on application forms and in interviews – which confirm positive attributes, expose derogatory information and deter unsatisfactory candidates.
- *Requiring the candidate to produce corroborative evidence* (such as educational certificates) that confirm his positive attributes.
- *Deciding on the external verifications* that will be carried out to confirm the integrity of candidates: these should be kept to the minimum and apply only to one or two candidates on the final list.

The objective is to reduce external checking to the minimum (this saves costs and time, and cannot be argued as being intrusive) i.e. to the finally listed applicants. This approach throws far more emphasis on the need for effective interviewing.

The process should be documented and approved at the appropriate level, and made available to managers and employees.

THE POLICY STATEMENT

The directors should specify a pre-employment screening policy:

DRAFT POLICY STATEMENT

In the interest of employees, shareholders, the organization itself, customers and suppliers we will only recruit stable, reliable and honest people. To achieve this objective, the backgrounds of job candidates will be thoroughly checked. The pre-employment screening processes will fully comply with data protection and other applicable laws.

A policy along the above lines should be given the highest possible profile and should be repeated in staff handbooks, job application forms etc.

DATA PROTECTION AND OTHER REGISTRATIONS

The appropriate registrations should be made with the Information Commissioner so that personal data can be used for screening purposes. Record retention periods (see page 346) should be agreed and maintained. Also, consideration should be given to registering with the Criminal Records Bureau or joining an 'umbrella organization' through which applications for basic and other disclosures can be made.

THE DECISION MATRIX AND JOB SENSITIVITY

Obviously some jobs (both at initial appointment and on subsequent internal promotion) are more sensitive than others depending on such factors as:

- access to children and vulnerable adults;
- financial responsibility;
- access to sensitive areas and assets.

The organization should determine – in advance – the sensitivity of jobs and the elements in the candidate's background that would disqualify him from consideration, possibly including:

- false data on an employment application form or submitted during the selection or screening process;
- undisclosed previous dishonesty, violence or other criminal conduct, malingering, trouble-making etc.;
- grossly irresponsible financial record;
- unexplained gaps in employment;
- serious drug or alcohol abuse;
- history of bad debts or financial distress.

Specifying and giving transparency to these factors ensures that decisions are consistent. It also enables the organization to carry out reduced checking for low-sensitivity jobs. A matrix along the lines of Appendix 2 also makes it less likely that claims of discrimination would succeed because it can be produced to show the reasons why a candidate was rejected.

A matrix eliminates subjective decisions

PREPARED BIOGRAPHIES

Candidates should never be accepted purely on the information provided on prepared biographies.

COSMETIC CVs

It is estimated that about 70 per cent of all *CVs are deceptive*. The deceivers rationalize that falsification is just a tool to get them into an interview; but once started they have to continue with their deception through to employment. This results in a serious breach of trust.

Prepared biographies also tell you a lot about the candidate if you read them carefully because they may be packed with subjective truths and Freudian slips:

Example.
- 'I revolved customer's complaints.'
- 'Planned a new facility at $5 million over budget.'
- 'Directed a $40 million anal budget.'
- 'Experienced manager, defective with both established employees and new recruits.'
- 'I am seeking a party-time position.'

In every case an application form should be required that contains some or all of the features set out below.

THE JOB APPLICATION FORM

An essential requirement
Every job candidate should be required to complete an application form. For part-time and temporary positions and for jobs that are not sensitive a shortened version might be used.

DOUBLE FORMS	
Some companies have two forms. One is completed at the outset and a second, shorter version filled in under supervision immediately before the screening interview.	The answers given on the different forms should be compared and the candidate questioned about any discrepancies.

All forms should be carefully designed, taking into account the features described below.

Visual impact
The form should have a strong visual impact, using graphics, colour and prints to provide a positive professional impression of the employer and to deter unsatisfactory candidates by raising the pavement.

FALSE IDENTITY	
Where false identification is considered to be a high risk, the application form may be printed with shiny blank spaces in the areas where the candidate would leave fingerprints while completing it. Alternatively these spaces could be sprayed before the form is issued with fingerprint-sensitive spray. After completion the	sprayed areas turn black, exposing the candidate's fingerprints. The candidate seeking to falsify his identity is unlikely to submit the form and this is all to the good. Similarly, forms returned without any fingerprint impressions should be treated as suspect.

There are other, less dramatic ways, of raising the pavement but the principle is to hit his subconscious so that the dishonest candidate is deterred.

Explanations and warnings
Subject to specific legal advice, application forms should contain a warning to the effect that it is a criminal offence to attempt to obtain employment by deception and this again may deter a dishonest candidate.

A form of wording is set out below.

Example: Thank you for your interest in ABC Limited. It is a very special company; we care very much about our employees, customers and suppliers and we intend to maintain the very highest standards. If you join us, we are sure that you will agree with our philosophy and with our objectives.

Because we intend to maintain these high standards, coupled with close and friendly teamwork, we must have absolute honesty in all of our dealings. There can be no secrets between members of our team and no surprises. For this reason, we urge you to complete the form fully and accurately. Take your time and if you have any questions or problems, please ask us. Do not put down information unless you are sure it is correct.

The fact that something may have happened in your past that you now regret need not rule out your employment with us. But we do need to know where we stand and to be absolutely honest with each other from the outset. Our initial selection of candidates for interview is based entirely on their qualifications and work experience as provided on the application form. If you are invited to attend an interview, you will also be asked to produce your birth certificate, marriage certificate, driving licence, and original copies of educational and other certificates and these will be verified with the agencies concerned. You will also be asked questions to corroborate details provided on the application form.

If you are subsequently placed on a shortlist, your background will be thoroughly checked and you may be asked to provide a disclosure from the Criminal Records Bureau concerning convictions for criminal offences. The fact that a candidate has been convicted of an offence or offences will not automatically disqualify him or her from employment with us, but we do need to know the truth. You will also be required to undergo a medical examination and testing for abuse of narcotic drugs and alcohol.

We will treat all of the information provided to us in the strictest confidence and will handle it securely. We will advise you of the result of our screening checks and, if you are the preferred candidate, give you the opportunity to explain or clarify any discrepancies.

The reverse of this form contains an extract of some important employment conditions, which we would like you to read carefully. If you have any questions we will be happy to answer them.

If you are employed, any contract of employment will be dependent on the accuracy of the answers provided on this form.

Good luck. We hope to have you working with us.

Some companies, especially those in California where employment laws could be regarded as somewhat liberal bordering on lunatic, have an additional page entitled 'Special concerns on background checking' which are prefaced by:

SPECIAL CONCERNS

'I have the following concerns or comments about potentially negative information that may be revealed during verification of this application for employment. I understand that I do not have to provide any personal information that is not relevant and I have been told that if I have any questions about what is relevant or not relevant, I should ask. I have no questions or reservations on this point. My questions or comments about potentially negative references or information are ...'

The form should also set out statements that achieve compliance with data protection, human rights and related legislation.

IMPORTANT EMPLOYMENT CONDITIONS

Principles
[Company X] intends to maintain its position as an exemplary employer. In the interest of other employees, shareholders, the organization itself, customers and suppliers we will only recruit stable, reliable and honest people. To achieve this, the backgrounds of job candidates will be thoroughly checked. The pre-employment screening processes will fully comply with data protection and other applicable laws.

False and misleading applications
The applicant accepts that errors or omissions will result in his application being rejected or his employment terminated without compensation and he understands that providing false information to obtain employment is an offence under the Theft Act 1968. He warrants that all information provided on this form and in connection with his application for employment is true and correct.

References
The applicant authorizes the company to contact referees (but excluding his present employer, until after appointment) and releases the company from any liability in this regard.

Probationary period
If employment is offered, it will be subject to a three-month probationary period during which time the employee's performance will be monitored.

Use of personal data
The applicant accepts that any data provided on the form or at any time during his employment may be used at any time for the purpose of preventing and detecting crime or losses and may be released to others for this purpose. The company will retain all personal data securely.

Compliance with security procedures
The applicant agrees to comply with the company's procedures on security and on the conduct of investigations (copies of which have been provided).

Conflicts of interest
Neither the applicant nor his close family members have any interests that could conflict with his employment and he undertakes to keep the company advised of any material changes in his circumstances including:

- change of address or significant changes in his domestic or financial circumstances;
- potential conflicts of interest that may arise during his employment including:
    - part-time or other employment,
    - appearances in court,
    - county court or other financial judgements made against him,
    - treatment or counselling for drugs or alcohol-related illnesses.

Rights to privacy
Employees and others are permitted to use company premises, telephones, computer systems, communications networks, postal, courier and other facilities on the specific understanding that there is no guaranteed right of privacy.

Any item on company premises or in any vehicle or craft owned by the company is subject to search for security purposes at any time. Personal information provided by employees and others may be used for data matching and other fraud prevention and investigation purposes.

Use of privately owned computers etc.
Employees are allowed to use personal computers on company premises, to download, process and upload data and programs on the basis that they will secure such data or programs and will permit inspection by the company at any time.

Registration of encryption keys
Employees using encryption or other security packages on company or their own computers for company work must register the keys or other devices with the IT manager and permit inspection at any time. If the key or other security feature has not been previously registered, the employee will immediately make it available on request by [state name and contact details]. Failure to comply will result in disciplinary action.

The closing certificate, signed by the applicant, should be along the following lines:

Example: 'I certify that the above replies are true, complete and correct. I understand that it is a criminal offence to attempt to obtain employment by deception and that any misrepresentation of a material fact or omission of relevant information will be cause for cancellation of consideration for employment, or dismissal. I have read and understood the employment conditions set out on page xx and I agree to abide them if I am employed. I also undertake to keep [the company] promptly advised of any change in my personal, financial or business circumstances that could have an impact on this application or on my suitability for employment.'

The form should be signed and dated. The agreement to provide information on changed circumstances is very important.

FALSE BANKER

Ricardo Garotte obtained work as a temporary employee with two banks and made off with more than $3.5 million – he was arrested when about to land a position with a third bank, and nearly secured a fourth banking position while on bail.

Questions
Questions should be relevant and focused on important issues:

- Is the question necessary to identify the applicant?
- Is the question necessary to assess his qualifications, suitability, experience, honesty or reliability?
- Is the question legal? Has the company the right to ask it in the country or state concerned?

Most application forms consist entirely of closed questions, often requiring simple 'yes' and 'no' answers which are easy to falsify. Sometimes it is more meaningful to include a number of open questions, leaving space for freestyle answers. For example, questions such as the following can provide a good insight into the candidate's honesty:

- How would you react if we discovered that you have not told the whole truth on this application form?
- On a scale of 1 to 100, how accurate are your answers?

A genuine applicant should not resent completing a detailed form. People who have something to hide may show more reluctance and fail to pursue their interest, perhaps alleging that the forms intrude upon their privacy or civil liberties.

MISSING APPLICATION FORMS

A company that uses a very detailed application form was concerned because around 10% of candidates failed to return them. The personnel director argued that the forms were intrusive. The backgrounds of the candidates who had withdrawn their applications were checked and in every case they had derogatory histories that would have resulted in their rejection.

Set out below, in Table 9.9, are the questions and elements that should be considered:

- on application forms;
- in interviews;
- by inspecting corroborative data (such as educational certificates);
- by external verification.

Items shaded in dark grey in column 5 highlight factors that would normally debar any candidate from employment. The legality of asking questions relating to items shown in BLOCK CAPITALS should be confirmed with local employment lawyers.

Table 9.9 Elements to be checked in a pre-employment screening process.

[The findings in column 4 may be obvious from the application form or interview. Disqualifying information may be uncovered from the absence of corroborating data or through external checks. For example, any candidate who gives a false name should be rejected, whereas an incorrect passport number may result in the candidate being asked for an explanation.]

1	2	3	4	5
Percentage of forms asking the question	Information requested on application forms and tested by corroborative data, in interviews or by external verification	How corroboration is obtained. Based on questions asked on application forms and interviews. *Objectives*	Recruitment decision based on the results of checking or interview. Findings	Decision
	Identification	*Make sure you are dealing with the right person*		
100	Full name	Birth certificate and passport	False	Reject
17	Previous name	Interview	False	Reject
50	MAIDEN NAME	Marriage certificate	False	Confront
100	SEX	Birth certificate and passport	False	Reject
74	DATE OF BIRTH	Birth certificate and passport	False	Reject
	Birth certificate	Failure to produce		Confront
33	PLACE OF BIRTH	Birth certificate and passport	False	Reject
15	CITIZENSHIP	Passport	False	Reject
2	PASSPORT NUMBER	Passport	False	Explain
22	Social security number	External verification	False	Confront
0	Fingerprints	Obtained covertly on the application form (see page 244)	False Hidden	Reject
11	PHYSICAL DESCRIPTION	Photograph and interview	Inaccurate	Explain
9	ENCLOSE CURRENT PHOTOGRAPH		Wrong person	Reject

continued

Percentage of forms asking the question	Information requested on application forms and tested by corroborative data, in interviews or by external verification	How corroboration is obtained Based on questions asked on application forms and interviews *Objectives*	Recruitment decision based on the results of checking or interview Findings	Decision
1	2	3	4	5
100	Current address	Electoral roll	False	Confront
40	Years at address	Utility bill	False	Confront
15	Previous addresses		False	Confront
37	Home telephone number	Telephone directory/invoice	False	Confront
26	Person to contact in an emergency	Application form	Does not exist	Confront
	Education	*Make sure the candidate is qualified*		
20	Names of schools attended		False	Reject
20	DATES OF ATTENDANCE	External verification	False	Confront
20	Names of universities attended		False	Reject
			False	Confront
100	Qualifications obtained (*What is your highest qualification?*)	External verification Examination of certificates	False	Reject
30	Name of teacher	External verification	False	Confront
Findings	Failure to produce original certificates	Interview	**Findings**	Confront
	Unexplained gaps in schooling		**Findings**	Confront
	Record of violence or insubordination	External verification	**Findings**	Reject
	Record of stealing or lying		**Findings**	Reject
	Record of serious drug abuse/dealing		**Findings**	Reject
	Record of truancy		**Findings**	Reject

Financial information		*Make sure the candidate is solvent and financially reliable*		
15	TOTAL FAMILY INCOME	External verification	False	Confront
15	REGULAR MONTHLY OUTGOINGS		False	Confront
15	NAME AND ADDRESS OF BANKER		False	Reject
	Bankers' reference			
7	CREDIT CARDS HELD		False	Confront
	What is the minimum income you require to cover your current financial obligations?		**False**	Confront
Findings	Excess of outgoings over salary offered		Findings	Confront
	Unexplained wealth or assets		Findings	Confront
	Undisclosed bankruptcy		Findings	Reject
	Bad credit record and court judgements		Disclosed	Confront
			Undisclosed	Reject
Criminal Convictions		*Make sure the candidate is being honest about problems in his past*		
Findings	Disclosed serious criminal convictions In last 5 years Earlier Minor juvenile offences	External verification Criminal Records Bureau; accessed by the candidate under the European Data Protection Laws	Disclosed	Reject Consider Accept
	Undisclosed criminal convictions		Discovered	Reject
	Pending litigation		Disclosed	Confront
			Undisclosed	Reject
Personal and family		*Confirm family stability and commitments*		
20	Personal referees	Written and telephone references	Negative	Confront

continued

Percentage of forms asking the question	Information requested on application forms and tested by corroborative data, in interviews or by external verification	How corroboration is obtained. Based on questions asked on application forms and interviews. Objectives	Recruitment decision based on the results of checking or interview	
			Findings	Decision
1	2	3	4	5
24	MEMBERSHIP OF CLUBS AND ASSOCIATIONS	External verification	False	Confront
40	MEMBERSHIP OF TRADE UNION		False	Explain
	Would you be prepared to join a trades union?			
20	Details of driving licence and endorsement	Driving licence	False	Reject
0	Directorships and private business interests of the candidate and immediate family members	External verification	False Concealed	Reject
0	Any potentially conflicting interest	External verification	Disclosed	Explain
			Undisclosed	Reject
	What are your main hobbies?			

39	MARITAL STATUS	External verification	False	Confront
20	NUMBER OF CHILDREN	Corroborative data	False	Confront
15	NAMES OF CHILDREN		False	Confront
17	DATES AND PLACES OF CHILDRENS' BIRTHS		False	Explain
15	NUMBER OF DEPENDANTS		False	Explain
9	DATE AND PLACE OF MARRIAGE		False	Confront
7	WIFE'S MAIDEN NAME		False	Confront
11	WIFE'S DATE OF BIRTH		False	Explain
0	Family member with a conflicting business interest		Undisclosed	Reject
4	DETAILS OF PREVIOUS MARRIAGES		False	Reject
4	NAMES AND ADDRESSES OF PARENTS		False	Confront
Findings	**Unstable family – criminal – background**	**External verification**	**Findings**	Confront
	Criminal associates		**Findings**	Confront
	Housing	*Needed to confirm credit history etc.*		
17	Owned or rented	Rating list	False	Reject
0	Number of years at each address	Corroborative data	False	Explain
7	Name and address of landlord		False	Confront
	Employment history	*Confirm experience, qualifications, reliability etc.*		

continued

Percentage of forms asking the question	Information requested on application forms and tested by corroborative data, in interviews or by external verification	How corroboration is obtained Based on questions asked on application forms and interviews *Objectives*	Recruitment decision based on the results of checking or interview	
			Findings	Decision
1	2	3	4	5
43	Name and address of present or past employers (normally for at least ten years)	External verification Corroborative data	False	Reject
24	Years service with the employer		False	Reject
61	Work responsibilities		False	Reject
31	Salary record		False	Reject
0	Sickness record		False	Confront
0	Name of supervisor	External verification	False	Confront
0	Non-competition agreement	Application form	True or false	Explain
		External verification	Correct	Accept
			False	Reject
0	Acceptance of a job with a lower salary, without a satisfactory explanation	External verification	False	Reject
10	Name of company referee		Derogatory	Explain
20	Reasons for leaving previous employers Resignation Redundancy Dismissal	External verification	False	Reject

	Item	Method	Findings	Action
Findings	Job hopping	External verification	**Findings**	Reject
	Unexplained gaps in employment		**Findings**	Confront
	Unsatisfactory performance		**Findings**	Confront
	Extended self-employment without supporting accounts		**Findings**	Confront
	Extended periods of unemployment		**Findings**	Confront
	Multiple employment with references that cannot be traced or checked		**Findings**	Confront
	Dishonesty/subversion/violence		**Findings**	Reject
Health		*Identify drug and alcohol abusers*		
20	PHYSICAL DISABILITIES	Medical examination	Concealed	Reject
11	NAME AND ADDRESS OF DOCTOR		False	Confront
0	USE OF NARCOTIC DRUGS OR ALCOHOL	External verification / Medical examination	Disclosed / Concealed	Explain / Reject
Findings	Any other undisclosed condition affecting the person's ability to do the job	**External verification**	**Findings**	Confront
Interviews		*Confirm positive and expose negative features. Assess overall good faith in the application*		
Interview	Does not answer relevant questions	Interviews	Findings	Reject
	Any deception			

Even in the most liberal parts of the world (i.e. Highgate and Cheam), once a person has been appointed (say as an employee or contractor) much of what might otherwise be regarded as discriminatory information can be requested. The reason for this is simply that after the person has been engaged, he cannot reasonably argue that he has been discriminated against. Some organizations attach a separate sheet for questions that are potentially discriminatory with an explanation.

Example: 'XYZ is committed to a policy of equal employment and non-discrimination. So that we can monitor the success of this programme, we would like you to complete the following details. You will not be penalized if you do not wish to provide some or all of this information at this stage.'

RECEIPT AND HANDLING THE APPLICATION FORM

Completed application forms should be reviewed by at least two people, working together in a brainstorming session. This approach is proven to be far more effective in identifying potential problems. Details on the form should be compared against any CV prepared by the candidate or by an agency on his behalf and any discrepancies highlighted, so that they can be raised in the interview.

If the candidate is invited for an interview, he or she should be asked to bring the originals of educational and other certificates, passport, driving licence, birth and marriage certificates, a recent utility bill and a payslip.

THE INITIAL INTERVIEW AND CORROBORATIVE DATA

A distinct portion of the initial interview for potentially suitable recruits (don't waste time on any screening if the candidate is not suitable) should be devoted to verifying details provided on the application form. Pre-employment interviews are discussed at page 419.

EXTERNAL VERIFICATION

For short-listed candidates, important data uncovered on the application form, from corroborative data or in interviews, should be independently verified, depending on the sensitivity of the job concerned (Table 9.10).

If the results of these checks contradict any detail given by the candidate he should be called back to attend a further interview and asked to give his explanation.

DRUGS TESTING

Experience shows a very close relationship between fraud and drug abuse: drug abuse can be the doorway through which serious criminals infiltrate an organization. Thus all candidates for sensitive positions should be required, as part of their medical examination, to be tested for symptoms of narcotic drugs or alcohol abuse.

Table 9.10 External verifications

Reference source METHOD	Areas to check and questions
Roll of electors • ONLINE ACCESS	• Check residency and years at address • Identify family members and neighbours • Speak to immediate neighbours
Housing or rating list • TELEPHONE	• Ownership and value of house • Confirm address and dates of residency
Telephone directory • ONLINE ACCESS	• Confirm residency • Check for businesses registered at the address
Schools and universities • IN WRITING AND BY TELEPHONE	• Confirm dates of attendance and qualifications obtained • Confirm attendance and disciplinary record • CHECK THE STATUS OF THE COLLEGE: is it bona fide?
Previous employers (for the past 10 years) • IN WRITING AND BY TELEPHONE	• Name, place and date of birth • If possible, obtain a copy of the employment application form from the previous employer • Confirm employment dates, positions held, salary and reasons for termination • Confirm work responsibilities • Check eligibility for re-employment • Check restrictive covenants on employment • If possible, speak to the applicant's immediate supervisor and colleagues
Bankers • IN WRITING (with permission of the candidate)	• Confirm financial standing
Companies house online	• Directorships of the candidate and close family members
Credit agencies (if allowed) • ONLINE	• Check financial history
County courts • ONLINE	• Check bad debt record and judgements
List of directors • ONLINE	• Check for present and past directorships for the candidate and his immediate family
Reuters Business Briefing or LexisNexis • ONLINE	• Media search
Internet • ONLINE	
Criminal Records Bureau (UK) • Applied for by the candidate	• Criminal convictions

DRUGS TESTING

There are four reasons why drug testing should be part of the recruitment process. The first is that narcotic users and alcoholics are more frequently absent from work than their colleagues. Second, their decisions can be adversely affected by narcotic drugs or alcohol. Third, the cost of drugs usually puts addicts under severe financial strain and this can be a motivation for fraud. Finally, organized crime uses drugs as a means of subverting employees.

There are a number of websites that have model policies on the control of narcotic drugs: one of the best is www.dfwp.utsa.edu.

THE SIGN OFF

A brief report summarizing the results for shortlisted candidates should be submitted to human relations or the line manager who will take the decision to hire or reject the candidate. Copies of the clearance report should be retained in a confidential security file and duplicated in the personal file for the applicant if he or she is employed. After six months, files should be purged of all sensitive personal information that is no longer required.

THE OFFER LETTER

The offer letter, which should be in a more or less standard form approved by lawyers, should make employment conditional on any outstanding references, results of medical examinations, the candidate's acceptance of a contract of employment, and satisfactory completion of a probationary period. The candidate should required to sign and return a copy of this letter, acknowledging his acceptance of the conditions and the fact that there has been no change in his circumstances since his application was first submitted.

EMPLOYMENT OF TEMPORARY STAFF

Specified procedures should ensure that temporary and part-time staff, especially contract programmers and secretaries, are not employed in sensitive jobs, unless their backgrounds have been checked.

INFILTRATION

One of the most common ways in which competitive intelligence is compromised, is by infiltration of the target company by its opponents. Wherever possible, short-term vacancies should be filled by rotating the duties of other employees, so that temporary staff take over the least sensitive jobs.

Companies should take special care where the employee has only been on the agency's books for a short time or has recently worked for a competitor. Both of these are red flags indicating possible infiltration.

Also, the integrity of the agency supplying temporary staff should be carefully checked and it should be required to sign a contract setting out its obligations, especially in relation to the screening of candidates. The agency should be required to produce a copy of any internal application form completed by the candidate and the results of its own background verifications.

The temporary employee should be briefed on the company's policy on business ethics, conflicts of interest etc., and asked to sign the appropriate declarations. Performance should be carefully monitored and, as a general rule, access privileges should be limited to those absolutely necessary.

At the end of the assignment, the line manager concerned should require the temporary employee to sign a termination agreement (see page 345). He should also prepare a brief appraisal, stating whether the person concerned is suitable for re-engagement.

BENCHMARKING

The following checklist (Table 9.11) should help you benchmark your existing pre-employment process.

How does your pre-employment screening (PES) process measure up?

Table 9.11 Outline of the PES process

Consideration or action	OBJECTIVES *Comments*	Yes or no
MANAGEMENT APPROVAL	*It is vital that the PES programme is approved at a senior level and **included in the appropriate policy manuals and training programmes***	
What job positions should be included in the programme? *NB: if the programme does not apply to everyone who is placed in a position of trust, there is the possibility that rejected candidates could claim for discrimination*	• Should it apply to **all employees**? • Should it apply to **agents and advisers**? • Should it apply to **temporary employees**? • Should it apply to **staff employed by contractors**, such as security guards and cleaners? • Should it apply differently, depending on the seniority of the job?	
Acquired companies and members of the extended enterprise		
When should checks be made?	• Prior to employment • Annual reviews for sensitive positions • Prior to promotion or transfer • On acquired companies (before or after acquisition)	
What factors – that might debar employment – should be checked?	See Table 9.9. It is important that these factors are agreed and used as a yardstick	
Do your fidelity insurance policies require background checks to be made?	*This is a condition on some policies* *If so, details of the checks made should be permanently retained*	

continued

Consideration or action	OBJECTIVES *Comments*	Yes or no
What are the legal implications?	*What questions are prohibited under law?* **Candidates should be politely alerted to the fact that it is a criminal offence** *for anyone to attempt to obtain employment by deception*	
Who will administer the programme?	Personnel department? Security? Compliance or internal audit?	
What external verifications (see page 316) will be made and who will carry them out?	• Internal by security or a special department • Through an external agency	
Has the process been documented and flow charted?	The process should be specified in policies and procedures	
Are the costs acceptable?	*Bearing in mind that the average employee will remain on the payroll for 10 years, earn over £200,000 and could involve the company in multi-million pound fines, is spending even £500 on checking his background excessive?*	
Company policy should be based on the answers to these questions. It should be incorporated in the appropriate manuals, included in an employee handbook and training programme and also summarized on job application forms		
LEGALITY	*The legality of the process must be confirmed*	
A decision matrix for rejecting candidates should be determined – as a specified standard and under legal advice. It should identify the derogatory data that would debar employment	*Too often organizations come to subjective decisions on a case-by-case basis. Specified evaluation criteria determined in advance minimize the risks of taking bad decisions and being accused of unfair discrimination*	
The legality of the programme should be confirmed with specialist lawyers. This does not mean that the process should be emasculated. In most cases, employers should assert their rights to take effective precautions. But care has to be taken over the human rights, data protection and other legislation	*Laws governing privacy and access to government information vary from country to country and care should be taken to confirm the legality of questions and the methods through which answers can be confirmed*	
Compliance with the Information Commissioners Guidelines and Data Protection Registration	*Ensuring that (data protection) DP requirements are observed and that personal data can be used for screening and other security purposes*	
APPLICATION FORM	*The application form should set out the basics of the process, what is expected of the candidate and his legal obligations to tell the truth. It should deter dishonest applicants and ask the questions necessary to enable effective checks to be made*	

Consideration or action	OBJECTIVES *Comments*	Yes or no
A clear, comprehensive and well-structured application form is essential. The appearance of the application form should deter dishonest candidates The form should be divided into: • a welcome; • warnings on false applications; • how answers will be checked; • detailed open and closed questions; • warranty of accuracy. *In some cases, companies have two forms. One is completed in advance of the first interview, and a second, and possibly shorter, version under supervision in the second interview. The answers given should be compared and the candidate questioned about any discrepancies*	Subject to legal advice, application forms should contain some **words of warning**. *Many applicants do not realize the serious criminal implications of false declarations and it is in everyone's interests that this position is clarified. Also, warnings raise the danger level for the dishonest candidate and may deter him*	
	The form should also refer to, or **summarize, the company's security and related policies** or refer the candidate to a handbook which he should be given as early in the recruitment process as possible	
	The questions most frequently asked on employment forms are listed in Table 9.9 together with the likely decisions based on replies to background checks	
	The form should require candidates – at the first interview – to provide copies of their educational and other **corroborative data**	
	Job application forms should also contain clauses giving the **candidate's permission** for checks to be made with previous employers, bankers, credit bureaux, schools, universities etc. They should also include a **release to third parties**, permitting them to provide information. *The exact wording of these releases should be drafted by qualified employment lawyers in the jurisdictions concerned*	
	Similarly the forms should contain **releases** under the Data Protection, Human Rights, Regulation of Investigatory Powers Act etc., especially regarding the interception of communications and computer networks	

continued

Consideration or action	OBJECTIVES *Comments*	Yes or no
	Where allowed by local laws, job applications should be structured so they become **part of the candidate's contract** if he is employed. Wording should make it clear that false information on the application form will be regarded as a breach of contract and will result in immediate dismissal, without compensation. The form may also contain an **undertaking that the candidate**, if employed, will observe the company's security, investigatory, compliance and related policies and will provide annual declarations of compliance	
	The candidate should submit the completed application form **at least seven days before** the initial interview and be asked to bring along the originals of all **corroborative data**	
BRAINSTORMING	*Analysis of the application form*	
For candidates who might be invited to an interview, the application forms should be reviewed by at least two people in a brainstorming session and possible discrepancies or problem areas identified. Corroborative data should be examined on the same basis	*Experience shows that such sessions are most effective on the grounds that the suspicion level of two people working together is at least three times higher than two working separately*	
DUPLICATE APPLICATION FORM		
The candidate is asked to complete a short application form immediately before the screening interview	*This should be compared with the original application form and any discrepancies highlighted. Deceptive candidates may be taken by surprise*	
INITIAL INTERVIEW	*A segment of the interview should be devoted to screening and corroborating attributes.* ***Training on how to detect deception should be given to people who conduct such interviews***	

Consideration or action	OBJECTIVES Comments	Yes or no
A distinct portion of the initial interview should be devoted to screening and the examination and copying of corroborative data	*The candidate may be given an **abbreviated application form** and asked to complete this while he is waiting to be interviewed. It should cover key aspects such as education, work history and finances. Refusal or hesitancy to complete the form should be treated with suspicion*	
	The significance of the company's policies on Business Ethics, Conflicts of Interest and Pre-employment screening should be discussed	
	The interview should be **conducted professionally** by employees who have been trained to detect dishonesty. Excellent courses and videos are available from John E Reid & Associates, Chicago. See www.reidsystems.com (telephone 001 312 938 9200)	
EXTERNAL VERIFICATION	*Written and telephone references should be taken up to verify the positive attributes and to uncover derogatory elements*	
References are essential, and must be rigorously verified to a specified standard and based on a checklist	*Applicants can and do provide telephone numbers of friends, relatives and even themselves as contacts willing to provide glowing testimonials. The prospective employer should check that the telephone numbers given are valid and get oral references from at least the last two employers, and ideally should speak to the applicant's previous managers*	
If the candidate appears likely to be offered a job, the application form and all supporting detail should be thoroughly checked against an agreed matrix (see page 302)	*These checks should be aimed at corroborating attributes and identifying derogatory elements. The candidate should be evaluated against an agreed matrix*	
MEDICAL EXAMINATION	*This is important to avoid malingerers and drug and alcohol abusers*	
All candidates should be required as part of their **medical examination** to be tested for the use of narcotic drugs and alcohol abuse		
CLEARANCE INTERVIEW (if necessary)	*To resolve any discrepancies in the background of short-listed candidates (see page 419)*	

continued

Consideration or action	OBJECTIVES *Comments*	Yes or no
If the results of these checks contradict any detail given on the application form or at the interview, the candidate should be called back to attend a further interview and asked to explain the discrepancies	*Again, these interviews are critical and employees who conduct them must be adequately trained. This stage is applicable only to short-listed candidates*	
CLEARANCE REPORT	*A formal clearance report should be prepared*	
Based on these external checks and interviews, a brief clearance report should be submitted to the personnel or line manager who will take the decision to hire or reject the candidate	*Copies of the clearance report should be retained in a confidential security file and in the personal file for the applicant*	
THE OFFER LETTER AND CONTRACT		
The offer letter, which should be in more or less a standard form approved by lawyers, should make **employment conditional** on any outstanding references, medical examinations, the production of a birth certificate and other documents, on the candidate's acceptance of a contract of employment, and on satisfactory completion of a probationary period	*The candidate should be required to sign and return a copy of this letter, acknowledging his acceptance of the conditions*	
PROBATIONARY PERIOD		
All employees should be required to serve a **three-month probationary period**. During this time his performance should be carefully monitored. At the end of the period, the candidate's security clearance should be reviewed. This is the final safety net	*This is the final safety net*	
REVIEW OF THE SYSTEM	*Assessing the effectiveness of the process*	
The acceptance and rejection rate should be reviewed at least annually		
TEMPORARY EMPLOYEES and CONSULTANTS	*The process for clearing temporary employees should be specified*	
The process described above should be adapted for validating the integrity of temporary employees and should be based on: • A detailed application form • Screening interview • Limited external verification	*The processes used by recruitment agencies should be audited and checked from time to time. The bona fides of the agency should be confirmed by purchasing as part of its vendor approval programme*	

Staff handbooks

The position on human rights etc. for existing employees should be clarified and brought up to date in staff handbooks, management meetings and training courses.

Training programmes

Training programmes on control should cover what is, and what is not, expected of employees in the extended company and should be implemented through some or all of the following methods:

- booklets on business ethics and security procedures;
- induction training of new employees;
- on-the-job training;
- security presentations at management meetings and seminars;
- reading files for senior managers;
- articles in house magazines;
- films and video tapes;
- security newsletters;
- e-training or Web-based training;
- posters.

In addition, companies should consider using banner messages on computer terminals or personal computers, special screen savers or electronic mail broadcasts to raise the profile of ethics, compliance and controls.

Most companies would dramatically improve their security if they held special briefings on the subjects listed in Table 9.12.

The objective is to increase the awareness of employees to risks and the need for control.

Job descriptions

Some organizations don't like job descriptions on the grounds that they reduce flexibility. However, it is essential that there is a formal record in place to establish ownership of assets and processes and responsibilities for control. Ideally, in addition to addressing the more usual aspects of authorities and responsibilities, job descriptions should state:

'x is responsible for maintaining security over all aspects of his work and for compliance with company security policy and procedures. Failure to observe these policies and procedures will be subject to disciplinary action. Specifically the employee is required to:

- report incidents of suspected fraud or malpractice;
- comply with all laws and regulations, on which he has been fully briefed;
- cooperate and assist in investigations when requested to do so, and to answer questions posed by management;
- refrain from discussing sensitive company matters with third parties etc.'

Table 9.12   Essential security training

Special training for	Coverage
Top managers	Special high-level briefing on the risks of fraud and dishonesty
Executive secretaries	General security awareness: handling confidential information; dealing with potential pretext enquiries
Management and financial accountants	Special briefing on how to detect the symptoms of fraud
Salesmen	Laws on corruption and how to detect unfair competitive activity
Personnel officers	How to detect and deal with deceit in interviews
Purchasing agents and other employees who exercise discretion in favour of third parties	The consequences of corruption; legal position; what to do when a bribe is offered; reporting suspected bribery
Security guards	General security awareness; the legal position on search and arrests; emergency procedures
Computer users	Requirements of the Data Protection and Misuse Acts
Cleaners	Security of waste paper
Auditors	Automated fraud detection programmes; conduct of investigations; interviewing

This simple statement ensures that responsibility for controls is assigned to line managers, as 'owners', and that penalties will be imposed for non-compliance. The manager of internal audit should draw problems concerning any employee to the attention of the supervisor concerned and this should be discussed, if not before, at his annual appraisal.

Wherever possible, job descriptions should be written so that they support, or are in lieu of, more formal contracts of employment. Where employees are issued with job descriptions in addition to formal contracts, the greatest care should be taken to ensure that they are compatible.

Contracts of employment

Contracts with employees in the extended company should contain specific reference to the requirement to comply with controls and should contain undertakings to:

- report changes in their financial or domestic circumstances without delay;
- answer questions and provide information when reasonably required to do so;
- provide annual declarations of compliance and letters of representation;
- comply with other legal agreements;
- submit any disputes to arbitration or a procedure for alternative dispute resolution;
- protect confidential information, both during and after employment.

Contracts of this nature serve a preventive purpose and are extremely valuable in legal proceedings taken as a result of the employee's dishonesty. They must be compatible with job descriptions.

Agreements by personnel

Where appropriate, employees in sensitive positions should be required to enter into agreements that may be included in a job description or contract of employment (see Table 9.13).

Laws in some countries prevent certain types of agreements being used. For example, in the UK, restrictive covenants after termination of employment are usually limited in scope and duration and advice should always be obtained on the applicability and legality of agreements.

Annual appraisals

Annual performance reviews are important control tools and a procedure should be specified under the ownership of human resources. All line managers – in addition to the more usual items – should appraise the employee's performance based on the following inputs:

- observation of the way in which the employee has discharged his control responsibilities, including his appraisal of his subordinates;
- the results of the control self-assessment programme;
- objectives set in previous years;
- input, if any, about the employee or the business unit in which he works from the manager of internal audit;
- analysis of the reporting of incidents and gifts declaration procedures.

Table 9.13 Agreements by personnel

Type of agreement	Purpose
Conflicts of interest	See page 328
Confidentiality	Undertakings to protect information during and after employment
Patents and inventions	To assign the right to all inventions and patents discovered by the employee to the employer
Secrecy	To restrict the disclosure of sensitive information during and after employment. Agreements should prohibit employees discussing matters of company interest with the press
Non-competition	To prevent diversion of business to a future employer
Consent to search	To require the employee to submit to a search when entering or leaving company premises and more importantly to accept that the company has the right to search anything on its own property, including desks, cupboards, offices, lockers or computers
Termination	To ensure that all company property is returned on termination of employment

The detailed approach in such interviews is explained in Chapter 10. The employee should be informed of any aspects requiring improvement and asked to make suggestions and set control objectives for the future. In sensitive cases the employee might be asked to sign a formal declaration of compliance (see www.cobasco.com).

Conflicts of interest

Procedures to prevent and report conflicts of interest should be specified and drawn to the attention of all job applicants at the earliest possible stage in the recruitment process (see page 304). The procedures should apply to employees, vendors, agents, distributors and other members of the extended enterprise both at home and overseas.

Each year the personnel concerned should be required to complete a declaration of compliance (see page 327).

Bribery

BACKGROUND

This is a difficult area, which calls for very careful treatment. Legislation has resulted in a patchwork quilt of what is and is not illegal (see page 275) and is therefore of little help. The principle is that *all* bribery is bad and should not be condoned. Some companies have totally different standards for benefits that can be received by its own employees and the benefits it permits its own employees to give to others. They seem to identify an ethical difference between incoming bribes that corrupt their own employees and their outgoing payments to corrupt others. Policies must be consistent.

BRIBES PAID TO EMPLOYEES

Procedures should be specified for employees in the extended company prohibiting them from accepting gifts, lavish entertaining or benefits of more than nominal value from those with whom they do business. From time to time there may be exceptions and, in such cases, employees should be required to submit a gifts declaration form stating from whom a benefit will be, or has been, received and its estimated value. The form should be prepared with an original and two copies and serially numbered.

The bottom copy should be retained by the employee after signature by his immediate supervisor. The supervisor should retain the second copy and submit the third copy, with his comments, to the manager of internal audit. Audit should log gifts declaration forms and monitor them for trends. *For example, for vendors who give lavish gifts and for those who are most successful, but don't.*

Obviously, if an employee or agent receives a corrupt benefit, he is unlikely to declare it. But if the truth is discovered, the employee is prevented from giving a plausible excuse. In effect, by failing to make a declaration he has marked his behaviour as dishonest.

On the other hand, the honest employee who declares that he has received a benefit is protected. Expense statements may be used as an alternative to a gifts declaration form (Table 9.14). For example:

During the period I have received and given gifts and benefits as follows:

Table 9.14 Expense statement

Date	Name of individual and COMPANY	Give Received	Details and approximate value
1.2.2002	Bill Smith SMITH'S STATIONERY CO	G	Day out at Wentworth, lunch etc. £200
5.2.2002	Bill Smith SMITH'S STATIONERY CO	R	Lunch at Langans £180

Again, such declarations enable an honest employee to clear his conscience and a guilty one to commit himself to a course of conduct he will find difficult to explain – especially if he has omitted important items.

BRIBES PAID BY EMPLOYEES

Small gifts and entertaining

Top companies, with brilliant policies on ethics, authorize subtle, and not so subtle, forms of bribery through lavish entertaining, sponsored business trips, expensive prizes, and marketing promotional schemes. These may be rationalized as acceptable, but if they are not carefully controlled they can lead to serious consequences and customers, suppliers, competitors or regulators can allege that they corrupted the recipient to act improperly to their disadvantage. Marketing and other schemes that involve significant benefits for third parties should be reviewed, in advance, by the company's lawyers, auditors and security advisers.

Employees who wish to entertain someone with whom their employer does business should be required, as part of a specified procedure, to justify the expenditure, in detail, through their personal expense claims and not through some obscure accounts payable dodge.

Facilitation or 'grease' payments

These are small payments, often to government officials to get them to do what they should do anyway, only more quickly. The UK is unique in making grease payments a domestic criminal offence, even if the act took place overseas. Although the Crown Prosecution Service has said it is unlikely to prosecute such cases, there is no guarantee. There is no legal restriction placed on grease payments by American citizens and companies, or by most other nationalities. Thus, the practical approach (to this nonsensical British position) is for British companies to craft their approach along similar lines to legal tax avoidance – for example, by having non-British companies and individuals making the 'grease payments'. The fact is that if such payments are not made, business in many countries would grind to a halt: that is the reality.

Wholesale bribery

Sometimes when bribery is challenged, the managers involved excuse themselves by saying: 'There is no use being uncommercial about it. If we don't do it someone else will. Besides that it is just part of the culture, which you don't understand.'

When outgoing bribes are approved by the top managers who have the appropriate authority, there is little in practice that junior employees can do about it, except become whistle-blowers.

EXPECT IT TO COME OUT

When bribery comes to light, legal actions are possible by the police, regulators, the company whose employees have been bribed, competitors who have been disadvantaged and shareholders. Employees in the organizations receiving and paying bribes can expose the crime. New management may decide there are political points to score by dumping their predecessors.

In emerging and transitional markets, bribers also have to remember that new regimes have big brushes. The purge following the departure of President Marcos and in Korea, leading to the arrest of President Roh, are good examples. The bottom line is that companies that pay bribes, or close their eyes to bribery on their behalf by others, are crooked and deserve to get caught.

Wholesale bribery, especially to get new business, presents the biggest challenge to an organization's ethical policies. It takes courage and strong principles to say: 'We will not do business under those conditions' and withdraw. But it is the right decision.

Incentive schemes

Some companies offer incentives to employees in departments or branches whose financial results, losses, fire or safety records meet predetermined standards. Sometimes such schemes seem to work in reducing reported accidents, but whether they reduce actual accidents is a matter of conjecture.

UNDER A BUS

A major manufacturing plant had a superb safety record and was in line for a special award. One day an employee fell from a storage tank and broke his neck. His colleagues quietly smuggled him offsite and dumped him in the road two miles away, telling him he had to report that he had been run over by a bus. Unfortunately the man died and the deception came to light.

Similarly, highly geared bonus schemes can be an open invitation for employees to falsify results. The case of Barings is a good example of the blindness that can afflict good people when they are all pursuing the common goal of high personal rewards.

Thus all incentive schemes should be carefully reviewed and modified if they have negative outputs.

Incident reporting and whistle-blowing

BACKGROUND

The notion that one person should spy on another, or a company probe into the lives of its employees, is abhorrent to many people, and there is a critical balance between the requirement of an organization to limit its losses and improper intrusion into the personal lives of others.

However, it is critical that employees and others are both required and able to report suspicions of fraud, either openly or anonymously. In fact the US Sentencing Guidelines make it clear that organizations that do not have reporting procedures in place can expect little sympathy (and possibly heavy penalties) in US courts.

MYTHS AND MISCONCEPTIONS

It is commonly believed that people who blow the whistle always end up in trouble. Although this is true in some cases, most whistle-blowers do very well, thank you.

TAP PHARMA

Douglas Durand worked in a senior sales position with TAP Pharmacueticals (a joint venture between the Japanese giant Takeda and Abbott Laboratoties) and became concerned over improper practices in its sales department, specifically that salesmen were issuing excessive amounts of free samples of the drug Lupron to doctors, enabling them to dispense them to patients and claim the supposed cost from the Medicare providers. Mr Durand, apparently without trying to deal with the matter internally, took action under the Qui Tam – False Claims Act – against his employer. The act, which is based on ancient English Law (which still applies), is intended to enable citizens to take legal action on behalf of the King when they suspect the government is being defrauded[5] (see www.falseclaimsact.com). The action was taken over by the American Federal agencies and TAP fined $875 million and put on five years' probation. Under the False Claims Act, whistle-blowers may be entitled to between 5% and 50% of the amount recovered by the government. In this case Mr Durand was paid $78 million which, after taxes and legal fees, left him with a cool $42 million. So who says that whistle-blowing does not pay?

The TAP case is by no means unusual: the Nashville-based Columbia/HCA agreed to pay fines and penalties of $745 million: Smith Kline Beecham Clinical Laboratories paid $325 million, providing the whistle-blowers (nicely called 'relators') a cool $52 million. In the defence industry, United Technologies agreed to pay $150 million (with $22.5 million for the relator); Lucas Industries paid $88 million (with $19.3 million for the relator) and General Electric (considered to be among the most ethical companies) paid $75 million with $13 million going to Chester Walsh, the whistle-blower.

---

[5]   Qui Tam provisions – giving private citizens the ability to bring actions on behalf of the government – have existed for centuries. During the Middle Ages, England did not have an organized police force to enforce laws. English common law, by adopting various qui tam provisions, attempted to provide for the enforcement of the law by those who were injured by violations of the law. Qui tam provisions allowed private parties to act like a policeman. The private party was paid a bounty to make the effort worthwhile and to give incentives to other individuals to bring similar suits

The essential element of all of these cases was that the US government was defrauded and there is no doubt that the False Claims Act and rewards offered directly by government agencies have both exposed massive fraud cases and motivated unscrupulous people to make false 'whistle-blowing' reports.

The US is also riddled with class actions, where groups of people who consider they have been disadvantaged claim against the corporations and individuals they regard as responsible. Many class action cases were originated by whistle-blowers who gave their employers no chance to deal with matters internally. For this reason alone, it is critical that all organizations have effective internal reporting processes and comply with legislation such as the Public Interest Disclosure Act.

POLICY STATEMENTS

The company should introduce policies and procedures for reporting and investigating incidents, which extend to employees, customers, suppliers and other third parties. It should also set up a hotline through which suspicions can be reported, anonymously if necessary. Details of the procedures should be reproduced on purchase orders, and other relevant documents.

REPORTING OF INCIDENTS

1   Objectives of the reporting procedure
The objectives of these procedures are to ensure that employees and others who suspect malpractice are able to report their suspicions without compromising their own jobs, and that the matters they have raised are placed in independent hands as quickly as possible and investigated thoroughly thereafter.

2   Hotline
The company recognizes that there may be circumstances where an employee who suspects malpractice has a good reason for not wishing to reveal his identity. It has therefore provided a hotline and PO box number to which suspicions can be reported anonymously.

3   Routine procedure
Every employee is expected to remain alert to the possibility that fraud will occur. When concerns are first aroused, the employee must:

- Treat his suspicions, including anonymous letters and telephone calls, with the utmost care and must not discuss them with anyone who does not have both an immediate and obvious need to know.
- Report suspicions without delay, directly to [name and contact details]. No employee will be criticized for not first informing his immediate supervisor. In fact, any manager who impedes or censures an employee for reporting directly to [name and contact details] will be subject to disciplinary action.
- Secure all information or evidence on which his suspicions are based, providing this will not alert the people under suspicion.
- *Not* take disciplinary, investigative or any other action against the person or persons suspected until the matter has been fully investigated.

Thereafter, the employee will be guided by the auditor or by his designated representatives.

Any employee who fails to comply with this paragraph will be subject to disciplinary action.

4   Other matters to be reported
Introduction
The company has a right to know of any circumstances that fundamentally change the basis on which a person was employed or that could have an adverse impact on its business or reputation.
Potential conflicts of interest
Employees who are contemplating engagement, or who are already engaged, in any commercial activity – either in their own names or through a nominee – which has the potential to conflict with their obligations to the company should report the facts to the auditor and legal adviser [or some other nominated function] without delay. Failure to comply with this procedure will result in disciplinary action.
Employees charged with a criminal offence or insolvency
Any employee who is charged with a criminal offence involving a potential exposure to a term of imprisonment, in a private or business capacity, or who may be subject to an action for insolvency or bankruptcy must report the facts, without delay and in total confidence, to [name and contact details]. Failure to comply will result in disciplinary action.
Employees required to give evidence in court
Employees required to attend court in a private or commercial matter involving an allegation of dishonesty – whether as a complainant, defendant or witness – which could have an adverse impact on the company's reputation must report the facts, without delay, to the auditor and legal adviser. Any employee who disregards this paragraph will be subject to disciplinary action.
Improper approaches and solicitation
Employees who are approached – either directly or through a nominee – to act in any way which could be to the company's disadvantage or who are offered a bribe or personal inducement, must report the facts, without delay, to the auditor and legal adviser. Any employee who disregards this paragraph will be subject to disciplinary action.
Medical and drugs
Employees must report any treatment or counselling in relation to drugs or alcohol abuse.

5   Protection of employees
Introduction
It is fundamental to this policy that employees should have total confidence in the company and the board's unconditional undertaking that internal reports will be dealt with, and that, where they act in good faith, they will be appropriately protected. Any employee who at any time in his career with the company believes otherwise, should discuss the matter with the auditor.
Public Interest Disclosure Act
The company will comply fully with the Public Interest Disclosure Act 1998 in the UK, and with equivalent legislation in other parts of the world. This legislation, which is concerned with what is known as 'whistle-blowing', sets out the circumstances in which employees will be protected against internal disciplinary action if, in good faith, they report suspicions of fraud directly to external bodies. It should be noted that neither the legislation, nor the company, will protect any employee who makes malicious, slanderous or libellous allegations whether they are made internally or externally. All employees are strongly advised to report matters internally before approaching any third party.

Protection of employees and whistle-blowing
General provisions: The company will comply fully with the Public Interest Disclosure Act 1999 in the UK, and with equivalent legislation in other parts of the world. This legislation, which is concerned with what is known as 'whistle-blowing', sets out the circumstances in which employees will be protected against internal disciplinary action if, in good faith, they report suspicions of fraud directly to external bodies. It should be noted that neither the legislation, nor the company, will protect any employee who makes malicious, slanderous or libellous allegations.

An essential feature of this whistle-blowing legislation is that employees making external direct reports:

- were acting in good faith in relation to a serious matter;
- believed that their information was substantially accurate and that:
    - a criminal offence has been, is being or is likely to be committed,
    - a person has failed, is failing or is likely to fail to comply with any legal obligation to which he or she is subject,
    - a miscarriage of justice has occurred, is occurring or is likely to occur,
    - the health and safety of any individual has been, is being or is likely to be endangered,
    - the environment has been, is being or is likely to be damaged,
    - information tending to show any of the above has been, is being or is likely to be deliberately concealed.

In making an external, direct disclosure, employees may, to achieve protection under the legislation, have to demonstrate that at the time they made the report they complied with the conditions set out overleaf [the employee's thoughts at the time are critical].
The employee must be able to demonstrate that:

- they reasonably believed that they would be subject to a detriment if they raised the matter internally;
- that the disclosure was not made with the intention of making a personal gain;
- if the disclosure was made solely for the purpose of obtaining personal legal advice.

Finally, disclosure must be considered reasonable in all circumstances.

6   Confidence in internal procedures
Employees should have total confidence in the company and its unconditional undertaking that internal reports will be dealt with, and that, where they act in good faith, they will be appropriately protected. Any employee who at any time in his or her career with the company believes otherwise should discuss the matter with the auditor.
Against the above background, any employee who makes a disclosure of fraud to an external party, without first giving the company the chance of dealing with it, will be subject to disciplinary action.

Any organization that does not have such a policy in place opens the way for maliciously or financially motivated employees to report externally. This is not a desirable position.

TYPES OF INCIDENTS TO BE REPORTED

The policy and procedures should set out (probably with examples) the types of incidents that have to be reported, including suspected fraud, compliance, safety and environmental breaches.

REPORTING CHANNELS

Routine reporting

A procedure should be specified to enable employees and other members of the extended enterprise to report suspicions of fraud and other problems. The elements to be considered are shown on Table 9.15 below. Shaded rows are also applicable to hotlines and annual reporting, discussed on page 327.

Table 9.15 Routine reporting

Element of the procedure	Comment
The procedure should operate under a defined fraud policy approved by the board of directors	Without specified procedures, the organization passively encourages employees to report their suspicions externally or to condone fraud. An effective reporting procedure is a deterrent to fraud
The procedure should have a designated owner *(internal audit, corporate security or legal department)* who should manage and monitor its effectiveness	The advantage of having legal department the focal point of the procedure is that reports may be protected by Legal Professional Privilege
The legality of (or requirement for) the procedure should be confirmed in writing for all of the jurisdictions in which the organization operates and should be, as far as possible, consistent with the culture of the country concerned	In some countries (and the UK is an example) organizations may be required to comply with 'whistle-blowing' legislation. Critical elements that should be addressed in both policy and procedures include the payment of rewards and protection of informants
Employees and other members of the extended enterprise should be made aware of the types of risks that could affect their areas of work. Training may extend from small booklets through to formal training programmes for internal auditors and others. Internal audit should consider circulating a quarterly bulletin on fraud (or an intranet site) drawing attention to risks and actual cases	Raising the awareness of managers and employees increases the effectiveness of reporting procedures
Contracts with employees (and possibly other members of the extended enterprise) should include a requirement that they comply with the organization's reporting and other procedures and provide assistance to investigators	Cooperation should be a condition of continued employment

continued

Element of the procedure	Comment
One procedure should cover the widest range of potential problems including fraud, suspicious losses, apparent conflicts of interest, health and safety and environmental matters. It is critically important to specify that all anonymous letters *must* be reported	Some organizations also require managers to report changes in their financial circumstances, potentially conflicting interests, appearances in court etc.
The procedure should be widely published in operation and human resources manuals, extracted on appropriate forms (such as purchase orders), on intranet sites, posters, pay slips, wallet cards etc.	Some organizations use display posters in all of their facilities offering rewards for information leading to the apprehension of offenders. They have been very successful
A specified format *(form or electronic mail template)* should be provided for making reports. The form or template must be pre-printed with the words 'Strictly Confidential' or an equivalent classification. It should also explain the 'non-retaliatory' protection for people making reports and the penalties for making reports in bad faith	This makes it more likely that all relevant detail will be provided The 'non-retaliatory' and bad faith provisions are vital (see a sample policy on page 334)
The form or template should give simple instructions, including the requirement to maintain confidentiality and to preserve documents and computer files. It should also specify how feedback will be provided to the person making the report	Feedback is very important and the employee making the report should be advised to take no action until instructed to do so
The point, job function or person to which reports are directed should be specified and must be independent of line management The initial report must be promptly recorded and acknowledged and the reporting employee advised on what further action is to be taken	Some organizations require reports to be submitted in parallel to two separate functions (for example, both internal audit and legal) It is critical that suspicions are reported outside the management line as quickly as possible and that the function of evaluating and processing the report is truly independent
A process for validating reports should be specified	It is essential that unverified information does not harm the reputation of innocent people
Procedures should specify (for each type of reportable incident) to whom further reports must be made (for example, regulatory agencies, insurers, external auditors etc)	Generally incidents should not be reported externally until the organization has established the facts. However, this process should be specified
A central record should be kept showing how reports have been dealt with	This should be analysed to detect trends and omissions
A summary of all reports should be reviewed each year by the audit committee	The lessons learned and corrections made to prevent repetition should be recorded

Organizations with specified routine procedures for reporting fraud and other problems claim very high success rates. Examples include money laundering reporting procedures in financial institutions, Exxon Corporation and IBM.

Hotline

The term 'hotline' applies to a procedure under which employees and others who do not want to be identified may report suspicions of wrongdoing. Their motivation extends from a genuine desire to help the victim, to outrage, vengeance or malice. The experience of most organizations using hotlines is that the overwhelming majority of reports are genuine and well intentioned.

The elements to be considered, *in addition* to those shown in shaded rows in Table 9.15 are shown in Table 9.16.

Table 9.16 Hotlines

Element of the procedure	Comment
The principle of using an anonymous 'hotline' should be agreed by the board of directors in conjunction with the audit committee and external legal advisers. The way it is presented must be consistent with the company's ethos. A critical point is to decide whether or not rewards will be paid for information	Important ethical conflicts should be resolved at a senior level. The fact is that the majority of international corporations do have procedures that encourage the reporting of suspicious incidents. In all cases they have been successful. Some organizations recognize the heightened sensitivity of anonymous reporting in Central and Eastern Europe but plan to introduce processes (based on success in other countries) over the next two to three years. Moreover, organizations that do not provide procedures for anonymous reporting may be exposed under the Federal Sentencing Guidelines and other legislation and permit 'whistle-blowers' to report externally in the first instance. *This is a serious danger*
Some multinational companies maintain separate 'hotlines' in all of the countries in which they operate: others coordinate on a regional basis and others internationally	Many people (especially in developing countries) do not have the authority to call international numbers and thus fail to report. However, experience shows that people are more inclined to make reports to centres outside their country of residence
The centre point or telephone number for receiving calls should provide a human response 24 hours a day 365 days a year. Outside normal hours the line should be diverted to a mobile, so that a human and multi-lingual response can be given at all times	Under no circumstances should the 'hotline' terminate at an answering machine
People manning the 'hotline' should be provided with checklists or report formats so that they collect all of the relevant information and give appropriate advice and warnings to callers. They should also be trained in behavioural interviewing techniques	A well-trained, human response is essential

continued

Element of the procedure	Comment
Where permitted, calls should be covertly recorded	Providing in the jurisdiction concerned it is legal to do so. Where it is not, the company should consider using regional centres where recording is allowed
The telephone 'hotline' should be supported by an email address and PO and suggestion box.	Email is a useful addition to a conventional telephone 'hotline'
The centre may be internal or contracted to a third party	Ideally, call centres should be maintained in-house

The successes and failures of hotlines can be summarized as follows in Table 9.17.

All users believe their hotlines also act as a deterrent, especially to collusive fraud. Such savings are unquantifiable.

Table 9.17   Types of hotlines

TYPE OF HOTLINE *Example*	Successes and failures
GOVERNMENTAL *US Department of Defence* *UK Department of Social Security*	The DOD line has successfully exposed hundreds of major frauds especially in the procurement area. Most reports are believed to have been made by employees working for contractors. Rewards are paid The UK Department of Social Security claims to have over 2000 calls a week. The vast majority lead to apprehension of false benefit claimants. Rewards are not usually paid
LOCAL GOVERNMENT *Tennessee*	'Tennessee Anytime' runs hotlines on a variety of topics from 'most wanted' criminals to school violence. The results have been excellent
TRADE AND ASSOCIATION *Federation Against Software Theft (FAST)* *Insurance industry* *Medicare*	All of these hotlines have uncovered losses running into millions of dollars
COMMUNITY *UK Neighbourhood Watch*	This programme has been an outstanding success and has resulted in the apprehension of thousands of offenders and in deterring robberies and burglaries
CORPORATE *Food Conglomerate* *Transnet (South Africa)*	This company displays posters in all of its facilities offering rewards of up to $100,000 for information leading to the apprehension of offenders. It reports very high success rates Transnet has run a hotline since 1995. 80% of reports are genuine and several cases have involved millions of rands. The head of internal audit has reported that, on average, frauds reported on the hotline have been detected within six months of commencement, against a norm by other detection methods of four years

TYPE OF HOTLINE *Example*	Successes and failures
OUTSOURCED *UK Forensic Accounting Limited*	This commercial hotline reports outstanding results for a wide range of commercial clients. There is a problem of confidentiality with all outsourced services
PUBLIC MEDIA *UK Television 'Watchdog'*	Many television and radio programs run hotlines. Unlike their commercial and governmental counterparts, they report a high level of frivolous and malicious reporting

The chairman's annual email

One leading British organization sponsors an annual email from the chairman to all employees, most customers and suppliers. It is an upbeat summary of his company's results but contains a closing statement to the effect *'if you have any concerns about the ethical conduct of X, or suspicions of any improper behaviour, you may report them directly to my office, in total confidence'*. Last year one fraud of over £4 million was uncovered in this way and many smaller, but still important, problems have been revealed.

Annual declarations

The trend is for directors to be required to certify the accuracy of their company's accounts and compliance with internal control standards (see page 271 ff.). Such declarations raise the stakes and focus people's minds and make malpractice less likely and less defensible when it happens. The principle of annual declarations should extend down the organization, requiring all line managers to sign an annual declaration along the lines of those in Table 9.18.

Such declarations should be discussed during annual performance reviews and filed securely.

Investigatory procedures

APPROVED METHODS AND RESOURCES

Procedures for conducting investigations should be in writing and based on specific legal advice. They are necessary to achieve proper control and to demonstrate, after the event, that proper authorization was obtained and that all processes and techniques were in compliance with the law.

All organizations should also have adequate trained resources to carry out investigations. Ideally, these will be provided internally through fully trained and experienced investigators in corporate security or internal audit. Where internal resources are not available the company should pre-qualify one or two specialist investigation firms.

It is critical that investigations are professionally handled

Table 9.18   Annual declarations

Aspect of the declaration	Consequences
That they understand the *significance of their declaration* and that their continued employment is conditional on their compliance with security and related policies	This is important. Annual declaration forms should spell out the serious personal consequences that can result from inadequate control
That they have *reviewed risks* in the operations for which they are accountable and are satisfied with the controls in place	This statement pins employees to the responsibility for CSA programmes
That they have fully *complied* with their control responsibilities	This enhances the profile of the control programme It makes all employees accountable for their control responsibilities It denies them the opportunity of a plausible excuse if dishonesty is discovered
That they are not aware of any *breaches in control*, compliance breaches, improper practices or weaknesses which have not been reported	This makes it more difficult for an employee, after his services have been terminated, to make wild allegations about improper practices in the company
That they have reported (n) *incidents* in the year	This is a cross-check. If an employee chooses not to report an incident he may always claim that the form has been lost. This annual declaration denies him such an opportunity
That there has been *no change* in their personal or financial circumstances affecting their declarations on conflicts of interest	This updates and reinforces previous declarations
That they have *received no income* other than that from their employer	This should be a specific declaration When there is any doubt, the employee should be asked to produce his tax return
That they have not *received any gifts* or benefits other than those (n) disclosed on gift declaration forms which they have submitted	This is a cross-check. If an employee chooses not to report a benefit he may always claim that the form has been lost. This annual declaration denies him such an opportunity
That they have not *given any benefits* to any third party with whom the company does business, other than those declared on their expense statements	This also is a final cross-check on the accuracy of declarations made throughout the year

POLICY STATEMENT

The policy statement on investigations should be along the following lines:

CONDUCT OF INVESTIGATIONS

All employees are required to cooperate with investigations conducted by the company and to secure and volunteer all records and other information that may be relevant. Any employee who fails to comply with this paragraph will be subject to disciplinary action.

Responsibilities of line management

Under no circumstances will an employee working in, or responsible for, an area in which fraud is suspected have any control over an investigation, unless specifically invited, in writing, by (name and contact details) to provide assistance. Any improper interference in an investigation by any employee will result in disciplinary action.

Similarly, employees are prohibited from retaining the services of external investigators or others providing similar services without the specific approval of the auditor. Any employee who disregards this instruction will be subject to disciplinary action.

Presumption of innocence

The rights of employees and others suspected of fraud, whether against the company or not, will be respected, based on a presumption of innocence. It is important to note that innocent people usually assert the right of explanation while offenders claim the privilege of silence. Thus failure by an employee to assist in an investigation will be considered a breach of contract. The company will terminate the services of any employee who refuses to answer questions on the grounds of self-incrimination.

Rights to representation

At fact-finding or investigative interviews, employees suspected of dishonesty will not normally be entitled to representation by a colleague, legal adviser or union official. (Name and contact details) will normally make exceptions in the case of employees under the age of 17, or for those with mental disabilities.

However, where:

- criminal prosecution is a likely outcome of an interview;
- *and* as soon as the auditor and legal adviser believe that evidence affording 'reasonable grounds' of guilt has emerged;

the employee will be told that he need not say anything further and may seek assistance from a colleague or legal representative.

Access to records of interviews

Interviews with people suspected of dishonesty may, at the auditor's discretion, be tape-recorded, with or (where permitted by law) without their permission, to ensure that an accurate record is obtained.

Providing, in the opinion of the auditor, this does not impede an investigation, the person suspected of dishonesty will be provided with notes or transcripts of his interview and a copy of any tape recording, notes or written statements.

A person suspected of fraud will not be entitled to copies of notes of interviews with other people, statements or investigation reports until such time as they are required to be officially disclosed to legal representatives.

Overall requirement

Procedures along the above lines should be issued to all employees, and part-time and temporary staff.

BENCHMARKING

Table 9.19 enables you to benchmark your company's investigatory processes and resources.

Table 9.19   Clearance of investigatory procedures

The aspect to be covered	Objectives and comments
AUTHORITIES	
Who is responsible for conducting investigations?	The designated person or department should be professionally trained
What are his authorities and his reporting lines?	These must be clearly stated, so that they cannot be effectively challenged during the heat of an investigation. Ideally, authority to conduct investigations should be given at the highest levels on a universal, rather than case-by-case basis
What is his authority to retain external lawyers and investigators?	Selection should be from a pre-qualified list of individuals (rather than firms). Working relationships should be established before the event
What is his authority to control budgets for external support?	The person given authority to conduct investigations should be provided with both annual and special budgets. Line management should not be able to intervene
What is his authority to report matters to regulators, police, external auditors and insurers	Ideally all disclosures to third parties should be through the company's legal advisers
What authority is necessary to commence pre-emptive legal actions?	This should normally be in conjunction with the legal adviser
What authority is needed to suspend and dismiss employees, terminate contracts with third parties and the processes for doing so?	The authority and procedures should be agreed by legal and human relations representatives
LEGALITY: Consider	
Data Protection Act registration of any computer or structured manual systems used in or for managing the investigation, if they have not already been registered	Registration details should be reviewed at least annually and amended if necessary
The computer and structured manual systems records investigators are entitled to rely upon and access	Special notification may be necessary for large cases where separate databases are created

The aspect to be covered	Objectives and comments
The external organizations with which personal data may be shared and the access rights to internal databases and personnel files	These should be fully covered in the basic Data Protection Act registration, so that information can flow freely
PROCESSES: Define	
The way new cases are registered	There must be a formal process for recording new cases. The record must state the purpose of the investigation. If it is other than for the prevention and investigation of crime, many of the techniques described below would be illegal or 'unlawful'. It is also important to record the size of the case as this will act as a measure of 'proportionality'
The procedure for issuing cautions to employees and others against whom there is evidence of crime	Ideally all people charged with the investigation of crime should be trained in the administration of cautions. This only applies when the objective is criminal prosecution
The processes for recording investigative interviews	For example, whether to tape-record interviews overtly, covertly or not at all
The general investigative techniques that are authorized	These should include most of the techniques shown below. It should be accepted that sometimes, robust and controversial methods must be used to expose fraud
The method of authorizing potentially controversial techniques in specific cases: • collection of call logging data • email interception • forensic examination of company computers • forensic examination of privately owned laptop computers • human intelligence sources • interception of post • interviews with suspects and witnesses • mail interception • other forms of eavesdropping • pretext investigations • rights of audit to third party records • searches of work areas • surveillance • telephone interception • trash searches • undercover investigations • use of closed-circuit television • vehicle tracking devices	Public authorities must align their procedures to the Regulation of Investigatory Powers Act (2000) – 'RIPA' – and the codes of practice (see www.homeoffice.gov.uk/ripa/codelett.htm). These should be based on the concept of 'proportionality' The process for authorizing sensitive techniques should be defined When the purpose is the investigation of crime by 'businesses' all of the techniques are legal and the results can be introduced in evidence

continued

The aspect to be covered	Objectives and comments
Records retention procedures for completed investigations	This may be necessary to comply with the records retention aspects of the Data Protection Act
INDEPENDENT REVIEW	
The results of the person or department charged with the responsibility of investigating frauds should be independently reviewed, at least once a year. Special attention should be paid to the control of controversial investigatory techniques	This review can be carried out by independent lawyers or by the audit committee

Failing to plan results in bad decisions being taken in the heat of the moment. These inevitably cause problems.

The investigations of most fraud cases are compromised within 24 hours of discovery

Replacement charts

The defection of key employees (see Chapter 10) is a problem for all organizations. Some defections can be classed as 'bad' because they involve collusion, theft of intellectual capital, poaching of customers and other malpractice. Most managers do not realize that they have a fiduciary obligation to the employer to report cases where they believe an employee is planning to leave.

Thus employees whose services are important or critical to the organization should be identified and replacements developed. This planning will reduce the effect of both 'good' and 'bad' defections.

Disciplinary procedures

Human resources department should specify a list of transgressions that will result in disciplinary action.[6] This should be checked by lawyers specializing in employment law. Details should be incorporated in the appropriate personnel manuals and training programmes.

The procedures should specify that an employee has no right to union or legal representation during an interview to establish the facts of an incident, but does have rights to independent counsel in disciplinary actions.[7] The procedures should also deal with the way appeals will be handled.

Policy and procedures *must* differentiate between investigatory and disciplinary interviews.

---

[6] Specifically, failure to cooperate in an investigation should be a dismissible offence
[7] Note the distinction between investigative and disciplinary interviews. The former is to establish the facts and the second to resolve them

DISCIPLINARY INTERVIEWS

When, in the opinion of the auditor and legal adviser, the facts of a case have been fully established, the employee will be invited to attend a disciplinary interview at which he will be entitled to representation by a colleague, legal adviser or union official. At such interviews, the evidence will be produced and the person invited to provide an explanation. Thereafter, he will be subject to the company's normal disciplinary procedures.

SUSPENSION

Employees suspected of dishonesty or wrongful acts may be suspended – with or without compensation – while investigations are being completed. If, on completion of the investigation, the employee resigns or is dismissed, compensation for any period of suspension will be deducted from his normal entitlement on termination of employment.

All employees and temporary staff should be asked to attend an exit interview and encouraged to comment on the company's control procedures. They should be specifically asked to report problems of a security nature.

Termination of employment procedures

Procedures should be specified for dealing with employees whose services are being terminated and should include the following (Table 9.20).

Table 9.20 Termination procedures

Procedure	Comment
The employee should be interviewed by someone other than his normal line manager as part of a formal *exit interview* process	In addition to other matters, the employee should be asked about controls and areas he would recommend for improvement A note should be prepared, copied to the manager of internal audit and placed in the file of the employee concerned
The employee should sign a *termination agreement* acknowledging that all company property has been returned	Where the employee had access to sensitive information, the name of his future employer should be established. The employee should be reminded (and a note made of this fact) that he is prohibited from disclosing classified information In serious cases a letter setting out details of any restrictive covenants should be sent to the new employer
All keys, identification cards, access codes, passwords etc. allocated to the employee should be *returned or cancelled*	Personnel department should initiate a system for automatically notifying central IT etc.

In most cases, employees whose service is being terminated should not be required to work out their period of notice.

Exit and transfer interviews

Some organizations have specified procedures for interviewing employees, and contract and temporary staff, on termination of their contracts or transfer to another location (see Chapter 10, page 408 for detailed recommendations).

All organizations should consider specifying a procedure for conducting exit interviews

Information classification

Procedures should be specified for protecting all confidential information and trade secrets.

ESPIONAGE AND WORLD TRADE COMPANIES

In April 2002, the *World Trade* journal reported there is nothing new about corporate espionage; stealing trade secrets is as old as the hills. But today the stakes are global and the difference between profits and heavy losses can be as small as the software encrypted on a microchip. In 1996, Congress and the Clinton administration made a gesture toward the situation by enacting the Economic Espionage Act. Now, six years later, there have only been a few dozen indictments and prosecutions and many of the accused have high-tailed it back to their home countries where their governments refused to extradite them.

So risks remain small while potential rewards skyrocket. The most recent survey by the American Society for Industrial

Security estimates *World Trade* 100 companies and other blue chips lose $45 billion a year from pilfered trade secrets. The ASIS survey says the annual loss among all US firms may run as high as $1 trillion.

Economic intelligence, as opposed to spying, concentrates on using legally obtained public information about competitors' activities to analyse their strategies for client companies. Intelligence professionals estimate that at least twelve of our top trading partners conduct systematic spying on major US firms. The top twelve include the seven largest European Community economies, plus Israel, Japan, China, Taiwan and Korea. Most are strictly company-directed attacks, but France and China most notably rely on government aid and direction.

A model information classification policy may be downloaded from www.cobasco.com.

Contracts

BACKGROUND

Contracts with senior managers, suppliers, customers, agents and other members of the extended enterprise are important building blocks in a control programme. First, they define the standards expected and deny people any plausible excuse for dishonesty. When this fact is made obvious, some potential violators will be deterred. Second, they provide a means of corroborating transactions with third parties and a platform on which legal actions can be launched or defended. Third, they help prove, after the worst happens, that the company at least attempted to act prudently.

INTEGRATION

Contracts should be clearly structured and integrated with related documents. For example, job application forms, job descriptions and contracts of employment should, if possible, be integrated into one document. When this is not possible, they should be consistent.

WARRANTIES

Facts or representations on which the company has relied should be included in a warranty section. For example, in contracts of employment, accuracy of the original application form and subsequent annual declarations should be warranted. Thus any false declarations should allow the company to terminate the contract, without penalty.

One international company requires vendors to warrant:

- that no customer benefits from lower prices for the same goods;
- no payments or commissions have been made to anyone to secure business with the company;
- no employee has benefited from entertaining or gifts valued in excess of $100.

The system seems to work well, but that is possibly because most of the company's suppliers are reputable corporations. It may not be so effective with less scrupulous companies.

COMPLIANCE WITH CONTROLS

Companies that are affected by the FCPA, and other potentially catastrophic legislation, should provide a written summary of their ethical code and legal requirements to third parties with whom they contract.

An unqualified requirement to comply with the laws and specified controls should be included in contracts with vendors, customers and other members of the extended family. The terms should bind them to policies on business ethics, compliance, quality, control and other procedures and obtain their undertaking to provide annual declarations or letters of representation.

THE RIGHT TO AUDIT

All significant contracts with:

- vendors, especially those who charge on a cost-plus or time-and-materials basis, including advertising agencies, consultancies, mailing houses, telesales and software developers;
- joint venture partners, especially those in emerging markets;
- customers, distributors and agents;

should provide the right to audit including:

- unrestricted access to all relevant books and records, including those of associated companies, parents and subsidiaries;
- all files relating to competitive bids obtained on the company's behalf and all delegated purchasing;
- invoices from suppliers, accounts and other data on which the above depend;
- correspondence and contracts relating to subcontractors;
- access to any relevant computer system, including permission to download data;
- office space in which to carry out the audit, copying and other facilities;
- technical assistance and all other facilities necessary to carry out the audit;
- an undertaking that managers and employees will attend interviews and answer questions;
- an undertaking that if overpayments are detected, these will be returned with interest; additionally the vendor will reimburse the costs of the audit.

Contracts should also require third parties to obtain similar rights to audit the records[8] of their subcontractors and suppliers and to retain records for a specified period.

The clauses should be carefully drawn up before contracts are finalized and at a time when the third party may be more cooperative, because it wishes to obtain new business. Consideration should also be given to incorporating audit clauses on purchase orders, invitations to tender and on other forms.

If a third party refuses to comply with the request to carry out an audit, it has technically breached the contract, which may then be terminated.

RETENTIONS AND DEPOSITS

Standard terms and conditions, where appropriate, should require a deposit or advance payment from customers or allow for retentions on purchase contracts. Alternatively, vendors should be required to enter into bank guarantees or performance bonds. Holding other people's money is a good control.

INDEMNITIES

Where appropriate, third parties should indemnify the company against losses, the results of its negligence and breaches of regulations.

ALTERNATIVE DISPUTE RESOLUTION

Litigation is easy to start, overly expensive and difficult to stop. Thus, wherever possible, contracts should specify that disputes will be resolved by arbitration or through an alternative dispute resolution (ADR) procedure. This provision is especially important on insurance policies and on contracts with third parties based in countries where the legal system is inefficient or corrupt.

---

[8] Especially time sheets and travel expenses

STANDARD CONTRACTS SUBMITTED BY THIRD PARTIES

In this area, what is good for the goose is not so good for the gander, and companies should take great care before acceding to standard contracts proposed by third parties. Dangerous areas include standard form insurance policies, leasing and consultancy contracts.

Great care should be taken over audit clauses incorporated in standard contracts proffered by third parties, such as advertising agencies, as they give very limited rights. Often advertising agencies will refuse to provide any supporting data on media costs, in-house production, inter-group charges, correspondence or other information on which the reasonableness of their final charges can be assessed. The usual argument is that such data is confidential since it identifies or relates to other clients. In such cases, the clauses should be amended to permit a full audit by independent specialists.

Hardware standards

The security adviser or another qualified person should specify standards to be maintained by owners of every building and other physical assets used by the organization (Table 9.21).

These standards should be issued to line managers responsible for the facilities of the type concerned. They can usually be introduced without delay and at minimal cost.

Table 9.21   Hardware standards

Hardware elements *All company facilities should be protected to a baseline standard*	Examples of specified standards *How implemented*
Buildings: exterior	Perimeter protection and access control External lighting and signage Burglar and other alarms Fire protection Emergency evacuation points and routes Car parks Assignment instructions for security guards *Procedures and recommended products* *Surveys by security*
Buildings: interior	Access control Reception areas Additional protection of high-risk internal areas Computer and telephone frame rooms Goods inwards and outwards bays Mail rooms Conference rooms *Procedures and recommended products* *Surveys by security*
Delivery vehicles	Locking devices Alarms GPS trackers and tachographs *Procedures and recommended products* *Surveys by security*

Equipment and processes standards

Similarly, standards should be specified for all commonly used equipment and processes (Table 9.22).

Table 9.22   Standards for commonly used equipment and processes

Examples of hardware elements *All company facilities should be protected to a baseline standard*	Examples of specified standards *How implemented*
Hardware examples	
Personal computers	Keyboard locks Passwords Encryption Back-up Chip security and secret marking Diskettes *Procedures and recommended products* *Spot checks by supervisors*
Laptops	Passwords Encryption Diskettes *Procedures and recommended products* *Spot checks by supervisors*
Modems	Unauthorized use prohibited Asset listing and controlled purchase Procedures for registration and use *Procedures and recommended products* *Spot checks by supervisors*
Telex machines	Physical security of communications lines Physical security of answer-back devices Continuous copy logs *Procedures and recommended products* *Spot checks by supervisors*
Cheque-signing machines	Asset listing Located in a secure area Dual custody of signature plates Continuous record of use *Procedures and recommended products* *Spot checks by supervisors*
Mobile telephones	Asset listing Bar on international calls Monthly bills provided on diskette and analysed *Procedures and recommended products* *Spot checks by supervisors*

Examples of hardware elements *All company facilities should be protected to a baseline standard*	Examples of specified standards *How implemented*
Photocopiers	Automatic power disconnection outside working hours Metered consumption Adjacent shredding facilities *Procedures and recommended products* *Spot checks by supervisors*
Filing cabinets Provided for every employee	Minimum fire and attack resistant Combination lock and locking bar *Procedures and recommended products* *Spot checks by supervisors*
Blank documents with intrinsic financial value	Controlled inventory and log of use In-built security features Secure storage under dual control *Procedures and recommended products* *Spot checks by supervisors*
Processes examples	
Goods inwards	*Secure areas* *Closed circuit television surveillance* *Warning notices* *Procedures for receipt*
Computer maintenance	*List of approved contractors* *Access control* *Supervision* *Procedures*
Cleaners	*Selection and approval of companies* *Pre-employment screening* *Undertakings on confidentiality* *Right of search and to cooperate in investigations* *Procedures*
Confidential waste	*Secure disposal* *Local shredders* *Spot checking by supervisors*

Again the standards should be issued to appropriate owners, possibly through an intranet. These standards ensure that hardware and processes are consistently controlled throughout the organization. They also result in the company being able to buy security hardware and services at discounted rates and to negotiate cheaper, company-wide maintenance agreements.

Fidelity insurance

The company's fidelity insurance policies should be reviewed generally and the subrogation clauses amended so that the carrier's rights to sue the company's directors and officers are removed. Also the clauses on 'prior dishonesty' should be limited to commercial dishonesty of the nature insured. Special care should be taken over the definition of 'employee' and 'director' and to ensure that all part-time and temporary staff are insured.

Conclusions

The processes explained in this chapter set the foundation for effective control. They invariably require supplementing by effective interviews: these are described in Chapters 10 and 11.

'BLOODY LIAR! I KNOW HE'S GOT WHISKY!'

10 *Other Applications*

If two wrongs don't make a right, try three

Background

The cunning plan can be used anytime you believe you might be told lies and it should become as much a part of your life as your mobile telephone, Filofax, PDA or even your Scotty Cameron putter. This chapter gives examples of how the plan can be applied in the business situations shown in Table 10.1.

Table 10.1   Coverage of this chapter

Types of situations and lies	Examples and *comments*
Achievement lies (see page 356)	Dealing with confidence tricksters or 'conmen', including job candidates
Anonymous letters (see page 371)	Resolving allegations made against employees etc.
Annual appraisals (see page 375)	Bringing risk, compliance and control issues to the fore
Debtors (see page 377)	Recovering bad and doubtful debts when the 'cheque is in the post'
Defections (see page 383)	Dealing with 'bad' defections and the theft of intellectual capital
Drugs abuse (see page 395)	Dealing with employees and others suspected of abusing narcotic drugs. Drugs abuse is corrosive and may lead to the infiltration of organized crime. It is a very serious problem
Elimination interviews (see page 400)	Eliminating innocent people from suspicion
Exit interviews (see page 408)	Developing intelligence on risk, compliance and control issues
Meetings and negotiations (see page 410)	Minimizing the risks of deception in meetings
Pre-employment screening (see page 419)	Identifying lies in CVs and job application forms
Witnesses (see page 414)	Obtaining intelligence and evidence from potential witnesses using cognitive techniques

Principles

The natural instinct of most people when confronted with a problem is to ignore it (known in the trade as the 'Chamberlain syndrome'[1]) or to address it in what they regard as a polite, low-key way. For example, the first step in dealing with someone suspected of sexual harassment or malingering may be to ask for his explanation. This is a dreadful mistake and is normally doomed to failure. It results in the guilty party walking away unpunished (with a negative effect on other employees who know the truth, and conclude that the organization has acted incompetently) or, probably worse, with a cloud of suspicion continuing to hang over the head of an honest person.

The object of any investigation is to find the truth

When a problem arises, you should consider your action as a two-stage process:

- finding the truth, to clear the innocent and expose the guilty;
- then, based on the truth, to take appropriate action.

You should never confuse or mingle these two stages. The fact-finding must be clinical, within the law and the techniques used proportionate to the seriousness of the suspected problem.

The steps we would always recommend are detailed in Table 10.2.

The idea of ambushing someone suspected of wrongdoing may seem unfair, but it is by far the best way of finding the truth. Based on this initial work you are much more likely to make subsequent interviews effective.

Interviews are 95% preparation and 5% execution.
Never go into an important interview without careful preparation

Achievement lies and dealing with conmen

BACKGROUND

Types of conmen and modus operandi[2]

The main focus of this section is on achievement lies, involving determined opponents often with large amounts at stake. The subjects, suspects and liars are referred to as 'suspected conmen' or 'conmen' and they come in all shapes, sizes and colours.

The difficulty arises in distinguishing conmen from people who may, or may not, fall into that category. Obviously, once you have determined that a person is a conman, as opposed to merely a suspect, you should have no dealings with him as you will always come out badly.

Never deal with proven conmen.
Don't play with fire

---

[1]   After the Prime Minister badly misled by Adolf Hitler in 1938
[2]   Just to remind you of the dangers of Latin

Table 10.2 Stages to getting to the truth

Stage	Action	Comment
1	Maintain absolute secrecy Determine your objectives	What are the policy issues? If there are none ask yourself if you had a magic wand how would you like to see the problem resolved? Bear in mind the effect your action, or inaction, will have on honest employees
2	Get the full background on the subject	Know everything about the person suspected
3	Consider the facts and formulate a problem theory and deception theory	Write down exactly what you think has happened on the assumption that the suspicions are true. If you were the subject, what explanation would you give? Consider how you can overcome false excuses
4	Formulate a resolutions plan	Identify the 'key points' that support your theory. Assemble them in a way that they can be presented to the subject at the appropriate time Think about the enquiries you can carry out (see Appendix 1) before the interview and especially how you can confirm the accuracy of the suspicions Is your approach proportionate to the seriousness of the matter suspected?
5	Plan the interview	Plan the interview carefully in the seven phases described in Chapter 7, page 167 ff.
6	Rehearse the interview	Carry out at least one practice run of the interview with a colleague
7	*The first step*: carry out the interview	Carry out the interview, giving the subject minimal advance notice
8	Review and follow-up actions	Complete any follow-up enquiries quickly. Check out all excuses carefully. If there are unresolved issues, ask the subject for his assistance in resolving them

Some people who fall into our category of conmen are, in day-to-day life, reputable businessmen, politicians, professional advisers and civil servants. They become tricksters only for a short time, possibly in relation to a specific transaction. The conman may operate alone, in a group or through a company, charity, or some other existing or totally false organization or 'front'. There are a number of conmen who are on the run and operate internationally, away from the scenes of their previous crimes and country of origin. A number use totally false identities (see the Paper Trip www edenpress.com).

In all cases, the conman's objective is to obtain an improper advantage by exploiting achievement lies. He succeeds because he knows you, as a potential victim, are facing a dilemma: in fact it is almost a pivotal point, in reverse. On the one hand you want the transaction to succeed and don't want to upset anyone in case you miss the opportunity. On the other, you have nagging suspicions that you are just about to sacrifice your house, dog and Scotty Cameron putter. A good conman will ruthlessly exploit this dilemma, knowing that most victims are unprepared to commit themselves sufficiently to walk away.

Types of achievement lies

There are thousands of ways in which you may be victimized by conmen in both your business and private life including:

- acquisitions;
- applications for loans or credit;
- discussions, meetings and negotiations;
- investments, *ranging from simple Nigerian 419 scams to complex financial deals with derivatives, prime bank guarantees, investments, venture capital etc.;*
- *job candidates, employment agencies, consultants and advisers;*
- procurement and purchasing involving salesmen from both good and dishonest companies.

The essential feature is that achievement lies are told before you make a decision or part with any money and with the intention that the liar will gain an unfair advantage. They usually have the following characteristics:

- an apparent opportunity for you to make *exceptional profits* or avoid exceptional losses;
- *artificially imposed deadlines* panicking you into making a quick decision before being able to check the facts;
- *alleged secrecy or confidentiality* of the transaction: to the extent that the conman may insist that you don't discuss anything with your family and colleagues;
- *vague promises of future benefits;*
- *penalties or adverse consequences* if you do not meet the deadline;
- *competitors* who are ready to seize upon the opportunity, should you fail to do so.

Once you have committed yourself and have parted with your money or acted in other ways which will turn out not to be in your best interests, achievement lies are characterized by:

- *failure to deliver the benefits promised*, usually for reasons supposedly beyond the liar's control;
- *failure to respond* to your complaints, to return telephone calls or requests for meetings – the liar deliberately remains inaccessible;[3]
- almost limitless *exculpatory lies*, including blaming you for any failure;
- changing the ground rules, *denying earlier promises* by suggesting loss of memory on your part;
- *feigned anger* if you question him, perhaps stating that he is 'sick of your insults'[4] and *claiming the moral high ground* to the extent that he is the injured party.

Finally, the victim usually loses and the liar escapes to fight another day. Often his goals are short term to the extent that he only intends to get your money and run.

> *If the deal looks too good to be true, it is too good to be true*

---

[3]   This is often for two reasons: the first is to avoid you and the second because he is busy ripping off new victims
[4]   Conmen seem to use this word rather a lot

PRIME BANK GUARANTEES

Over 20 years ago, shady American loan brokers and advance fee scamsters hit upon the idea of Prime Bank Guarantees (PBGs). These fictional 'bank instruments' are supposedly issued by 'prime banks' as a method of raising off balance sheet funds. The scamsters claim to have an inside route for obtaining these for 'self-liquidating loans'. Essentially the scheme is that a person or company that wishes to raise finance (usually in 'tranches' of $100 million) can buy for $85 million a PBG from a leading bank which has a face value of say $100 million, bearing interest at 4% per annum and being repayable in ten years' time. This instrument can then be used as collateral for a loan of $100 million from another bank. This money is then used to immediately liquidate the loan, leaving the borrower with an immediate 'fall out' of say $10 million after all fees have been paid. It all sounds a great idea and many victims have fallen for it, but the logic is fatally flawed[5] and PBGs, in the form suggested, don't exist.

Tricks of the trade

The most important attributes of a conman are that he is plausible and determined, with an extremely thick skin, ruthlessly exploiting the greed and gullibility of his intended victims. The conman may use fine words and appear to be your dearest friend, but his intention is simply to do or say anything necessary to gain an advantage.

Sometimes the conman will inveigle his victims into illegal acts, in the process knowingly depriving them of any form of redress.

OFFSHORE TRANSFER

In a recent merger, one of the negotiators suggested that he could pay the seller for his shares through an offshore tax haven. 'We do not even have to describe the transaction as a share sale. If you set up an offshore vehicle, you can transfer the voting and dividend rights in the shares to us and then invoice my offshore vehicle for goods or services. We can pay it and you will save the tax. We can think about formally transferring the shares later.' What he really meant was if the victim transferred his voting rights through an illegal deal he would never be able to enforce the debt and thus would lose everything.

Agree to anything illegal and your rights of recovery go out of the window.
There is no such thing as a free lunch

The victim may be sexually compromised or led astray in other ways: again the conman's objective is to deprive the victim of his rights of redress. This is sad, but true, of many achievement lies.

Never compromise your own position

---

[5]   When you look at the instrument in terms of net present value, why should one bank give a value of $85 million and another $100 million?

The higher-level conmen often retain superb legal advisers who will go on the attack immediately a victim starts to complain. In a process known as 'papering' they flood everyone with threats, letters before action, injunctions, writs, complaints, summonses and subpoenas as diversionary tactics. Conmen know they can outrun their victims in terms of legal costs, especially when they don't intend to pay them.

Conmen often sting reputable lawyers for their fees: this is the ultimate irony

Conmen seem to have no difficulty convincing very reputable people and pillars of society to join the boards of their companies or back their schemes. The names of worthy citizens are used to add credibility – and to provide a 'front' – for very shaky deals. Thus the fact that the conman has retained the best lawyers, accountants and advisers and is surrounded by dignitaries means nothing, since it is likely that they have all been deceived. Once one victim or sycophant has been conned, he will be used as a reference or 'bait' for others.

THE NATO FRAUD

In 2001 a group of con men set up a dummy North Atlantic Treaty Organization and fooled a number of suppliers into bidding for a multi-billion dollar contract. They were required to send vast amounts of equipment (estimated to be in excess of $100 million) for testing to destruction to Military Testing Laboratories in Belgium and Italy. Unsurprisingly, the equipment was sold off for cash. one leading American defence contractor who was misled put details of the contract on its web site asking for bids from subcontractors. As a result, many were drawn into the scam.

In some instances, conmen are supported by violent criminals who will not hesitate to maim or murder anyone who stands in their way. Sounds dramatic, but it happens.

SERIOUS AND ORGANIZED

A British company was approached by a group of organized and violent criminals to buy its scrap products, which were virtually worthless. The gang negotiated with Freddy who was a junior manager in one of the victim's factories, and paid him personally £3000 in cash to ease the deal through. Without consulting his managers, he signed the contract. However, he did not know that other members of the gang who were posing as a competitive bidder had signed a national contract to buy the scrap with another manager. The gang then sued the victim company for breach of contract and produced false affidavits to show losses of £5 million. They put pressure on Freddy to support their claim and he initially became a witness on their behalf. Coincidentally, when he lost his enthusiasm, Freddy was involved in a serious car crash. Although this had been a pure accident, the gang convinced him that he should take the crash as a warning and his resolve in the gang's favour was quickly reinstated.

The hard facts
The fundamentals
There are some hard facts to remember about achievement lies and conmen. The first is that you will be chosen as a victim not because they like your Hush Puppies and purple flared trou-

sers but because they believe you are a 'soft touch'. You also have to accept that conmen live by different rules from honest people. They are quite prepared to lie and cheat and then to move on to new victims. Very seldom do they have long-term friends or business associates.

> *Conmen pick soft, gullible and vulnerable victims.*
> *They live for the short term*

Awareness and counter-surveillance

The second hard fact is that you should never underestimate the skill and determination of conmen. The good ones seem to be able to react instinctively to any situation: or maybe it is just practice. They use counter-surveillance techniques, including bugging the victim's telephone, accessing his computer and picking up trash thrown outside his office or house. They are on the lookout for that tiny bit of information that adds to their advantage or warns them that you are suspicious.

> *Good conmen always seem to have their senses finely tuned,*
> *whereas the victims are blissfully unaware*

A numbers game

The third hard fact is that you are likely to be one of many, possibly hundreds, of victims all simultaneously suffering the same fate. The conman may not have a defined endgame but he will know, from experience, that most victims fail to pursue their rights quickly enough or with sufficient determination.

THE DEAD DONKEY

A truck driver moved to Texas and bought an old donkey from a farmer for $100. The farmer agreed to deliver the animal the next day but he telephoned to say it had died in the night. 'Don't worry,' said the truck driver, 'just deliver the dead body'. The puzzled farmer asked what he intended to do and the truck driver said he planned to 'Raffle him off'. 'You can't raffle a dead donkey', said the farmer. 'I sure can', said the truck driver, 'just watch me. Of course, I won't say it is dead.'

A month went by before the two men met again. 'What happened to the dead donkey?' asked the farmer. 'I raffled him off and sold 500 tickets at $2 a throw and made a profit of $996.' 'Didn't anyone complain?' the farmer asked. 'Sure,' replied the truck driver, 'the winner was really pissed off, so I gave him back double his money and kept the rest.'

Although the conman may have to repay some victims, or deliver some of what he has promised, the majority of losers will fund the few winners, leaving him with a substantial profit.

Safe money

The fourth hard fact is that conmen usually put their money in safe havens where the victims have little chance of recovering it. The current classic is to have the proceeds of crime laundered through false identities, nominee companies, international business corporations or asset protection trusts, so that while the villains retain control, their ownership is obscured. Thus the chances of most victims getting their money back without positive assistance from the conman are remote. Even then, one of the characteristics of a good conman is that once his scam has been exposed, he feigns bankruptcy.[6]

The bottom line

There are classic situations in which conmen operate, and standard profiles. But the bottom line is that – before entering into any significant personal or business transaction – you must consciously examine the fundamentals: take a step back and ask yourself: 'Am I being had over?' This, in more polite terms, is known as remaining alert and it is the first step in the cunning plan.

For every credibility gap, there is a gullibility fill.
If they accept your first offer, you gave away too much

OBJECTIVES

Your objectives in the area of achievement lies, and suspected and actual conmen, are three-fold. The first is to establish the truth so that you can make a balanced decision based on fact rather than on fiction. This means that you want to avoid bad deals and close those that could be good. The second objective is to decide whether the potential reward from the proposed deal is worth the risk. The third objective is to determine whether or not, by catching the con-man with his pants down, you can turn the tables and obtain a far better deal than he ever intended. This is a potentially dangerous and unusual objective, but remember that a person is at his most vulnerable when he has been caught out in a lie.

ANOTHER 419 SCAM

A great example of the Nigerian 419 scam is given (www.scamorama.com) where x convinced the fraudsters that he had murdered his wife (attaching a photograph of her 'dead' in the bath) and needed money from them to escape. He also got another fraudster who wanted to meet him in Amsterdam to dress in an all-yellow outfit and hop on one leg down the main thoroughfare so that he would be able to recognize him. X did not get the money, but he had great fun.

Remember, everything is easier to get into than out of, and attaining your objectives in the face of achievement lies is all about timing.

In most cases, your fervour, gullibility and the fervour of the conman are related.

In the early stages of the scam, he is the most eager; then you get bitten and become more committed than him. If you are not careful, your eyes are closed to reality and all you can see are the benefits. Then, when reality strikes, your enthusiasm hits rock bottom. There are two rules you most follow. The first is to make sure that on the upward curve, you ask detailed questions about everything, keep an open mind and control your enthusiasm.

If something does not look right, politely question it

---

6   Although very few are and feigning financial distress is part of the scam

The second rule is that once you have made your decision or parted with your money, you are vulnerable and it is imperative that you take your time and plan an ambush. If, at that point, you act in haste, or let the conman know you have suspicions, he will just walk away and you will lose everything.

Timing is critical

METHOD BEFORE THE EVENT

Principles
The majority of conmen can be detected or deterred before the event, providing you take a few elementary steps.

Remain alert
You must remain alert to the circumstances in which you might be deceived and, as usual, elevate your suspicions to a conscious level. Once you have done this, and suspect the conman without his knowing that you have questions about his integrity, you have the advantage and can ambush him in the ways discussed later. However, if you are careless and let the conman know you suspect him, he is likely to fight or flee before you are ready to act. If you are not sure whether you are being told lies or not, get some of your female colleagues, or your wife or mother-in-law, involved. 'Women's intuition' is a fantastic tool (see page 37).

Get females involved and follow their advice

Assessment of risk and reward
Remember, risks and rewards are symbiotic and if you cannot afford the pain of the potential loss, don't chase after the gain. Further, if the suspected conman lies to you at any point about any important aspect, you know his motives are bad and you must plan to take action at the appropriate time.

Develop a fraud theory and minimize the downside
Develop a fraud theory and think carefully about the liar's endgame; in most cases it will be to take your money and run or to hide behind a thick legal shield. Pay particular attention to pieces of the jigsaw that don't appear to fit and try to find an explanation for them. Assume everything that happens, and does not happen, is part of the conman's scheme and remember that in deception, there is no such thing as a coincidence.

Assume everything happens for a reason and is part of the conman's plan.
Stand back and ask, 'Is it viable?'

Always try to make sure you owe the conman more than he owes you. You may do this by or through:

- retentions or payments into an escrow account;
- performance bonds;

- personal guarantees;
- agreed performance timetable and penalties.

If he is really a conman (rather than just a suspect) he is likely to protest that you don't trust him and make some sort of emotional attack. Don't panic and, if your requirements are reasonable under the circumstances, don't weaken. Make sure he delivers what he has promised before you part with your money.

Appoint an ogre

It does not matter whether the deal is being handled with the assistance of a professional team of advisers or not, or if it is in your business or private life. If you believe you may be seriously deceived, you should consider appointing an ogre[7] to your side who will stand slightly off line, be a pain in the neck for the suspected conman and question everything. You can then maintain a friendly relationship with the suspected conman, while blaming the ogre for any difficulties. In extreme cases you can pretend to side with the conman against the ogre, requiring him to convince you of his bona fides.[8] This is a variation of the 'good guy/bad guy' approach suggested in some poor books on interviewing as a method of dealing with fraud suspects.[9]

An ogre enables you to take a neutral position

Get the background

Obtain as much background as possible on the suspected conman and the proposed transaction. Carry out a full due diligence audit: get bankers' references and speak to his other clients, but remain alert to the possibility that they are part of the scam or have themselves been misled.

Check everything

Make sure you positively identify the conman, for example, by covertly collecting his fingerprints and handwriting and craftily let him realize you have done this.

THE WINE GLASS

The victim admired the glass that contained the conman's vermouth and asked the waiter in the bar of a posh London hotel if he could buy it to take home for his wife. The conman, realizing his fingerprints would be all over the glass, deliberately knocked it off the table. This raised the victim's suspicions and he pulled out of the deal before he lost his shirt.

Get a detailed written biography of the principal conman and all supporting players[10] and check them line for line, getting as much detail and personal information as you can. Most

---

[7] Possibly a female
[8] Comer was right: Latin is just everywhere
[9] And which we do not recommend except in dealing with suspected and actual conmen
[10] Especially people in the shadows who may be the real principals

conmen are garrulous, so whenever you have a spare moment together, find out everything about him, where he has assets invested, his favourite haunts, the countries in which he has lived for extended periods,[11] details of his mother, father, brothers, sisters, children, spouse, ex-spouses, lovers and ex-lovers: his hobbies, interests etc. Write all of this down and note any changes to his story and remember if he gives you any false background, he cannot be trusted.

One serious lie should be enough to tell you his intentions are not honest

Also try to identify other people with whom he is working and other potential victims. Note all of this information down. If it all goes wrong, it will be invaluable in both tracing him and his assets.

Get details of the competitor allegedly waiting in the background if you do not seize the opportunity the conman is kindly offering you. Speak to the managing director of the competitor or its bankers or accountants and, if you cannot do this, consider retaining investigators to get the full story. Pin everyone down to detail, preferably in writing. Let the conman know you are taking up these references and ask him to explain any discrepancies but do not burst the bubble until you are ready.

Get the answers and retain the evidence

Ask the conman detailed questions at every opportunity. You must also carefully document every 'fact' on which you are relying and get the conman's written acknowledgement of it. If he does not put things in writing, you must write to him and retain proof that he has received it. Also consider covertly recording meetings, retaining the tapes and transcripts securely. If things go wrong you must have an overwhelming, watertight case. Make sure your correspondence and computer files are complete and accurate and are kept securely. Keep back-up copies of important documents in a secure location unknown to the conman.

In complex cases, keep a detailed chronology recording meetings, correspondence and promises made but not kept (Table 10.3).

Table 10.3 Tracking evolving stories

What I have been told	When and how I was told it			
RATE OF RETURN	Date	How		
The rate of return would be 80% pa	1.1.2003	Prospectus		Meeting
The rate would be 40%	1.2.2003		Contract	
The rate would be 8%	1.3.2003			
HIS BACKGROUND				
PhD from Cambridge	1.1.2003	Prospectus		
O level in woodwork	2.4.2003		Bill Smith	

---

[11] If the going gets tough, they will flee to a country where they have connections

Try to make sure he answers every question and every point in every letter. Don't let him escape with concealment lies.

Not answering difficult questions is a characteristic of a conman

MISSING CORRESPONDENCE

A typical trick of conmen is to say that they never received a particular letter or email and thus their failure to respond did not imply that they agreed. Obviously, you can avoid this problem by sending important communications by registered letter or through a secure courier but this may alert the conman that you have suspicions and cause him to flee before you are ready to pounce.

A less obtrusive way of achieving proof of delivery is to ensure that every important communication also contains something the conman would like to know or have, such as an invitation to the theatre or a golf match. If he reacts to the bit that pleases him, he cannot later deny receipt of the part he would prefer not to acknowledge.

In some cases you may let the conman discover that you are building up a dossier that could 'paper' him if he does not deliver what he has promised. This is akin to 'raising the pavement'. If you are right and he really is a crook, he may divert his attention to another victim and this is to your advantage providing you have not already parted with your money. If he is genuinely honest, he will understand the reasons for your caution. Always try to have the detail at your fingertips.

Analyse the paperwork

Pay special attention to accounts, proposals, projections, spreadsheets, surveys, brochures, contracts, letters and other documents provided by the conman and on which you are expected to rely. Stand back, and again ask yourself: 'Is the basis of this transaction sound? Is the story believable and consistent?'

ENRONESQUE DEFINITIONS

Feudalism. You have two cows. Your Lord takes some of the milk.
Fascism. You have two cows. The government takes both, hires you to take care of them and sells you the milk.
Communism. You have two cows. You must take care of them, but the government takes all the milk.
Capitalism. You have two cows. You sell one and buy a bull. Your herd multiplies, and the economy grows. You sell them and retire to play golf.
Enronism. You have two cows. You sell three of them to your publicly listed company,

using letters of credit opened by your brother-in-law at a Luxembourg bank, then execute a debt-equity swap with an associated general offer so that you get all four cows back, with a tax exemption for five cows. The milk rights of the six cows are transferred through an intermediary to a Cayman Island company secretly owned by the majority shareholder who sells the rights to all seven cows back to your listed company. The Enron annual report says the company owns eight cows, with an option on one more and has securitized the income on all twelve cows.

Pay the closest attention to detail

If there are important documents of title which are central to the deal, such as share certificates, deeds to gold mines in Clapham, debentures, proof of asset ownership or custodial receipts, inspect the originals and have their authenticity confirmed, possibly through your bankers or professional advisers. Make sure you keep copies securely.

Remember that vital documents may be forgeries. So check them out

Don't be tempted

Do not be tempted into doing anything that is illegal and do not compromise yourself in any way. In fact, if you are dealing with a suspected conman, don't let your guard drop for a single moment.

You can never cheat an honest man, but it is always worth a try

Raise your concerns in a low-key way

As soon as you have specific concerns you must raise them in a low-key way, and commit the conman to more and more detail, which you must document and preserve. However, it is critical, unless this is part of a planned ambush, that you don't frighten him off. You can take an approach much like the fictional detective, Colombo, by saying something along the lines:

BLAME THE OGRE	
'Bill (the ogre) is very concerned that the custodial receipt from the Bank of Credit and Commerce may not be genuine and he	is advising me to pull out. I have told him I have total confidence in you. How can we reassure him?'

The chances are the conman will comply with your request (because he still believes you are gullible and on the hook) and this is precisely what you want and will add to your case if the worst happens. He may also approach the ogre to strike a side deal and, again, this will tell you all you need to know.[12]

The more evidence of gross deception you have, the more likely you are to get your money back

If you have reached the point where you have serious concerns, don't make the matter worse by parting with more money. As Edward de Bono, the originator of lateral thinking, said: 'You don't dig a better hole by digging the same hole deeper'. This may mean you have to tell a few white lies to keep the conman in play while you plan your ambush.

Contracts

Good conmen are great at contracts and usually have had years of practice developing subtle phrases that appear to say one thing but mean another. Thus, in important deals, you must get a good lawyer to review every document and assess the significance of every word and

---

[12] Unless he succeeds

phrase. He should also pay very close attention to standard clauses that don't appear. In short, he should continually ask himself the question: *'If I were a crook, how could I weasel my way out of this clause, statement or contract?'* Then he should make sure you are fully protected, either in the contract itself or in some other document signed by the suspected conman.

Preparing for the ambush

If the time comes when you are sure the liar is a conman, rather than just a suspect, you must plan your action carefully. Ideally you want him on tape and in writing, telling outright, indefensible lies for which he can have no plausible excuse. This will probably result in the conman being exposed to criminal prosecution under the Theft Act and will give you significant leverage if you decide to negotiate with him or litigate.

Don't give references

A common conman's tactic is to get one victim to give references that can be used to mislead others. If you are less than 100 per cent certain about anyone, do not give references. If you are asked to do so by a suspected conman, you can quite reasonably say:

> *'When our deal has been completed to everyone's satisfaction, we will be more than happy to consider giving a reference. As you know we have not yet reached that stage. Now tell me again, when can we expect completion?'*

Do not waver from this course, under any circumstances, because if you do you may be liable for your own losses, plus those of other victims. This is a bad scene and also, whatever you do, don't join the board of his companies, however flattering that might be, until you are absolutely sure of his honesty.

METHOD WHEN IT GOES BELLY UP

The dreadful realization

Let's hope your fears were misplaced and the breathtaking deal comes to fruition, proving that the person you thought was a liar is a pillar of virtue. However, the chances are that sooner or later you are going to take the hit and this is where you must react quickly. There are two things you must remember. The first is that the conman is likely to have scores, if not hundreds, of victims in just the same position as you. If you sit back and wait you will fall to the end of queue and will never succeed: the victim that causes the biggest fuss is most likely to prevail.

> *You must become the conman's biggest problem*

The second point is that the conman is likely to have pending deals in progress with other victims and he will not want these upset. This is his Achilles heel. However, as in all cases of deception, you must plan to ambush him with a knockout blow from which he never recovers. This is akin to the *first step* in fraud investigations.

Objectives and action plans

A victim's initial reaction when the bubble bursts is to panic and rush around like a headless chicken, blaming everyone in sight, especially the innocent. This is a natural reaction, but you must get over it quickly and plan an effective and unemotional reaction.

Nothing useful is achieved by self-flagellation

You must also set realistic expectation levels and if you have been stung, the chances of getting all of your money back are remote. Ideally, put someone in charge of the recovery plan who was not party to the transaction concerned and who has no vested interest in covering his ass. He is in a good position to assess the position and whether it is worthwhile devoting time and effort to chasing a lost cause.

Depending on the facts of the case, your priorities might be:

- To prevent further losses and cancel transactions that are still in progress.
- Minimizing your liabilities to others. For example, in some recent banking cases, victims had to pay other victim banks for fraudulent letters of credit that fell due for payment long after the dishonesty was exposed.
- Minimizing your liabilities for legal and regulatory breaches.
- Recovering the amounts that have already been lost.
- Exposing and prosecuting the conman.
- Minimizing adverse publicity.

The first three points are really important, because it is extremely exasperating for any victim to have to continually pay out after the conman has been exposed.

Possible approaches

You have a number of possible approaches, which are not mutually exclusive, and all are based on the principle that you must ambush the conman with overwhelming force and become the biggest problem in his life. You must convince him it is not in his interest to engage you in a battle.

The options are given in Table 10.4.

In most cases, you must retain the very best, blood curdling litigation lawyers and set them loose as part of an integrated action plan. All actions are obviously dependent on whether you believe the conman has assets and part of his plan may have been to falsely convince potential litigants that he is penniless. Thus it may be worthwhile for you to retain investigators to see if they can trace his assets.

Budgets for recovery

Bear in mind that investigation and litigation costs can be crippling and there is no point in throwing good money after bad. A worksheet that may help you decide whether a potential loss is worth pursuing or not can be downloaded from www.cobasco.com.

Don't throw good money after bad

Table 10.4   Options for dealing with conmen

Method of approach	Success rate	Examples
Negotiation	20%	Using your overwhelming case, you can take the conman by surprise and let him know that unless he makes good your losses he is in serious trouble
Legal	20%	You may mount an ambush through the civil courts by obtaining search, seizure and freezing orders that enable you to enter his premises, car, bank, golf bag etc. and remove evidence that assists your case. The freezing order will also compel the conman to disclose his assets and if he fails to do so, he can be imprisoned for contempt of court
Police and regulators	2%	You may make a report to the police or regulatory agencies concerned. However, even if they are interested action is likely to be slow, allowing the conman to escape
Media	2%	You can report the facts to a friendly journalist and expose the conman, thus frustrating any deals he has in progress
Disruption	20%	You can harass the conman, by having him followed, making it clear to him that any deals he has in progress will be disrupted

If you decide to press for recovery, it is essential that you set a realistic legal and investigative budget. This should be under the control of the person put in charge of the recovery action plan and not line managers who were deceived; this may be you!

ESCORTS GALORE

An investigation was moving along just fine, driven by a team of external lawyers and consultants under the control of a director of the bank. He had been very positive throughout and the team was confident it would recover many millions of dollars under fidelity insurance. Then, all of a sudden, client support disappeared. Invoices from the lawyers and consultants were not paid and the credit head's deputy nit-picked every line of enquiry and its cost.

Before long the case ran out of steam and then collapsed. The director blamed the consultants for the failure, saying that they were 'too greedy, had lost focus and were going nowhere'. His managers accepted this excuse, since they didn't like paying consultants, either.

A few months later the real reason for upsetting the lawyers and consultants emerged. It appears that one evening the main suspect working for the bank called on the director and warned him that if the investigation continued, some very fruity photographs and tape recordings of his sexual misbehaviour with escorts while he had been travelling overseas on the bank's business might surface. The director was terrified and wanted to comply but did not wish to put his neck on the line by terminating the investigation. However, he achieved the same result by not paying the advisers' bills and by nit-picking, causing them to withdraw.

The bottom line was that preservation of the director's career cost the bank $20 million. But the problem has not really gone away and if the shareholders were ever to discover the truth, all hell would be let loose.

Another normal reaction of victims to gross deception is to join together and pool their resources to share legal costs. Banks do this all of the time and it never produces results. This is because multiple victims are all chasing after the same assets and in the end, fight over them. If you are one of a number of victims of the same scam, you must act alone and stay ahead of the chasing pack. Do this and you might just succeed.

Joining forces with other victims to save recovery costs is a waste of time

CONCLUSIONS

Recovering after you have been victimized is a nasty and costly experience. It is always preferable to avoid getting into bad situations in the first place through effective due diligence and other procedures and by asking the right questions at the right time.

It is always easier to fall into the crap than to get out of it.
Prevention is far better than cure

Anonymous letters

BACKGROUND

In most frauds there are people on the sidelines who know what is going on but are frightened to make a direct report. However, they may do so anonymously through letters, emails or telephone calls. Obviously, some allegations are malicious or improperly motivated by the chance of a financial reward, but these are in the minority. The allegations usually relate to employees, although they may be made against companies, including vendors and customers. Experience shows that most anonymous communications contain at least a grain of truth and therefore must be taken seriously.

IGNORED ALLEGATIONS

An investigation revealed that a senior manager in a company's treasury department had defrauded over £2 million, by working in collusion with a brokerage firm of which his wife (using her maiden name and her parent's address) was the co-owner. A review of his personnel file showed that four years earlier an anonymous letter had been received setting out the precise mechanics of the fraud and naming the brokerage firm. It had been filed with the annotation 'Rubbish, GG is a senior officer of the company and these allegations are malicious.'

Never ignore anonymous allegations of wrongdoing

OBJECTIVES

When an anonymous allegation has been received, there is an obligation to find the truth in the interests of the victim organization and of the subject. Thus, the objectives are to:

- establish whether the allegations are true or false;
- establish the facts of a possible 'worst case' (see Appendix 1);
- identify the informant, to see if he can provide further information or to censure him for making a false allegation.

Responsibility for investigating allegations should be passed to internal audit, corporate security or to external advisers and handled by trained investigators in strict confidence: under no circumstances should the allegation be handled by managers in the business line concerned. Ideally the company's reporting of incidents procedures should cover anonymous allegations (see page 335).

METHOD

Initial handling

It is critical that the forensic integrity of the physical media on which the allegation is communicated is maintained. For example, anonymous letters and envelopes should not be touched unnecessarily, so that fingerprint and other evidence are not compromised. The originals should be copied and placed in a cardboard-reinforced envelope.

Try to trace the informant

You should consider having the letter and envelope forensically examined to see if there are any clues that could identify the author. For example, an Electrostatic Document Examination (ESDA) may reveal impressions from writing on other documents.

HOW ON EARTH DID YOU TRACE ME?

An anonymous letter was subject to an ESDA examination. In the top right-hand corner, the examiner discovered the impression of an address which had been made when the author had used an earlier page in his notepad to write to his mother. From this investigators traced and interviewed him: 'How on earth did you trace me?' he asked.

Also, the syntax of the letter, its layout, the typeface, the precise nature of the allegations made and *not* made, the time frame to which they relate and the possible motivation of the informant should be considered. These may lead to identification of the author.

Always try to identify the informant

You should check to see if other allegations have been made about the same person or relating to the area in which he works. If these were fully investigated and proven to be untrue, this will obviously influence the importance you attach to the current information but, even so, don't simply dismiss it.

Obtain full background on the subject

Without alerting the subject of the complaint, find out as much background information as possible about him, from personnel files, telephone call logs, expense statements etc. Review his authority levels and the transactions he handles. These details may help you decide whether the allegations are true or even feasible.

Develop a fraud theory

List the allegations which have been made and note alongside each one the evidence that supports or contradicts them, and assess whether they are credible. In the first instance, assume the allegations are true.

Do not dismiss allegations without investigating them carefully

If possible, you should review audit and performance reports for the area in which the subject works. Develop a fraud theory of the 'worst case' and assemble any 'key points' (see page 138) that support or rebut the allegations. In some cases it may be possible, without alerting the subject, to review transactions for which he is responsible. Again the objective is to test the accuracy of the allegations.

Prepare a brief investigations plan and consider actions you might take (see Appendix 1), including test purchases or sales, interception of communications, examination of telephone call logs, personal computers etc. prior to interviewing anyone. However, remember that the action you take must be proportionate to the seriousness of the allegations concerned.

TAPE RECORDING

It would be proportionate to intercept the communications of an employee where massive corruption was potentially involved, but excessive if the only suspicion was a minor expenses fiddle.

You should plan the *first step*, as you would for any other investigation. This would normally involve interviewing the subject and, assuming he has been identified with reasonable certainty, the informant.

Interviewing the subject

Your approach to the subject will depend on the strength of the evidence and the fraud theory but in most cases it should be based either on blocking questions (see page 198), or on a low-key opening statement and then conducted along the lines laid down in Chapter 7. If his reaction tells you the allegations are likely to be true, you must press on to try to find the deep truth.

The greatest difficulties arise when you are not sure, one way or the other, about the accuracy of an allegation. In these cases, it is usually best to explain the allegations in detail and to ask the subject to cooperate fully, by making bank and other records available and to work with you to disprove them and to help you identify the informant.

Innocent people usually fight to clear their names

Interviewing the informant

In many cases, the identity of the informant will become obvious and you should always try to interview him. Again your approach must be carefully planned and will depend on:

- the degree of certainty that he is the informant;
- the credibility of the information provided;
- his apparent motivation.

If you merely suspect that a person is the informant, you should still interview him but in a very circumspect way, using open questions about the area in which the subject works. You should not mention the subject's name unless he raises it first, nor should you show him the anonymous letter. If the person appears cooperative you may then move on to discussing the specifics of the allegation, but again avoiding the subject's name: his reaction should tell you whether or not he is the informant.

If you are reasonably certain that you have identified the informant you may take a more direct approach, but you must be careful not to put words in his mouth or slander the subject. Again your approach should be adapted to suit the circumstances. For example, if the information appears correct and the informant not motivated by malice you might take a low-key, empathetic approach from the outset, whereas if the allegations are false, you may treat the informant as a suspect and interview him accordingly with the objective of exposing and, in due course, punishing him.

In any event you should probe the information in depth, looking for supporting evidence and exploring other matters. If it emerges that the allegation is false and the informant is motivated by malice, consider obtaining a retraction in writing.

Follow-up action

It is imperative that allegations are not left on the subject's personnel file unresolved, and in all cases a report on the investigation should be prepared. Other closure action is essential and can be determined on the following matrix (Table 10.5).

If the allegations are unfounded, the subject must be told and asked whether he wants the report retained in his personnel file and it is usually in his interest to do so.

Table 10.5   Likely closure actions

Motivation of the informant	Evidence supporting the allegation and worst case		
	Accurate revealing malpractice	Accurate But not revealing malpractice	Inaccurate
Genuine	Investigation	Investigation	Close the file
Malicious		Action against the informant	
Not identified		Investigation	

DESTROYED RECORDS

In 1995, allegations were made against an employee, investigated and proved to be untrue. However, the human resources manager at the time[13] destroyed the letters and investigations report on the basis that they were 'personal data' that should not be retained any longer than was absolutely necessary.

In 2001, the employee was being considered for promotion to a senior overseas position. A junior employee in human resources department submitted a note to the effect that: 'Suspicions had been raised about this employee some years ago, but there is nothing on file'. This spooked the senior line manager who was making the appointment and another employee was selected for promotion.

Cases such as this show that some of the data protection laws are counterproductive (see page 298).

Annual appraisals

BACKGROUND

Annual performance appraisals can be extended to include a discussion on risks and control weaknesses. The benefits of such discussions are that they heighten employees' awareness to their control obligations and make it easier to prove wilful intent if problems emerge later on.

ANNUAL DECLARATION

For five years an employee complied with his company's policy and submitted an annual declaration that he had no private interests that could conflict with his obligations to his employer. When it subsequently emerged that he was effectively the owner of a company supplying industrial gloves and protective clothing to his employer: that he had pre-qualified the vendor and approved most of the contracts, the declarations came back to haunt him. They proved his dishonest intent.

Annual declarations raise the pavement for liars because they commit them to a falsification

OBJECTIVES

In addition to the normal objectives, annual appraisals can be used to:

- identify control weaknesses, possible compliance breaches and risks;
- draw employees' attention to their compliance and control requirements;
- commit liars to falsifications which they cannot defend.

---

[13] He moved on in 2000

The appraisal interviews may be linked to a written declaration of compliance along the lines of Table 9.13, page 327. Experience shows that there is a vast difference between expecting an employee to volunteer information and his revealing it in response to specific questions. Many routine appraisal interviews have resulted in serious frauds being exposed.

METHOD

The interview

A discrete part of the annual appraisal interview[14] should be devoted to risks and control issues and may be based on a standardized checklist of questions[15] consisting of:

- An opening statement, drawing the employee's attention to the company's business ethics and other control policies.
- A release under the Data Protection Act along the lines of:
  'This section of the appraisal may relate to confidential personal data which may be used for the prevention and detection of crime. Do you have any objection to this?'
- A reassurance statement along the lines:
  'During these appraisals, information often emerges of problems in our business. This informa-tion is always treated in confidence and we never reveal our sources. Are you aware of anything that is going wrong in the company?'
- Specific control-related questions such as:
  - Where do you see the risks in your area?
  - What improvements do we need to make to our controls?
  - Do you think problems are being reported?
  - In your appraisal interviews with subordinates, have any risk and control issues been raised?
  - Can we go through the results of those interviews?
- Compliance questions such as:
  - Do you understand the company's policy and procedures on (price fixing etc.)?
  - Do you require additional training?
  - If you suspected something was going wrong, do you know how to report it?
  - Have you ever made a report?
  - Is there anything going wrong now?
  - Do you or your immediate family have any interest that could conflict with your work here?
  - Are you aware of any abuse of drugs in the company?
- A final open question along the lines:
  'Are you aware of anything else that could have an impact in the control and compliance area?'
- A closing, thanking the employee for his cooperation.

The checklist should be annotated with the employee's replies and he should be asked to sign it. Usually, appraisals will be conducted by line managers and this results in a risk that information might be suppressed. Thus, from time to time, a representative of internal audit

---

[14]   Some of which should be conducted in the presence of a member of internal audit or human resources
[15]   This is one of the exceptional cases where checklists are useful because they ensure that coverage is consistent

or human resources should re-interview a small number of employees and confirm that appraisals have been fairly conducted and reported.

Follow-up action

A short file note should be prepared after each interview and placed in the employee's personnel file together with the annotated and signed checklist. If the subject has given information that justifies follow-up action, he should be kept informed of the results.

Debtors

BACKGROUND

Possibly the most common business lie is: 'The cheque is in the post,' and in recent years it has gone from being vaguely funny to catastrophic as more and more businesses are forced into liquidation because of cash flow problems. Often the largest companies and government departments are the slowest payers. Creditors, especially small ones, are reluctant to press too hard because they fear that by asserting their right, further business will be jeopardized. It is a Catch 22 problem and, at best, an example of organizational bullying.

There are four main categories of potentially bad debts:

1 Fraudulent trading, long firm and Phoenix frauds where the debtor never had any intention of paying.
2 Where the debtor does not have the money to pay and may itself face bankruptcy.
3 Where the debtor has money available and deliberately holds back payment to improve its own cash position or to apply leverage to get better terms on future transactions.
4 Although the debtor organization has a fair payment policy and the funds available, a manager deliberately holds back payment because:
   • he does not have the budget or authority to pay, or
   • wishes to solicit a bribe in return for authorizing payment.

Your method of approach, as a creditor, has to be adapted to suit the category concerned.

COLLECT QUICKLY: PAY SLOWLY

One leading company uses: 'Buy cheap, sell high: collect quickly, pay slowly' as a key phrase in training its managers and takes great pride in its aggressive management of cash. It has purchases of over £200 million a year and by deferring debts, so that on average it pays after 80 days, it reckons to save around £4 million per annum. However, if you read its annual report and accounts, it claims to pay suppliers, on average, after 28 days. Ironically, both statistics are true.

This smoke and mirrors illusion is possible because:

• it pays its associated companies within 7 days;
• it pays everyone else within 90 days.

This results in an average settlement period of 28 days and the distortion is the result of a deliberate plan to make its small suppliers, as one senior manager says, 'Sweat, as it makes them more appreciative of our business'.

The fact is that in the UK, like most other sensible countries, it is a criminal offence for anyone to obtain services or to defer payment of a debt by deception. Thus a person commits a criminal offence if he says the cheque is in the post when he knows it is not.

It is very serious to say: 'The cheque is in the post' when it's not

THE LEGAL POSITION

Obtaining services by deception

Section 1(2) of the Theft Act 1978 states that it is a criminal offence for anyone to obtain services where the provider is induced to confer any benefit by doing some act on the understanding it will be paid for. To succeed with a prosecution under this section, the victim has to prove:

1   The accused's deception induced him to actually confer a benefit by:
   * doing something,
   * causing some act to be done by another,
   * permitting some act to be done.

> E*xample*: A car is taken in for repair, a taxi hired or a consultant retained when the buyer has no intention, nor the means, to pay.

2   The benefit conferred must be on the basis that it will be paid for and it is not an offence to obtain *free services* by deception.

It does not matter that the transaction involves a contract that is unenforceable or even illegal. Thus a man who by deception induces a prostitute to provide services when he has no money to pay may be convicted under this section. Equally, where a consultant is retained, without a contract or on an oral understanding, and the client does not have the funds or budget to pay, the basis of a criminal offence can be established.

However, the prosecution has to prove that the accused's deception was deliberate or reckless and that he obtained the services dishonestly. If the prosecution succeeds, the accused my be fined and imprisoned. Where a person obtains property, rather than services, by deception, the charge is usually under Section 15 of the Theft Act 1968.

Evasion of a liability by deception

Section 2(1) of the Theft Act 1978 deals with three offences that are all concerned with evading a liability by deception. This is a typical 'The cheque is in the post' lie.

It is an offence where any person by deception:

1   Dishonestly secures the remission in whole or part of any existing liability to make payment, whether his own liability or another's. For example, this section applies where a person untruthfully says he cannot pay his bill because his cat has died, because he has not been paid by a customer or because invoices have been lost or have to be reissued for some spurious reason.

2 With intent to make permanent default on any existing liability, dishonestly induces the creditor to wait for payment or to forgo payment. This includes cases where the debtor delays a debt in the hope that the creditor will be forced into liquidation and therefore will not have to be paid at all.

3 Dishonestly obtains an exemption from or abatement of liability to make payment.

A liability to make payment is restricted to a legally enforceable obligation and thus does not apply to cases of, for example, prostitution or gambling. Again, the prosecution must prove that the accused acted dishonestly or recklessly. This standard can be proved quite easily by showing that the debtor told lies. Saying that 'The cheque is in the post' when it is not, is thus a very serious matter.

Remission of a liability

Section 2(i)(a) of the Theft Act 1978 relates to cases where dishonest deception by the accused results in the remission of an existing liability.

Example: A persuades B, who has lent him money, that the loan cannot be repaid by telling him a false hard-luck story. Another example is where a debtor gives a false story to his creditors to the effect that his business is in trouble and convinces them, dishonestly, to accept settlement for less than the actual amount owed.

The bottom line

The bottom line is that where anyone obtains services or property by deception, or tries to deceive creditors into deferring or writing off a debt by giving a false explanation, he commits a criminal offence subject to heavy financial and custodial penalties.

Late payment of commercial debts

The Late Payment of Commercial Debts (Interest) Act 1998 is also relevant.

The purpose of the Act
The Act provides a statutory right to claim interest on late payment of commercial debts.

Definitions of key terms
• *Late payment.* A payment is late when it is received after the expiry of the contractually agreed credit period; or the credit period in accordance with trade custom and practice or in the course of dealing between the parties; or the default credit period defined in the legislation.
• *Commercial debt.* The Act applies to a debt under a contract for the supply of goods or services where the purchaser and the supplier are both acting in the course of a business.

Territorial extent and applicable law
The legislation applies across the UK and to any commercial contract, including imports and exports, written under the law of part of the UK, except where there is no significant connection between the contract and that part of the UK, and, but for the choice of law, the applicable law would be a foreign law. Where the choice of law is a foreign law, the Act applies if, but for that choice of law, the applicable law would have been a law of part of the UK and there is no significant connection between the contract and any country other than that part of the UK.

> *Interest*
> The Act seeks to recompense creditors for the cost of the payment delay. It provides a power for the Secretary of State to set the rate of statutory interest. Currently this is base rate + 8%, reflecting the rate at which the smallest and most vulnerable businesses are generally able to borrow from the banks.

On the face of it, the Act is a powerful weapon for creditors, but in practice it is far from perfect because when it is enforced, commercial relationships may be irreparably damaged.

TO HELL WITH IT: LET THEM GO BUST

A large management consultancy outsourced part of a sensitive investigation to a small firm and allocated a budget of $50,000. The enquiries moved forward and the consultancy agreed – orally – that the budget could be extended. Invoices from the small firm were submitted but not paid and when things became desperate, a partner in the large consultancy asked that the invoices should be redrafted before submission to its client, which was an international institution that makes great play of its integrity. Invoices were resubmitted four times over a period of eight weeks, but still payment was not forthcoming.

The partner said that the invoices were being processed by his client and that payment was imminent. This statement was not true and, on the contrary, the partner was concerned that he had seriously overrun his budget with his client and had chosen not to submit any of the subcontractors' costs, lest this should cause him further problems.

After five months, without a penny being received, the small firm spoke directly to the client who arranged a meeting with the large consultancy. At this meeting the partner and his assistant presented the subcontractors' bills for the first time and there was a furious argument about them. The partner said: 'To hell with it, if you don't pay us we can't pay them. They will go bust and no liquidator would be prepared to spend legal fees chasing this, because the extensions to the budget were not agreed in writing'.

And what, you may ask, was the client's reaction to this? It basically agreed. So much for business ethics.

Business ethics are great until money is involved

The bottom line

The law is more than sufficient to ensure that creditors are paid on time. However, debtors are able to avoid their obligations through a number of ruses. The first is to claim, usually long after the event, that the goods or services were defective and that payment is therefore not justified. The second is to delay payment[16] by asking for invoices to be resubmitted, possibly to a different subsidiary or parent company, with or without VAT, in dollars rather than sterling or sterling rather than dollars. Some debtors systematically and routinely reject invoices, asking for them to be reissued over and over again.

---

[16] To improve its own cash flow and earn interest on deposits

However, the most cynical and criminal organizations are those that deliberately string out small suppliers, knowing that when they go into liquidation, payment can be avoided altogether.

THE CONSTRUCTION COMPANY

One major construction company has worked competitive bidding and credit management to a fine art. It deliberately bids low for major contracts and when it is successful appoints a manager whose main job is to find ways in which specifications can be changed, and confirmed in writing, thus allowing additional invoices to be submitted to its clients. The manager is paid a bonus based on his success in negotiating 'overruns'.

At the same time the construction company passes out most of the work to subcontractors and agrees budgets with them. It avoids, almost at all costs, putting specification changes in writing, but assures the subcontractors orally. Initially it pays subcontractors on time, but as work moves forward it systematically builds up its debts. Invoices from subcontractors are quickly submitted to the client, long before the subcontractors are paid, again improving the construction company's cash flow.

At the end of the job, the contractor prepares a final bill for its clients, which is often a work of fiction. In one case on an initial budget of £4 million the final claim was for £12 million. The company has two people working in a department whose only role in life is to prepare final claims for arbitration or litigation. The authors of the claim are, again, paid a percentage based on their success. Clients are told that if they do not pay the final amount, legal action will be taken against them and most offer to make a settlement which is far in excess of the value of the work done.

When subcontractors finally press for settlement of their invoices they are told that their work was not satisfactory and if payment is offered it is for a fraction of the amount already paid by the client. In one case genuine bills from a subcontractor amounting to £800,000 were paid by the client but were 'spot settled' for £200,000, giving the construction company an additional profit of £600,000.

Many subcontractors are not paid at all and are forced into bankruptcy. If the liquidator presses the construction company for payment, he is told that the work was not satisfactory and that the claim will be disputed. Most receivers don't bother, again providing the construction company with pure profit.

You may ask, with such an appalling record, how the construction company survives. The answer is that there are thousands of subcontractors all anxious for business and who do not check deeply enough into the payment records of their customers. If they do check, they are assured that a particular subcontractor was not paid because his work was not up to standard and the gullible believe it.

For liars, when one door closes, two more open

OBJECTIVES

Your objectives are to ensure that debts are paid on time and that, in turn, you pay your creditors promptly. This can be achieved by before and after the event procedures.

Method before the event

Prevention is obviously better than cure and good credit control and due diligence are essential. If you find (or have previous experience) that a particular customer deceptively defers debts, you should not deal with him unless you have advances, binding personal guarantees, or his money in your pocket. These days, turning down business is a difficult decision, but it is better not to have it than to deliver what was asked for and then not get paid.

The cost of doing business with some people is just too great

Another essential is to ensure that the terms of business are in writing, including the price and payment terms. Any changes to these must also be in writing and signed by the other party. If you fail to do this, the unscrupulous debtor will claim he never received the document or received it but never agreed to it. Unfortunately, courts do not regard failure to respond as an agreement and conmen know this. Thus from the outset you must build up a watertight case and make sure every aspect is documented.

Retain accurate documentation

It is also vital to ensure that you get proof, as soon as you can, that what you delivered was up to standard and complied with the agreement. You might achieve this by terms and conditions on delivery notes or in contracts that require customers to report any defects within a specified period, which should be as short as possible. Alternatively, before things go badly wrong, you may speak to the customer and tape-record his assurance that you have fulfilled your part of the deal. Whatever way you do it, you must have this proof before payment becomes delayed, and retain it.

Get proof that you have delivered

You should also keep up the pressure to get the debt paid. If you send reminders and make chasing calls after 14 days you might receive payment after 28. Start pushing after seven days and you may get paid in 14.

Keep up the pressure to get paid

Method after the event

The normal methods of collecting a debt include negotiation, legal action and making offsets against any money you owe the debtor. All of these can be improved if you are prepared to play a little hardball. You can do this by getting someone, and preferably a senior manager working for the debtor, to lie to you and to have this preserved in writing or on tape. To succeed with this tactic by asserting your rights you are likely not to get any other business from the debtor, but do you really want it?

The debtor's lies help your case

Thus, as a minimum, covertly tape-record all conversations with the debtor and pin him down to as much detail as possible on:

- the fact that the goods or services you delivered were satisfactory;
- the debt is owed;
- the reasons for delayed payment;
- when payment will be made and how.

Preserve this evidence and, if you have retained lawyers, make it available to them.

You may then speak again[17] to the debtor or get your lawyers to write to him personally, preferably at his home address, and tell him that you have tape recordings of your conversations in which he has lied and that unless payment is made forthwith you will:

- make a formal complaint to the police;
- send copies and transcripts to the board and audit committees of his company;
- send copies to the trade and national press;
- send copies to credit agencies;
- send copies to any professional organization of which he is a member and make a formal complaint, to have him disbarred.

This approach is likely to raise the temperature, but don't worry, as it is critical that you become the biggest problem in his life and you must make it very personal. It is also likely to get a result but if it, legal action and negotiation all fail, your only hope is to send in the heavies.

Make it personal

Defections

BACKGROUND

Obviously employees are entitled to better themselves by moving on to another employer (defined as 'good defections'), and there is little an organization can do to prevent this other than to be a genuinely good employer. There are other cases, called 'bad defections', where employees commit wrongful acts such as stealing intellectual capital, customer lists and breaching their employment contracts in other ways.

Defections can be categorized as follows in Table 10.6.

Dishonesty is often a factor in bad defections (shown in italics in Table 10.6) and is most common when a team of employees plans to defect to start up or join a new business or to work with a competitor.

The usual flow of bad defections

Most bad defections can be viewed in the eight steps described below.

Step 1: What sets the mind thinking

Bad defections can be triggered for many reasons, some of which are under the control of the employer and some are not (Table 10.7).

---

[17]   This conversation must be carefully planned and tape-recorded

Table 10.6   Good and bad defections

One or more employee plans to leave the employer:	Category of defection in % Subjective estimates	
	Good	Bad
To support a **hostile acquisition:** *the employee covertly assists the acquirer by providing assistance and intellectual capital*	0	100
To create, or become a shareholder in, a **new business:** *start-up ventures where intellectual capital is stolen to give them a flying start*	20	80
To contrive a **management buy-out:** *where employees covertly provide information to the acquirer or falsify performance records to their own advantage*	50	50
To join a **fledgling business**, attempting to enter the employer's sector: *where employees covertly steal intellectual capital to assist it*	60	40
To work for a customer or supplier: *stealing intellectual capital in the process*	60	40
To join a legitimate competitor: *stealing intellectual capital in the process*	90	10
To join a legitimate business in another sector	99	1

Table 10.7   The start of defections

Reason	Examples of driving forces and result
Dissatisfaction with the existing job or employer	Inadequate job satisfaction Being overlooked for promotion Perceived low rewards, especially annual bonuses Lack of recognition Poor working conditions
Unacceptable changes to the existing job	Promotions of other employees Appointment of a new supervisor Transfers to a new job or new location
Getting out before the collapse	Knowledge that poor personal performance is about to be uncovered Inside knowledge of poor financial results, affecting bonus or share option schemes
Acquisitions and disinvestments	Resulting in uncertainty and unacceptable changes
Defection of other employees	Envy and uncertainty
Competitors	Encouraging the employee to consider a move
Incoming teams	Causing uncertainty or a change in responsibilities
Suppliers and customers	Encouraging the employee to consider a move
Envy of the employer's profits	Resulting in employees believing they can do the same
Approach by headhunters or merchant banks	Encouraging the employee to consider a move

Effective HR policies minimize bad defections

Headhunters are probably the largest single cause of team defections, closely followed by merchant banks. A recent full-page feature advertisement by the 3i Group plc reads:

BE YOUR OWN BOSS

'The advertisement your boss doesn't want you to read? Why? Because he knows that the combination of your ideas and 3i's backing could mean he's not your boss for long. The chances are he knows that we're Britain's leading specialist investor in private businesses. That we've invested in over 4000 new and emerging businesses. That we invest nearly £3 million every working day and that we've invested over £8.5 billion since we started. His problem now is so do you. We want you to succeed.'

This is tempting stuff for any employee and a perfectly honest invitation to defect. However, it does not say that 30 per cent of start-up ventures fail within the first 18 months.

Step 2: Discussion and collusion

An employee will usually discuss his intention to defect with his family and then with his immediate colleagues. The initial discussions, although innocent, can lead to collusion and to very bad group defections.

THE LEGAL POSITION

It is worth noting that the legal position in the UK on such discussions is clear. An employee who learns of an intended defection is required to act honestly and to report the facts to his employer, but very few do so, even when they are not interested in defecting themselves. Where a director hears of a planned defection and does not report it, he may be personally liable for the consequences.

Some employees who have been involved in discussions to defect may decide to remain in place and to wait and see what happens. Others will use inside knowledge of the planned defection to improve their own position, and unusual assertiveness or ambition by previously passive employees may be a sign that a mass defection of his colleagues is imminent.

There are always clues …

Step 3: Detailed planning

The extent to which employees' discussions about plans to defect are legal or illegal varies from case to case. But in bad team defections, experience suggests illegality is the rule rather than the exception. Most bad defectors will obtain legal advice, although the experience is that they are often reluctant to incur significant costs or to follow the advice they have been given.

For example, it is not unusual to find that they tell their legal advisers only part of the story and, while appearing totally honest, engage in improper practices including those shown in Table 10.8.

Table 10.8 Examples of improper practices

Type of improper or illegal practice	Purpose and comment
Running down the business	To assist hostile acquirers To reduce the cost of a MBO
Ramping up the business	To achieve incentive and bonus targets To improve their track records and CVs
Jumping the gun with part-time working and conflicts of interest	To springboard a new enterprise
Skimming income or diverting costs of a planned new enterprise to the employer	To springboard the new enterprise To create working capital
Stealing information such as customer lists, pricing details, new product plans	This is one of the most common problems

Obviously evidence of such malpractice significantly improves the employer's position if the case gets to court.

Deception by the defectors assists your case

Step 4: Counter-intelligence and getting protection
In some cases, defectors will prepare to protect themselves by obtaining evidence of misdeeds by the employer, to discourage legal or other action being taken against them. In one case, the defectors bugged conference rooms and copied sensitive files, proving that the employer had paid bribes to civil servants. When this evidence was revealed, the employer's enthusiasm for pursuing its rights quickly evaporated.

Step 5: The decision to go
The first time most employers hear about a planned defection is when the person or persons concerned hand in their resignations. This is too late. The result is that the employer can be panicked into action it later regrets. A common reaction is for the employer to make a counter offer in the hope that the employees concerned will be persuaded to stay. A second common reaction is for the employer to adopt a hostile and aggressive attitude, immediately threatening litigation, doom and despondency. Neither approach works.

Plan carefully and unemotionally

Step 6: Running in parallel
As soon as possible, defectors will start their new jobs but the chances are they will not have the immediate impact on its business that the former employer feared. Customers resent change and even when they have a close personal relationship with the defecting team they may be disinclined to transfer their business.

However, the start-up period in a new venture or with the new employer is critical for the defectors and, to an extent, for the former employer. It is usually a time for rumour and speculation. It is important that the employer does not overreact, but focuses on its relationships both with customers and remaining employees.

Focus on retaining business and the support of good employees

Step 7: Further poaching

If the defectors are successful in their new venture, which they will usually claim to be whether true or not, they may try to poach other employees. This, again, is a sensitive period. Waverers will watch the situation carefully and defectors in place may provide assistance and support.

Watch for defectors in place

Step 8: The longer term

Experience shows that over the longer term, good companies recover from bad defections. Convincing senior managers of this , when they are in the middle of a defection crisis, is not easy, but it is a fact.

Clues that defections are imminent

Often the clues that a defection is probable, if not imminent, are obvious and include those in Table 10.9.

Table 10.9   Signs of defections

Clues that a defection is imminent	Significance	Illegal
Unexplained failure to close important transactions by employees, customers and suppliers	Holding back income to springboard the business with a new employer	Possibly
Unexplained refusal to enter into long-term commitments, promotions or transfers		
Unwillingness to recruit staff		
Poor performance by hitherto high-performing employees	Disinterest Running down the business	Possibly
Unexplained errors, discrepancies and failure to submit accounts		
Senior employees taking on responsibilities below their rank	To learn or obtain new skills or resources in preparation for a move	Possibly
Unusual requests to attend training courses		
Unusual requests for information, outside the employee's normal area of responsibility		
Strange alliances: for example the managing director of a subsidiary company inexplicably becomes close to the data processing manager		
Odd decisions, agreements or contracts affecting third parties and especially customers, suppliers and employees	Granting favours in the expectation that they will be returned later	Possibly

Clues that a defection is imminent	Significance	Illegal
Rumours	Disrupting the employer's business to encourage other employees to defect	Possibly
Dissatisfaction		
Following a major structural change to the organization such as an acquisition, disinvestments, merger, re-engineering	Uncertainty	No
Employment of an incoming team or a senior manager	Uncertainty Disappointment that their own contributions have not been recognized	No
Defections of key employees working for a competitor	In turn the competitor will seek to find replacements	No
Situations vacant advertisements placed by a competitor	These will be seen by key employees who may be attracted	No
Entry of a major player into the employer's market	New vacancies	No
Calls to and from headhunters and merchant banks	Encouragement to defect	No
Unexplained absences of groups of employees	Off-site meetings to discuss the defection	Possible
Unusual working hours for a group of employees	On-site meetings to discuss the defection	Possible
Team meetings held off site or outside normal working hours		
Missing contracts and legal agreements	To prevent the enforcement of legal contracts with employees, suppliers, customers	Yes
Missing books and records		
Missing fixed assets or inventory	Skimming: theft of inventory to springboard the new venture	Yes
Excessive photocopying or microfilming of sensitive records	Theft to springboard the new venture	Yes
Access to premises, papers and systems at unusual hours	Theft to springboard the new venture	Yes

Prompt recognition of such clues enables the employer to plan ahead and minimize the damage of defections.

Incoming defectors: key employees who join you

A serious blind spot, for some organizations, is that they fail to appreciate the problems with incoming defectors, especially when the new employees arrive in teams.

INCOMING DEFECTIONS

Barings was a classic example, and the operations in Singapore, which were eventually to lead to the bank's downfall, were centred on a group of employees which had been imported from a trading company run by Christopher Heath.

The report into the Barings crash, prepared by the Board of Banking Supervision of the Bank of England, commented on the cultural clash between the robust marketing focused, highly incentivized team from Heath and the more blue-blooded, laid-back Barings style. These differences, and the underlying cultural gap, was manifested in unwillingness to report, or to be held accountable, leading to serious political dogfights and turf wars. It was a recipe for disaster and it happened.

Top management's joy in capturing a winning team from a competitor should not blind them to the fact that serious morale and control problems can result. The incoming team may be heavily ego driven, see themselves as superior to existing employees and a law unto themselves. They may not integrate easily.

Incoming teams are not all sweetness and light

The problems are amplified when an incoming team is rewarded through a highly geared, short-term incentive scheme, perhaps based on the number of new accounts they obtain, or new business generated. They may take dishonest routes to achieve their targets, falsely account for their achievements and engage in other malpractice. Such transgressions expose the new employer to loss and penalties for breaches of the law and other regulations.

CLOSED GROUPS

The recent scandal surrounding the supposed 'mis-selling' of pensions contains many examples of where sales teams, imported *en masse* from other companies, ignored the rules so that they could profit for themselves.

Typically incoming teams will canvass clients and customers of their ex-employer, with the intention of persuading them to transfer their business to the new employer. This again, as illustrated by the pensions scandal, may not be in the customer's interest, although obviously it will be to the employee's advantage.

An incoming team may unsettle established employees, in turn causing them to think about defecting. An endless spiral can be triggered between competitive organizations in the same industry. And what security of tenure does the new employer have, knowing that if the incoming team defected once, it can do so again? The bottom line is that incoming defections call for very careful handling.

Attitudes of the employer

Even honest defections can raise the heat. By resigning, the defector announces to his colleagues he is no longer part of the team. Their feeling of rejection, and sometimes envy, can result in animosity and this, if not carefully controlled, can result in serious problems.

A CASE OF VENGEANCE?

In one case, where the defection was overwhelmingly honest, senior managers of the employer put round a circular warning remaining employees that were they even to speak to their ex-colleague, they would be instantly dismissed. So paranoid were the managers about any contact that internal telephones were tapped and mail intercepted.

The home and mobile telephone bills of employees and of the ex-employee were obtained, with questionable legality, and audited to detect if there had been any unauthorized contact. Trash bins, left outside the ex-employee's home, were searched for incriminating evidence. Even worse, a campaign of hostility was mounted, resulting – during the period of gardening leave – in his new employers withdrawing their offer. Legal action is now pending.

The big question is what effect does such hostility have on other employees if they see the employer acting improperly or unfairly towards their ex-colleague? Some may take his side and thus the alliance that the employer was most trying to prevent is forged.

Typically defections are dealt with by legal action with the employer trying to enforce restrictive covenants on the ex-employee's future activities. These are intended to protect the legitimate business interests of the employer and not to stifle honest competition, nor to make life impossible for ex-employees. In any event, enforcement of restrictive covenants is not easy and even if successful, merely shuts the door after the horse has gone.

OBJECTIVES

An employer's objectives are normally to:

- identify key employees, make sure they are motivated and that succession plans have been developed;
- minimize the impact of defections, especially of teams;
- recognize the importance of employees, especially those who choose not to defect;
- protect its intellectual capital;
- retain customers;
- not to drop its guard with incoming teams that have defected from other employers.

The ways in which these objectives can be achieved for bad team defections are discussed below.

METHOD: OUTGOING BAD DEFECTIONS OF TEAMS

Starting position

You must recognize that all of your employees are key assets that require both nurturing and control. Thus, fair employment practices are essential, including an awareness that apparently small organizational or other changes can create a climate for mass defections. Once the defection ball starts rolling in a company or department it is difficult to stop.

When it happens, it is too late

You should consider putting a procedure in place that identifies key employees, and prepare succession plans. Often quite junior members of the company are among the most critical.

THE ELECTRONICS GIANT

A few years ago a major electronics company introduced a downsizing programme and offered retirement packages to anyone over fifty years of age and most jumped at it. It then had a very serious problem[18] trying to establish ownership of a particular invention but no one could find the files or remember who worked in the department at that time. Eventually an ex-employee was traced who was able to guide the employer to the information concerned.

Retiring all of the elderly may result in throwing out the baby with the bathwater

Information protection

All organizations should specify a procedure for protecting confidential information, in all of its forms, starting with the recording of new ideas,[19] patents, and copyright through to electronic data and archives (see Chapter 8, page 346). In addition they should:

- register all databases with the Information Commissioner: thus if defectors misuse your data, they may be exposed to criminal prosecution;
- seed all mailing and customer lists with a few false names: if lists are stolen, mail sent to the false seeded names will expose the theft;
- carry out routine and surprise audits to ensure the standards are observed. For example, maintaining a 'clean desk' policy.

Limit the damage

Telephone call logging

You should consider enabling telephone call logging software on telephone systems to record the date, time, sequence, and caller's number of incoming and outgoing calls. Retain these logs, preferably in computer form, for at least five years.

Where telephone conversations are routinely tape-recorded, such as in a dealing room:

- make sure recording equipment cannot be deactivated;
- ensure that recordings are securely retained for at least two years;
- identify, log or monitor extensions in adjoining conference rooms and public areas, which are not recorded. *Experience shows that these extensions are used by defectors and others to make sensitive calls.*

Consider installing monitoring equipment to capture an image of all faxes sent and received to and from sensitive areas or operations.

---

18 Potentially involving billions of dollars
19 Especially important in research and development organizations

Legal agreements and contracts of employment

For key employees, have contracts of employment reviewed by a specialist human resources lawyer. Confirm that they are appropriate and filed securely. Under no circumstances should any employee be allowed unrestricted access to his personnel file.

Intelligence

Great care has to be taken to avoid unjustified intrusion in the lives of employees but good intelligence can ensure that problems are avoided, or quickly detected.

1   Consider running regular audit tests against telephone and fax call logs. Identify calls from key employees to:
    • competitors,
    • ex-employees and earlier defectors, at their homes and offices,
    • headhunters,
    • company formation agents,
    • office accommodation bureau.

    Examine suspicious patterns in detail, especially around sensitive times such as on the announcement of an acquisition, the termination of employment of a key employee or group of employees, a restructuring, a re-organization, or immediately before and after annual bonuses have been announced.

2   Routinely check with company registration databases for new directorships accepted by key employees or their wives, and directorships registered at their home addresses.
3   Monitor newspapers, trade and professional journals for job advertisements placed by competitors.
4   Remain alert to any of the symptoms of possible defections shown in Table 10.9.

As soon as you have a firm indication that a team defection is imminent, you must act quickly.

When a bad team defection appears imminent

If you suspect a possible bad defection of a team of employees:

1   Assess the position carefully:
    • A good or bad defection?
    • A single or team defection?
    • What are the possible consequences?
    • Is dishonesty suspected?
    • How strong are non-competition restrictions and would you wish to enforce them?
2   Develop an action plan focusing on:
    • the customers who might be affected:
        – develop a plan to get them onside,
        – play it low-key and don't overreact.
    • The remaining employees:
        – develop a plan to get them onside,

- do not defame the defectors or exaggerate the impact their leaving will have,
- don't give in to blackmail by waverers.
- Any improper or illegal acts by the defectors.

3 As soon as possible have a trusted senior manager interview and covertly tape-record the potential defectors. He should:
- be low-key and as friendly as possible, using blocking questions, giving them the chance to volunteer the truth,
- establish what they plan to do, when and with whom,
- determine if they have taken legal advice and if so, from whom, when and its nature,
- remind them of any restrictive covenants and their responsibilities as employees or directors,
- ask for their suggestions on how their area should be managed in their absence,
- ask if they have discussed their departure with any other employees/customers or suppliers,
- try to agree an exit plan on the most amicable terms possible.

In bad defections, it is unlikely that the employees involved will be truthful and it may thus appear that interviews are a waste of time. However, lies told at this stage will act to the defectors' disadvantage later on.

4 If there is any chance of the defection turning hostile or illegal, prepare for a fight:
- Retain top employment and litigation lawyers, without delay.
- Under legal direction, think about assigning the defectors to a high level project that keeps them fully engaged during their period of notice. The project might focus on requiring them to assess the opportunities in the market they intend to enter, or the employer's competitiveness vis-à-vis the new employer. *This is something of a double bluff. If they give a misleading report, it may be a breach of their contractual duties.*
- Subject to legal advice, provide a special project room, remote from their normal work areas, which is under audio surveillance.
- Require them to return all company property (and especially personal computers and laptops) to their project office *(where it should be forensically examined)*.
- Retain specialist investigators to audit their last twelve month's work in detail to detect any irregularities by the defectors or by their new employer, including:
  - expense statements,
  - telephone call logs,
  - diaries,
  - requests for bulk copying or microfilming of documents, such as customer lists,
  - mobile and home telephone bills,
  - any underperformance or 'held back business',
  - negotiations and the validity of any discretion exercised in favour of third parties,
  - missing documentation and company property,
  - forensic examination of computers to which they have had access and especially their own personal computers and laptops:
    ~ dump and analysis of email correspondence,
    ~ dictation tapes and answering message tapes,
    ~ memories from telephones and faxes.

Any evidence of wrongdoing will be invaluable in subsequent negotiations or legal proceedings

5   Change access codes to premises and computers and generally tighten security. Remain on the lookout for signs that the defectors are running a counter-intelligence operation or are trying to persuade other employees to join them.

6   Consider meeting with the defectors' new employer:
   • point out any restrictions on the defectors' future activities,
   • try to establish as much as possible about their future intentions,
   • give them the opportunity to tell lies; this will serve to their disadvantage in any subsequent legal proceedings.

7   Brief the remaining employees and seek their support. Don't make heroes or villains out of the defectors. Concentrate on re-establishing the business. Consider revising budgets and other performance targets.

8   Require the defectors to return all company property: get them to certify that the list is complete and correct.

9   Hand them and their new employers a letter, describing what they can and cannot do and specifically what information must be kept confidential.

10 Consider limited periods of surveillance and other enquiries to ensure that the defectors have not broken (and do not break) their non-competition restrictions.

11 Consider retaining commercial investigators to report on the progress of the defectors in their new positions and particularly any misuse of confidential information.

12 Monitor call logs carefully for evidence of 'defectors in place'.

13 Don't try to prohibit social contact between the defectors and remaining employees.

The art is to get evidence of any malpractice by bad defectors, to pin them down to detail and deception. Do this and your rights of action are improved.

METHOD: INCOMING TEAMS

When defections go the other way and your organization acquires a team, possibly from a competitor, don't let the benefits blind you to the realities. Get all of the incoming team members to go through the normal (hopefully, thorough) pre-employment screening programme; don't take anything on trust.

Ask them to warrantee the accuracy of their biographies and to certify that they are not aware of any transactions with their past employer which could emerge to cause them problems.

Watch for abuse of earn out results or other incentive schemes and don't encourage or condone breaches of obligations to previous employers.

Try to integrate the new team as quickly as possible. Make sure they understand the company's policies on business ethics etc.

CONCLUSIONS

These simple measures will avoid most of the problems of incoming and outgoing defections. They are mainly additional to the conventional approach based only on enforcing restrictive covenants and must be coordinated with your legal and HR advisers.

Drug abuse

BACKGROUND

It is reliably estimated that, by the age of 24 years, almost half the population in the UK will have taken illegal drugs, with many becoming addicted to a greater or lesser degree. Organized crime is always at the front end of the supply chain and its members routinely exploit and blackmail users.

Drugs in the workplace are a serious problem because:

- they adversely affect the performance of employees;
- addiction is corrosive and creates a destructive, conspiratorial sub-culture;
- it creates financial pressure;
- it exposes the users to blackmail.

Drug abuse also results in the infiltration of organized crime into the workplace.

WIRE TRANSFER FRAUDS

John was a young employee working in the cables room of a London bank. He regularly took drugs, which he bought in East End clubs and discos. One of his suppliers asked him where he worked and what he did; John told him and thought nothing further about it until his debts got out of hand. The supplier said John could solve his problems by working with him and his colleagues to 'pull a little scam'. This involved falsifying a $100 million wire transfer instruction. Fortunately, the attempt failed and John and his supplier were prosecuted.

However sympathetic or apathetic an employer might be it is foolish to ignore the fact that drug abuse is a serious criminal offence, as is allowing premises to be used for that purpose.

Drug abuse cannot be ignored

THE COMMONLY ABUSED DRUGS

Ecstasy

Ecstasy or methylenedioxymetheamphetamine (MDMA) was first patented by Merck pharmaceuticals in 1912 and acts on the brain's neurotransmitters to produce serotonin, creating a feeling of well-being; and dopamine which acts as a pain suppressant. Both types of neurotransmitters regulate body temperature and may cause dehydration.

Many users therefore consume excessive quantities of water to counteract this effect but this causes the brain tissue to expand and press against the skull, resulting in irreversible damage to the parts of the brain that control heart rate and breathing.

Possible long-term effects include depression, anxiety and psychosis, all of which could be permanent. Users can become psychologically dependent but not usually physically addicted.

- *Highs*: Feeling of well-being. Lots of energy. No pain.[20]
- *Lows*: Severe reactions include hypothermia, convulsions, blood clotting, liver and severe kidney failure, which can be fatal.

Acid or LSD

Albert Hoffman, a pharmaceutical chemist working for Sandoz took the first 'trip' on lysergic acid diethylamide (LSD) in 1943, when he accidentally ingested the drug during tests. He experienced strange hallucinations that transformed sounds into optical illusions. LSD was originally seen as a potential cure for mental illness and many UK institutions used it, ignoring the evidence that it often made patients worse.

In its purest form LSD is a white, tasteless powder, which can be dissolved in water. Consequently, street-bought LSD could be mixed with other substances such as speed, PCP or even strychnine. LSD increases the heart rate, blood pressure and body temperature but most deaths are the result of hallucinations (for example, people falling to their deaths convinced that they can fly). Other deaths include suicide during the deep depressions that can follow a bad trip.

- *Highs*: Heightened self-awareness and possible mystical experiences. Feeling of euphoria.[21]
- *Lows*: The trip can trigger paranoia, fear and illusions so intricate that the user cannot distinguish them from reality.

Cannabis

Until recently, the effects of delta-g-tetrehydrocannabinol (THC or cannabis) were the least understood of all drugs. The first clinical description of being 'stoned' was recorded by American psychiatrist Walter Bromberg in 1939. It is almost impossible to overdose on cannabis although heavy users can suffer from lethargy, apathy and a lack of ambition. Cannabis psychosis is rare but psychological dependence is common.

- *Highs*: Euphoria, increased self-confidence and relaxation; increased ability for intense concentration.
- *Lows*: Anxiety, depressions, paranoia. Possibility of amotivational syndrome (i.e. becoming engrossed in something of little value to the detriment of something important).

Heroin

Diamorphine or heroin was developed in the 19th century as a painkiller and its name was taken from the German word *heroisch* meaning hero, such was the belief in its miraculous properties. Pure heroin causes no physical damage to the body although it is highly addictive, causing physical and psychological dependence.

An overdose results in the user feeing drowsy, slowly slipping into a coma. Heroin depresses the cough reflex and the unconscious user may suffocate by inhaling their own vomit.

- *Highs*: Immediate rush of intense euphoria subsiding into a relaxed feeling or warmth, optimism and confidence. Detachment from pain, desires and anxiety.

---

[20]   i.e. just like being an investigator
[21]   i.e. like working in human resources

- *Lows*: Vomiting, sweating, anxiety and abdominal cramps.

Speed

Amphetamine sulphate (speed) is one of the cheapest stimulants and was first marketed as Benzedrine in 1932. It is still prescribed for hyperactive children and accountants. Approximately 70 million pills were sent to American, British, German and Japanese troops during World War II to increase alertness in the field. Later it was prescribed to cure obesity.

As users do not need to eat, the withdrawal symptoms can include nausea. In extreme cases, amphetamine psychosis can occur, a state similar to schizophrenia with paranoid delusions and hallucinations. It causes profound psychological dependence but no major physical addiction.

- *Highs*: Exhilaration, increased energy and self-confidence. Increased awareness and alertness. Suppresses appetite and removes the need for sleep.
- *Lows*: Because the effects last a long time, there is almost a continuous demand on energy supplies. Regular high doses can cause lesions in the brain and damage to its structure. Mood changes, including maniacal depression, aggression, over talkativeness and excitability are common.

Cocaine or crack

Bought on the street, it has been found to contain a mixture of manganese carbonate (a cause of Parkinson's disease) lidocaine, ephedrine and PCP as well as dextrose, glucose, talc and caustic soda. When 'snorted' only 20–30 per cent enters the blood stream with the majority remaining in the nasal cavity. The first rush is felt in 1–4 minutes, but will then start to fade. Tachycardia is common because cocaine constricts the blood vessels hampering the supply of blood to the heart but it also releases adrenaline which makes the heart beat more rapidly

Long-term use of cocaine, speed and ecstasy may also permanently damage the production of dopamine. This can lead to depression and Parkinson's disease.

- *Highs*: Intense stimulation resulting in euphoria, sexual arousal, increased energy and feeling of well-being.
- *Lows*: Dehydration, psychosis (hyperactivity and delusions such as insects under the skin), convulsions and the 'crash'. This can include anxiety, sadness, apathy, anorexia, insomnia and increased aggression.

OBJECTIVES

An organization's objectives are to ensure that:

- it does not recruit drug users;
- it detects and deals with drug abuse at work.

These objectives are necessary to provide employees with a safe working environment and to ensure that human resources are optimized. Also they ensure that the organization is itself not liable to prosecution for allowing its premises to be used in connection with illegal drugs and reduces the risk of infiltration by organized crime.

COMPANY POLICY

Every organization should set out its policy in relation to drug abuse. The following is based on a template provided by www.dfwp.utsa.edu.

Purpose

X is committed to providing a safe work environment and to fostering the well-being and health of its employees. That commitment is jeopardized when any employee illegally uses drugs or alcohol on the job, comes to work with these substances present in his or her body, or possesses, distributes, or sells drugs in the workplace. *Drug abuse is a serious criminal offence, as is allowing any premises to be used for the illegal taking or distribution of drugs.*

Violations

It is a violation of company policy for any employee to possess, sell, trade, or offer for sale illegal drugs or otherwise engage in the illegal use of drugs, intoxicants, or alcohol on the job.
It is a violation of company policy for anyone to report to work under the influence of illegal drugs or alcohol – that is, with illegal drugs, intoxicants, or alcohol in his/her body.
It is a violation of the company policy for anyone to use prescription drugs illegally. However, nothing in this policy precludes the appropriate use of legally prescribed medications.
Violations of this policy are subject to disciplinary action up to and including termination of employment. *In addition, X will report all cases of drug abuse on company property or in working time to the police.*

Policy on recruitment

X will not employ any candidate who takes or distributes drugs or who has been convicted for any drugs-related offence in the previous ten years.

Supervisor/management responsibility and training

It is the responsibility of the company's supervisors to counsel employees whenever they see changes in performance or behaviour that suggests an employee may be under the influence of alcohol or other drugs. Although it is not the supervisor's job to diagnose personal problems, the supervisor should encourage such employees to seek help and advise them about available resources for getting help. Resource lists will be available to supervisors during training sessions held throughout the year.

Employee education

The company will provide drug and alcohol awareness information to all employees. This will include the company's policy on drug and alcohol abuse, information on the magnitude and dangers of drug and alcohol abuse, and the availability of counselling and treatment through the employee assistance programme.

Co-worker responsibility

All employees share responsibility for maintaining a safe work environment and should encourage co-workers who use alcohol or other drugs in the workplace to seek help.

Drug testing statement

Company X is committed to safeguarding the health and welfare of our employees and to providing a safe working environment. Drug and alcohol testing assists us in ensuring our commitment to our employees, customers, and the public. Thus, all job candidates will be required to provide medical and other evidence that they do not and have not abused drugs. Employees will, from time to time at the discretion of the company and at its expense, be required to undergo medical testing for drug abuse or to provide written declarations of compliance with this policy.

Employee assistance programme

The company recognizes that drug and alcohol abuse can be successfully treated and is committed to helping employees who suffer from these problems, while holding them responsible for their own recovery. The employee is responsible for the full cost of these services.

Closing statement

The intent of this policy is to offer a helping hand to those who need it, while sending a clear message that the illegal drug use and alcohol abuse are incompatible with employment at X.

The policy should be summarized in staff handbooks and training programmes for all employees. No one should believe that drug abuse will be tolerated.

JOB APPLICATION FORMS

Job application forms should set out the organization's policy on drug abuse and should specifically ask questions about it:

- Do you use drugs such as cannabis, ecstasy, crack, etc.?
- Have you taken any of these drugs in the past five years. If so please explain the circumstances?
- Have you even been arrested or prosecuted for the use of such drugs?

Also, a section of the pre-employment interview (see page 415) should focus on drugs abuse. For sensitive jobs, the pre-employment medical should test for drug abuse. The employment decision matrix (see page 302) may permit the employment of former drug users. However, it should disqualify from employment any current user and any applicant who attempts to mislead.

MAINTENANCE

Employees in sensitive jobs should be required to sign an annual declaration (see pages 327 and 338) to the effect that they have not used narcotic drugs and should be politely questioned on the subject in their annual appraisal. If routine medical examinations are held, they should be extended to check for drugs abuse. For most organizations this level of control may appear extreme, but for banks and financial institutions it is critical.

WHEN ABUSE IS SUSPECTED

Any signs of drug abuse must be taken seriously and acted upon without delay. However, experience shows that when most drug abusers are questioned, they make strong denials and counter-attack, resulting in the problem remaining unresolved. An overt approach merely forces the problem underground and can make matters much worse.

Once suspicions have been aroused, your objectives are:

- to find the facts;
- ask for the subject's explanation;
- based on this, to decide what action should be taken.

Thus you are strongly advised to try to obtain evidence, covertly, that either confirms or rebuts the suspicions, possibly by retaining investigators or advising internal security.

If covert enquiries indicate that the subject is not abusing drugs, you may still wish to interview him about the behaviour that led to suspicions being raised. If evidence is uncovered indicating drug abuse, the subject should be interviewed and ideally brought to the point where he admits his problem and gives details of how and where he obtains supplies and who else is involved. You should also carefully explore the possibilities that his work and honesty has been compromised by his suppliers and, in due course, audit the processes for which he is responsible. It is important, if you can, to get to the deep truth.

The action you take will depend on the circumstances, but if drugs have been used on company premises, you should normally report the matter to the police as failing to do this could leave the organization exposed to criminal prosecution.

If you decide not to dismiss the employee, you are strongly recommended to suspend him until he has completed a course of counselling. But remember, the action you take will have a serious impact on other employees and showing too much sympathy for the admitted drug abuser may simply encourage others.

Elimination interviews

BACKGROUND AND NATURE OF THE PROBLEM

There are occasions when a number of people *could* be responsible for a crime or some other problem: for example, cash may have gone missing from a cash register to which four or five people had access.

OBJECTIVES

There are three main issues involved in elimination interviews:

- identify the guilty party and clear people who are wrongly suspected;
- obtain admissions and other evidence;
- make financial recoveries.

To achieve these objectives, it is essential that the anxiety of the guilty party is increased so that he reveals himself and there are three ways of doing this.

METHOD 1: ELIMINATION CHECKLIST

Background and planning

You should obtain as much information as possible about the problem in question, and about any similar incidents, develop a fraud theory and prepare single-sheet summaries of any 'key points' which can be shown to the subjects at the appropriate time. You should also get as much background as possible on each of the potential suspects along the lines of Appendix 1.

Preparing the checklist

Prepare a checklist on the lines of Table 10.10 below, tailored to the facts of the case concerned.[22]

Reformat the table on to sheets of A4 paper and prepare a clean copy for each interview.

Table 10.10   Potential elimination questions and profiled answers

No.	Nature of question or statement	Indicative reaction	
		Indicative of responsibility Little detail Lack of commitment No volunteered information	Indicative of innocence Detailed Committed Volunteered information
1	2	3	4
1	The opening statement	Anxious Defensive body language Appears threatened	Interested Open body language Relaxed
	Do you know why I have asked to see you?	Will usually prevaricate and say 'no'	Will usually know; he admits there is a problem
	Is there anything you want to ask me?	Unlikely to ask a question or asks one which is irrelevant	Asks a sensible question
2	Did you do it?	Prevarication Not a clear binary answer	A committed 'no'
3	Have you discussed this case with your colleagues?	Prevarication	A committed 'yes' or 'no'
4	Have you had any contact with [names of people already interviewed] since I spoke to them?	Prevarication	A committed 'yes' or 'no'
5	If so, what did they say?	Prevarication Unlikely to give detail	Likely to provide detail
6	Do you think the [actual losses] are deliberate and premeditated theft?	Prevarication or may minimize the seriousness of the case	May ask for clarification or a committed 'yes'

continued

---

[22]   The checklist should jump from topic to topic as shown

No.	Nature of question or statement	Indicative reaction	
		Indicative of responsibility Little detail Lack of commitment No volunteered information	Indicative of innocence Detailed Committed Volunteered information
1	2	3	4
7	Do you think there is any chance in this case that there could be an error?	Possibly	May ask for clarification or a committed 'no'
8	If we don't catch the [thief] do you think it will happen again?	Probably 'no'	Probably 'no idea' or 'yes'
9	List the names of possible suspects and say:' 'It has to be one of you, doesn't it? Who do you think is responsible?'	Unlikely to name anyone	May name someone
10	How would you react if we asked everyone who could have been involved to compensate us for the losses?	May consider	Unlikely to accept
11	Is there anyone you are sure did not do it?	May not name himself	Normally will name himself. 'I know I did not do it'
12	Where were you and what were you doing when this happened?	May produce an alibi too readily	More likely to seek clarification
13	How would you react if I told you a number of people believe you are responsible?	Defend or object	May seek clarification, or become genuinely angry May ask for the names of the people concerned
14	Show the subject the evidence ('key points') [List what it is] Xxx Xxx Xxx xxxx and ask him detailed questions about it	Reactions indicating responsibility (see Chapter 4)	Reactions indicating innocence
15	Do you think the evidence points towards you?	May give an explanation	May seek clarification or become genuinely angry
16	Tell me why you could not have done it?	Possible objections such as 'because I would not be so foolish'	Probably a committed denial

No.	Nature of question or statement	Indicative reaction	
		Indicative of responsibility Little detail Lack of commitment No volunteered information	Indicative of innocence Detailed Committed Volunteered information
1	2	3	4
17	If you had been involved in this, how would you have done it?	May suggest a method May reveal information known only to the guilty person May make a stupid suggestion	Unlikely to consider the possibility
18	In forgery cases, ask the suspect to make 10 or 12 copies of the forged signature in writing	May make a poor attempt to copy the forged signatures	Likely to make a good attempt
19	Would you be prepared to give us access to your bank accounts to check this?	Probably 'yes'	Probably 'no' Possibly angry
20	How would you feel if we subsequently prove that what you have told me is untrue?	Prevarication	Committed response to the effect that you would be wrong
21	I have to tell you I think you did it	Pseudo-denial (see page 88) or objection	Committed denial Genuine anger
22	Would you be prepared to take a polygraph test?	Prevarication Asks for clarification	A committed 'yes' or 'no'
23	Can we do it this afternoon?	Very unlikely and will give a reason for stalling	Probably a firm 'yes' or 'no'
24	If you were responsible for [xxx] would you admit it?	'Yes' or 'what do you expect me to say?'	Probably not. Would depend
25	Why should I believe you?	More likely to make an objection such as 'Because I didn't have the keys'	'Because I am telling the truth'
26	You look really worried about this. Has it been bothering you?	Without considering probably 'no'	Considers and then probably 'yes'
27	Would you like to change your explanation	Pause and may discuss the possibilities or say 'yes'	A firm 'no'
28	Do you have any other information that might help us identify the [thief]?	*This is a purely informational question*	
29	Do you think this interview has been fair?	Probably 'yes'	May be upset

Control interviews

You should interview two or three people, ideally of around the same age and rank as the potential suspects, using the approach set out below. Use their reactions as a baseline for evaluating the responses in the relevant interviews.

INTERVIEWS WITH THE POTENTIAL SUSPECTS

Invitation

Invite each potential suspect to an interview. If possible all of the interviews should be conducted simultaneously but where this is not possible, it is essential that subjects who have not been interviewed are prevented from speaking to those who have.

Don't let the potential suspects compare notes

The opening statement

It is imperative that you do not allow the subject to interrupt at any point, by saying something along the lines: 'Please let me finish. We have to go through a set process which will get to the truth'.

You then make an opening statement.

Example: 'I am Bill Smith from internal audit. I am investigating a very serious case where [confidential company information has been passed to X, a competitor]. This theft could result in our losing a large contract in the Far East, to loss of jobs and other problems for everyone. The company will spare no time or expense in finding the truth and we have investigators working on this throughout the world. The top management of X is also very concerned and is cooperating fully. In fact, my colleagues are working with X as we speak.

We know the information was removed from the office in which you work and we hope to recover the original documentation, which we will have tested for fingerprints. We are also analysing telephone, Internet and computer records, expense statements and bank accounts. I am confident that we will find the person responsible.

There were only ten copies of this confidential report and we have recovered nine of them, so only the one is missing. We believe that the missing copy was taken from the office in which you work. There are only ten people who have access to that office and we are interviewing each of you to try to identify responsibility and to clear those who are not involved.

I am going to ask you some questions and note down your responses in one of two columns on this profile. Do not worry about what I am writing down. What I plan to do is go through the same process with everyone and then analyse the results. I promise you we will find the truth and put this very unfortunate problem behind us.'

You should adapt the opening statement to suit the case concerned and then pull out a clean copy of the checklist and use red (indicative of responsibility) and green (indicative of innocence) highlighter pens to mark the subject's reaction to the opening statement and then ask:

'Is it possible that, by accident or otherwise, you released the copy that is now with X?' (i.e. 'Did you do it?').

Again note down the response and continue with the remainder of the questions, marking the appropriate column in red or green as you proceed. If a response does not fit either column, put a small mark between them.

Watch the subject and monitor his reaction

Innocent people are much more likely to ask about the significance of the checklist and the coloured pens, whereas the guilty party will watch your every move, but is unlikely to say anything. If you are asked, play it low-key along the following lines:

'This is a really brilliant method that enables us to clear people who are innocent. Now let's move on.'

If the subject's reactions indicate that he is innocent (see Chapter 4) you should say so:

'I am pleased to tell you, Bill, that it looks fairly certain that you are not responsible but I will probably have to see you again when we have moved forward with the investigation. Is that OK?'

You should then spend a few additional minutes to see if he has any information that may assist you. Most innocent people usually do.

In most cases, if the fraud theory is correct and the guilty party is among those being interviewed, his responsibility will emerge and you should then raise the pavement possibly through a bridging statement or direct accusation.

The bridging statement

The bridging statement might be along the following lines:

'I have to tell you it appears that you were involved in this. How did it all start?'

Depending on his reaction (for example, failure to deny, lack of commitment or feigned anger) you should move into Phase C and proceed as with any other tough interview (see Chapters 6 and 7).

METHOD 2: THE FREESTYLE STORY

An alternative approach is to ask all potential suspects to a meeting and deliver an opening statement along the lines suggested above. They should then be asked to write down: 'Everything you know about the matter' and each one sent to a private room, where they cannot consult with each other, and allowed as much time as necessary. You should analyse their stories carefully and interview the person whose response is most indicative of guilt.

METHOD 3: THE STRUCTURED CHECKLIST

You should consider designing a form specific to the case concerned, and issuing it to all of the people under suspicion and to three or four people you know are innocent.[23] Again you should deliver an opening statement along the lines of the example on page 404.

The purpose of the form is to:

- increase anxiety in the guilty party;
- identify responses that are indicative of guilt or innocence;
- use the form as a 'key point' in confronting the guilty party.

The form should be laid out carefully, so that it has the maximum visual and emotional impact and should consist of separate pages, each with marginal notes, boxes for official use and colour coding:

- an opening, setting out the background of the case and the purpose of the form.
- a release under the Data Protection Act along the following lines:

DATA PROTECTION ACT

'I understand that the information I provide on this form may be classed as personal data under the Data Protection Act. I agree that this data may be used for the prevention and detection of crime and released to law enforcement and other agencies, to graphologists and forensic laboratories.

- If you do not agree to such a release please tick here .... ❑
- If you have put a tick in the box, please explain your concerns.'

- Questions covering the person's attitude such as:
  - Why did this happen?
  - Did you do it?
  - Do you think it will happen again?
  - If you had to investigate this case, where would you start?
  - Have you discussed this case with your colleagues?
  - If you were to do (the dishonesty suspected) how would you do it?
  - Would you do it by yourself or would you involve others?
  - Do you know anyone who has done this (the problem suspected)?
  - Is there anyone you know who could not have done this?
  - What should happen to people who do (the problem)?
  - Where were you when this (the problem) happened?
- Closing pages:
  - Would you like to change any of the information you have provided?
  - How did you feel when you were completing this form?
  - How do you think the person responsible would feel?
  - What would be your reaction if we found that the answers you have given are incorrect?

---

[23]   A sample form and worked example can be downloaded from www.cobasco.com.

   – If all employees were asked to (repay or take a pay reduction) to cover these losses, how
     would you feel?
   – Would you be prepared to take a lie detector test?
   – Is there anything else you think might be relevant?

At the end of the last page, two horizontal lines should be drawn in the place normally used
for entering a signature and date. However, no explanation should be given.

_____   _____

    Innocent people are more likely to use the lines to enter their signature and date, whereas
the guilty party will leave them blank. Again, the subject whose guilt appears most likely
should be interviewed along the lines of Chapter 7.

    A structured checklist was used in a wire transfer fraud investigation, with interesting
results:

THE WIRE TRANSFER FRAUD

Around $10 million was transferred from a London bank by a fraudulent wire transfer instruction entered into a computer input queue: one or more of twenty employees had to be involved. Each was asked to write his or her explanation on a specially designed form. Although this was not exactly a freestyle document, it was designed to elicit freestyle explanations. One completed form stood out from the rest, because the author:

- Disputed that there was 'evidence' that the case was an inside job and presented a complex (and highly unconvincing, bordering on silly) case for responsibility being outside the bank.
- He responded to many questions with a question.
- He sought clarification of points that were obvious to all of his colleagues.
- He used the phrase 'to be absolutely honest' in reply to two questions.
- He used the phrases 'to the best of my recollection' and 'I don't really remember', when none of his colleagues had memory lapses.
- He used a number of discontinuity phrases (see page 97, Table 4.5) when accounting for his movements on the day

in question.
- Many answers contained an unexplained change from past to present tense (when describing past events).
- He used generalizations ('I usually') and conditional phrases ('I would have gone to lunch') in explaining specific actions on the day, whereas none of his colleagues did the same.
- He consistently avoided using the pronoun 'I'.
- In response to the question 'How do you feel now that you have completed this form?', he responded with the word 'nothing' whereas all of his colleagues expressed a strong positive 'good' or bad 'angry that I am being accused' reaction.
- He admitted discussing the possibilities of fraud with others.
- In responding to the question: 'Should we believe your answers to the questions?' he responded: 'Yes, but you don't think someone would honestly omit [sic] to fraud' and continued: 'I've never done anything to prove I am dishonest'.
- For reasons best known to the bank, they disregarded the clues in this response and a few weeks later the man resigned and went to work in the US.

CONCLUSION

Although, in the cold light of day, the methods suggested may appear superficial, they work in practice and usually the guilty party quickly identifies himself.[24] However, we must always bear in mind that there is an exception to every profile.

Exit and transfer interviews

BACKGROUND

Even the most honest people are reluctant to report their suspicions of malpractice, because they fear that they have the most to lose by doing so and to an extent this is true. On the other hand, once they know they are moving on to a new location or new employer, they are usually prepared to assist and talk freely. Exit interviews are an important source of information.

OBJECTIVES

The control objectives of exit interviews are to:

* obtain information on risks and control weaknesses;
* leave the ex-employee with a better impression of the organization by showing that it is interested in hearing his views;
* keep communication channels open for the future;
* minimize the risk that the ex-employee can raise false allegations in the future.

In addition, exit interviews can provide useful information for management and human resources.

METHOD

Overall

Every substantial organization should have a specified procedure (see page 346) for conducting interviews with employees whose services have been terminated, on retirement, dismissal, resignation through ill health or on transfer to another location. Ideally, the procedure should also apply to long-serving temporary employees and contractors.

The usual background

The employee's personnel file and audit reports for the area in which he has worked should be reviewed and any points relating to control issues noted. The types of fraud that are most likely in the operations concerned (i.e. a 'fraud theory') should be noted down.

The interview

Interviews should be conducted as soon as it is known that an employee is leaving the organization and by someone senior to him, other than his line manager. At least one hour should be allowed for each interview.

The important rules for exit interviews are:

---

[24] See the example at page 407

- they should be non-accusatory;
- they should focus on weaknesses in processes and not on personalities;
- you should not mention anyone's name unless the subject has raised it first;
- you should not make anything but the briefest trigger notes until the end of the interview;
- you should not discuss the reasons for the termination of the employee's services until the closing stages of the interview and then only if it may produce relevant information.

Under no circumstances should you give the impression that the interview is to 'dig the dirt' or cause trouble for anyone. The purpose is to listen to the subject's recommendations for improvement.

The interview should be opened in a unassuming way.

Example: 'We are always sorry when employees leave us and meetings like this are to give us the chance to learn lessons, especially in relation to risks and control and things that may not be going as well as they should. Anything we discuss will be treated in the strictest confidence and I will not make notes unless you agree I can do so. I have held a number of meetings like ours and I believe they have proven very useful for both the organization and the employee concerned. Thanks for meeting me.'

The interview should start off with a number of open questions.

Example:
- What did you like best about working in department x?
- What do you believe are the department's strong points?
- What can we do to improve things for your colleagues?
- Were there other departments in which you would have preferred to work?

These are all non-threatening and the replies will enable you to assess the subject and how cooperative he might be on more sensitive matters. You should then turn to processes:

Example:
- I believe you know a great deal about [the accounts payable] procedures. How effective are they?
- What can we do to improve them?
- Did you discover any problems or weaknesses in the way they operate?
- Do you think we are losing money through poor control?
- Were you ever concerned that things may be going wrong?

These questions give the subject the opportunity to raise specific concerns about processes but, more importantly, his colleagues and third parties. You must treat these very carefully and quietly press for more and more detail.

Depending on the openness of the subject you may move on to elements in your fraud theory, but again doing so in a low-key way.

Example:
- I remember that sometime ago there was a problem with [x]. What was that all about?
- What were the feelings in the department at the time?
- Do you think we got to the bottom of that case?
- Is it still going on?
- What was the worst thing you ever discovered?
- Was it resolved satisfactorily?

Towards the close of the interview you should say something along the lines:
'I would like to make a few notes of what we have discussed. Do you have any objection to this?'

You can then write down the action points and get the subject to agree them and close the interview by thanking him for his time and wishing him good luck in the future. Finally you can ask if he would be agreeable to your calling him if anything else arises in the future and get his mobile telephone number and give him yours.

Follow-up action

It is imperative that any concerns raised by a subject are treated in confidence and checked thoroughly. If it is appropriate, wait for three months and call him, enquiring how he is progressing in his new job and seeking his help on any points that you have been unable to resolve. These follow-up calls have generally produced the most valuable information.

Meetings and negotiations

BACKGROUND

Cynics say that meetings are usually a displacement activity for people who have nothing better to do and that standing committees are the worst of all.

RED TAPE COMMITTEE

At a recent meeting of the Red Tape Committee it was unanimously agreed (with four dissenting votes) that unnecessary meetings cost the UK taxpayers between £1 and £50 billion per annum. The committee thus reported a mean loss of £25 billion.

The intelligence of a committee varies inversely with the number of people on it.
Never underestimate the power of very stupid people in large groups

There are many different types of meetings, some of which are more exposed to deception than others, depending on whether they are internal and involve only employees or external with the participation of third parties, and whether they are:

- *Decision related*[25] when the purpose is to agree on some future action such as whether a new product should be launched or a new procedure put in place.

---

[25]   Including negotiations

- *Informational*, when the main purpose is to advise people on a decision that has already been made, such as announcing the creation of a new department or putting a redundancy programme in place.
- *Task related* to produce a desired detailed output, such as finalizing a legal contract or designing a new brochure.

The possibilities and estimated levels of potential deception, varying from good lies to hot air and outrageous trickery, can be summarized in Table 10.11.

Table 10.11   Types of meetings

Type of meeting *Examples*	Potential for deception			
	Decision related	Informational	Task related	Other
Internal (involving employees)				
Team meetings	High	High	Low	Varies
Annual budget meetings	High	High	Low	Varies
Bid evaluation meetings	High	High	High	Varies
Detailed work on legal agreements	High	High	High	Varies
External (involving third parties)				
Negotiations	High			
Assessment of a vendor's quality control procedures				
Discussion of a customer's warrantee claims				

This section deals with most types of meetings and suggests how you can handle them to minimize the risks of being deceived.

OBJECTIVES

Your objectives, for most meetings, are likely to be:

- to ensure you take decisions based only on the truth;
- to influence the meeting in a way that achieves your objectives;
- to minimize the amount of time you and your subordinates spend on pointless meetings;
- to ensure that an accurate record is kept of all important meetings.

These objectives can be achieved by a slight modification of the cunning plan and will depend on whether you call (and are thus in charge of) a meeting or are merely a participant.

Stay neutral in a conflict so you can win whichever way it goes

METHOD

Background

The steps suggested below are mainly relevant to important meetings where gross trickery or deception is possible. However, they can be adapted to most meetings, including those of the Hush Puppies Appreciation Society.

Determine your objectives

Before any meeting, decide on your objectives and success criteria by asking yourself, 'If I could wave a magic wand, what result would I like to achieve?' Then consider if the meeting is necessary at all or whether the same or better results could be obtained by a telephone call, exchange of memos or by doing nothing. It is usually to your advantage if you can avoid a meeting and play golf instead.

HAVE YOU NOTICED?

When you received the email inviting you to a meeting at your office in Birmingham, you just knew it would be a waste of time. But, being a diligent employee, you cancelled your golf, got up at 5.30 in the morning and returned home at midnight. The day was a total waste of time. You told yourself you would never do the same again, but you will. Why? Because we are all scared of missing something.

If you believe a meeting[26] is going to be a waste of time, it invariably is.
Unless you are convinced a meeting is necessary, don't go

However, if a meeting really appears necessary, list your objectives in the left-hand column of a piece of A4 paper (or a Mind Map) and in the right-hand column show the 'key points' that should swing the meeting in your favour.

Also consider the objectives and success criteria of other potential participants and the approaches they might take. Again, list these on a sheet of A4 paper, showing their 'key points'. You can extend this sheet so that, in effect, it becomes a deception theory.

Sometimes your position may appear weak or even hopeless and if this is the case, you should:

- list all of the key points in your favour and support them with detailed evidence;
- list how you can defeat the opponent's strong points;
- consider how you can divert attention away from your weak position.

---

[26] In both your business and private life

THE CUSTOMS LAWYER

Years ago most of the worst smugglers and purchase tax evaders would consult an elderly, butter would not melt in his mouth, London solicitor. He was a star. When accompanying his clients at interviews with customs lawyers and investigators he would always take a passive role and get them to produce their most dreadful evidence against his clients. From time to time he would make 'tutting noises', look towards his client and shake his head, but say nothing else.

When his turn came he would select the weakest element in the case against his client and build it up into a hanging offence: sometimes haranguing his client along the lines 'This is much worse than I believed. I did not know that you had done this'. In eight-, ten- or twelve-hour meetings he was able to prevent the officials from asking his clients any meaningful questions about the more serious aspects by interrupting and saying, 'No, we must deal with this really important matter first,' and then continue to beat the least relevant issue to death.

The proposed participants

Take great care over the proposed participants in any important meeting and don't just throw out invitations willy-nilly. Think of the participants in three categories, those that:

- are likely to support you (usually around 10 per cent);
- are likely to oppose you (usually around 11 per cent);
- are likely to sit on the fence (usually around 79 per cent).

Your success in meetings and negotiations is likely to depend on having more, or more powerful, people supporting you than opposing you, so plan carefully.

Try to identify the opposing power player – who may dominate the meeting by adopting a critical parent role – and there may be more than one. From the outset you should consider ways in which he or they can be marginalized and the easiest way of doing this is to get someone on your side who is more powerful than him.

Indecision is the key to flexibility

If your research indicates that there are other people, supposedly on the power player's side, that don't really agree with him, consider the ways that you can invite them to the meeting even though their presence may not be justified. On the other hand, if there are people supposedly in your team that might subvert you, try to make sure that they are excluded.

Your chance of success in any meeting varies directly with the number of participants who support your view

Always consider the cost of the meeting. If it involves lawyers, consultants or even investigators who charge an hourly rate, don't agree to their attendance en masse.

Always consider the cost of meetings

If you are calling the meeting, you can list the participants and move forward on that basis. If you are a guest, you might suggest rearranging the meeting for a date when you know the power player is not available or try some other ruse to swing the balance in your favour. If you have no alternative but to attend in a minority position, don't panic, as all is not lost.

Getting the background

If you don't already know it, obtain as much background as possible on the proposed partici-pants, including their career histories and private interests. See Appendix 1. As always, even small details can make the difference and may be used to your advantage.

> *Example*: If you discover that the opposing power player disappears every Thursday afternoon to play golf, and you want a nice brief meeting, you should try to fix it on a Thursday morning.

You should carefully research the rules of formal meetings and understand the procedures, so that you know more about them than the other participants. Then, if you want to create a critical parent role, you can point out some procedural gaffe and throw your opponents off track.

Attention to detail pays dividends.
The harder you work, the luckier you become

Strategy

Fight, flight or appease

Deciding on your strategy is akin to specifying an investigations plan. You should think about this carefully and there are essentially three options which, as always, are based on the animal instincts of fight, flight or appease. Are you going to swing the meeting in you favour by taking a tough attacking position or by playing possum? You must decide.

Decide on your strategy

Be prepared to alter course during the meeting if your approach does not work, but re-member changing from an attacking role to appeasement can be a serious climbdown so, to successfully attack, you must be absolutely sure of your facts and remain committed.

Strong and weak points

If you are in a very strong position, you may decide to go for a knockout blow using a very powerful opening. Alternatively, you may let your opponents make the running and then shoot them down in flames. If you are in a weak position, consider whether you can hijack the meeting with some diversionary tactic.

If you are in a desperate position, consider how you can avoid the meeting altogether, pos-sibly by submitting a brief note setting out your arguments or defences and then disappearing on an important business trip to Bulgaria. This is much better than getting your ass kicked and if you are not present, and the others ignore your memo, you can claim the Nuremberg defence and live to fight another day.

Relax time pressures

Many negotiators[27] impose unrealistic deadlines, for example: 'If this deal is not closed by tomorrow, we will have to go elsewhere'. You should weigh up whether the deadline is valid

---

[27]   and conmen

and pin down the reasons. If the timescale is unrealistic and puts you at a serious disadvantage, you must extend it or pull out.

Never act in panic.
When in doubt, pull out

Set the agenda

Try to make sure that there is a written agenda (ideally only listing the points you want to cover) for every important meeting: even the most obdurate participant will find it difficult to disagree with this, and you should also try to set a time limit. It is often a good idea to expand the agenda and to state specifically what the objectives are and how decisions will be made.

> *Example*: 'The purpose of this meeting, which is scheduled to last for 30 minutes, is to decide whether we are going to open a branch in Cheam. The decision will be taken on a vote of the participants and proxy votes will be (if they are in your favour) or won't be (if they are not in your favour) allowed.'

Also ensure that a chairman is appointed as well as someone who will take the minutes. Ideally you should either be chairman or minute taker and, given the choice, the latter is usually more influential than the former.

He who takes the minutes, has control

If you are not in a position to submit an agenda before the meeting, prepare one anyway and produce it immediately the meeting opens. If an agenda has been provided by someone else, don't just accept it. Read it carefully and think how you can swing it in your favour. Also make sure that the topics to be discussed in 'any other business' are listed in full. This will prevent you being ambushed, which is always a bad scene.

Always pay attention to 'any other business'

Decide on the venue
The location

If you are in a position to decide on the venue, so much the better and again think carefully. If you want to impress outsiders, consider holding the meeting in the presidential suite of the Ritz. If you want to deflate someone who believes he is the most important person in the world, choose the scruffiest room you can find. In dealing with all forms of deception, small points matter, and your objective may be, in the nicest way possible, to marginalize your opponents and make them slightly anxious.

If you have to hold the meeting in your own office, make sure it gives the impression you want it to give. For meetings with third parties (as well as many internal meetings) the big question is whether you go to their premises or they come to yours. The protocol[28] appears to

---

[28] Inherited through evolution

be that the senior participant, or the most important party, is saved the trouble of having to travel. But you should think about this.

The timing

If the opposing power player is an owl, fix the meeting for as early in the morning as possible and in a location where he has to get up early to travel but with no justification for staying overnight. Do the opposite if he is a lark. If you know he is a heavy drinker, fix the meeting in the early morning in a posh hotel that stocks every brand imaginable of his favourite drink. Make sure that one of your supporters, who is not critical to the meeting, takes him for dinner the night before and gives him a heavy alcoholic marinating. Remember, everything is fair in love, war, in business meetings and, of course, *golf.*

> *There is no such thing as a free lunch*

Summarize the history

Make sure you know the facts that are to be discussed in the meeting inside out, backwards and forwards. Most participants don't prepare sufficiently and the rule is 'Who knows, wins'. In complex cases, consider preparing schedules of events, correspondence and detailed chronologies. Think about summarizing key facts[29] on a PowerPoint presentation or fancy handout, but make sure that everything you say is accurate.

> *The person with the better detail is in command*

Pay particular attention to mistakes, errors or omissions previously made by your opponents and make sure you have them summarized on single sheets of paper or in a PowerPoint presentation that you can thrust under their noses at the appropriate time.

> *Having to admit to a mistake may destroy a person's credibility.*
> *Being shown to have lied is fatal*

Watch for dirty tricks

You should remain on the lookout for dirty tricks played by the opposition, including:

- bugging hotel bed rooms and rooms used for pre-meetings by your side;
- glamorous blondes sat next to you on the aircraft while travelling to or from the meeting or in the bar, restaurant or bingo hall;
- briefcases, pens, coats etc. containing tape recorders left behind by the opposition when your side remains in the meeting room during adjournments;
- collection of waste paper from bed and conference rooms (including partly used notepads which will contain ESDA sensitive impressions);
- theft of personal computers;
- arranging social trips for the participants' wives so that they can be pumped for information.

---

[29]   Especially those in your favour

Fortunately, most opponents don't stoop to such tactics, but some do: so don't let your guard drop.

Preparing the meeting room

You should always be the first to arrive at the venue and, if possible, enter the meeting room before anyone else and generally check it out.

THE SAUSAGE CASE

A post-acquisition meeting was planned with a father and son who had sold their sausage making business to a British company at around four times its real value, mainly because assets had been grossly inflated. The listed company's team arrived early in the room and heard shuffling noises, which appeared to be coming from a void in the gabled roof of the office. They looked around and found a microphone hidden in an exotic plant connected to a cable going under the carpet and then into a cupboard and up into the roof void.

A vigorous pull on this cable resulted in a scream from the roof void, then a loud crash and the words 'Oh shit!' Further investigation revealed a young man who had concealed himself in the roof void, wearing earphones connected the cable. When this sad creature was interviewed he admitted that the father and son had intended to start the meeting, then adjourn it, leaving the listed company's team alone to discuss their position. They then planned to react based on this inside information.

If you have called the meeting, consider setting out place names, putting the opposing power player to your right and as far away as possible from his supporters. If you cannot do this, get your team in their seats before the opposition arrives and try to marginalize them. If you know the power player is deaf in his left ear, sit him to the right of everyone else and preferably near a noisy window.

If you plan to use PowerPoint, video conferencing or any other equipment, check it out because if you are unable to operate it, you look a plonker and are thus put in the role of a child: this is not good news.

The meeting

Basic principles

If you have planned effectively the meeting will be a cinch but you must:

- deal quickly and politely with anything you think is untrue;
- never let anyone conceal the truth but raise the pavement by requiring them to falsify details.

You should also carefully monitor the transactional dynamics of the participants and change your role accordingly. Also remember that the opening and last 20 per cent of a meeting are the most critical.

Openings and closings are critical

Demand equivalent concessions

If you are involved in a hardball meeting or negotiation, you should only make a concession when an equivalent benefit is obtained.

> *Example*:
> - 'We are prepared to reduce the price by 2 per cent, but need payment in advance.'
> - 'I accept that we should open a new office in Cheam, but [think of something you would like[30]].'

In some instances the psychological gains from insisting on a reciprocal concession will far outweigh the financial benefits. However, in financial negotiations, you should make sure that the concessions you make are in the smallest possible increments.

> *Example*: A builder quotes you £30,000 for erecting an indoor driving range at your home. You think this is expensive and should be no more than £20,000. Thus you start by offering him £12,000 and concede that you will pay him a 50 per cent deposit. He is not prepared to accept, so your first increment is to £12,100 and his to £27,000. If you are advancing in increments of £100 and he is reducing by £3000, you should come out a winner.

In negotiations, the party that concedes the smallest increments usually wins

Watch for legitimization

Negotiators frequently use legitimization statements (see page 98) to justify their position, by claiming, for example, that they can only work from a standard price list, that company policy does not permit discounting or that the terms of a contract are non variable. Legitimization also pops up in other meetings with statements such as: 'We cannot do that because of the Data Protection Act or human rights legislation.' If these go against your objectives, you must question them and press for more and more detail. In most cases you will discover that the person concerned is unsure of his facts and that his legitimizations can be dismissed. This also seriously reduces his credibility for the remainder of the meeting.

Raise the pavement

Many people are unclear where the line is drawn between trade puffing and criminal deception but the fact is that a criminal offence is committed if anyone tells lies to obtain a pecuniary advantage and this includes retaining his job.

If you believe that someone is trying to deceive you over an important matter, you should consider raising the pavement with a statement along the following lines:

---

[30]   e.g. a new Calloway driver

Example: 'Can we stop there a moment, Bill, because I want you to be absolutely sure of your facts. You realize that if what you have just said is untrue and we rely on it, you could be in very serious trouble [long pause]. If, on reflection, you are not sure and may have made a genuine mistake, then we can start over again and no damage has been done.' [Note the rationalization statement.]

The chances are if his statement was untrue, Bill will soften and you can move on from there. If he continues with what you believe is a significant lie you should consider delivering the ultimate statement along the lines:

'So if we find out that what you have said is untrue, the only explanation is that you have told a barefaced lie that may amount to fraud. Am I correct in this?'

If the reply is a binary 'yes' without any unnecessary words before or after it, you can assume you are being told the truth. Any deviation from this and you must remain on your guard.

A single exchange along the above lines is likely to keep people far more honest for the remainder of the meeting, but it will raise the temperature, so be careful.

Closing the meeting

The way you close any meeting is important and you should summarize the key points and any proposed actions: make sure that everyone present agrees or that their dissenting view is recorded.

Follow-up action

Accurate and timely minutes should be prepared and circulated after every important meeting and you must check them carefully. If you do not agree with anything, suggest amendments and if these cannot be agreed immediately, prepare a dissenting report, submit it to all of the participants and put it on the agenda for future meetings. If minutes have not been taken, make sure you preserve your notes; they may be very important one day.

Never agree to minutes that are not totally accurate

Pre-employment screening interviews

BACKGROUND

Interviews with candidates are a critical part of the pre-employment screening process (see Chapter 10, pages 316–323) and yet in most cases they are ineffective, with 95 per cent of the time taken by the interviewer and 5 per cent by the candidate trying to get a word in. The fact is that the vast majority of unsuitable applicants can be eliminated by effective pre-employment screening interviews and without any need to waste time and money on external verifications or even reference checking.

OBJECTIVES

The objectives of pre-employment screening interviews are to:

- confirm key facts presented by the candidate and on which his suitability will be determined;
- test his honesty and good faith by a mixture of control and relevant questions.

To achieve these objectives, a section of the first and any subsequent interviews should be set aside for screening purposes.

METHOD

Preparatory work

Interviews should be conducted against the wider policy and procedural issues discussed in Chapter 9 and particularly:

- a decision matrix of factors which would debar employment;
- a brainstorming review of a detailed application form and any prepared biography;
- examination of corroborative data such as original educational certificates.

You should review these documents carefully and prepare a list of discrepancies or aspects that require clarification. Pay special attention to subjective truths, omissions, inconsistencies and to entries that may be difficult to verify externally. For example, a period of work for a company that has gone out of business or a gap year when the applicant says he was studying anthropology in Benedorm. Highlight and use coloured Post-it tabs to annotate the application form to remind you of these points.[31]

The opening

You should explain the purpose of the interview with a comprehensive opening statement and monitor the subject's reaction closely.

> *Example*: 'I would like us to spend the next twenty minutes on making sure we have accurate information about you and that nothing important has been overlooked. Some of the areas we will cover involve personal data and the data protection laws. We keep all personal data confidential and handle it securely.
>
> Do you have any objection to our discussing and recording personal data?
>
> I believe X is a very special company and we care very much about our employees, customers, shareholders and suppliers and intend to maintain the very highest standards. If you join us, we are sure that you will agree with our philosophy and with our objectives.
>
> Because we intend to maintain the highest standards, we must have absolute honesty in all of our dealings. There can be no nasty secrets between members of our team and no surprises.
>
> We recognize that sometimes people do things that they later regret and that we all make mistakes. The fact that you might have done something in the past that you now feel ashamed of does not mean that you will not be able to join us. However, if a candidate is deliberately dishonest over the information provided to us on an application form or during

---

[31]   The anxiety of the dishonest candidate may be increased when he sees these

interviews such as this, his or her application will be rejected. If employment has commenced before we find out, he or she will be subject to instant dismissal.

We carry out detailed checks before we finalize job offers. These include access to a large number of public records, databases and checks with past employers and colleagues, bank references and so on. In some cases, we ask shortlisted candidates to produce a certificate from the Criminal Records Bureau proving that they have not been convicted of a serious offence. If someone has been convicted of even a serious offence and can show that he has reformed, we will still consider him for employment with us. But again if important facts like this are deliberately hidden, there will be no future with us.

For obvious reasons, we do not employ people who are addicted to narcotic drugs or who have [other items from the decision matrix].'

A candidate's reaction to such a statement – especially his body language – will often give you a good idea whether he is hiding something nasty.

Basic questions

Your questions should focus on two aspects. The first is to obtain corroboration that what the candidate has put in writing is true. The second is to test his honesty generally and his good faith.

During the early part of the interview you should adopt the transactional role of a nurturing parent and must not take notes. You should observe the candidate carefully and determine his baseline communications code and particularly his hand and body movements. *Do not refer to the application form or biography* but work from your checklist, using open questions and jump from topic to topic.[32] For example:

- When you were at the Sussex College of Technology, where did you stay?
- What dates did you attend?
- What school did you go to before that?
- Who was your closest friend at the college?
- What makes you angry?
- Were you in the cricket team at Sussex?
- What is the most successful thing you have ever done?
- What is the thing you are least proud of?[33]
- Have you ever been subject to disciplinary action?

Expand each question looking for consistent, volunteered detail and commitment. A dishonest candidate is likely to become irritated over questions he has already answered on the application form, possibly untruthfully, and is more likely to use referral statements such as 'I am not sure, but I put it all down on the application form and it is in the biography I sent you.' If this happens, you should respond along the lines: 'I know that, but I want to go over it again with you.'

---

[32]   Working from an application form imposes a sequence and a template for deception
[33]   If he says his pencil-thin moustache, you know you have a problem

Verifying the application form and biography

At the end of a period of open questions, you should pull out the application form and any other written material submitted by the candidate. You should concentrate on the statements and answers you have highlighted, asking both open and closed questions, pressing for the finest detail. The dishonest candidate is likely to be preoccupied with the papers you refer to and what you write down and when, whereas honest people are usually less concerned.

If you detect any discrepancies you must point them out.

Example: 'In your biography you stated that you worked as credit control director at XYZ but on the application form you said you were credit control manager. What exactly was your title?' You should continue asking detailed questions on this discrepancy until you are satisfied.

Again, pay close attention to the candidate's reactions and depending on his response you may raise the pavement a little higher.

Example: 'I understand. So, saying you were a director was over-egging the cake a bit, wasn't it? [Pause] Are there any other areas on the form where there is just a little too much egg? I understand how these thing happen, but we need to know.'

If you get any signs that the candidate has been less than truthful you must concentrate on important statements that will be difficult to verify. For example, he may have claimed to have worked for ABC (which has gone out of business) to cover a period when he was unemployed or in jail.[34]

Example:
- Who was your manager at ABC?
- Have you kept in touch with any of your colleagues?
- Do you have contact numbers for them?
- We may have difficulty checking with ABC, as I believe it is no longer in business. How do you suggest we confirm this period of your employment?

Again you should assess his reaction and if you have any doubts, ask for more detail. It is critical that you do not permit a dishonest applicant to succeed through concealment lies.

Examination of corroborative data

You should carefully examine any corroborative data that the applicant has available (Table 10.12).

The originals should be examined for signs of alteration or falsification and copies should be retained.

---

[34] As has happened on many occasions

Table 10.12   Sources of corroborative data

Item to be examined	Areas to check and questions
Passport *Produced at the interview or, in jurisdictions where this is not allowed, upon commencement of employment*	Name, place and date of birth Citizenship Names of spouse and children Physical description
Birth certificate	Name, place and date of birth Names and addresses of father and mother Maiden name
Marriage certificate	Names, place and date of birth Name of spouse and any previous names Addresses
Driving licence	Name, place and date of birth Addresses Endorsements and convictions
Educational and other certificates	Name Schools attended and dates Qualifications obtained
Utility bill	Address
Payslips	Name of employer Job or reference number Salary Tax paid and tax code

Closing questions

You should thank the candidate for his cooperation and say something along the lines: 'For insurance and other purposes, I have to ask all candidates:

- Have you ever been convicted of a criminal offence?
- Have you ever used narcotic drugs such as cocaine, heroin, crack etc. *(If the candidate volunteers in response to this question that he has taken drugs other than cocaine or heroin, put a big tick in his approval box.)*
- Have you ever used cannabis or ecstasy or any other narcotic drug? *(If he replied 'no' to the previous question and 'yes' to this, you know he is not being entirely honest.)*
- Do you or your immediate family members have any private interest that could conflict with your work for us? *(The honest applicant will usually ask what sort of interests you are talking about.)*
- Is there anything you have told us that you would like to correct or qualify?'

Finally, if you believe the candidate has told lies, you may consider asking:

- 'What would your reaction be if we find that some of the information you have provided is not accurate?'

The honest applicant's response is most likely to be totally committed, maybe suggesting that you are wrong. He may also become genuinely angry. Liars are much more likely to prevaricate and suggest that they have made a mistake.

Honest people will blame you: liars will blame themselves

However, it is a high-risk question that you would only use when you had already, more or less, come to the conclusion that the candidate is not being honest.

FOLLOW-UP

You should prepare a brief note of every interview, but bear in mind that it may have to be made available to the candidate under the subject access rights of the Data Protection Act so don't put down that: 'He is a lying toad'.[35] Review your findings and opinions against the decision matrix and note whether you believe the facts presented by him are truthful or not and what external verification would be necessary to complete the clearance, if the candidate is to be added to a final shortlist.

If you know the candidate has been untruthful on a significant point, you should not employ him.

A candidate who lies to you cannot be trusted

Witnesses

BACKGROUND AND OBJECTIVES

A 'witness' is any person who is able to provide information, possibly intelligence or evidence relating to a matter of concern such as:

- a person who saw a car accident;
- an accountant who can explain how the sales invoicing system operates;
- an interviewer who can say what a suspect admitted to him;
- a doctor who can explain the reasons why someone died.

There are three main problems with witnesses. The first is that a person may not wish to become involved, for reasons ranging from apathy to fear, and in the corporate fraud area, because he has been bribed or pressurized. The second problem is that some people genuinely cannot remember what happened and when they think they can, get it wrong. The third problem is that in high-profile cases, including frauds, witnesses come forward with false or malicious evidence to get their moment of glory or payment.

This section is concerned with getting reliable evidence from willing and unwilling witnesses in complex fraud cases and obtaining a written account of their evidence. This may be in the form of a Proof of Evidence, affidavit, statement or CJA statement (see page 438) and is required by lawyers to assess the strength of their case, pre-trial, and to know what the witness is expected to say during it.

---

[35]   As has happened

COGNITIVE INTERVIEWING

In olden days, statements would be taken by police officers, lawyers, investigators or even accountants, based on simple question and answer interviews, which often contaminated the witness's memory or failed to produce accurate detail. The witness evidence in the assassination of President Kennedy illustrates the weaknesses.

Witness evidence is vital

Nowadays, more sophisticated methods are available, the most popular being 'cognitive interviewing'[36] (CI) which was invented in the US by Geiselman and Fisher.[37] CI is a little like NLP to the extent that the phrase is often bandied around but seldom defined: 'cognitive', much like 'initiative', 'issue' and 'fury', is a vogue word. The best explanation of what practitioners mean by CI is paraphrased from a paper by Brian R Clifford and Amina Memon[38] as follows.

WHAT IS CI?

The 'cognitive' components of CI draw upon two theoretical principles. First, that a memory retrieval cue is effective to the extent that there is an overlap between it and the information encoded in memory (see page 52), and that reinstatement of the original encoding context increases recall. Secondly, the multiple trace theory suggests that there are many ways in which memory can be cued and that if one cue fails, another may succeed.

For our own purposes we can define CI as: 'A structured, holistic process, based on an understanding of the brain's operation, in which a person's memory is stimulated by a combination of retrieval cues.'

There is no question that CI assists recall:

- for eye witnesses who can be compelled to assist;[39]
- who are not themselves under threat or maliciously motivated;
- in simple, single event cases.

Improvements in memory recall of between 35 and 46 per cent have been claimed,[40] and some academics suggest that CI is almost as effective as hypnosis. However, the basis on which measurements have been made are, at best, subjective and, more likely, suspect. Also, recent research[41] indicates that CI results in higher error rates, especially among young children and mentally handicapped witnesses, as a result of a process[42] in which pure memory is contami-

---

[36] Cognitive is defined as 'knowing, perceiving or conceiving as an act or faculty distinct from emotion or volition... a notion, intuition, perception.'
[37] See Geiselman, R. Edward and Fisher, Ronald P., 1985, *Interviewing Victims and Witnesses of Crime*, National Institute of Justice, Washington, USA
[38] Analysing Witness Testimony, Blackstone Press ISBN 1 85431 731 8
[39] e.g. police cases
[40] These figures are virtually impossible to verify
[41] Higham and Roberts 1996
[42] Usually called 'reminiscence' or 'reiteration'

nated by what the witness, or someone else, has said before. So even in the applications for which it is recommended, CI has its limitations and is not a panacea.

Neither are conventional CI tools particularly relevant in serious fraud cases because, among other things:

- complex, multiple incidents are usually involved over extended periods of time in different locations;
- eye witness evidence is likely to be a small part of a much bigger picture (for example, the primary evidence in fraud cases is usually documentary, technical or verbal);
- even if he is not a participant, the witness may have personal reasons for not telling the truth (for example, he may want to hide his own poor performance).

The method proposed below advances CI into the fraud world to deal with witnesses who find it difficult to impart the truth because:

- of poor memory: as in conventional CI cases;
- of the complexity of the case;
- they are defending or improving their own positions;
- they are emotionally involved or fearful of the suspects or have been bribed by them;
- they are not required to provide assistance and, on the contrary, may have a legal obligation of confidentiality to the suspects.

Since these days everything must have a title and an acronym, the process described below is called 'cognitive interviewing for fraud' (CIFF) and its objectives are to get accurate evidence from witnesses in the business world.

> *CI is about enhancing recall.*
> *CIFF recognizes other recall problems besides memory failure*

THE CIFF METHOD

Overview

CIFF can be viewed in a number of stages. As always, the most important are getting the background and effective planning.

> *Inexperienced interviewers are too casual with witness interviews*

Doing the background

The fraud theory and investigation plan (see pages 138–140) will usually result in the identification of people who are not themselves under suspicion, but who might be added to a list of potential witnesses in the categories shown in Table 10.13.

Table 10.13 Willing and other witnesses

Category A Probably cooperative witnesses	Category B Witnesses requiring persuasion
Position An employee of the victim organization or an associated enterprise (such as its bank) An expert witness	Position A third party such as a customer or vendor, who is under no obligation to assist
Nature of case Relating to a minor matter, such as an accident injury	Nature of case Relating to a serious matter, such as a serious fraud
Type of evidence Has formal evidence, such as explaining a process or producing records, supported by written or computer records	Type of evidence Has sensitive or emotionally laden evidence against the suspect, such as what he did or said. Usually such evidence is not supported by formal, written records
Personal interests Has nothing to hide	Personal interests Wishes to hide poor performance or a personal ambition Possibly malicious Emotionally or financially involved with the suspects
Relationships Has no relationship with (or often personal knowledge of) the suspect	Relationships Is known to the suspect
Nature of suspects Suspects are ordinary business people, citizens or employees	Nature of suspects Suspects are violent criminals

You should obtain as much background information as possible on all potential witnesses (see Appendix 1) and think about the evidence they might be able to give on the 'worst case', bearing in mind the factors in Table 10.10 at page 401. You should also fully understand the case and its 'key points', having summaries and exhibits available to show to the witness at the appropriate time. If the witness has made previous statements on the matter, or other witnesses have, you should analyse these in a way that makes it easy to highlight the essential facts and discrepancies.

If you believe, for any of the reasons set out in Table 10.13, that the witness might be unwilling to assist, you should plan and rehearse persuasive arguments for delivery in the interview. The persuasion may be along the lines shown in Table 10.14.

Table 10.14   Potential persuasive arguments

Category B Witnesses requiring persuasion	Possible persuasive arguments You should make it clear that:
Position of the witness	
A third party such as a customer or vendor, who is under no obligation to assist, may refuse to do so	Persuasion Failure to assist may result in the termination of all business relationships You will invoke the audit clause in contracts You will have no option but refer the case to the police A witness summons may be issued that will compel the witness to attend court Civil action will be started which will require the production of records
Nature of the case	
Relating to a serious matter, such as a serious fraud	The witness will not be alone but will be supported by other witnesses, documentary and technical evidence. You must make it clear that the witness will be one of many
Type of evidence Has sensitive or emotionally laden evidence against the suspect, such as what he did or said. Usually such evidence is not supported by formal, written records	
Personal interests of the witness	
Wishes to hide poor performance or a personal ambition	Rationalization: The reasons for any genuine mistakes and poor performance are understood and are not a problem providing they are openly admitted. Subject to legal advice and management approval you may give the witness immunity in relation to genuine mistakes
Emotionally or financially involved or has been compromised by the suspect	This is a very difficult situation and you must decide whether to treat the subject as a witness or suspect. Unless you have specific legal and management authority you must not give any witness immunity for his dishonesty[43]
Is known to the suspect	Persuasion A witness summons may be issued, compelling him to attend
Payment of a reward	

---

[43]   If you do so, it is likely to prejudice a fidelity insurance claim and lead to problems in court

The witness demands payment for giving his assistance	Again a dangerous area. Payment should only be made with specific legal and management approval. Also remember if the case goes to court, payments have to be disclosed to the opposing parties. This fact often exposes the witness to attack and reduces the credibility of his evidence
The witness demands immunity from prosecution	Unless you have specific legal and management authority you must not give any witness immunity for his dishonesty. If the case goes to court, the complete story has to be disclosed to the opposing party
Nature of the suspects	
Suspects are violent criminals The potential witness has been threatened or pressurized, but does not appear to have acted dishonestly	Conduct the interview informally, promising the witness anonymity and total confidentiality and that his evidence will not be used overtly. Ultimately, cases of organized or violent crime should be reported to the police

Sometimes it may not be clear whether the person should be treated as a witness or a suspect. For example, you may have specific concerns or even an intuition that he is less than innocent. In such cases, you should interview him as a suspect using the techniques described in Chapters 6 and 7.

Unless you are absolutely sure that the witness is innocent, interview him as a suspect

You should consider the timing, sequence and location of interviews very carefully and unless you are absolutely sure[44] that a witness will not alert the suspect he should not be seen until after the first step (see page 168).

Principles
General
All witness interviews should be conducted in private and should normally be non-confrontational, based on all of the rapport-building techniques described on pages 9 and 132–133 and an adult-to-adult transactional relationship. Important or complex interviews should be covertly tape-recorded. You must be careful not to reveal sensitive information, nor make derogatory comments about anyone, including the suspects. You should have all of the documents and other evidence you plan to discuss with the witness assembled in the way in which you plan to produce them as key points (see page 162).

Keep it at an unemotional level, but very professional

---

[44]   Unless such an alert is part of the investigation plan to panic the suspects into action

In complex cases, the chances are that you will not be able to complete the interview and draft Proof of Evidence in one session. This does not matter, providing you:

- complete the freestyle version in one continuous session;
- get all documentary evidence from third party witnesses as soon as possible;
- make sure that any draft statements you prepare in the absence of the witness are subsequently agreed by him, line by line.

Thus you may arrange the detailed reporting phase, external stimulation sessions etc. on separate days and start completing and updating a draft Proof of Evidence after each one, rather than leaving it until the end.

Monitoring and remaining aware

In every interview you should keep all of your senses switched on and monitor the subject's responses. However, in the early phases, you should not challenge anything that he says. Let the subject tell his story in a truly freestyle way and ideally do not take notes, other than simple bullet points[45] and Mind Maps. Actively listen to every word he says and evaluate his non-verbal communications.

Stay alert

The opening and freestyle story

As always, you should carefully plan and deliver an opening statement including:

- who you are;
- what you do;
- the reason for the interview and possible duration (always allow sufficient time);
- the structure of the interview;
- establish common objectives;
- emphasize confidentiality and security.

For example, in a simple case, with a witness you have evaluated as willing (Category A in Table 10.13 on page 427), the opening might be as follows.

Example: 'I am Bill Jones from internal audit and I appreciate your seeing me. As you know, we are investigating a case of suspected fraud in accounts payable. I understand that you handle maintenance of the vendor master file and have worked for the company for the past five years. I would like your help in understanding how the system operates and any problems you have had. Our meeting, which is in total confidence, will take around an hour. In cases like this it is vital that we find the truth, so that we can all get on with our lives. So can you please tell me everything you know about x?'

---

[45]   And only then when the witness has paused

Chances are the subject will ask for clarification and you should keep this to a minimum, so that you get a pure version.

> *Example*: 'I don't know, Sam, you are the expert. Just go over it in any way you want. How it works, what you have seen going wrong, anything about the current case. Just let it all hang out.'

The witness's freestyle story is likely to contain the following elements:

- background or context applying to the story as a whole;
- clarification including his reasons for doing things, excuses and assumptions;
- emotions, including the way he felt throughout the time period concerned or in individual scenes;
- scene, topic or event detail.

In each of these aspects, the witness's recall is likely to be less than perfect, sometimes for reasons other than pure memory degradation. Try to identify the reasons why a witness is being less than open: is it a memory problem or something else?

A CASE IN QUESTION

More than two million pounds were electronically transferred from the accounts payable system of a British company. Investigations, some five months later, indicated that standard settlement instructions hade been amended and false vendor files created. All of the documentation had been destroyed and there was absolutely no audit trail. However, investigations suggested that a temporary employee, called Robin Blind, appeared to be behind the scam. The problem was that his name and biographical details were false. Undercover investigation and intercepted communications established that employees working in accounts payable and in the wire transfer room were innocent and were totally devastated that they had reacted to instructions from Mr Blind without checking.

Let the witness complete a freestyle story uninterrupted

Detailed reporting: CI tools and techniques

When the freestyle approach has been exhausted, move into the next phase and provide the subject with as many memory retrieval cues as you can. In an interview with an employee in the Robin Blind case, cues might be introduced as follows.

Explain the process to the witness.

> *Example*: 'We are going to try some memory retrieval techniques to see if we can dig more deeply. Some may seem a bit strange, but don't worry. I guarantee some of them will work and you may be surprised just how much detail we find.'

Then try the techniques in Table 10.15.

Table 10.15   Memory retrieval cues

Memory retrieval cues *Objective*	Example of your prompt
Context re-instatement *Replicate the scene and circumstances when the witness encoded his memory*	Go back to the very start of that day and speak it out loud as though it were happening now in the present tense. 'Robin Blind is walking into my office … I am speaking on the telephone…'
Visualization *Picture the scene* *Draw diagrams* *Get the witness to access his visual memory stores by getting his eyes to focus upwards*	Try to picture the scene. You were in your office. Let's do a Mind Map of all the things that were there when Robin walked in … Did he touch anything? What was odd about him? How would you imagine his wife and family? What sort of things do you think he likes doing? What would his house look like? I am going to play your role. I am sitting at the desk and you are Robin. Now go on
Change perspective *Get a different view*	Just imagine you were Robin. What would you have noticed most in your office? What would your secretary have seen?
Reverse or random sequence *Break the chronological sequence*	Let's reverse things. Start from the moment Robin walked out of your office and let's go backwards
Humour (of the gallows variety) *Cue the humour memory stores*	Imagine Robin at a fancy dress ball. What would he be dressed as? Complete the sentence, Robin has had a bad day because …
Peripheral cues *Trigger memory on dates, weather etc.*	Can you remember what was in the national papers that day?
Emotions, feelings and thoughts *Cue the witness's emotional memory stores by looking downwards*	How did you feel when Robin asked you to sign the form? What did you think was going on? What did Robin smell like?
Non-happenings	What did Robin not do that he should have done? Why didn't he ask you to go to his office?
Parallels	What did the incident most remind of you of? Have you ever seen anything like this before? Who did he sound like? Did he have squeaky shoes?

Holistic	Looking back, what are your most important thoughts on the case? On Robin?
Opinions and theories	Why do you think this happened? What exactly do you think happened? Do you think anyone else would have seen Robin?
Scene visit	Not appropriate in the Robin Blind case, but consider taking the witness to the scene
Names	Was it a long or short name? Did it begin with A, B, C etc.? What did it sound like? What would be your best guess? Why do you think that guess is not correct?
Repeated event	If Robin were to walk into your office tomorrow, what would you do differently? Why didn't that happen at the time?

In practice, most of the cues will produce no result and expect that the witness may think you have lost the plot: don't worry, because some additional detail will emerge, often in areas neither you nor the witness expected.

CONTINUING WITH ROBIN

Q: What date did Robin come to see you?
A: I am not sure.
Q: Was it this year or last?
A: Last.
Q: Winter or summer?
A: I can't remember.
Q: Did he come to your office?
A: Yes.
Q: Can you picture the scene?
A: More or less.
Q: Were you with anyone when he came in?
A: No, I was on the telephone.
Q: Can you remember who you were speaking to?
A: No, but I remember I was really pissed off and was shouting: it may have been my mother-in-law. [Laughs]
Q: Did Robin sit down while you finished your conversation?
A: No, he walked over to the window and stood there looking out: actually I thought he was looking over my shoulder.
Q: Was it day or night?
A: It was daylight.
Q: Sunny or overcast?
A: No, very sunny.
Q: So do you think it was summer?
A: Yes, because after he left [Pause], I walked into the park and fed the birds. It was the day before my wife's birthday.
Q: Which is when?
A: 4th June.
Q So would your meeting with Robin have been on 3rd June?
A Yes.

The witness's response to your prompting will tell you a great deal about him and his motivation. Usually people who don't want to recall, don't even think about the cues, whereas genuine people do.

If the witness makes no effort to think about cues, he may have other reasons not to remember

However, even if you conclude that the witness is being less than honest, do not challenge him at this stage, but press on.

External stimulation

You should next produce exhibits, schedules and key points and ask for the witness's comments on them, using open and closed questions. Identify any discrepancies and seek clarification, again using memory retrieval clues.

Press for detail.
Note discrepancies and the subject's reaction

Records retrieval and anything else?

Principles and formal records

It is vital that you obtain copies of relevant documents and any other evidence in a witness's possession. For example, in a corruption case, you might want copies of the vendor's cash book, cancelled cheques etc. showing payments to a corrupt employee. If the witness refuses to produce these, you have a number of options based on your powers of persuasion.

Always consider obtaining personal and informal records such as:

- expense statements;
- image copies of the witness's computer;
- diaries;
- telephone call logs (including mobile telephone records).

ROBIN BLIND

In this case, telephone call records confirmed the date of the meeting on 3 June at 11.34am, when the witness terminated a call to his mistress (just who can you trust?). More importantly, analysis of all telephone logs around that time showed a call from an internal conference room to a number which subsequently proved to be Robin Blind's home in the Channel Islands. He was traced through this and arrested.

Effective investigation is all about detail

In due course, you should analyse all records and make sure nothing has been missed and that they are consistent with the fraud theory.

The little black book (almost like the white van)

Innocent people on the edge of frauds often keep 'little black books' or private notes to protect their backsides if things go wrong. You should always ask about these.

Example: 'I have been involved in lots of cases like this and usually innocent people keep little notes, or bits of correspondence as insurance. What did you keep?'

THE PA TO THE SALES DIRECTOR

A terrifying woman who was the PA to the sales director who had just been fired for fraud was asked: 'Jennifer, you are a very clever and prudent person and will have kept personal notes. Can we see these in confidence?' She subsequently produced diaries for the past five years that proved her boss's dishonesty beyond doubt.

Try to get the little black book: someone will always have one

Interim summary

When all detail has been exhausted, you should prepare a summary of the witness's story. In a simple case, an annotated Mind Map or bullet point list may be sufficient. In more complex cases, you should consider drafting an outline Proof of Evidence or file note. Either way, you should have a list of:

- the people involved;
- the actions that took place;
- the objects involved;
- the conversations that occurred;
- other detail;
- emotions, thoughts and feelings.

You should then move on to the next stage.

Detail on critical factors

You should again use memory retrieval cues to obtain detail on people, objects, actions and conversations etc. that form part of the witnesses' stories. You should cross-reference this detail with other evidence and resolve discrepancies.

ROBIN BLIND

Various witnesses gave detailed descriptions of Robin Blind as shown in Table 10.16.

Table 10.16   Descriptions chart

Factor	Description given by witnesses			
	Witness 1	Witness 2	Witness 3	Witness 4
Age	30 to 35	30 ish	Over 40	38 to 47
Height	5.7	5.9	5.10	5.975
Weight	150 lbs	180 lbs	180	189
Hair	Brown/black	Brown	Brown	Tawny
Glasses	Rimless	No	No frames	YSL Type 52
Reminds you of	Robin Day	Robin Day	No one	Plato
Sounds like				
etc.				

Charts of this type help you to build up a picture of each of the important characters and objects in the witnesses' evidence. Someone, like Witness 4 in the above table, always seems to appear to have more precise information than others or provides significantly different recollections. Do not dismiss this: in every fraud theory, you are completing a jigsaw puzzle and if a piece does not fit, don't bash it into position. There is always an explanation and by identifying it, you could open up critical new lines of enquiry.[46]

Deviations always open up new lines of enquiry

You should continue with the same process on objects, actions etc. In most cases it is critical that you compile a detailed chronology of events that should be cross-referenced and annotated in tables summarizing the recollections of different witnesses (see Table 10.16 above).

Challenging discrepancies and deception

You should not challenge discrepancies or suspected deception until you have covered everything that could be relevant and obtained and reviewed all documentary and other evidence. Then, your approach will depend on the circumstances and may range from low-key questions seeking clarification to direct confrontations on deception.

If your initial appraisal of the subject was wrong, you may decide to treat him as a suspect and to interview him along the lines of Chapters 6 and 7. The critical point is that you try to resolve all discrepancies, so that the final Proof of Evidence is as accurate as it can be.

---

[46]   In this case, witness 4 was a plonker!

Homework

Finally, at the close of the interview or at overnight breaks in multiple interviews, you should thank the witness for his help (assuming he has given some) and neurolinguistically programme him to get his subconscious monkey working overnight.

> *Example:* 'I am sure that when you get into bed tonight, your mind will race over the things we have missed. I know your wife will think you are barmy, but keep a pen and pad alongside your bed and when you wake up thinking about this, as you will, jot down anything that comes to mind. It always happens. I will do the same, so let's talk and compare notes at around 8.30 tomorrow. Is that OK?'

Getting a witness to think overnight pays dividends

STATEMENTS AND PROOFS OF EVIDENCE

The principles

A *Proof of Evidence* is a written account of what a witness can say in court and which may contain hearsay and other details not directly related to the facts in issue. The Proof of Evidence may support your case or destroy it. Either way, if it is relevant to the matters in issue, it must be fully documented.

Do not close your mind to anything.
Don't reinforce prejudices

Although in both criminal and civil proceedings in the United Kingdom, formal statements usually have to be disclosed to the opposing side, this is not always true of Proofs of Evidence, providing they are prefaced as follows:

STRICTLY CONFIDENTIAL

'This Proof of Evidence has been prepared for the legal advisers of X Ltd for information and in contemplation of legal proceedings relating to the matters referred to in it.'

This caveat should establish the privileged nature of the document. It is therefore much safer for inexperienced investigators to obtain Proofs of Evidence, rather than formal signed statements. However, the decision on whether or not anything has to be disclosed to the other side must be made by an experienced lawyer, so you must make sure that everything is drawn to his attention.

Failure to disclose is a mortal sin that can destroy even the best case

Preparing the final draft

You may draft the proof or statement in the presence of, and with the cooperation of the witness, although in larger cases this is seldom possible and you will have to prepare a number of drafts as you progress. The critical point is that the final version is not closed until every point and every discrepancy that could be relevant has been resolved. Documents and other exhibits referred to in the Proof of Evidence should be accurately cross-referenced and attached.[47] Normally, lawyers will use the Proof of Evidence for preparing a formal statement or affidavit and will also decide what has to be disclosed to the opposing party.

Always keep your legal advisers fully informed.
Avoid surprises in court

Refusal to sign a proof

If a witness refuses to sign a Proof of Evidence, you should read the draft to him – word for word – and then ask him to check it himself. He should be asked if it is correct and, if not, any corrections or additions should be made and initialled even though he may refuse to sign the statement as a whole.

Criminal Justice Act statements

When criminal proceedings are contemplated in the UK, witnesses may be asked to sign a *CJA statement*, bearing an endorsement under the Criminal Justice Act (CJA: see www.cobasco.com).

> 'This statement consisting of … pages, each signed by me, is true to the best of my knowledge and belief, and I make it knowing that if it is tendered in evidence, I shall be liable to prosecution if I have wilfully stated in it anything which I know to be false or do not believe to be true.'

Statements of this type are sometimes invaluable because they can be introduced directly into evidence without the need for the witness to attend, but they should only be taken by experienced investigators and then under legal advice. They are particularly useful if you believe a witness may be lying. The statement can be drafted and the pavement raised by pointing out the seriousness of the perjury provisions. This has caused a dramatic change of direction by some deceptive witnesses.[48]

UPDATING DOCUMENTATION

In complex cases, it is vital that you keep the fraud theory, chronology, investigations plan etc. up to date and that files are maintained and kept securely.

ADVISING AND PREPARING THE WITNESS

Normally, lawyers will decide which witnesses will be called, but this can be a traumatic time for those who have helped you. You and your lawyers should make sure the witness is still prepared to give evidence and you should explain the process to him. You should again check the accuracy of his statement or Proof of Evidence with him and if there have been any

---

[47] Usually in indexed binders
[48] But you must keep the original draft and disclose it to your legal advisers

changes in the facts or in recollection, these should be recorded and drawn to the attention of your lawyers: preferably in writing.

There is no reason why you cannot accompany the witness to and from court. This has a two-way benefit. First, to make sure he does not lose his nerve and buzz off to the Canary Islands to avoid giving evidence. Second, he will appreciate your support.

Finally, when it is all over, it does no harm to drop a line of thanks to the witness for his help and, if the case has been stressful for his family, to buy his wife a nice bunch of flowers which you can describe on your expense statement as a 'rail fare'.[49]

TAKING STATEMENTS FROM EXPERT WITNESSES

Normally witnesses can only testify to facts from their first-hand knowledge and cannot give hearsay evidence, nor can they express an opinion. The one exception to this rule arises in the case of *expert witnesses* who have a recognized expertize in a particular subject and who are allowed to express *an opinion* and advise the court generally. For example, a medical doctor may give an opinion as to the cause of death; an accountant can express an opinion about the reasons for a company's failure or the efficiency of its controls.

Before being called to give evidence, the expert witness must satisfy the trial judge that he is qualified by learning and experience to give an opinion within his field. Any statement taken from him should set out his qualifications in full and his past experience as an expert witness. It is absolutely vital that the background of an expert witness is checked out thoroughly and that any padding of his qualifications or experience is removed. It can be catastrophic if an expert witness is discredited in court: this sometimes happens.

Statements by expert witnesses will usually be taken under the guidance of lawyers, although the task of interviewing and obtaining a draft Proof of Evidence might be delegated to an investigator, auditor or manager.

Expert testimony is intended to inform and be helpful, and not simply to impress the court with the skill of the witness, nor to bamboozle the jury. The quality of expert testimony can be measured by its simplicity.

The objectives of simplicity and clarity can be achieved as follows:

- He should be given copies of anything that could be relevant in forming his opinion and especially anything that is unfavourable to your case.
- The expert should understand the case concerned and exactly what is required of him. Each question should be framed *in writing* and should deal with a single matter upon which an opinion is required.
- The conclusions that the expert is expected to reach should not be suggested to him. He must be free to make up his own mind.
- The expert should be given a realistic amount of time to study the facts and to form an opinion.
- The expert should provide an initial report, addressed to the company's lawyers, which should be read carefully and all ambiguities resolved.
- Technicalities, acronyms and abbreviations should be avoided.
- If the subject is complex, charts, diagrams, a glossary or working models should be used to assist in the understanding of his testimony.

---

[49] Just kidding to make sure you are still awake

- The draft Proof of Evidence should be submitted by the company's lawyers to two or three laymen who are not familiar with the case. They should be questioned on their understanding, and the Proof of Evidence revised if necessary.

The procedures outlined above should result in clear-cut and simple evidence, and not, as often happens, in technical gobbledegook which confuses the judge, jury and even other expert witnesses.

Conclusions

The cunning plan is already flexible but you should adapt it to suit your personality and style. However you do it, getting to the deep truth is 95 per cent preparation and 5 per cent execution. You will find that the harder you work, the luckier you will become, especially at GOLF.

4 *In Court*

'I KNOW THE PARROT HAS CLAIMED THE FIFTH AMENDMENT, BUT I HAVE TO WARN YOU, CAPTAIN BLYTHE, THAT WHAT YOUR MONKEYS SAY MAY BE USED AGAINST YOU'

11 *Giving Evidence*

*A person who laughs in the face of adversity
has not understood the problem*

Background

The day will come when you, your colleagues or, heaven forbid, your lawyers[1] are called into court to give evidence. Although this is a terrorizing prospect, your ordeal can be made easier if you heed the following warnings. They are deliberately written in a very personal way, because at the time you will need to refer to them, the issues will indeed be very personal.

Giving evidence is a very personal experience: much like torture

Giving evidence is a great example of the saying 'What goes round, comes round' and you just have to accept it is your turn in the barrel. If you have done your job professionally and fairly, the pain about to be inflicted on you will be unpleasant but tolerable. If you have been un-professional or unfair, this is the time when your ass is going to get severely kicked and it serves you right. We trust you will not be in this position, so your anxiety should be tolerable.

Everything is easier to get into than to get out of

Prepare carefully

CHECK YOUR PAPERS

Always prepare for court carefully. Know your statement, Proof of Evidence or affidavit, back-wards, forwards and inside out and the exhibits to which they refer. Double check all sched-ules, calculations and conclusions you have made in your statement or which you might be required to comment on during your evidence. If you believe that a source of your information should be protected, or if you have some other problem, speak to the lawyer representing your side. You must also make sure that you have told him about every piece of evidence, intelli-gence or rumour so that he can decide what has to be disclosed to the other side. If something has not been disclosed that should have been, he will blame you. Remember, lawyers are very clever and never responsible for any failure.

Check your notes, and other records you may be allowed to refer to in the witness box to refresh your memory; make sure you can read and understand them.

---

[1]   They usually just hate being in the witness box

MAKING NOTES AT THE TIME

An investigator was asked in cross-examination: 'You have said that you wrote your notes at the time; that they were contemporaneous. Is that correct?' 'Yes,' replied the witness. 'And was the interview conducted at normal conversational speed?' Counsel asked and the witness agreed that this was the case.

'They are very neat and tidy, Mr Jones, aren't they?' 'Yes', replied the witness and then added a fatal piece of humour: 'Unlike lawyers and doctors, I have been trained to write nicely.' 'Very good, Mr Jones. I am now going to dictate a passage to you at normal conversational speed and I would like you to write down notes of everything I say.'

Within two minutes the witness was a blubbering wreck, because he could not keep pace with the dictation. The case was thrown out.

Also anticipate that your notes will be taken from you while you are in the witness box and scrutinized by opposing counsel and possibly a forensic document examiner acting on his behalf. This makes it imperative that they do not contain embarrassing things such as details of your Swiss bank accounts, notes about your neighbour's niece or golfing results.

Experience is something you don't get until after you need it

GET IT IN YOUR DIARY

Make sure you have multiple reminders– in your diary, filofax, PDA and on the back of the fridge door – of the date and time you are required to attend court. If you forget to appear and instead buzz off to play golf with your pals, you will be in very serious trouble.

THINK ABOUT THE QUESTIONS

Develop a fraud theory in reverse and think, if you were the defendant, how your evidence might be attacked. Consider the questions you might be asked and discuss them with your colleagues and, if he is willing, with your lawyer. If you have weak points or have made mistakes, be prepared to admit them and apologize if necessary. It is much better to make an open and contrite admission than to have the truth painfully dragged out of you in cross-examination.

Plan ahead

CHECK OUT THE COURT

Familiarize yourself with the court, how to get there and how long the journey takes even when you have to stop every ten minutes for anxious lavatorial breaks. If you have not given evidence before, sit in on another trial[2] for a couple of hours before your big day. Watch and get the hang of things. It is pretty awesome; lawyers are clever and very smart.

---

[2] You will not be allowed to sit in on the trial in which you are a witness until after you have given evidence

On the day

APPEARANCE

On the day you are required to give evidence, arrive at court really early and make sure you dress sensibly. Your wife may tell you that you look wonderful in your yellow waistcoat, pink suspenders, Gucci sunglasses and Hush Puppies, but it is doubtful that the court will appreciate their sartorial elegance. Wear loose clothing and comfortable shoes, just in case you have to make a run for it. Also wear clothing that – unlike Tony Blair's – does not show how profusely you are sweating. Like fierce hunting dogs, lawyers smell fear and, if they see signs of your terror, it will just make matters worse.

If you wear dentures, a glass eye or a hairpiece, make sure they are firmly affixed. It will not be good for your credibility if in the heat of the moment an appendage becomes detached and the judge and jury (but, obviously, not the barristers) have to chase around trying to find it.

Beware of your emblems

If you are a member of the Surbiton Train Spotters' Club, however proud you might be of this rare distinction, don't wear the lapel badge, tie or cap. This is not impressive. All you will achieve is to mark yourself out as a plonker and thus damage your credibility before you even open your mouth. If you must have facial hair, make sure you do not look like a member of the Taliban and your court appearance may be the excuse you need to shave off your pencil-thin moustache. You always knew it made you look like a ballroom dancing teacher.

WAITING TO BE CALLED

You can guarantee you will be kept waiting outside the court, possibly for hours if not days. Don't worry about this, it is all part of the softening up process. Do not read sensitive papers in public areas and be careful with your mobile telephone and laptop computer. Do not engage strangers in idle conversation because the delightful blonde sat next to you in the waiting room, who tells you she finds fat, old, grey-haired men an aphrodisiac, could be a plant by the opposing side to get you into a compromising position. Believe it or not, this sometimes happens and what you tell her may be used against you when you are impaled in the witness box.

Don't speak to anyone: pretend you are an accountant

In fact, do not discuss your evidence or the case with anyone else waiting around the court and especially with a witness who has not completed his evidence and been released. A little paranoia does no one any harm, and waiting about makes matters worse. This is the time to read *this book* or have a nap: the two things are closely related as a neurolinguistic programming feedback loop.

While you are waiting, you will see barristers, solicitors, and even ordinary humans walking around, clutching papers and always looking either very happy or very anxious. It will help you if you try to picture the very impressive, robed and wigged figures as they would appear in real life: on the golf course or in the bath. This bit of NLP will help you set the right transactional relationship when you get into court. Although lawyers are very clever, they do have human tendencies, so don't be misled by their emblems which are a historical relic meant to increase your anxiety – as is the layout of the court. If you did not believe how important venue and emblems are in increasing anxiety, you are about to find out. Courts are nasty places, full of nasty people: much worse even than the lodge.

ENTERING THE COURT WITH PANACHE

Do not go into the court until your name is called. When this happens your legs will crumple and the past will flash before your eyes, so much so that you may wish you had heeded your mother's advice and, like your uncle Alf, become a butcher: but it's too late.

Make sure you pick up all of your belongings[3] – TURN OFF YOUR MOBILE TELEPHONE – and walk into court nice and slowly; don't panic. Take your time and grab some deep breaths. Wait to be spoken to and don't start off with a cheery 'Good morning, judge. I like your wig' or with some flippant remark to the defendant like 'Guilty bastard'. Neither will go down well. Also, if you are a Freemason, don't be tempted to give the secret gesticulations to members of the jury, the judge or anyone else. This will not be appreciated, especially if you outrank them. Stand still and wait until you are spoken to and take a few deep breaths, without overt panting or gasping.

A closed mouth gathers no foot[4]

GIVING YOUR EVIDENCE IN CHIEF

You will be asked to take the oath or to make some other form of esoteric incantation, depending on your beliefs. Do this very carefully and remember that first impressions count; so that within seconds the judge, jury and counsel will have unconsciously categorized your emblems and formed an opinion of you. If you get off to a bad start or anyone senses any weakness, your ass will get kicked: that's a promise.

You will be asked your name and there is not much you can do about this, but it does have an effect on the way you are perceived, especially by the jury, which is made up of ordinary folk from Cheam and Islington. If your name is Peregrin Anstruther Tarquin Jocelyn Maltravers-Blythe, you might want to abbreviate it a bit. On the other hand, if your name is Richard Head, you should avoid shortening your first name, even though your wife says she likes it a lot. If you served in the armed forces and reached a commissioned rank, don't say you are 'Major Jones' or 'Field Brigadier Nonkins'. Similarly, don't append your educational qualifications to the end of your name, such as 'Dick Head, BA, MA, PhD'. Unquestionably, you and your mum are proud of your achievements, but most people won't give a damn, but will mark you down as a plonker.

In court, you must appear ordinary

In normal circumstances you will be led through your evidence by counsel representing your side, but don't be thrown if as soon as you enter the witness box, opposing counsel jumps up and makes an objection. This is usually because the defendant's case is hopeless and his only hope is to argue some esoteric legal point. The judge may ask the jury to leave while the

---

[3]   Especially your spectacles, hearing aid and hairpiece
[4]   Based on 'A rolling stone gathers no moss'

fine legal point is being considered. Don't worry and just stand there, look around the court, and answer any questions you are asked. This is the time for you to watch the lawyers closely and you will discover that many are more nervous than you. If fact the only person who is really cool is the judge.

If all goes well and under normal circumstances, you will then be asked questions by counsel representing your side. This is called your 'evidence in chief'. Your counsel should be friendly, or superficially so, and he may smile from time to time, nod his head and give you positive non-verbal feedback. Don't relax, because if things go wrong, he will drop you like a hot potato. Remember, lawyers are very clever, intelligent and smart and that you are a guest in their world. If a scapegoat has to be found, lawyers close ranks and turn on you or some other poor bugger who is not a lawyer. It does not matter who he is, how old, or how innocent; his only qualification is that he is not a member of the legal profession.

A good turn never goes unpunished

Direct all of your answers to the judge and try to establish eye contact with him and members of the jury from time to time, but don't glare or wink. Keep your answers simple. Most honest witnesses genuinely want to assist the court and thus volunteer things they think could be helpful. Don't do this, just answer the questions you have been asked, preferably with a binary 'yes' or 'no'. Remember, lawyers don't necessarily want to hear the truth but just want their questions answered.

If – at any point – you are not certain of a fact, ask the judge if you can refresh your memory from your notes. Under no circumstances should you guess or try to crack a joke. Humour, especially, will backfire on you, although you must always laugh at the judge's humour.

Counsel for the other side may continue to jump up and down and make objections to your evidence. This is a good sign, unless he has a gerbil in his underpants in which case it means nothing. When you have finished your evidence in chief, wait in the witness box and whatever you do, don't look smug because the ambush is just around the corner. Never forget that lawyers are clever and the older they are the more clever they become.

The bodies of lawyers deteriorate much faster than their brains

CROSS-EXAMINATION

The big problem comes with cross-examination by opposing counsel and, if there are a lot of defendants, each one will have a personal monster who will attack you. It is one of life's great truths that opposing lawyers always appear bigger, better, cleverer and more determined than yours, but don't worry. They are all very smart: you are fodder for their cannons – they are the hunters and you the huntee. Just accept this and adopt the transactional role of an adaptive child and you may just survive.

Opposing counsel will ask you lots of dreadful questions, try to trip you up, and make you appear an incompetent idiot or much worse. Remember this is his job and he will be doing his best. Just remain calm and don't take it personally and remember when you get home your dog will still love you. Tell the truth and if you have made a mistake admit it and, if necessary, apologize. Lawyers are not used to apologies and your candour will impress them if only for the microseconds before they kick your ass.

Don't argue the case or matters of law – you are not an advocate; appear impartial and concede points genuinely in favour of the defendant whom, deep down, you know is a loathsome lowlife who pulls the legs off spiders and picks his nose. Just stick to the facts, remain emotionally detached and *never look* at the defendant because, if you do, he will have a face like thunder and this could unbalance you.

Occasionally, counsel will make mistakes and if this happens don't laugh because if you do, he will get you later. Lawyers are very clever and have long memories.

THE HEARTBEAT

An unusually uppity lawyer was cross-examining a coroner about a man's death:

Lawyer: So, Mr Jones, you signed the death certificate without taking his pulse or temperature?
Coroner: Yes.
Lawyer: Did you listen for a heartbeat?
Coroner: No.

Lawyer: So when you signed the death certificate you did none of the things your professional training would require you to do, did you?
Coroner: Well, let me put it this way. The man's brain was sitting in a jar on my desk, but for all I know, he could have been out there somewhere practising law.

When opposing counsel sits down, you remain standing. Don't move.

RE-EXAMINATION

Next you may be re-examined by counsel for your side. You can tell how badly you have been dented in the cross-examination by the number of questions he asks and the way he avoids eye contact. If there are a lot of questions, you can assume you have not been impressive. Don't worry: that's life, and lawyers are very brainy.

Finally, you may be asked questions by the judge. These are really important and take care as judges are cleverer than anyone else and they have unlimited power to kick ass. Simply tell the truth.

BREAKS IN THE CASE

You can almost guarantee that you will not complete your evidence in one session and will have to worry through a lunch, overnight or some other adjournment. George Carman QC – perhaps the leading advocate and cross-examiner of his generation – used to love this, if not contrive it. He used to say, 'It will give the witness time to worry' and he was right.

Don't speak to anyone during breaks in your evidence. Politely ignore and avoid eye contact with members of the jury and the defendant if you happen to bump into them in the pub, bingo hall or lodge. Just get out of their space as quickly as you can and pretend you haven't seen them.

During longer breaks – however tempting it might appear at the time – don't console yourself by a prolonged session in the pub. Keep off the juice overnight and arrive at court the next day nice, fresh and preferably celibate. Tell your spouse you have a migraine and get a good night's sleep; if that's at all possible. If you just cannot doze off, start reading this book and that will do the trick, because NLP feedback loops are wonderful things.

LEAVING THE WITNESS BOX

Don't try to leave the witness box until the judge says you can. He may or may not thank you, depending on how well you have performed. Pick up your stuff, glance confidently towards the jury and walk slowly away, taking care not to fall over or faint. If it is possible, sit down at the back of the court and wait until the next adjournment. Most witnesses leave the court after completing their evidence and this is a big mistake because in the animal kingdom – which is where you are – this is interpreted as desertion of territory and a cowardly flight response. So stand your ground and look occasionally towards the jury, but again avoid eye contact and Masonic signs.

THE DEFENDANT AND DEFENCE EVIDENCE

At the close of the prosecution case, evidence will be called for the defence, including witnesses, experts, other defendants and even the malodorous villain himself may be brazen enough to take the stand. Last time you saw him he was six foot nine tall, with muscles like Popeye, a dark Benidorm tan, pencil-thin moustache and oozing with jewellery and fancy feet. In court he will present himself as a fragile old gentleman, about to pop his clogs and in whose mouth butter would not melt, so don't be taken by surprise. This is life.

If you have the time, sit in court while defence evidence is being given, but don't glare at the witnesses even though they may be telling dreadful lies and poking holes in your brilliant case. From time to time you can nod your head in disagreement, put your hand over your mouth, or affect a sickly smirk, but don't overdo the acting. Just sit back and wait, because your counsel will be able to cross-examine them and this is where the fun should start. If you discover that any of the witnesses are telling lies, try to get a message to your counsel, but don't keep bobbing up and down like a gerbil on minor points. Chances are, in any case, he will ignore you. Lawyers, like waiters, are trained to be deaf and blind when it suits their purpose: they are very clever.

THE SUMMING-UP

Eventually, at the close of the defence case and submissions, the judge will sum up the evidence and this will reveal just how clever he really is. You may have thought he was an old codger who was asleep for most of the time, but now you will discover he has a mind as sharp as a razor and the recall of an elephant. Keep your eye on the jury during the summing-up but again don't nod, wink or make Masonic signs. Just watch and try to look really confident.

It always seems to be the case, whichever side you support, that the judge's summing-up is against you. Don't worry because it is much like watching the England football team on television to the extent that the action is always worse than the result.

THE DELIBERATIONS

When the judge has finished, he will send the members of the jury out to consider the evidence and the court will adjourn to wait for the result. This is a bad time for everyone, so just relax. Many jurors, who have boring lives in Cheam or Islington, will see their noble calling as a chance to stay overnight in a fancy hotel, all expenses paid while they 'deliberate'. This is especially likely if one or more of the members has sexual aspirations towards one or more of his or her colleagues because it is a great excuse for a serious amount of rogering, at the state's expense. Don't worry about this: it is life.

After what will appear a lifetime's wait, the court will reconvene and the jury will amble in. It's strange, but jury members always look sheepish and have their heads down, especially if they have had boozy nights 'deliberating' in a luxury hotel. When the verdict is announced, grip your seat really hard and don't leap in the air and shout, but just accept it and remember this is justice.

If subsequently you happen to bump into a member of the jury, don't ask him anything about the case or the nights in the expensive hotel. Just acknowledge him and walk away because what happened in the jury room is secret: what happened in the hotel is even more of a secret, so don't even think about it.

After the event

Chances are, at the end of it all, you will leave court feeling drained and with acutely hurt feelings because unfair allegations have been made against you. Even when you know you have carried out your tasks honestly, professionally and to the best of your ability you will still get pulped. Exceptionally, especially if you have been discontented with your own work or the result of the case, you might get commended by the judge. Don't wallow in false pride because commendations are but temporary intervals in a life of having your ass kicked.

Because of such systemic pulping, witnesses and others involved in investigations might wonder whether the whole episode, and especially the torment in court, was worthwhile. The answer is overwhelmingly affirmative, because someone has to take a stand against fraud. Besides that, if there were no witnesses, there would be no lawyers and where would we be then?

Witnesses are to lawyers what plankton is to whales

As ordinary folk we are in the firing line and if any human wants an easy life he should become a lawyer or politician or, if they are clever enough, a judge: now that is a really good job. True, the pay is not great but the perks, like unrestricted ability to kick ass, having your jokes laughed at, and unlimited free tea and cream scones with strawberry jam, more than compensate.

Finally, remember that courts are the lawyers' hunting ground and that witnesses are their next meal. Lawyers always win, whatever the outcome. But every dog has its day and that's why this chapter has been a little bit rude to them.

'PLEASE MAKE UP YOUR MIND, YOUR HONOUR. DO YOU WANT
THE TRUTH, THE WHOLE TRUTH OR NOTHING BUT THE TRUTH?
REMEMBER I AM AN ACCOUNTANT'

1 *Suspects Checklist*

Stage	Page	Action	OK
Investigation planning	152	**MAINTAIN ABSOLUTE CONFIDENTIALITY** Do not tell anyone who does not need to know Protect the rights of honest people wrongly under suspicion Assume that everything you do and do not do will be scrutinized by a court Do nothing that might compromise your position Take no action unless it conforms with your objectives and is part of the investigations plan Remember that most investigations are compromised within 2 hours of discovery Plan to catch the suspects by surprise as part of the FIRST STEP (see below)	
		Assume the suspicions are true and probably worse than you currently know. This is the safe course	
	150	**Determine the objectives of the investigation** To get money back To expose and punish the offenders To clear innocent people Other	
	152	**Obtain the necessary authority to act (if you do not already have it)**	
Legal framework	146	**Understand the legal framework** Criminal proceedings: and whether or not a caution has to be administered Civil law: and possible channels of discovery of documents Human rights Investigatory powers Proportionality Interception of communications Other investigative methods and resources Internal disciplinary procedures	

Stage	Page	Action	OK
Case analysis	147 149	**Understand the weight of evidence necessary to achieve your objectives** Criminal prosecution: beyond reasonable doubt Civil action: balance of probabilities *Ex parte* orders: arguable case	
External reporting	154	**Decide whether you will advise the police, when and by whom** If criminal prosecution is an objective, advise the police as soon as possible Agree the objectives and methods of investigation	
	154	**Decide on when you will advise regulatory agencies and by whom** Remember you may be under an obligation to advise regulators without delay Failure to report promptly may result in penalties	
	154	**Decide on when and how you will advise your external auditors, but do not employ them to conduct the investigation (simply because this may result in a conflict of interest)**	
	154	**Decide on whether you will advise your fidelity insurers and when** You do not have to advise insurers of mere suspicions Advising insurers too soon may compromise the investigation	
Fraud theory	138	**Develop a fraud theory and write down the *precise mechanics* of the worst case** Identify who may be involved List the evidence you have Consider other potential methods of fraud List the evidence that should be available and how you can obtain it List details of potential witnesses Consider what plausible excuses the suspects may offer and how these can be disproved by blocking actions or some other method *Keep this theory under review as the investigation moves forward*	
		Start to compile an EXCEL or Case Map (see www.casemap.com) chronology of events, showing every action relating to the case. Keep this updated as the investigation continues	

Stage	Page	Action	OK
Investigations plan	140	**Write down an investigations plan for all of the suspects: obtaining critical evidence** How can critical evidence be obtained? Prepare lists showing how evidence you don't currently have can be obtained If you can do so without alerting the suspects, secure vital internal records such as telephone logs and expenses statements Consider having important evidence forensically examined Personal computers Electronic address books etc **Resources and management** What resources are necessary? Who will direct the investigation? (This should be a senior line manager not responsible for the operations concerned. Investigators, lawyers and managers involved in the operations concerned should not control the investigation) Consider retaining external advisers, but qualify them carefully	
		Actions to improve your chances of success Consider monitoring the suspect's internal telephone (but make sure it is legal and 'proportionate' to do so) Analyse telephone call records Consider searching the suspect's work area, desks and files Under legal advice, consider setting traps to catch the suspects in the act	
		Planning the first step Decide when you will take the FIRST STEP that will catch the criminals by surprise Determine the order in which suspects and witnesses will be interviewed Identify other actions that must take place as part of the FIRST STEP	
Legal advice		Obtain top-level legal advice on the investigations plan This is especially important in large-scale investigations	
Background		Fully **research the background** of each potential suspect and witness Work, personal and other history Maiden names of his wife and married names of daughters Covertly inspect his home: look for cash improvements Check company registration records	
		Obtain evidence of **minor breaches** by suspects and witnesses Expense claims frauds Misuse of discretion Other Arrange this so that it can be presented in interviews	

Stage	Page	Action	OK
Interview planning	151	Determine whether a confession is important If the evidence is already conclusive, you may decide to conduct a low-key formal interview, simply to give the suspect the opportunity to explain	
		Decide when, where and by whom each interview will be conducted Assign suitably qualified investigators to each interview Assign and brief interpreters	
	162	Consider how the evidence will be presented in each interview Summarize evidence in easily understood schedules Translate all important exhibits Decide whether to display the evidence or hold it back until the suspect has given a false explanation Consider enlarging important documents for display Consider preparing bulky evidential files or labelling filing cabinets Arrange the evidence professionally in the order in which it will be presented in interviews Select the best pieces of evidence you have (the 'key points') and enhance their impact Enclose in exhibit bags Enlarge Enclose in bulky files Summarize on schedules	
	167	Consider how and when the suspects will be invited to attend interviews: Give the minimum advance warning Try to catch them in a dishonest act Do not deter them from attending	
Arrange the interview room	160	Prepare the interview room(s) Lay out the room carefully Ask a colleague to give you his first impressions of the room Make sure the room is clear of distractions and audio interference Check and replay recording equipment	
Record of the interview	161	Decide how and by whom a record of the interview will be maintained Is covert tape-recording allowed? Don't make detailed notes at the time	

Stage	Page	Action	OK
Detailed interview planning	191	Decide on your opening approach Introductory statement Blocking questions Direct confrontation Probing approach	
	191	Write down and rehearse your introductory statement and decide how you will progress depending on the suspect's reaction	
	191	Determine how many topics you will cover and in what order Base these around the 'key points' Make sure you have documentary or visual evidence of each one Produce these in conjunction with questions	
	191	Determine the questions you will ask and statements you will make to increase the suspect's anxiety to the point where he loses his confidence to continue with deception. Pay particular attention to visually reinforcing important questions with the production of exhibits	
	191	Decide how you will phrase soft and direct accusations	
	191	Decide how and where you might use enticement questions	
	191	Decide how you will phrase rationalization statements	
	191	Decide how you will deal with negotiating questions	
	191	Decide how you will handle the pivotal point and the first admissions	
	191	Decide how you will close the interview	
Rehearsal		Rehearse the interview with interpreters and corroborating witnesses Brief the interpreter on the tactics Brief the corroborating witness to remain silent Also carry out a rehearsal with you taking the role of the suspect Refine your approach	

Stage	Page	Action	OK
Interview		Conduct the interview according to the plan If the suspect continues to lie, force him into detail and indefensible positions	
		Close the interview Agree future meetings and action	
		Agree the record of the interview with the suspect Oral summary Copy of tape recording Joint notes Admissions repeated before an independent witness Statement	
Follow-up		Update the fraud theory and investigations plan	

2 *Evaluation Matrix*

Attribute List other attributes you think important	Weight 100 = High 0 = Low	Option 1 Jones & Co		Option 2 Plan Inc		Option 3 BYK Inc		Option 4 Panel and Co	
		Score	Total Col 5*Col4	Score	Total Col 7* Col4	Option 3 BYK Inc	Total Col 9* Col 4	Score	Total Col 11*Col 4
1	4	5	6	7	8	9	10	11	12
PRE-QUALIFICATION and ABSOLUTE REQUIREMENTS (This is a "Yes" or "No" decision)									
Financial capacity to handle the project	Need	Yes		Yes		Yes		Yes	
Licensed and qualified in the country concerned	Need	Yes		Yes		Yes		No	
Registered for tax purposes	Need	Yes		Yes		Yes		Yes	
Financial stability	Need	Yes		Yes		Yes		Yes	
Membership of professional associations	Need	Yes		Yes		Yes		Yes	
OTHER NEEDS (Scored on the basis of 100 for fully satisfies the need to 0 for total failure)									
WANTS: These are desirable attributes. Each one can be allocated a 'Weight' to show its relative importance								**NOT QUALIFIED**	
Reputation in the trade	100	90	9,000	50	5,000	100	10,000		
References from clients	100	90	9,000	80	8,000	70	7,000		
Technical competence	100	100	10,000	80	8,000	60	6,000		
Clearly defined and enforced ethical values	80	50	4,000	70	5,600	60	4,800		
Quality of management	100	70	7,000	50	5,000	60	6,000		
Health and safety record	100	80	8,000	100	10,000	80	8,000		
Environmental record	100	80	8,000	100	10,000	90	9,000		
Acceptance of bonds and guarantees	60	100	6,000	50	3,000	90	5,400		
Supply chain integration	60	70	4,200	70	4,200	100	6,000		
Price	80	100	8,000	90	7,200	80	6,400		
Through Life Cost	90	100	9,000	90	8,100	70	6,300		
Record of on time delivery	100	80	8,000	100	10,000	100	10,000		
Good record of avoiding litigation	100	50	5,000	40	4,000	50	5,000		
Successful track record on similar projects	80	75	6,000	100	8,000	100	8,000		
Successful relationship with the client	50	80	4,000	50	2,500	100	5,000		
Willingness to accept standard contract terms	50	80	4,000	30	1,500	80	4,000		
Willingness to provide rights of audit through open books	100	100	10,000	50	5,000	90	9,000		
Good public relations record	100	100	10,000	80	8,000	80	8,000		
Nominated subcontractors	100	60	6,000	60	6,000	80	8,000		
Good record with subcontractors	100	60	6,000	70	7,000	90	9,000		
Transparent process for appointing subcontractors	100	60	6,000	60	6,000	90	9,000		
Compatible contract with subcontractors	80	60	4,800	50	4,000	60	4,800		
Willingness to provide rights of audit to subcontractors' books	80	100	8,000	100	8,000	60	4,800		
Fair system of selecting subcontractors	100	50	5,000	40	4,000	70	7,000		
Quality of ideas and innovation	70	50	3,500	100	7,000	80	5,600		
Flexibility	70	70	4,900	100	7,000	80	5,600		
Total			173,400		162,100		177,700		
							Highest score = Preferred vendor		

Scores should be entered in the values 100 = Fully achieves requirements to 0 = Does not meet requirements

Total is calculated by multiplying Weight by Score

Index

If you have found this book useful you may be interested in other titles from Gower

Corporate Fraud 3ed
Michael J. Comer
0 566 07810 4

Investigating Corporate Fraud
Michael J. Comer
0 566 08531 3

Statistical Sampling and Risk Analysis in Auditing
Peter Jones
0 566 08080 X

Managing Communications in a Crisis
Peter Ruff and Khalid Aziz
0 566 08294 2

**How to Keep Operating in a Crisis:
Managing a Business in a Major Catastrophe**
James Callan
0 566 08523 2

Data Protection for the HR Manager
Mandy Webster
0 566 08596 8

**For further information on these and all our titles visit our website
– www.gowerpub.com
All online orders receive a discount**

GOWER

Join our email newsletter

Gower is widely recognized as one of the world's leading publishers on management and business practice. Its programmes range from 1000-page handbooks through practical manuals to popular paperbacks. These cover all the main functions of management: human resource development, sales and marketing, project management, finance, etc. Gower also produces training videos and activities manuals on a wide range of management skills.

As our list is constantly developing you may find it difficult to keep abreast of new titles. With this in mind we offer a free email news service, approximately once every two months, which provides a brief overview of the most recent titles and links into our catalogue, should you wish to read more or see sample pages.

To sign up to this service, send your request via email to info@gowerpub.com. Please put your email address in the body of the email as confirmation of your agreement to receive information in this way.

GOWER